Sermons On The Second Readings

Series II

Cyc

D1269612

Donald Charles Lacy
John T. Ball
Maurice A. Fetty
Richard Gribble, csc
Lee Ann Dunlap

CSS Publishing Company, Inc., Lima, Ohio

Second Printing, 2005

Copyright © 2005 by
CSS Publishing Company, Inc.
Lima, Ohio

Some scripture quotations are from the New Revised Standard Version of the Bible, copyright 1989 by the Division of Christian Education of the National Council of the Churches of Christ in the USA. Used by permission.

Some scripture quotations are from the Revised Standard Version of the Bible, copyrighted 1946, 1952 ©, 1971, 1973, by the Division of Christian Education of the National Council of the Churches of Christ in the USA. Used by permission.

Library of Congress Cataloging-in-Publication Data

Sermons on the second readings. Series II, Cycle B / John T. Ball ... [et al.].
   p. cm.
  Includes bibliographical references.
  ISBN 0-7880-2369-1 (perfect bound : alk. paper)
  1. Bible. N.T. — Homiletical use. 2. Lectionary preaching. I. Ball, John T., 1933- II. Title.

BS2341.55.S47 2005
252'.6—dc22

                     2005009630

For more information about CSS Publishing Company resources, visit our website at www.csspub.com or e-mail us at custserv@csspub.com or call (800) 241-4056.

Cover design by Chris Patton
ISBN 0-7880-2369-1

PRINTED IN U.S.A.

Table Of Contents

Sermons For Sundays
In Advent, Christmas, And Epiphany
Paul's Pastoral Passages Of Promise
by Donald Charles Lacy

Preface   **15**

Advent 1   **17**
Thanksgiving And Thanksliving
1 Corinthians 1:3-9

Advent 2   **25**
Taking The Long View
2 Peter 3:8-15a

Advent 3   **33**
Apostolic Instruction
1 Thessalonians 5:16-24

Advent 4   **41**
Secret Revealed
Romans 16:25-27

Christmas Eve/Christmas Day   **49**
Training For A Purpose
Titus 2:11-14

Christmas 1   **57**
Precious And Privileged Children
Galatians 4:4-7

Christmas 2   **65**
Deep Calling To Deep
Ephesians 1:3-14

The Baptism Of Our Lord   **73**
Epiphany 1
Ordinary Time 1
Taking A Necessary Step
Acts 19:1-7

Epiphany 2   **81**
Ordinary Time 2
Getting It Straight
1 Corinthians 6:12-20

Epiphany 3   **89**
Ordinary Time 3
Being Single-minded
1 Corinthians 7:29-31

Epiphany 4   **97**
Ordinary Time 4
Looking Out For Others
1 Corinthians 8:1-13

Epiphany 5   **105**
Ordinary Time 5
A Man For All Seasons
1 Corinthians 9:16-23

Epiphany 6   **113**
Ordinary Time 6
Plea For Discipline
1 Corinthians 9:24-27

Epiphany 7   **121**
Ordinary Time 7
   Gift Of Positive Thinking
   2 Corinthians 1:18-22

Epiphany 8   **129**
Ordinary Time 8
   Making Disciples
   2 Corinthians 3:1-6

The Transfiguration Of Our Lord   **137**
(Last Sunday After Epiphany)
   Proclaiming Jesus Christ
   2 Corinthians 4:3-6

Sermons For Sundays
In Lent And Easter
Faith As Alternating Current
by John T. Ball

Ash Wednesday   **147**
   Selling Sin In A Celebrative Age
   2 Corinthians 5:20b—6:10

Lent 1   **153**
   Listening To Minority Voices
   1 Peter 3:18-22

Lent 2   **161**
   Abraham: The Near Death Of God's Promise
   Romans 4:13-25

Lent 3   **167**
   Finding Our Salvation In Today's World
   1 Corinthians 1:18-25

Lent 4   **173**
Goodness — A Way Of Life
Ephesians 2:1-10

Lent 5   **179**
Mediating The Grace Of God
Hebrews 5:5-10

Sunday Of The Passion/Palm Sunday   **187**
(Lent 6)
Palm/Passion Sunday And Today's Faith
Philippians 2:5-11

Good Friday   **193**
Dave, Tell Me About The Cross
Hebrews 10:16-25

The Resurrection Of Our Lord/Easter Day   **199**
True Resurrections
1 Corinthians 15:1-11

Easter 2   **205**
On Having A Good Church Fight
1 John 1:1—2:2

Easter 3   **211**
Salvation Is A Journey, Not An Arrival
1 John 3:1-7

Easter 4   **217**
Faith As Alternating Current
1 John 3:16-24

Easter 5   **225**
Love — The Only Absolute Commandment
1 John 4:7-21

Easter 6   **231**
The Commandments Are Not Burdensome
1 John 5:1-6

The Ascension Of Our Lord   **237**
All That Goes Down Must Go Up
Ephesians 1:15-23

Easter 7   **245**
The Blessings Of Writing
1 John 5:9-13

**Sermons For Sundays
After Pentecost (First Third)
Birthpangs Of The New Age
by Maurice A. Fetty**

Preface   **253**

The Day Of Pentecost   **255**
Birthpangs Of The New Age
Romans 8:22-23

The Holy Trinity   **265**
From Father Failure To Divine Father
Romans 8:12-17

Proper 4   **273**
Pentecost 2
Ordinary Time 9
Parades And Crosses — The Challenge Of Ministry
2 Corinthians 4:5-12

Proper 5   **283**
Pentecost 3
Ordinary Time 10
Looking To The Unseen
2 Corinthians 4:13—5:1

Proper 6   **289**
Pentecost 4
Ordinary Time 11
   No-fault Religion
   2 Corinthians 5:6-10 (11-13), 14-17

Proper 7   **297**
Pentecost 5
Ordinary Time 12
   The Acceptable Time
   2 Corinthians 6:1-3

Proper 8   **303**
Pentecost 6
Ordinary Time 13
   Are You A Taker Or A Giver?
   2 Corinthians 8:7-15

Proper 9   **311**
Pentecost 7
Ordinary Time 14
   The Paradoxical Power Of Weakness
   2 Corinthians 12:2-10

Proper 10   **319**
Pentecost 8
Ordinary Time 15
   A Time For Us
   Epesians 1:3-14

Proper 11   **327**
Pentecost 9
Ordinary Time 16
   Modeling A Necessary Future
   Ephesians 2:11-22

Sermons For Sundays
After Pentecost (Middle Third)
Jesus Is The Recipe For External Life
by Richard Gribble, CSC

Preface   335

Proper 12   339
Pentecost 10
Ordinary Time 17
    Let God Do The Rest
    Ephesians 3:14-21

Proper 13   345
Pentecost 11
Ordinary Time 18
    Finding Unity Through Christ
    Ephesians 4:1-16

Proper 14   351
Pentecost 12
Ordinary Time 19
    Jesus Is The Recipe For Eternal Life
    Ephesians 4:25—5:2

Proper 15   359
Pentecost 13
Ordinary Time 20
    Make The Most Of God's Gifts
    Ephesians 5:15-20

Proper 16   365
Pentecost 14
Ordinary Time 21
    God Our Protector And Shield
    Ephesians 6:10-20

Proper 17   371
Pentecost 15
Ordinary Time 22
    Living The Word Of God
    James 1:17-27

Proper 18   377
Pentecost 16
Ordinary Time 23
    Strength Through Diversity
    James 2:1-10 (11-13) 14-17

Proper 19   385
Pentecost 17
Ordinary Time 24
    Engage Mind Before Putting Mouth In Gear
    James 3:1-12

Proper 20   391
Pentecost 18
Ordinary Time 25
    God's Wisdom Or The World?
    James 3:13—4:3, 7-8a

Proper 21   399
Pentecost 19
Ordinary Time 26
    Prayer: A Way Of Life
    James 5:13-20

Proper 22   407
Pentecost 20
Ordinary Time 27
    In Solidarity With Jesus
    Hebrews 1:1-4; 2:5-12

Sermons For Sundays
After Pentecost (Last Third)
Travel Tips For Fellow Pilgrims:
Lessons Learned Along The Way
by Lee Ann Dunlap

Introduction   **417**

Proper 23   **419**
Pentecost 21
Ordinary Time 28
   Like A Child
   Hebrews 4:12-16

Proper 24   **425**
Pentecost 22
Ordinary Time 29
   Power And Compassion
   Hebrews 5:1-10

Proper 25   **431**
Pentecost 23
Ordinary Time 30
   The Unshakable Foundation
   Hebrews 7:23-28

Proper 26   **437**
Pentecost 24
Ordinary Time 31
   Where Is Love?
   Hebrews 9:11-14

Proper 27   **443**
Pentecost 25
Ordinary Time 32
   Dots On A Screen
   Hebrews 9:24-28

Proper 28   **449**
Pentecost 26
Ordinary Time 33
    Practicing God's Presence
    Hebrews 10:11-14 (15-18) 19-25

Reformation Sunday   **455**
    Looking In All The Wrong Places
    Romans 3:19-28

All Saints   **461**
    Our Ultimate Destination
    Revelation 21:1-6a

Christ The King   **469**
    Grace To You, And Peace
    Revelation 1:4b-8

Thanksgiving Day   **475**
    Our Prayers Are Our Thanksgiving
    1 Timothy 2:1-7

Lectionary Preaching After Pentecost   **483**

U.S. / Canadian Lectionary Comparison   **485**

About The Authors   **487**

Sermons On The Second Readings

For Sundays In
Advent, Christmas,
And Epiphany

Paul's Pastoral Passages
Of Promise

Donald Charles Lacy

*Dedicated to
the United Methodist Church
of Yorktown, Indiana*

Preface

It is a joy to present this volume to clergy and laity alike. It is my tenth book of sermons, seven of them for CSS Publishing. I trust these pages will come alive for the reader's nourishment, especially providing ideas for speaking and writing.

The Advent/Christmas/Epiphany season is indeed a precious time for all adherents of the Christian faith. The texts, almost totally from Paul, offer special opportunities and challenges for us as we live out our lives in this always surprising world. At the beginning of the church year, the foundation is laid for future growth, offering unlimited potential for Christ and his church.

Generally, sermons are intended to put both pastor and people in touch with the living joys and concerns of the faith. For us who preach and write sermons over the years, it is so refreshing and exciting to experience the Word of the Living God speaking to us here and now.

While I have published well over 100 sermons, the next one being preached and written is always potentially the best one. In this case, Paul's pastoral passages of promise are placed before you in an "attitude of gratitude." Furthermore, I hope and pray they will help you cope with today's often hectic circumstances.

I especially want to recognize the United Methodist Church of Yorktown, Indiana, where I spent four beautiful years among loving, caring, and sharing people. I am indebted to their administrative secretary, Judy Marsh, for preparing this manuscript.

May the Holy Spirit abide with you, provide for you, and guide you now and forevermore.

Donald Charles Lacy

Thanksgiving And Thanksliving

Introduction

Don't you just love times of thanksgiving? Yes, and Saint Paul is a genius at reminding us of this component to victorious living. His "attitude of gratitude" finds its way throughout his letters, except possibly for Galatians.

My first response to all of this is "what a wonderful way to live our lives." Of course, he is rooted and grounded in his Savior and Lord. It is a natural — most likely spontaneous response — to the depths he discovers in Jesus.

Perhaps the most missing ingredient among those who profess the faith, is thanksgiving. In short, there appears to be a generous amount of complaining with loads of dissatisfaction, even among God's elect.

If God has truly come to us in flesh and blood as a Jewish male, we are the most blessed of all peoples. For the opportunity is at hand to receive the Messiah. Mary's son makes his entry and we have the great privilege of saying "Yes" to him.

Why should anyone who has received him be dejected and without hope? We know Paul's answer. There should be continued thanksgiving but that's not all. There must be thanksliving as well. Don't they belong together?

Focus

Thanksgiving and thanksliving are supposed to exist at the same time.

17

Body

1. Wholeness and holiness are manifested to the community at large.

Pause and reflect on your parish or parishes. Isn't the coming of Jesus Christ historically and personally a cause for precious people to become much less fragmented? With the potential of total integration we can observe at times our people becoming not only whole but holy. Thanksgiving reigns in the hearts and minds of parishioners, as this happens. Talk about being born again and again! Some will even exclaim, "I don't know him or her anymore!" A new human being emerges and a new personhood never witnessed before is there for all to see. Then we rediscover the magnificent power of our faith.

But that's not all. Pastors who know their flocks well see this happen — and indeed are a part of this — at a congregational level. Each church has a personality all its own. People become one in community. Old First Church that used to be that grouchy and stalemated organism becomes a unique creation. The old has gone and the new has come! It is much less interested in projecting a proper image and far more concerned about something (someone) else. The wholeness and holiness comes not so much in radical changing of structures as it does in experiencing the vitality of openly expressing thanksgiving born of thankful hearts and minds.

While I believe deeply in the spiritual changes occurring in an individual, there is always that further step to the entire community. A Christian in isolation is a contradiction in terms. Even those cloistered bear responsibility for making contributions to others. Their thanksgiving is also thanksliving as it rubs off on others in a monastery or convent. The greatness found in these institutions is always somehow and some way been in a body of people living in Christ. Such people as Thomas Merton are internationally known. However, that does not mean they were formed in a vacuum. They were invariably in contact and some relationship with their brothers or sisters. Wholeness and holiness has a way of rubbing off!

Can we apply this to denominations as well? I believe so. The Wesleyan family can point to John and Charles Wesley. It was obvious to them that the Church of England in their day and time had drifted far from a sense of serious Christianity. It needed to be made whole and holy again! So they sought to bring about needed changes. Their successes are legendary. While this eventually meant a new denomination, that was never the intent of the Wesley brothers. Some years ago, I met the Archbishop of Canterbury (George Carey) who indicated to me one of the worst things the Church of England ever did was to let those Methodists get away. Perhaps we should recognize we Methodists are in need of recapturing the emphasis on the Eucharist taught and practiced by the Wesleys. Then thanksgiving and thanksliving will come in a new thankful way.

2. Thanksgiving is intended to be extended.

"The testimony of Christ," as Paul says, means spiritual gifts are among us. The babe who was born in Bethlehem has provided us through the Holy Spirit a means of telling others. This within itself is one of the gifts. Our culture, just like others who have followed Christ, tends to surround us and even engulf us. This means our communicated testimony can be seriously influenced by matters such as bad timing, indifference, hesitancy, and incompetence. For those dear people who are spiritually oriented, such considerations can be seriously overrated. At the same time we are called to be cognizant of everything that will aid us in our mission to share. Thanksgiving and thanksliving.

Holding back or limiting the story and power of the faith can be tragic. We have this timeless gift in the person of Jesus the Christ to share with others. Our beginning point can be his birth to a Jewish maiden and all that surrounds this one of a kind breaking into history. After all, who wants to shun a lovely and holy young woman's baby boy? There is a certain magnetism about this special event that has been on the world scene for most of 2,000 years. Our destiny is tied to this little fellow, who comes among us as a human being. We have received in thanksgiving and we are called to share him in thanksliving. The angels sing and we shout, "Joy to the world!"

"To keep something you have to give it away" is a cliché that bears repeating. I believe this is especially true of the faith we proclaim. It sounds like Paul was much in agreement. Even as we

19

acknowledge this, it can be one of the hardest things — in fact — to do. If something is really valuable to us, sometimes it is only in real hesitancy we share it with anyone else. That's the way we are and yet the Christian dynamic enables to see the imperative of such a matter. We have this treasure we are called to spread around, as the Holy Spirit directs. In particular, we do this by interacting with others. Paul says, "In every way you have been enriched by him, in speech and knowledge of every kind." Yes, it is time for "show and tell!"

"Extension ministries" or something similar is common terminology to most of us. Usually this means a position beyond serving the local church. While it seems accurate enough in terms of institutions and categories, I like to consider all ministry as an extension into the lives of people. That may sound "picky" until we see our understanding can be one of a local congregation being mostly static, raising money for those ministries considered "extension." The implication of that is a subtle way of blighting a much more thorough and complete "outreach!" Ponder that for a moment. You may discover our church has taken the easy way out!

3. A truly grateful person spontaneously desires to share.

Ideally, in the hearts and minds of Christians is an unending flow of "great thanksgivings." This is seen so distinctly in the writings of the Apostle Paul. It seems as though he can't stop giving thanks, especially for what he has found in Jesus the Christ. He overflows with expressions that inspire us, as well as other readers for centuries. He does so, even though clouds of imprisonment and shipwreck hang over him. He is the "Apostle of Gratitude" *par excellence*. The source is found in the Lord Jesus Christ. There is nothing fabricated or questionable about all of this. It is just there and he wants others to know.

If you are like I am, sometimes I get impatient with those who provide an artificial and syrupy thankfulness. It seems they are trying too hard to evidence something that just isn't there. The mere reading of this text does not mean we automatically capture the spirit of it. There is a spirituality at work calling for our entire being to shout into the heavens and also among our fellow women and men. It is getting beyond theory that counts in the long run. Genuine thanksgivings born of a right relationship with God the Father through his Son cannot be faked! Paul understood so well it is in paying the price for us by Jesus of Nazareth that the door opens to an "attitude of gratitude." Rejection and/or indifference speak for themselves.

Isn't it amazing what we communicate, often without knowing it? "He will strengthen you to the end, so that you may be blameless" is not for the light-hearted and those espousing a minimal Christianity. It is my experience we do not often fool "the world," so to speak, in our thankful expressions. If we really ascribe to Paul's approach, which means to live for Christ is also to die for him, even hardened secularists silently applaud our style. It is our spontaneity that sells others. There is nothing quite like a disciple who tells others how grateful he or she is for Christ and his church. "Sinners" may know a great deal more about the quality of our faith than we are willing to admit.

A thankful style of living that exudes from our innermost being is an evangelistic program all by itself. In a striking and masterful way, others catch this spirit in time and some even say excitingly they want what we have. It can even be reminiscent of the very early followers, who evoked a response from pagans saying, "See how those Christians love one another." No writer or painter can adequately depict such gloriously delightful scenes. That's how Christianity is supposed to work. Others are to seize our spirit, especially because our witness is unfeigned and inspirationally natural. The best sermons are those when few — if any — words are spoken and the power of the living God descends upon the moment. Great laity at times have to show clergy how and why this happens.

4. The world yearns for those who practice what they preach.

"Hypocrisy" is such a nasty word! In my long pastoral ministry of well over forty years I have come into contact with numerous people who spend virtually a lifetime dealing with it. They always seemed to look upon the lives of church people they knew and said — in one way or another — the Christian faith isn't lived.

They go to church and go through the motions; then on Monday a different life is lived. While we may say that is no justification for shying away from Christ, the point is well taken. There are those who seriously search for the power and purity of the gospel message. Sadly, often they do not seem to find it in their church-going neighbors and friends.

The hunger for genuine and vital Christian living is all about us. People feel — sometimes deeply — a void in their lives. Some read everything they can find on spirituality and do all the one/two principles. The discovery is made but the void is still there. Their search for "the grace of God that has been given you in Christ Jesus" eludes them. Books, various other publications, videos, and television/radio become more entertainment that anything else. What does the latest guru — Christian or non-Christian — say? Show them one solid honest-to-goodness disciple of Christ and lives can be changed overnight. The veneers and fabrications slip into the background. Thanksgiving and thanksliving become flesh and blood.

Perhaps the worst offenders of putting faith and practice together are clergy. Laying aside the political realities of the parish life, our people want to experience pastors who are thankful and live in that mood. Such sends an aroma throughout the parish. Even those who dislike us will honor and respect our styles of living. Our failures along this line are frequently closely related to upward mobility as professionals. We try too hard to succeed in wrong ways and end up failing in matters that really are crucial. I do not believe there is a more serious vocation or profession than being a clergyperson. We "walk the walk and talk the talk" or we become "a noisy gong or a clanging symbol."

In recent years, we have learned the mission fields are not abroad. They are next door, down the block, in the office, and at the coffee shop. Some who reside near us have even lost or never had the vocabulary to talk about Christ and his church. American culture has so changed in a couple of generations, that we can be caught off guard. Saint Paul was close to his churches and he taught them carefully and thoroughly about his Lord. They, too, faced a predominantly secularized society and emerged time and again faithful to what Paul taught them. We have come so far now that competing theologies even tend to blur any solid teaching we have for the world. We need to learn from the foreign mission fields the fact that we are all in this together. Go next door and proclaim Christ not Methodism!

Summary And Conclusion

So, "what has been joined together, let not man put asunder" is excellent advice. Thanksgiving and thanksliving belong together in one workable way of living. There is both substance and style. The legitimacy for this is a heavenly mark on our foreheads. We drink deeply and eat with inspired selection. Jesus and his ways are born among us and we are reminded of both his birth physically and our birth spiritually. Praise God we don't have to live with a set of principles. We can date our rebirth to his flesh and blood coming among us through blessed Mary. It is a relationship that never grows old. It is a highly productive marriage that passes from generation to generation.

Near the center of the city in Dallas, Texas, is an area called "Thanksgiving Square." It is a witness to the sameness of the world's religions at one point. All of them — in some form — espouse thanksgiving. It is a very moving experience to be there and share what seems to be something akin to holy ground. As you and I go about our lives, calling upon the wisdom of Saint Paul, just maybe life becomes worth living in ways we had only wondered about. Every community can have a thanksgiving square that is committed to Christian discipleship and interreligious dialogue with those who do not see things the way we do. We are so privileged to know the route of the babe in Bethlehem open to us.

Taking The Long View

Introduction

So much seems to press upon us in our daily living that "taking the long view" may not only be remote but considered impractical and therefore shelved. A thousand years equals one day and one day equals 1,000 years. It all sounds so mystical and unscientific! Do you mean we have to rethink being captains of our own ships? That is so basic to the American way and you are suggesting we give it up? After all, we can accomplish anything we set out to do — that is if we just try hard enough. Planning is done and realizable results in a given time frame are necessary.

Well, as some of us have learned, God does not see things and people the way we do. Whether it is Jesus' first or second coming, it happens on God's terms. I have heard it said some have been greatly disappointed he chose the particular time he did to bring his Son into the world. Why couldn't that have happened in time and space that was not nearly as male-oriented, even dominated? Equality of the sexes, especially in religion, could have thrived at a different time and place. Why didn't he return to us during the Second World War or some other cataclysmic moment in history? But he didn't.

Focus
We must seek to view things the way God does.

Body

1. Our God is before the beginning and after the ending.

As this soaks into our limited brains, we begin to have — at least — a clue to his bigness and our littleness. After all, aren't we supposed to do our measuring in starting and stopping points? To view life, especially cherished projects, in any other way is to ask for trouble. The boss sets goals and limits. We had better abide by them or, sooner or later, get fired. It really isn't going to help much to plead our case by maintaining, "But, God doesn't see it that way!" To live in a real world demands we adjust to the ways and means of the workaday world. Some people have to be kept happy, just for us to support our families. God may be God, but tell that to General Motors!

Questing of the sort the writer is speaking can be placed in a corner of the mind and never called upon again. It is labeled miscellaneous and perhaps even hurtful to one's progress. Before "the beginning and after the ending" is for a handful of philosophers to meditate upon. For John Q. Public and those primarily interested in "running the show" it is nothing more than unwanted stretching that goes no place. In truth the man or woman of faith is always more or less influenced by the idea presented. What appears to be so impractical must be considered for the health of our souls.

Could it be our real value and destiny are tied to the God who takes a view we cannot begin to measure? The words, "is patient with you, not wanting any to perish, but all to come to repentance" enter the picture. If he operated on our timetables, even our own salvation would be in jeopardy. In revival meetings I used to hear as a boy fiery evangelists say — in effect — be born again here and now or run the risk of spending eternity in hell. Frankly, such words scared me half to death! Emotions ran high and the old-fashioned mourner's bench was in clear view. God had spoken and no other chance to come to terms with him would be given.

Even after retirement, patience is often in short supply. The grandeur of the Creator with all his omnipotence and omniscience begs to be heard and believed. There are competitors. If I live ten more years, how much money will I need? Will my children pay attention to me as I am restricted to a nursing home? All this grandeur stuff is fine but who is going to pay the bills? It seldom seems to occur to us that God is God and sooner or later he supplies our needs. We don't want to be dependent on anyone and that is understandable. Yet, if God has taken care of you for seventy, eighty, or even ninety years, won't he continue to do so? Are faith, hope, and love mere words that begin to dissolve as we get so old? The text says, "regard the patience of our Lord as salvation."

2. Our God created time and therefore is master of it.

This thought can be life-changing! To begin to probe an infinite mind that knows no beginning and ending and — in fact — creates what we understand as time itself has a jarring effect. In a way it is much like a spectacular trauma carrying the revelation of God's greatness clearly exceeding our boundaries. Adjustments to this can be a conversion experience. Our measuring sticks tend to become laughable, as we get a peak at the long view. Clocks and all time pieces seem so trivial; yet we know we must cling to them in order for our brief life on this earth to go on.

To look into the heavens with the psalmist and worship God the Father who gave us Jesus the Christ in the form of a baby strains our ability to articulate. That foremost of all babies became a part of time that God created. It is as though he utilizes his powers in such a way that Jesus becomes compliant to the Father's wishes. In still another way, the ages come together to provide humankind's Savior. It is enough to give us a headache, isn't it? It is as though God refuses to allow what he has created to get in the way of his Son's entrance. So, Mary is utilized with her permission to conceive and bear a child in time and yet out of time for he is the second part of the Eternal Trinity.

Regardless of the period in which we are born, live, and die, the long view soon catches up with us. We eventually recognize we are "dust and shall return to dust." We also are alerted to an undying soul, created by the *Almighty*, that has life beyond our measurements. God set the perimeters. Then we discover he is Master, regardless of time or lack of it. For the Christian this is very comforting because we can rest in the assurance love is at work, especially in the birth, death, and resurrection of the Christ. Our hope is in the everlasting love of God the Father, Son, and Holy Spirit. Our souls are worth more to God than we can comprehend.

The persistence and consistence of such a view envelops both the good and evil. Struggle as we may, this Creator is at every turn. Our calling is to be found "without spot or blemish." Our free will, also given by him, is exercised and hopefully in ways that promise an eternal home. If it seems we are being crushed by all of this, in a way we are. Nevertheless, our assurance is found in him who goes to prepare a place for us. If a place is prepared for us, then he will come again and take us unto himself. Mystery in all of this comes and goes. We are able to see in a mirror dimly. What more can we ask? Our destiny is at stake and who better to trust than the God who created time and is master of it? As we struggle less and appreciate more, our death becomes powerfully positive.

3. Our God yearns for his children to catch a glimpse of his all-knowing powers.

The Almighty allows you and me the freedom to explore his greatness. We seem often afraid of all of this and end up either in predestination or license! Nevertheless, the windows of opportunity come and go, as we live out our lives. Each and every moment of the day (night) provides something or someone to aid us in a partial understanding of not only the creative process but of salvation history as well. Of course, we have to be alert and sensitive. This may or may not mean the disruption of our vocations and professions. The point is the ongoing availability of potential discovery in all our lives.

Just where is Jesus the Christ in all of this? Well, if God comes to us in flesh and blood in the person of Mary's baby, then he has a great deal to say. Our Lord's birth, ministry, crucifixion, resurrection, and ascension all enable us to catch a special glimpse. The privileges herein are remarkable for those who profess his name and seek to live by his commandments. In fact, they are unlimited! When we are ready to give up in attempting to make sense of life (and death), where do we go? We go to Rabbi Jesus. Through the Holy Spirit the needed understanding of the Father's will and ways are forthcoming. That does not necessarily mean clarity and specificity. It does mean an abiding presence that motivates us forward and upward.

Debates have raged for centuries about God's action or lack of action. As we live longer and are more absorbed in the Christian faith, I believe there is a certain peace that settles in. We hope we can live one more day but are thoroughly convinced we are not going to live 1,000 years in this life. In our twenties with — major and miraculous — medical advances we thought ten centuries was a possibility! I do not view this as resignation. If it is, it is a special type of succumbing to who and what God was, is, and shall be. Cynicism may rear its weighty head, but for those rooted and grounded in the faith, this is passing. The Father of our Savior and Lord will do whatever he chooses to do — whether it suits our fancy or not.

It seems to me the nature of God is such that we sooner or later pick up the truth that he seeks to woo us to him. Some would say this is a weakness and wishful thinking. It is put in the category of him laughing and crying. Perhaps such people would much rather deal with a first cause that simply does not communicate with his creatures. This denies the humanity of the one who created all of us and comes to us in the person of a baby, born of a woman. "Behold, I stand at the door and knock" is not an empty phrase that depicts a human god, devoid of any real power. It is a cardinal illustration of someone whose vast powers tell us there is providential care and concern, coming to us in a form we can understand.

4. Our God knows us thoroughly and totally, but respects our free will.

We are to "strive to be found by him at peace, without spot or blemish." Striving means it is definitely — to some extent — our doing. Our spiritual formation in the likeness of Christ may very well be a gift but our cooperation is imperative. God does not force his will upon us. In the end, of course, his will is done but let that not be a means to shove responsibility and even authority aside in our pilgrimage. As we, clergy and laity, labor to become more like our master, there is a certain grace that appears. It is as though our destiny is determined by the cooperation of God and man. Give thanks!

A real shocker is forthcoming as it dawns upon us the truth of the Creator's omniscience. Our privacy becomes non-existent. All that we do, say, and think is seen by the one who gave us life. For some this comes early in life and for others quite late. Then, I suspect for some it never comes at all. That is of tragic proportions! What do you mean there is some god out there who knows everything about me? That is sheer nonsense! Well, we know in the deepest part of our beings this is not all nonsense. The everlasting one who put us together in our mother's womb knows everything about us from conception. Is that something that should cause us to be in constant fear? Perhaps the best answer is: only if we belligerently insist on our unenlightened ways.

I am among those who find great comfort in God's knowledge of me. In that approach I discover his love and power coming together for my own good. Do I want it any other way? Frankly, the answer is, "No." There is grand joy. Only the one God of us all has the stature for this. Turn your imaginations loose and ponder a different arrangement. Are you willing to be tossed to and fro by elements and spirits? Are you really the captain of your own ship? In our prayers it helps to put in the beginning words which are obvious. Lord, you know all about me. Once this is unequivocally admitted, prayers take on the clothes of universal and personal reality. We know where we stand!

In the "long view" how much should others know about us? Having dealt with God's complete information bank on us, there is this related question. The sheer fact of the matter is that we are seen many ways by many people. How we perceive God's assessment of us may be tied to what we think others think of us. Wow, that is a conundrum of major proportions! I am reminded of a brother minister who maintains his next appointment is based on about half what he thinks of himself and half what others think of him. There is substantial wisdom here but in the "long view" it leaves little or no room for God. The quicksand becomes manifest, as we enter our prayer closets for extended periods of time. Then and there the Spirit of the Living God helps us to sift and sort.

Summary And Conclusion

This view is one of coming to terms with the way our Judeo-Christian background has informed our journey. From the inspiration of the psalms to the promises of the one who called himself the Son of Man, and abiding truth emerges. It has a way of explaining both our Lord's first and his second coming. In all cases it has to do with "holiness and godliness." Our hope is encompassed in an eternal love that can give us untold joy, as generations pass. No one is above this view and in one way or another all are ultimately subjected to it. There is a call for celebration not because we emerge as people of hope but as the Holy One reveals himself both as God and man.

All of this leaves us with more open doors than we can possibly enter. It is not lack of opportunity to come to grips with this; it is virtually too much which strains our often impotent powers. The fixing of this understanding to take the "long view" is maybe the most crucial and relevant doctrinal principle that waits to be fully received. Its benefits are too numerous to mention. Perhaps to make the mistake of not wholeheartedly accepting it is akin to splashing in the Pacific Ocean alone, shouting your independence. Today can very well be a brand new beginning because, at last, we have seen the light of his mercy, love, and never-ending powers. Humility of heart and mind should very well carry today and all the tomorrows.

Apostolic Instruction

Introduction

Saint Paul is "on a roll!" He keeps on coming with what he expects of the followers of Christ, as he has nurtured them. It is as though in a breathtaking fashion he wants to be sure his dear people are instructed properly. The words ring with excitement. Today's readers also feel the holy heat that is generated. The words are not theologically demanding as the same found in some of the passages from both Galatians and Romans. The elementary way we can experience the passage is very helpful. In short, it is difficult to misunderstand what is being conveyed. While it might appear a bit simplistic for veteran theologians, it touches the essence of Christian discipleship!

The generous expression, found in easily understood words and phrases, is thrilling to anyone seriously seeking to follow the Christ. We discover so much in so few words and are brought face to face with the contemporary scene and living out the faith. It is class 101 in the exercising of a way of life couched in terms so dynamic even non-believers could get excited about the life we profess! Furthermore, we are given a springboard that encourages and enables us — here and now — to be Christ's people not merely in theory, but in fact. Friends, for the kingdom's sake, this is all very important and helpful. Give thanks for such motivating inspiration.

Focus

We are called to exercise a formula for right living.

Body

1. Commands are required for our well-being.

Like rifle shots, the Pauline teaching comes to us hitting its mark again and again. Do we feel like we are at a remarkable shooting gallery, being hit by blessed requirements? Well, that might be a bit of a stretch for the imagination but it seems to me the point is well taken. Over and over we are pelted by commanding and forceful language. The apostle doesn't want us to get away and run the danger of languishing in fields of indifference. Such fields "miss the mark" and — at best — allow for a temporary respite from the insistence that comes from his teaching. We are privileged people, as the shots hit us and provide spiritual direction!

We are naturally resistant to anything or anyone telling us what we can or cannot do and perhaps think. Many of us take the attitude that since we are being told, we are not going to succumb for any amount of reward! Of course, the beautiful and awe-inspiring part of the passage is "the one who calls you is faithful...." This gives purpose and even glorious sequence to our following orders. We belong to the Lord and he belongs to us. So, why shy away from that which brings us fulfillment under his lordship? Resist long enough and we are going to "backslide," as old-time Methodists would say. Reluctant and belligerent children of the Father create their own problems.

Is there self-interest in all of this? Well, yes, I do believe so. Some of you may be tempted to say "but don't go there." I think it necessary we do that very thing. It is immeasurably inspirational and satisfying in the best sense to "rejoice always, pray without ceasing, and give thanks in all circumstances." It is as though we are enveloped by a teaching much bigger and better than we are. We have tapped into a stream of living water and it really and truly feels good! In reality it is doubtful we do anything completely free from self-interest. Otherwise, we would be sacrificing our personhood, given to us by the Father, and intended to be molded after the one who gave his life for us. Who and what we are is at stake and that is preciously powerful.

Are we dealing with indoctrination? If we are, it seems to me we have to label it "necessary and vital." In a sense, the faith is

34

transmitted by indoctrination that includes commands in addition to the Ten Commandments. Saint Paul is a great teacher and his rabbinical skills show in his writings. In a magnificent way such requirements are given birth by a spiritual dynamic that propels them into our midst for consideration! His people are already a part of God's kingdom. What they need now is "apostolic instruction" to carry them forward. It is training that is "basic" and promises more than the world can ever give. While they may never have noticed it, they were very privileged to have been taught by a brilliant practitioner of the ancient faith.

2. In capsule form we are given the ingredients for successful living.

The birth of a single baby boy launches a more complete way of living out our lives. In a way, we discover an evolution of vast and permanent proportions is taking place. This Jewish child, who became immersed in a Judaism of truly fascinating value, "fulfills the Law." It is a complicated relationship with those who cling to Moses and the prophets and yet the reality is quite simple. We are called through Christ's revelation to live in a certain way and that can — for the most part — be put in a capsule. In some respects, it is almost like holding these priceless gems in our hands and gazing upon them.

To my knowledge, American culture has always said we are born to be successful. It is even maintained that the Puritans thought anyone who wasn't a success was either lazy or sinful! Of course, we have definitely tended to see and measure success in monetary or other material ways. This very strong part of our psyche has led to some living that has not only been unhappy, but even disastrous. Failure after failure can be seen for anyone to observe. This is not judgmental; it is a way of knowing people by their fruits. One of our monumental problems in America is having the strength and fortitude to unlearn what we have been taught about success. It appears we have been inflicted by a persistent ailment: You must succeed "the American way" or indeed you have failed.

The apostle maintains "this is the will of God in Christ Jesus for you." So, in a pointed way he seeks to convey the road to living that is successful. It transcends the common and well-worn path of a secular world that aids and abets misery born of a misunderstanding. The ages and our history speak often, and sometimes in picturesque ways, of the tragedy of turning one's back on a few words geared to set us straight with the Father. Is there any doubt in human sin and the desperate need of a Savior? Isn't it shockingly amazing the way even professing Christians have refused to follow such a simple and practical teaching? How can humankind be so stupid? Yet, but for the grace of God there go you and I!

Those men and women who cook, know about ingredients. Mess up a little and you can have something indescribable. Mess up a lot and you run the risk of total embarrassment. It is likewise true in our spiritual lives, as we seek to be successful in God's sight. The Christian life requires flesh-and-blood living. Anything less reduces it to propositions that give enjoyable moments of mental gymnastics but little in pulsating behavior that elevates the Christ. There is an enormous and crucial difference between Christianity that stops in attitude with Good Friday and one that celebrates the Resurrection and all that follows. Our dear Lord is the chef and Saint Paul is the waiter. Taste and see that is good!

3. It is in the give and take of living that saints are born.

During my doctoral program, a special and lasting lesson was learned. Simply stated: Preachers must be in touch with the living concerns of their parishioners in order to be effective. The finest homiletical and theological works of art will fall on deaf ears, unless such concerns are addressed. Paul must have been an expert at correcting this! By his own admission, he was not much of an orator and hardly an average speaker. What he did understand was the necessity of being in touch with the overt and latent pressing interests of his people. He knows firsthand how saints were born.

Take out spiritual formation and discipleship and what do we have? Well, if our emphasis is the academic and theoretical, most likely we produce people who are stunted in their spiritual growth. Flesh and blood participation, yes, and immersion in people's lives — in time — mean so much to others. Granted, there must be a balance to our ministries, but let us never skirt the issue of the joys and sorrows of humankind, as lived day-by-day. The text is very clear about practicality in the parish and beyond. Some preaching is geared toward excellence in a narrow professional sense. We must be professional but always being sure we are assisting our people in their lives, so they can become more like Jesus the Christ. We preach to and for others, not merely to impress in wrong ways.

"Saints" was a rather common term in the ancient church. To live as the apostle suggests and requires, a lofty level of living those outside of the faith could hardly miss. "Giving thanks in all circumstances" was something most unique in a world of rudeness and crudeness. Someone must be out of his/her mind to live that way! Of course, how many people do you know who would agree with the ancients? My guess is that a very large number of people would insist on the sheer impracticality of it. It's a fine idea but it won't work in a real honest-to-goodness world. We serious-minded Christians have been in that bind for years. The world tells us in many ways that we should provide instruction that will work.

Like Advent, Paul's teaching is intended to be in preparation for the coming of the Lord. We are to be "blameless at the coming of our Lord." Whether we are looking to the first or second arrival of this God/man, our calling is to be in a period of preparing to greet him on bended knees. We have anticipated him and our readiness for the event will be manifest to the Savior of humankind. If it is the manger scene, our task is clear. If it is his appearing in the clouds, our task is also quite clear. Don't be caught unprepared! The utmost seriousness of this cannot be underestimated. However, by way of a precaution, we are counseled to "test everything." Remember, when he did not return in the first century, some Christians were caught off guard.

4. The beautiful spiritual life can be awesomely simple.

The Amish people are both striking and remarkable. This is especially evident among the "old order" group. Having served churches in northern Indiana, their presence was often a joy to me. The horses and buggies sometimes seemed to inundate the countrysides. The plainness of their attire was an inspiration to many of us. It wasn't that they were without problems. In fact, some of their youth from time to time were singled out for their rowdiness and intemperate drinking. However, the overall impression certainly seemed positive. Few people poked fun at them and many admired them. Along with Paul, their priorities were clear.

The call to us is not to be anti-intellectual and irrational. It is one that bulldozes away the debris of impractical theology that tends either to appeal to the ego only or a certain onesideness, freezing out the easy to understand. Granted, there may be those who find this a veiled attempt to put down time-honored theological education. That in no shape or form is my purpose. Falling in love with the finer points of in-depth study of religious doctrines is not inherently evil. But if that is all there is to one's life, the problems of genuine Christian practice can become colossal. After all, a simpleton can be just a simpleton and reflect little or no understanding of Pauline teaching! There is always the dilemma of leaning too far in any direction.

Untold numbers grew up on the pithy saying "Jesus loves me this I know for the Bible tells me so." While many of us smile at the rudimentary nature of these words, there is a mysterious way in which they provide both an entrée and closing to our lives. Indeed, spiritual living at the highest levels can be both awesome and simple at the same time. In parishes across our land there are those devoted Christian soldiers who know little beyond the necessities of which Paul speaks but they do them. They also know what it is to experience them at work! Is this a means of elevating uninformed and misinformed souls who mean well? Quite the contrary, it is a way of accepting Jesus' invitation to be like children.

There is a radiance to some people, isn't there? Their faces glow. Their eyes are bright. Their smile is infectious. Their gait is noticeably confident. Perhaps there are not as many as we would like, but they are among us. We only have to be alert, sensitive, and observant. The magnificence of the apostolic instruction before us really calls us to newer depths of behavior, built upon profound understanding of the gospel witness. The preciousness, vitality, and wholesomeness are there for all to see. Such people do not set out to impress anyone, especially their Lord! It is with the abiding of the Holy Spirit that their gift is presented to be appreciated and imitated. There is such a naturalness to all of this it can escape our full attentions. May God forbid!

Summary And Conclusion

To share and absorb one of the most colorful and yet profound passages in Holy Scripture is a blessing in numerous ways. The various opportunities for good it spontaneously created give us a peek into the unlimited storehouse of the blessed Lord. The formula is there. It is not the entirety of the gospel message but it is imperative to an abundant life here and now. Can it be this has escaped vast multitudes, even in the churches? I strongly suspect the answer has to be in the affirmative. The numerous one-syllable words that come to us greet us much like prized roses in a garden filled with many varieties of flowers that are attractive but at a closer look are mostly lackluster.

Saint Paul places his lesson, leading to victorious living, squarely before us. To every age his challenging invitation bids us to accept and practice ideas emerging from his relationship with Jesus the Christ. By now, some of us are probably saying to one another by look and/or word, let's give it a try. He is like that in most of his writings — and in effect — is proclaiming, "Well, come on let's get with the program." Even as this highly motivating message is considered, we dare not miss the concluding part of the text. Recall, "May the God of peace himself sanctify you entirely." He is well aware of the goal present and the fruition of practicing what he preaches. Try it, you will like it, now and forevermore. Our spirit, soul, and body are to be kept sound. Amen.

Secret Revealed

Introduction

At last it happens! Jesus the Christ is born of a woman and is here for all to see in flesh and blood. Paul, as is often the case, is in a celebrative mood. It is as though all of creation is pulsating with his entrance into history.

Human nature has a way of enjoying secrets and naturally wants exposures to occur. We are fascinated by the possibility of something or someone being revealed. In this case it is far more than fascinating. It is thrilling beyond adequate words to depict. History seems to stop!

Our faith is deeply enriched by accepting and believing the revealed secret is for all of humankind. While it is "my gospel," as the apostle says, it is also a universal and one-of-a-kind happening that he simply attests to. But we would be impoverished without his special touch.

His words are heavily freighted in a brilliantly cast look into what God the Father had finally decided to do. It is not just a prayerful affirmation. It is a theological gem that says so much so quickly we can be caught off balance. Of course, Romans is known for that and this passage especially calls for our complete attention and study.

Focus

God's Son visibly comes on the stage of history.

Body

1. What was shrouded in holy secrecy becomes evident.

God has a way of doing these things to us, doesn't he? By this is meant, of course, not in the same magnitude as our Lord's coming but in our own personal and professional lives. For example, some of us may have learned more about ourselves and others after sixty years of age than before. Some of our questing and inquiries of a lifetime find us with answers and explanations hitherto unknown. Sometimes we discover that what we wanted to know is simply not available to us, until we have lived many years. Sometimes the surprises are so wonderful and at other times far less than wonderful! All in all, this is God's doing.

Had God been keeping something or someone from us in this holy secrecy? Well, yes, I guess so. After all, who has all of the answers here and now and forever and ever? It isn't you and me. Our experience and formal education, regardless of its quality and quantity, are never enough to make us reliable experts on much of anything. We may act like that is not true and parade our resumes across the Internet for all to admire. The reality is if the Creator of the universe and the Father of our Savior and Lord wants to keep a secret, there is nothing we can do about it! Therein lies our security and peace, as we humbly acknowledge his greatness and our littleness.

Dare we talk about or perhaps even debate the timing of the event? As we understand history, we might very well conclude the coming of Jesus and his ministry should have happened in some other generation or century. Is that blatant arrogance? I don't think so, as long as we admit our views are always severely limited and our understandings less than perfect. Frankly, I think it is healthy to theorize about other periods in history for his entrance, as long as we are willing to admit to what we are doing. Whoever became any less by testing revelation in a way that can cause us to refine our faith? Such struggles under the lordship of Christ are therapeutic and can be delightfully helpful.

The weaknesses and, I dare say, the sins of all humanity allow us to stand just so much in the ongoing and colossal conflicts of the world. If God gave us more than we could bear, he would be untrue to his word to us. Therefore, his refusal to make manifest to us people, places, and things that will strongly influence our destiny is necessary to his providential care. This is truly a safeguard for all his children — past, present, and future. We should be on our knees thanking him for omniscience solely found in the Creator of all. Have we forgotten? God does not make mistakes and with that as a part of our basic thought patterns, we are equipped to conquer all under the powers of the Holy Spirit. Failure to believe this sets us up for human errors and perhaps a lasting pattern of disappointments.

2. An extraordinary person at a particular time in history was born among us.

The Judeo-Christian tradition had already witnessed the likes of Noah, Abraham, Moses, and David. Who could ever possibly forget their genius and contributions to all of us? Then, to broaden our perspectives, we discover such luminaries as Socrates, Buddha, Confucius, and Mohammed. Mysteries and miracles surround all of them. To debate who is right or wrong becomes mostly irrelevant, largely because their impact on world history is well known. Some can and do make a case for their entry on the world scene being something of a "Christ event." Of course, much of this is well beyond our puny minds to comprehend.

There are any number of people, especially reputable scholars, who would draw comparisons. They would include Jesus in a pantheon and find him just one among several. On an intellectual level among those who seek to know world religions and philosophies in an objective sense, this seems to work very well. For those of us — including some of the intellectuals — our values in a personal Savior and Lord come to the forefront and may very well collide unceremoniously. To know Jesus as a person who continually is present in one's life means differing from others who can be what they are, with certain lines drawn. This interaction is increasingly true in our lives.

Is it tenable or even possible to absolutize, so to speak, our loyalty to the babe born in Bethlehem? This is invariably present as a problem for Christians. Yet, as those of us deeply involved in ecumenism over the years know, there is a practical answer. The search for Christian unity is just what it says it is. The focus is on Christ who wants all of us to be one. Beyond that clear understanding is the imperative of interreligious dialogue. We can do both! In fact, I do believe, we must do both. The complicated world in which we live will tolerate little else. Realistically, our "head in the sand" approach can make us virtually irrelevant to untold numbers. We proceed with such an approach, inviting perilous times.

Who are we to say our "holy secret" provides us with a monopoly on God's wisdom? Are we privy to all of God's secrets? Having stated those inquiries, I would not want to belittle in any way the revelation we have most assuredly received. The followers of Jesus, born of Mary, are special people that want to share their faith. If this creates arguments and even conflict, so be it. To do less is to deny the very extraordinary person to whom we have vowed allegiance. Faith and works come into play. We see if there is faith, then there must be works and that means some form(s) of witnessing. Hopefully, we also see that legitimate works are born of genuine faith. It is a distinct privilege to be a disciple of the "Lamb of God, who takes away the sins of the world."

3. What God's people had been yearning to see becomes reality.

We can only imagine in faith the yearning that had taken place through centuries for the Messiah. Judaism always had a faithful remnant that was sensitive to God's promise of someone who would come and save his people. We see this especially in the prophets with Isaiah standing out. Their faithfulness generation after generation, as they waited, is certainly one of the brightest lights in all of the history of religions. Some charismatic personage would come on the scene and even do wonders for a time. It wasn't long, however, until it was evident their Messiah had not arrived. But the Jews were tough people who refused to give up, so it eventually happened.

They didn't know and probably didn't even suspect he would also be made known to non-Jews. The apostle tells us "made known to all the Gentiles." Then, he wants his Jewish brothers and sisters to know this is "according to the command of eternal God." It is a way of conveying to them that they should not look for another. Jesus the Christ was there among them. He was preaching, teaching, and healing. At times he performed miracles and the firmly entrenched Jewish hierarchy had to deal with it. Reality of messiahship was all about them but relatively few of his people believed. Then, the Gentiles are invited and guess what? They began to be believers and followers in the millions.

This is so like God, isn't it? The way is being prepared and finally is concluded with John the Baptist. The Jews had long been hungry and thirsty for their fulfillment to an already great religion. After all, didn't Jesus say quite directly that he came to "fulfill and not destroy" the Law? It is like a momentous evolutionary force was set in motion after the fall of man and is now completing its mission. Was Jesus a revolutionary? Yes, in a way, but Holy Scripture brings us a message of evolution, also. He carried with him in his teaching and behavior characteristics not unlike what they had for many, many years. So, at the end of the preparation Mary gives birth to her baby, who in most ways is a natural result of all that had gone on before.

We must never be too hard on our Jewish friends. For, after all, haven't we been guilty of refusing to see and accept the reality of our spiritual lives? Admittedly, our lack of vision may not at all be at the level of their blindness but let us not brag about our superiority. My Jewish colleagues tell me that "triumphalism" angers them more than anything else about Christians. We have seen the light and they haven't! We received, as Gentiles, the revelation secondarily. To put this matter in perspective it helps to read and ponder Romans 9, 10, and 11. While Paul must have had many enemies among his countrymen who hated him, he never gave up hope for them. Salvation is originally from the Jews and not the Gentiles. Who better to spread the gospel than a former Jewish rabbi?

4. God leaves no doubt that he has acted in a singular fashion.

The words "according to the command of eternal God" have a way of telling us this is the way it is. The will of the one and only true God, the Father of our Savior and Lord, has been done for all to see and make response. We are to have no doubt about the coming of

Jesus, born of the Virgin Mary, among us. Some would label this the Almighty's unilateral action. Christians of all persuasions know this to be true and bet their lives and deaths on it. It is a sobering and awesome declaration. If you are looking for someone else, forget it. If you want to continue to expect a future Messiah, don't waste your time and energy.

The Lord God of the universe has spoken now and forevermore. Mary's son is the one, the only one Christians are called to follow. Others, such as Peter, James, John, and Paul, will provide guideposts through their witness and writings, but this Jewish baby boy is the one who provides salvation. Through him comes forgiveness of our sins. Our repentance that is made to anyone or anything else will not fall on inconsequential ground. What is needed to be brought into full view has happened. No more wandering for those waiting for the ultimate to appear. He is among us and the heavens shout their approval. Praises be to God the Father for his Son, Jesus the Christ! For those of us living it is a preeminent privilege to know the event happened once and for all.

The "only wise God" reveals his secret at precisely the right moment he has chosen. It is not one of generalities but one of the decidedly particular. All wisdom that matters resides in him and is dispensed as he deems fit. What greater security can there be? We have hope in someone far bigger and better than ourselves. Those who seriously follow Christ have a peace that does surpass all understanding. It is not as the world gives. Its peace evaporates in both good and bad times. Our peace remains steadfast, as long as we cling to him and carry our crosses in victory. What the world calls wisdom must fall by the wayside. It must never be allowed to set our priorities or get in the way of serving the one, the only one.

The foundation is firmly in place and sinners, both Jews and Gentiles, are beckoned to come and believe. They are also inspired to turn their faith into action and make love a vital and healing energy for all to observe. Will there be other secrets and mysteries? Of course, the answer is an uncomplicated, "Yes." Our incompleteness will not go away, because as yet, we are not what we are intended to be. Full perfection eludes us. Nevertheless, to be convinced we are on the right road to eternal glory is enough. What more can humankind ask? Think of the millions over the centuries who wanted — sometimes in agony — what you and I have. What shall we do with so great a salvation? Our answer should be just as clear as God's explicit revelation.

Summary And Conclusion

The culmination of ages of yearning is now at hand. The great and often unfathomable streams of human experience and God's omnipotence seem to come to a unique intersection in time and space. The forces and energies of all that "was, is, and shall be" have brought to humankind the gift above all gifts. The Word came and dwelt among us. Considering the day and time, eyewitnesses were many. Let there be no doubt the Savior is on the scene. He comes in flesh and blood. Institutions of that day and time would not be able to defeat him. His body, the church, in its broadest and most diverse forms would continue, victorious even against the gates of hell.

So, the continual challenge is put forth to humankind. The secret has been revealed. Will you receive him as your Savior and Lord? To reject Mary's son is not to prevent him from knocking at the door of your heart. The invitation will go on unabated, at least, in this life. The magnitude of this divine enticement to come and live as a new being continues, at times, to enthrall even the most hard-hearted souls. Their rejection stands side by side with the Father's Son wooing them. And, at times, they blow their cover and are on the verge of accepting him, only to return to their former selves whimpering, "Not yet." What shall we do with him? The word is out and has been for 2,000 years. The Lord calls and death comes. We are intended to live for him and spend eternity with him.

Training For A Purpose

Introduction

Some years ago, many of us, like others before and after, went through basic training or boot camp. It was a time to get thoroughly acquainted, usually with either the army or navy. It was also a time of endurance. The hardened and veteran men of years' experience sought to teach us the elementary principles of living in the military. The "old salts" in the navy used to delight in bringing us down several notches. This was their method of clearing away obstructions to the teaching they were providing. Was it fun? Not really. Did funny things happen to us? Well, yes and some were embarrassed to tears. Some could barely contain their anger.

What I remember most about my boot camp was the closeness I felt to the living God. Truth was, I didn't have anyone else that would listen in compassion to my groans of awkwardness and reluctance to give up a comfort zone. At Christmas time we were given liberty to be with our families. With little hair and a face somewhat scarred because of a straight razor, my appearance was not that of a wise and proud public school teacher. In retrospect, it was one of the best times with my family I had ever had. Their son, grandson, and brother was in training. His, and their, Savior — Jesus Christ — was present in a new way. It was as though he had been reborn among us.

Focus

We are trained in order to be useful to others.

49

Body

1. A negative individualism is counterproductive.

When Christ was born among us, he began early on to have apostles close to him. While they were strong individualists, not one was allowed to go it alone and be the only spokesperson for our Lord. Even Peter, who seems to be dominant in the gospels, is not allowed to tell the others what to do. And when we visit with our Catholic friends, we discover — for the most part — the holy father in Rome is held in high esteem but is not experienced as a leader who "lords" it over them. As we study Catholicism we see checks and balances in the Vatican that do away with negative individualism.

As we read the New Testament, there is the witness of the four gospels. Even the synoptic gospels show some differences among them. Then, John comes along and thrills us with both mystery and mysticism! However, when we read and study them together, what a magnificent narrative we receive. We are not disciples of Matthew, Mark, Luke, or John. We are disciples of the babe in Bethlehem, born to bring us the good news that is always more than a single individual, except Jesus the Christ. Our training is not allowed to become negative under a single point of view. Christ "gave himself for us that he might redeem us" and that is the most powerful idea humankind has ever heard. Praises be to the Father for sending his Son among us!

There are those who believe they have a "corner on the market" and seek to absolutize the entire religious experience by sectarian teaching and training. Witness the numerous evangelists and revivalists who have "converted" people to their way of thinking. Sometimes their narrowness only becomes apparent years later, as followers cling to disciplines more inflicted upon them than given to them. Our history is filled with examples of those who allowed their egotism and perhaps self-righteousness to get in the way of the true training of Jesus the Christ. So often it seems those who begin with purity of motivation, sooner or later, are overcome by self-importance. Not only is this negative, it is very sad. We are first of all trained to serve the Christ!

50

If we seek continually "to go it alone," how can we possibly witness in helpful ways? The point is not to negate personal evangelism; it is simply to point out the pitfalls of one who loses contact with others, who are just as much committed or perhaps more so. Christ persists in purifying "for himself a people of his own." Highly individualistic models of discipleship tell me the plural "people" may be considered of secondary importance. To be sure, the babe in Bethlehem calls us as individuals but we are parts of the whole and not the whole! Creativity and innovations can be wonderfully valuable gifts for Christ's holy church. They can also be ways for precious human beings to be misled in directions that produce questionable fruit.

2. A singleness of purpose leaves no doubts.

The reason for our training is to make of us people "who are jealous for good deeds." Salvation has come in the person of Mary's son and is intended to be spread among the lives we touch. We are not lethargic people. We are zealous people! Our good deeds are given birth by a right relation with God the Father through his Son, Jesus the Christ. There is excitement and love in all of this that lays before the world, acts of kindness for the spiritual benefit of everyone. No one should be confused by our lives, as we go about being empowered by the Spirit of the holy God. Nonbelievers are to view in their midst actions and even reactions by those redeemed.

There will be criticism for those of us who go about practicing our faith, usually by calling into question our motivations. This is unavoidable and to be anticipated. Nevertheless, in time, doubts will be diminished as the world sees consistency and persistency in our talk and attitudes. Then, the reality of Christ coming can be seen because there are those in flesh and blood who practice his teaching. The birth of the Savior of the world is seen as more than Christmas presents and carols for once-or-twice-each-year Christians. One of the great victories in our pilgrimages is to experience those critics who finally are willing to accept the generosity of God in our lives. The training has gone well and victorious people learn anew that the awesome everyday power of committed Christians is among us.

To win at anything requires concentration. This is certainly true with our walk with the Lord. We cannot be wandering here and there, indecisive about our gift of salvation. Not only did God's Son come to us centuries ago, he has come into our lives and is a living, vibrant presence at this very moment. We are neither to veer to the left nor to the right. We are to walk the straight and narrow pathway that eventually leads to eternity with our blessed Lord. We are in the harness, so to speak, like any race horse who strains down the track to receive the reward. Some of us know what it is to take our eyes off the prize and lose ground in the most crucial race of all. Sometimes it is devastating.

Congregations and pastors should always move forward together. Internal and external unity is decisive in our quest to show the world that Christ has — in fact — come into our lives. The truly spiritually successful bodies of believers are united and move like a mighty dynamo throughout their communities and beyond. Why? Largely because there is no question about the direction they are moving. Even those who never enter a church building have good things to say. A dysfunctional church is never a positive sight. It conveys quickly the fact that those folks are not together and cannot seem to settle on a clear purpose for being. Their deeds in the community cause confusion. If we are ever at fault for such a situation, may God be merciful! We do not want to be the cause of Christ's sorrowful tears.

3. A ministry to others under the inspiration of the Holy Spirit validates itself.

Serving others is articulated by numerous clichés. Obviously, it is part of the air we breathe. Think of the service clubs, such as Rotary and Kiwanis, who promote and practice serving others. They use the same carefully worded phrases that communicate to the faithful that it is very important to put others above yourself. Is this the work of the Holy Spirit? My own experiences and perceptions are affirming because the Spirit flows where it flows. Strange as it may sound, these clubs and those similar in nature are a training ground. Good deeds are all about! In a way, the invisible church, the one without steeples and pulpits, is hard at work.

Solid and genuine ministry, wherever it takes place, has a way of validating itself. The quality is there and manifest to anyone with serious interest. Our lives are to be lived as "self-controlled, upright, and godly" and that can happen in any set of circumstances. The secular and sacred have their boundaries blurred. It is hard to tell one from the other. The Spirit of the living God will not be denied. Christ was born into this world so that others who follow him will look after their fellow men and women. To accept life and live it in that fashion means Christmas is always with us. Why? Because the gifts of serving others are continually being bestowed upon humankind. So, be alert. There are a lot of really good deeds all about you.

Believe it or not, the world and Christians have need for a sign that calls attention to happenings truly benefiting others. Enough of this theoretical stuff; we want that which is real and evidences gems of legitimacy. It seems we all go through periods in our lives that are filled with spiritual mediocrity or worse. We desperately need a sign that shows God still cares about us and ministers through us. When this happens, what a great day it is! All at once what appeared so average or even sub par comes to life and we are thoroughly reminded God has not abandoned us. The validation for which we were looking virtually stuns our senses and thought categories. Christmas wrappings and the gifts contained therein go together in cohesive beauty.

Being zealous in the right ways is a pure work of art to watch. Demagoguery doesn't rear its ugly head. Our works are free from egotistical yearnings. Our love is for more than a bit of kindness. Our motivations are pure and undefiled. Aggressiveness and helpfulness do not collide in bitter disagreement. We know who and what we are. The babe in Bethlehem is elevated for all to see how beautiful it is! Now it can be said and felt that those Christians have something I don't have and I want it! The stars in the heavens sing out in perfect harmony that Jesus Christ is born, and that everlasting love, as practiced in human relations, is possible because we witness it in action.

4. A wholesome sense of service is among those few essentials of the faith.

The long and short of it is we are intended to be useful to and for others in the highest and best sense. Jesus did not just come to us to be adored in a manger. He came to you and me that we might have life and have it abundantly. His promises are a sterling part of the revealed gospel. To sit by the hour and marvel by the hour at an exquisite crèche may be inspirational for us but whom else does this benefit? To laud to the heavens pictures — even icons — of the blessed Virgin and Jesus weeping, is marvelous for us, but for whom else? The grandeur of striking architecture thrills us beyond words. Frankly, what does it do for your neighbor with cancer?

It usually takes the common and human touch to strike a chord in those who are needy and perhaps on the verge of self-destruction. I believe we frequently underestimate ourselves here. The quiet pat on the back sometimes works wonders. No amount of money could have bought the positive sensation. Whisperings of appreciation with deep emotion can send many devils in hell running. Yes, there is a wholesomeness that is essential for anything significant to happen. Praises be to God, the Father of our Lord and Savior Jesus Christ, simple kindness with sensitivity to the Holy Spirit can carry the day! The world yearns — sometimes in agony — for just these simple but very powerful good works.

Christ keeps on asking us, just as Peter, if we love him. If our answer is in the affirmative, we are to feed and tend his sheep and lambs. Through this endeavor we act as vehicles or channels of "bringing salvation to all." Isn't this what we are always to be about? Indeed, how else can we justify our existence as those professing the name of Jesus the Christ? Funny how we keep evading and avoiding that which is of the essence of our being in Christ, as Saint Paul put it. Loving others in a sincere and wholesome way, bears fruit in ways people can view. The Spirit will seek to guide them to accept and understand that this is why Jesus was born among us.

Are we able to enter the "pearly gates" without taking others with us? That question has been posed numerous times. Frankly, I believe it is possible but highly improbable. Why? Largely because it tends to contradict our vocation as Christians. Of course, if we are not formed after Christ's likeness and only play at religion for our own benefit, it is common sense we are going to fail spiritually. Without being judgmental, take an objective look at yourself. What do you see? Better continue to look some more and with intensity. In order to help Christ, we must continually give him away in thoughts, words, and actions. Believe me, the ages prove there is more than enough of him to go around! Stretching beyond these poor and weak spiritual muscles of ours, nevertheless, is to aid and assist our precious brothers and sisters.

Summary And Conclusion

Our dear Lord's coming throws into operation the possibility and probability of good deeds unlimited. His birth has made the difference between the ongoing and pagan understanding of existence and another way of living, replete with precious persons giving themselves in the name of Christ. The pragmatic and useful characteristics of our ministries, lay and clergy, are evidence his coming was and is not in vain. His birth shattered the assumption that life, even for morally upright people, had to be lived stoically with bravery. This is not to discount those religious beacons coming before him. It is to emphasize that his coming brought us a whole new dimension, namely, love in action freely doing good deeds.

So, the "grace of God has appeared" in the person of a Jewish baby boy. In accepting him as personal Savior and Lord with renunciation of "impiety and worldly passions" we are born anew for the benefit of others. Lives that are "self-controlled, upright, and godly" bring to the world a magnificent and yet practical way of serving humankind. The question is: Do you and I believe this? If we don't, why not? The revelation of his salvation to us should not only stagger us with its uniqueness, but empower us to take upon ourselves as many crosses as are laid upon us and be thankful! The call is for a decisive decision to discipleship that upon being fully accepted — leads to untold riches for others. Indeed, how shall we escape if we neglect so great a salvation?

Precious And
Privileged Children

Introduction

The remarkable world of children has always fascinated me. Their naturalness and innocence — in particular — thrills me and serves as a reminder of the intended relationship between us and our Father. Even more, when they are pouty and sometimes destructive, there is a genuineness about them that is so winsome.

Regardless of our attainments, we never seem to rise above the fact we are simply the Father's boys and girls. The great and the less than great are called to admit to this eternal verity, in time. The famous and infamous, sooner or later, understand in some intuitive way their perpetual childhood.

Some of us wish we could experience more childlikeness in our churches and less childishness. There is a huge difference. One is ready for orders from the Almighty. The other complains the orders received are inappropriate or worse! Childlike congregations and pastors are always learning and growing.

Our destinies are tied to being precious and privileged children. The Father's love is always accessible and it always works in perfect harmony with his crucified and resurrected Son. We have so much for which to be grateful! Kneel some place this day and pour out your heart in thanksgiving for your special place and relationship.

Focus
Our dependency on God is the key to our success.

Body

1. The Father wants us to imitate his Son.

He "has sent the Spirit of his Son into our hearts...." That simply and unalterably means we are to be like Jesus, as nearly as we can. Through our joys and sorrows we are to remain steadfast in seeking to practice the teachings given to us. Through our good times and bad times we are to stay close. Through our successes and failures we are to hold up mirrors now and then to test our faithfulness to the highest and best we know. There is always another virtue or attitude for which to strive. We like to think in terms of attainment and soon admit we are only going to improve, humbly conceding our incompleteness.

Imitating a person you highly respect may be the most flattering action to the man or woman you have chosen. In Jesus' case it is more — much more — than a lofty level of respect. It is seeking to become like one who came to us as God in the flesh. This is a lot more than trying to become like a Michael Jordan, Barry Bonds, Ronald Reagan, Hillary Clinton, or even Billy Graham! Models of people in our midst and people long gone may be helpful, but they do not have the substance of our Lord and Savior, Jesus the Christ. Even denominations have to be careful that Martin Luther, John Calvin, and John Wesley are not placed ahead of Christ. They are not the source but merely offer commentaries in print and behavior. We are to remember who the priority is.

Perhaps the greatest teaching devotional is the *Imitation of Christ* by Thomas à Kempis. The centuries of readers bear witness to the profundity of this book. In my own experience, I find it second only to the Holy Scriptures. Page after page, in dialogue form, the author drives home the truth that we are to be like Jesus and we do so by being childlike. Who can even estimate the good that has come from this publication, which has been through countless editions? Protestant, Catholic, and Orthodox all benefit. It is more than a rare book; it is inspirational and instructional beyond anything, other than our Bibles. Its thrust is invariably the same as disciple and Christ visit: We are to imitate our Master and Friend.

World history has been influenced and perhaps shaped by those who have imitated others. Kings, queens, presidents, popes, prime ministers, ayatollahs, writers, artists, and scientists all learned from those they sought to imitate. On the more down-to-earth side of life, many of us found Harry Emerson Fosdick a homiletician worthy of imitation. In fact, go to any walk of life and we discover this phenomenon at work. Even the Mafia chieftains patterned their evil ways after those already successful in corrupting human lives! The Almighty knew the power of imitation far better than any of us. So, the best — the perfect one — was sent into our midst that we might know the way of spiritually happy life. The New Testament with the Old Testament (Hebrew Scriptures) sets the stage for us.

2. The Father seeks to be our parent.

We are no longer slaves! We are children and eventually we are heirs. The Father's heart pulsates in loving energy to draw us to him in a relationship, both meaningful and everlasting. Christmas is the beginning of this love story and it continues to work itself out all our lives. It is the parental approach that wants his offspring to return to their rightful place in the scheme of things. The fall of man is reversed and the opportunity — indeed invitation — to rediscover what was intended to be ours is centered upon a Father's love and the gracious gift of his Son. The fallen kingdom so long in force can now be conquered. Talk about faith, hope, and love!

What does a really good parent do? He looks after his precious children, who are the most privileged in the entire creation. This means and implies many things but probably above all is protection and sustenance. Have we not been given minds to protect us from all adversaries? Have we not been given a vineyard that provides for our welfare? In a different way we are protected by a spiritual heart, given to us by our parent known as "Abba! Father!" Then we are sustained by the many spiritual disciplines, especially prayer and Holy Communion. Our God provided again and again. He is the totally good Father whose loving power and powerful love comes to us now and forever and ever. Hallelujah and amen!

Many older parents are being cared for today by their children and to a lesser extent other relatives or friends. As our population grows older and older, there will be greater need for this. It may take the form of a nursing home and/or assisted living quarters. Regardless of the health care configuration, it is coming and with question marks all up and down the line. Attempt, if you will, to relate this to our heavenly Father who is our parent. We will never have to be responsible for his care, or will we? The heart of God yearns for the children of the world — young, old, or otherwise — to come to him. So, his need for us to come to a shelter that protects from hell needs to be met. Just maybe we can minister to the Almighty and have never felt comfortable with that idea.

Even though the New Testament throughout designates God as the Father or in male-oriented language, this must be tempered by maternal and typically female characteristics present. The mystery involved here, especially in light of some theological controversies, is indeed substantial. We are working through a period of history and culture of immense confusion and disagreement. Hopefully and prayerfully, we will not lose our way and move precious children to a chasm that promises nothing but chaos and lost souls. In these days of questing it is good to be reminded that God comes to us as Father, Son, and Holy Spirit. In a sense, there is a parental relationship here that communicates our imperative need to be in a parental-child mode, always dependent on that for spiritual success.

3. The Father desires we huddle close to him.

To cry to one's Father is a fascinating way to depict our closeness to the everlasting God. Jesus knew more about this than you and I shall ever know. There is an almost indescribable intimacy and at times we are simply at a loss to tell others of God's presence. When pushed to describe this experience, I usually acquiesce into trying to say that I know beyond all doubt he is present. There is a sense that someone far bigger and better than yourself is there. It may be for quite sometime, perhaps minutes or even hours, or it may be only for a brief moment. The treasure is one that neither money nor self-help books can bring about.

His image as a faraway God, maybe perceived in a deistic fashion, does not exist. There is the Spirit of Jesus in our hearts, that glorious Son given to us by the Father through dear and blessed

Mary. Don't you feel sorry for those who never seem to get beyond a distant deity, who neither feels nor handles anything or anyone directly? Some have said the founding fathers of our nation were mostly deists. Frankly, that is debatable. Read the original materials of Franklin, Jefferson, and Washington more carefully. Do not depend on those who want to tell you their feelings and thoughts. Evangelical Christianity, to my knowledge, has always preached that God is very familiar with his children. Only as we persistently reject his gracious invitations do we began to perceive him in an abstract manner. Yes, draw near to God and he will draw near to you.

Some saints could hardly tolerate the pressure of his presence. The light and the heat were so intense it became virtually unbearable. Would that every one of us could have that experience! They had snuggled up so close, they felt encompassed and God-intoxicated. To be drunk with the Spirit of which Saint Paul is speaking is one of ecstasy, elation, and elevation. We learn in a sublime way that our spiritual success is, indeed, brought about by our full dependency. A man was asked why he couldn't stop weeping with joy. He said quickly that he had gotten too close to God and was now receiving the aftermath. Thomas Merton knew about this as he penned his many books. For some saints, every day is Pentecost.

We have all heard at sometime or another that God is closer than our very skins. There isn't much eloquence or theological precision in that but it is a way of delineating a blessed connection like no other. My own spiritual journey has many such highly charged human/divine events in it. That does not automatically make me special in a category not permitted to others. It does make me more and more grateful for salvation history that culminated with Jesus Christ. The ancient church was visited time and again by such phenomenon. There is the search, sometimes excruciating among people today, for intimacy with God. It is more than for reasons of secular ambition. There is a groaning after the ways and will of their maker. They have come to their senses and really want to return to their Father!

61

4. The Father pursues us in loving understanding.

"The fullness of time had come" and there is no object in looking or waiting for the Jewish Messiah. He has come by way of the virginal conception. Blessed Mary was the channel. In a sense she was the mother of God. The early fathers of the church have said so and with powerful emphasis. This indicates we have moved from slave to child to heir and we are not second-class citizens in the kingdom of God. The eternal love has been manifested in a particular and concrete way no human being can annul or invalidate. We find ourselves in a love that knows no bounds and an understanding of his children totally unique, and the angelic hosts sing with divine joy!

His pursuit never relents, even at a death's door. We have known those who regularly put off the requirements of the Christian life. God remains faithful. So, you thought you got away? Does that sound just too pedestrian and secular? I hope not. Why? Because there is a profound truth here and it will not be cancelled out. It has to do with the innate preciousness and privilege we have. One thing God is not: He is not a liar. We ought to see clearly that God will do whatever he decides to do and with whomever he has chosen. There is a great and undeniable life lesson in all of this. While we are pursued in loving understanding, this does not imply we are with God as one buddy to another. To carry that concept very far leads to perversions and prevarications.

God's patience is a virtue of such profundity we can understand it only darkly. Nevertheless, we do have a glimpse. What father desires to have even the most obstreperous child lost forever? Now, we get even closer to the fatherhood of God whose heart is in it! It makes a difference — a big one — whether or not each of his children sidles up to his side and pleads to be in the arms of the only one who can really care indefinitely. This is so deeply personal and requires we consciously become vulnerable. He has more patience than Job! How much more privileged can we possibly be? Yet, often, and probably most of the time, we hold him at a distance, either totally petrified or fiercely independent.

Most of us understand amazing grace just enough to know God cares about us. We have a bit of trouble with a love that has no boundaries. Then, in our most lucid moments it dawns on us the great God of the universe understands and loves us far beyond our wildest dreams. Some very fine churchgoers that I have known say such moments are far and few between. My belief is this is a problem with human perception. God is as near as we want him to be. There is no scarcity in this love that knows no bounds. There is no limit to his understanding of our lives and loved ones. We must learn to cry out more often, "Abba! Father!" It is a wonderful exercise for our vocal chords. It is the means our heavenly daddy uses to take us in his arms and hold us tightly with a supernatural love.

Summary And Conclusion

Say what we will, those professing Christ find great security, stability, and satisfaction in being the Father's boys and girls. Such dependency has been with us in the Judeo-Christian as long as anyone can recall. "The fullness of time had come" and humankind feels the full weight of God's omnipotence, omniscience, and omnipresence. He gives us our worth and identity, specifically as we relate to his Son — our Savior and Lord. All spiritual successes — in a way — are directly related to this understanding of the Christian faith. Are we precious and privileged? Of course, we are! Men and women over the centuries have attempted to find solace elsewhere. But we are extra-special. We have found more than easing of our discomfort.

So, the message is quite clear. We are called to be sons and daughters in the highest and best sense. This royal invitation is given to us by Jesus the Christ coming among us. Yes, we are given the opportunity to become spiritual royalty. Of course, the decision is ours. Jews and Gentiles have access to the gift above all others. What shall we do with the babe in Bethlehem now among us? Today is the day of salvation not only for you and me. It is such a day for others throughout the world. When in doubt as to how to bring this about, fall on your knees like children. Names and faces will come to you, some you will know and others you will not. Appreciate your lowliness. Christ did! Remember we have "the Spirit of his Son" in our hearts. All things are possible with God.

Deep Calling To Deep

Introduction

Wow, our text is not only challenging, it is a momentous portion of scripture that keeps spreading and giving! The profound theology expressed is in some ways more than we are able to handle. Yet, we are called to make an honest and forthright attempt. A conscientious rendering of the passage is in order that others may, at least, taste such wisdom is our goal.

To be chosen "in Christ before the foundation of the world ..." is both awesome and ominous. It is as though our free will has been suspended and a ring of unpredictability floods our souls. Nevertheless, we must live on and seek to fulfill our destinies. We must also work with the knowledge that there is something very special about us Christians.

While John 3:16 has been quoted for centuries as the quintessential statement of understanding God's relationship to us, it both tends to evade and reduce problems in our salvation history. Saint Paul wants more than it offers and yet is not in any sense wanting to contradict it. He seems never to be frightened by those really big ideas. In fact, he insists on providing explanations that make sense to him and should as well make sense to us. Christ's coming completely changed his life in terms of motivations and goals.

Focus

Probing at deeper levels gives a more complete understanding of our faith.

Body

1. To be too simplistic tends to produce spiritual pygmies.

This is not to infer or imply esoteric information is necessary in order not to wallow and eventually die with simple answers to huge and complicated problems. I believe our dear Lord would say to follow such a road is to shut out the "little ones" he came to save. Having admitted this, we must not be reduced into a Pollyanna that sings optimistically day-after-day whatever will be, will be! Such a practicing of our blessed Lord's faith may not be blasphemous or heretical but it will undoubtedly be minimal. This we must shun and be on our guard against. Our spiritual growth demands we keep moving on, hopefully upward.

As a boy, I remember honest people during the time of testimonials saying exactly the same thing at each and every service. It is not that they were in any sense wicked people. However, surely there could have been some indication of change, showing they had moved deeper with their Lord. As a lad, not even into my teenage years, I observed in respect but vowed I would go deeper, much deeper. This was not seen at the time as an attempt to be better than someone else but to acknowledge the enormity of the field with the ground hardly broken. It was a moment of awakening that was only barely a part of my consciousness at the time.

To be blessed "with every special blessing" conveys to me we are to labor in all times and places, and yes, with whomever we find ourselves. This is the best prevention against becoming spiritual pygmies. If we are to be six-feet tall, why settle for four-feet? Unused potential in the personal spiritual realm is a tragedy here and now and forever and ever. May God forgive us! Such work, of course, is not necessarily the visible kind. It may very well go unseen, only to be revealed on the last day. Many experience their labors in vain, only to learn later, frequently much later, that is not the case. Timing is really God's business because we have so little control over circumstances. More than that, we may not even know what they are!

Studying theology and philosophy among seminary students is always a serious task. It is the hope they wrestle with the profundity of the Christian religion in order to understand it in ways that cut below the surface. In our preaching and calling — in particular — the need is for pastors to be able to field questions and comments made by their parishioners. In a way preaching is group pastoral care every Sunday and at other times to enable the person in the pulpit to provide more than clichés. Seminary education is so important in aiding precious human beings in their spiritual formation. Repetition is essential and yet it can also be deadening. Of course, we are reminded to repeat the Lord's Prayer and the creeds with regularity, knowing their basic place in the deposit from which we all eat and drink.

2. We are called to work out our salvation in fear and trembling.

"We have redemption through his blood" is our assurance but it is also a prodding to a more complete understanding of how our salvation is to be treated. To be redeemed by his blood is no small matter! It is here that the ever-popular power of positive thinking types can be stumped and fail to come to grips with something far more significant than a tool for getting our way. To be afraid and trembling means our very personhood is in some way threatened. To become uneasy and yearn for better days under the banner of a nominal faith is no answer. Of course, we should not treat our salvation as a possession, but as a gift that spiritually forms us.

To be called to become more like Christ is to probe so deeply we not only learn of our crosses, but receive them with gratitude. We carry them and are educated in the ways of the master. The saints testify to the magnificence of these crosses. Their sainthood most likely depended on them carrying such uninviting objects that have truly taken on many forms throughout the ages. What for one was a cross for another was not. What one would have chosen for himself or herself was not the one selected by him. Saints have been known to cry out in gratitude for those burdens that turned out to be loads of love. We have much to learn here! Perhaps we must persist in getting a legitimate definition of sainthood back into our vocabularies.

The birth of Christ flung into motion "the mystery of his will." How can an innocent Jewish baby boy have anything to do with the excruciating and totally uncivil experience of crucifixion? It seems to me this only illustrates the greater the sacrifice of the innocent, the greater the power of that person. The Eucharist or Holy Communion speaks to this. The death of spotless animals could never be enough to atone for the sins of humankind. It took the pure and holy Son of the Father. There is a depth to this that is never fully discovered. Our Catholic and Orthodox friends understand that better than any Protestant I have ever known. To take the Sacrament in the understanding of Christ's "real presence" is to begin to get at these depths of which we are speaking.

A crucifix can speak countless words to the believer. An empty cross speaks of Easter. A crucifix conjures up images of Good Friday and that horrendous death scene. Frankly, we can't have one without the other. The "fear and trembling" of the crucifixion is built into the fabric of our fabulous faith! How else can we "live for the praise of his glory"? Note the ongoing depth of Saint Paul's lengthy passage. We have a crucified/resurrected Lord, who began his journey on this globe at Christmas. The most epochal of all presents is his salvation brought by who and what he was, the Savior of humankind. As we exercise in humility and sincerity our hearts, minds, and souls we begin to scratch the surface of a depth mostly beyond us. Nevertheless, the exercise is indispensable to our well-being.

3. Pleading ignorance in spiritual matters can be disastrous.

In dismay, my discoveries lead me to any number of church people, who appear not to have the slightest notion of the depths of our religion. A once each day devotional is about as far as they get. Even those who are fairly regular in worship attendance can embarrass themselves. Naming the gospels and the golden rule may be about as far as it gets. I am not trying to be unkind. Certainly my purpose is not to be judgmental. My great concern is how can such persons defend our precious faith. It becomes "oh you know" kind of thing.

We all have wide and deep gaps in our knowledge of spiritual matters. We can rightfully excuse ourselves upon occasion. However, to drift along in some dreadful bliss can be a disaster. For example, how can we answer basic questions asked us by inquiring people in search of salvation? When asked about our current passage, what can be intelligently stated without study and pondering? We are supposed to know our Lord in more than the ways taught us in a manner that eventually produces more heat than light! People need answers today and they generally want them from other lay people. The most professional thing a clergy person might do is take all of his/her members through Christianity 101 again, or the initial time for some. We clergy can be seriously at fault for our parishioners not knowing as much about the Bible as Oprah or David Letterman.

The riches of our faith are priceless and cannot be measured in secular terms. The deep waters are there to be explored unhurriedly. Anyone can take difficult passages, after just becoming thoroughly acquainted with Holy Scripture, and be blessed many times over. In view of the fact large numbers of church members have blocks of time and financial resources, we are brought face-to-face with something quite unpleasant. Well, let's go ahead and ask the question. Are we ignorant of large areas of the spiritual life because we want to be? Perhaps it is because we simply — by design — have other priorities more pressing. Since we "were marked with the seal of the promised Holy Spirit," how can any of these inquiries by relevant? May our dear Lord be merciful!

The resolution to our ignorance is mostly found in prayer and study of Holy Scripture with the added ingredient of congregational worship. To take these areas seriously is to banish ignorance in spiritual matters. We are enabled to probe at the deeper levels and begin to enjoy the excitement of what it really means to be a disciple of the Christ. Then Saint Paul's brilliance may not become crystal clear, but at least we are familiar with the magnificent and marvelous theological artistry put before us. Yes, and when we are stumped, we are to go to prayer, not as an escape but as a tool to continue our in-depth excursions. We value the news in-depth. Why can't we do as much for our spiritual lives? It seems to me the choice is plainly before us.

4. Everyone — in a sense — is his/her own theologian.

Ideally, every person who professes Jesus Christ as Savior and Lord is on a theological journey that makes him/her a student of God. It is a beautiful and even sacred phenomenon to observe some laity commit themselves to study the Father, Son, and Holy Spirit. They are never ordained but do they ever look like and act like trained and vibrant clergy! We owe the small group movement a debt of gratitude. Of course, it is not that different from the vital societies given birth in England by John and Charles Wesley. Spiritual sensitivities are brought to the surface. Both personal and group growth is seen. They are "God's own people," who either are or are becoming their own theologians!

Some of our laity will wrestle with passage after passage. They refuse to run away from the noble task of becoming theologically literate. Such men and women have always made me shout for joy! I believe some understand the meaning of being colleagues together better than some clergy, especially those who are turf conscious. We are blessed today with them taking courses in colleges and seminaries, sometimes on a non-credit basis. We clergy can learn from them, provided we are humble and honest. Their voyage takes them into the depths of theological inquiry and understanding. Think how proud the apostle would be! While we have enormous pockets of illiteracy in our flocks, we also have quite the opposite. There are adults determined to call unto the deep.

There are those who would maintain this only leads to private interpretation that can take valued disciples in too many hurtful directions, including toward hell. We do need to admit church history is filled to overflowing with those who go so far as to build entire denominations on a few verses. Such radical movements, I fear, have more to do with egotism and pride than anything else. The absolutism of one or a few can build cages for all those who are willing to agree and adjust accordingly. But let's not be too harsh in our day and time. We have checks and balances today that provide stopgaps for those who are traveling toward a dead end. We are helped greatly by knowing we were marked with the seal of the promised Holy Spirit.

We ought not to frighten our flocks by telling them they are expected to become their own theologians! Pastoral guidance is often necessary and this means clergy who are rooted and grounded in the faith, refusing to be threatened by bright laity. My experience tells me we always have some men and women who know more about certain areas than we do. As hard as it is to admit, that is even true in a spiritual sense. They are willing to dig deeper and will do so! Never underestimate the work of the Holy Spirit in parishes, and any place, for that matter. Secure within their own theological understanding, pastors can lead and enable magnificent blessings to occur among their precious people. At times the dear Lord just prods us to turn them loose!

Summary And Conclusion

The apostle's gift to us in this portion of Holy Scripture provides a cutting edge of growth for many of us. His emphasis is Christological and offers the opportunity for us to kneel and worship our Savior and Lord more completely. In addition, it especially provides a thrilling time of study that makes us forget all about the light-weight stuff we have been reading in popular devotionals! With heart and mind perfectly attuned to the Holy Spirit our labors become more and more fruitful. We are brought in touch with understandings — indeed wisdom — that enable us to celebrate Christmas on a daily basis, recognizing in joy our greatest gift is the Christ.

The challenge to the pastors and key laity in our time is much what it always has been. We are to know about Jesus Christ and accept him in our hearts and minds without reservation. We must not be spiritually starving people, refusing the royalty in our midst. A lazy and unsettled mind is a negative force in our quest to know our Lord. A heart that is barely lukewarm is a major problem — if allowed to continue — because we can never tell where we are going to land in matters of spiritual depth. Often, the Holy Spirit leads some of us to focus on disciplines that will move us into those heavenly lands where untold riches are plentiful. We must move from our glasses of skimmed milk to steaks perfectly cooked and ready for our consumption. Time is passing, so we must be at work.

Taking A Necessary Step

Introduction

The closeness between John the Baptist and Jesus can hardly be overemphasized. It was true from the time of their conceptions and the evident, close relationship between their mothers. It is said that in certain parts of the world there are still a few who follow only the baptizer. After 2,000 years the transition apparently has not been made.

Among those disciples that Paul found, they had no clear witness of the far greater one who would follow John. This may very well be a special word for those today who are good, morally upright people but have not made the discovery of Jesus the Christ. Our duty to instruct and inspire is an extraordinary opportunity.

It is likely these twelve or so knew of Jesus and had awesome respect for him. What they apparently did not know was that salvation was found in him and only him. Paul took the situation as he found it and made one of spiritual progress, doing so without denigrating John. Would that all spiritual transitions could be as smooth as this one!

The wise student and teacher attempts to preserve what is good and useful. They seek to improve and make additions with some needed corrections. There was no reason for competition between John and Jesus. That would be counterproductive or worse. The moment was crucial and Paul did not fail.

Focus

What we have may be good but it is only a beginning.

Body

1. We made a good start and then things began to fall apart.

How often this is true for you and me! The Christ is born in us and we begin to experience signs that everything he says is true. It isn't that the baptist is vying for our full attention. Some person, organization, or idea is making a move to loosen the relationship with our Lord. A pastor, who is charismatic and demanding, may become our sole interpreter of the Christian faith. A sectarian group, emphasizing certain points of scripture to the detriment of others, may become our only home base. An idea of genuine worth is allowed to become virtually the only one that guides our lives. The subtleties are numerous.

My experiences over more than four decades of pastoring churches tell me goodness is usually shattered by what Saint James labels the power of the tongue. We are moving in our spiritual lives really well and along comes someone who verbalizes something that becomes a bone of contention. Before you know it, the peace that passes all understanding is not only gone, it is so far removed that the people involved have moved beyond the perimeters of practicing the faith. What happened? Those who have a courageous spirit and real humility begin to retrace their steps. Eventually the discovery is made. Christ was sidestepped. His primary place had become optional and certainly his lowly, forgiving heart had been crushed. The good start had been compromised and a loss of faith was at hand.

"Backsliding" was a fairly common term at one time in our country, especially during revival meetings. The gist was usually the same. A precious person had received Jesus Christ as Savior and Lord. That person had begun to practice the Christian life in ways noticeable to others. Then, something happens and there are about as many reasons as there are people. While this may have little directly to do with John the Baptist, it strongly suggests a falling away of something good and supremely meaningful. We may not especially care for such revivalistic overtones, but the message is clear. We are created and intended for spiritual growth. To be seriously thwarted, regardless of how, becomes a sad state of affairs.

74

The more sophisticated and ritualistic parts of society are not that much different. A daily early-morning mass is not only avoided but becomes strictly an optional experience of the disciple. In time even regular Sunday mass is put on a take-it-or-leave-it basis. So, after some months the one, holy, catholic, and apostolic church has become mostly just another set of buildings and doctrinal concepts best evaded. May God be merciful! In mainline Protestantism this can be seen by secular politics and power struggles within the churches beginning to dominate good people's will and time. Even clergy begin to question their ordination vows and wonder that perhaps God did not call them after all! It's familiar territory, isn't it? Pray often — yes incessantly — that you will not fall by the wayside.

2. The sufficiency of Christ alone is illustrated.

We are born again to be faithful and forever attentive primarily to one person. We know his name and his way. While all the prophets and seers coming before and after Christ make their contributions, he and he alone brings completeness. True, the church — both visible and invisible — enters the picture but without him it has no real power or relevance. Paul found his way in Jesus Christ the crucified. So, our rebirth is an experience that gives us the reason and format for continuing our lives in a victorious manner. We must move beyond John the Baptist or anyone else who has given meaning to our lives.

Many of our parishioners tend to go through years of their lives never coming to terms with the truth of which we are speaking. It is as though a curtain drops and prevents them from fully receiving their Savior and Lord. It is not that they have no knowledge of him, of course; it is that they have a problem of readiness. Perhaps this is the work of Satan that likes things the way they are. Whatever it is, faithful clergy and laity are responsible for leading others to accept the sufficiency of Christ alone. It may be a bigger and more intricate problem than we are willing to admit. I suspect the best way to tackle this is to confess our sins of omission. We knew the right thing to do but we did not do it. As we are forgiven, let us vow to do better for the sake of the kingdom of God.

For those of us who have spent many years in formal education and have decades of experience, it is humbling to recognize this only has practical meaning as we relate completely to Christ. The Lord Jesus is the centerpiece and from him our lives and deaths are made acceptable to the Father. For some still wandering to find another and better messiah it becomes a heart-rending scene for those looking on. We want desperately to do something about this potentially tragic state of affairs. Have we run the race, only to have left Christ off to the side? In our quest for a secular success, have we been blinded by ambition, greed, and status? These are hard questions but they must be asked and more than once.

Sometimes we see and deeply appreciate the kingship of Christ, only to turn a deaf ear to his lowliness. We shy away from a man who was virtually pulverized by the power structures of his day. Yet we are told we must suffer with him in order to rise with him. The crucifixion must never be seen divorced from the resurrection and vice versa. The twin events illustrate in a realistic and graphic way what it takes to understand such all-pervasive sufficiency. Our acceptance of this truth gives us doctrinal grounding that is good forever and ever. To plead the weakness of humanity can only be a trapdoor that acts as a preventative in receiving his gift of baptism and the Holy Spirit. The gift wants to be given. Shall we go through most of life rejecting it? I humbly pray that will not be the case.

3. So much of life is a rewarding preliminary leading to something or someone better.

This concept takes time to ponder. The truth of it is not likely to come quickly. In honesty, perhaps we all need to live long enough to be able to perceive it and the value. Counting our blessings is one way to begin positive pondering on such a matter. Then, we see the connections of how one set of events leads to another and so on. Those who don't have a sense of growth, of course, will have some problematic times trying to deal with this. In terms of the truth of the text we understand John's baptism of repentance was not wrong. It just didn't go far enough. More — substantially more — was in the offing and it would potentially lead to fulfillment, at least, in this life.

From one valid viewpoint our lives are a series of beginnings and, therefore, endings. As times come and go, our lives are impacted and — to some extent — we impact the times. We were never intended to stalemate and live in little more than a parasitic existence. That is a tragedy! In the Methodist connection we move from church to church. We begin and we end. We move into new parsonages and churches, understanding one ministry is finished and another is beginning. My experience has been one mostly of celebration and a sense of accomplishment. Sometimes there are bumps at both the start and the finish but there has been learning and improvement in most cases. I cannot adequately speak of other polities but trust it is much the same.

As the Holy Spirit abides and provides, the awareness of a rewarding preliminary to something and/or someone else is frequently present. We may not know what or who but with our lives thoroughly in the hands of our Savior and Lord anticipation is in the air. Hopefully, this is a common experience for all brothers and sisters. I always looked forward to new appointments, largely because I knew there would be some truly good people ready to greet me. Not only would they provide a welcome, they would minister with me and — if need be — forgive me. Praises be to the mercies of God who enables this to happen! The ordained ministry is so precious and at times we make it more difficult and complicated than it is. This is because we do not trust fully in the one who called us.

Paul's friends in Ephesus did not appear to be unhappy solely with John's baptism. It took the apostle to point to the fact they were actually living in a preliminary period, awaiting more. He was emissary, teacher, and ordained clergy at the same time! Sometimes you and I are put into places where we fulfill the same functions. A key layperson doesn't know about the spiritual riches available to him or her. How can that person know? He/she needs someone to be put in his/her pathway to reveal the need. That person needs someone for instruction, and finally he/she needs a clergy person to put the three together and provide under the guidance of the Holy Spirit for his/her spiritual welfare. Is this only theory or inadequate discipling? No, it allows the Holy Spirit to work for everyone's benefit.

4. We are to acknowledge our mission as agents of introduction.

The input we can insert in others' lives is an area for close inspection. In short, what can we do even now to foster improvement in our brothers and sisters? What ideas or issues or maybe disciplines can enhance others? Well, let's admit this is a wide and deep area of ministry. For example, how can we be sure we are not simply attempting to influence others with our own pet prejudices? Do we have an agenda that doesn't resemble what Christ has in store for us? Yet, we must not go away or perhaps run frustrated in defeat. Only by staying close to Christ will we have the proper words, thoughts, and feelings. Anything less may cause a hailstorm of ill will brewed and stewed by Satan!

It is prudent to be reminded that the Holy Spirit does not make us timid. Instead, this Spirit fills us with power, love, and self-control. We can enable precious people to take a necessary step to substantially improve their spiritual lives. Timidity and essential humility are not synonymous. To be sure, within our strength we are going to fail in the long run. With the strength given us by God we are going to be successful, at least, in terms of right attitudes. Along the way in our lives these happenings occur again and again. Missed opportunities can be the worst of all admissions as one nears the end of his/her life. In our ministries as agents of introduction we are given what is imperative to say and do. Sometimes this means little planning on our part.

Note what a substantial and qualitative difference Paul made. He was an agent of introduction *par excellence*. An amazing and powerful change took place. Do you and I underestimate ourselves? Maybe a better way to phrase it is: Do we question our relationship with God the Father through Jesus, his Son? Still better, is our problem one of needing spiritual validation? Then, we are in crucial need of an agent to introduce us to the finer points of what it takes to improve our ministries! So, it works both ways and this is a means to instruct us in honesty and humility. Praise God from whom all blessings flow, praise him all creatures here below! Our ministries are so multifaceted and fascinating. Who can say what we will be asked to do or refrain from doing tomorrow?

It has been my philosophy since a college student to try to make the good better. This was partly ambition, pure and simple. It was also the sincere recognition that God still had changes to make in me and I had better listen ... carefully. There is that ominously wholesome craving to be more and better. It likely has nothing to do with money and property. It has a great deal to do with the evolution and improvement of one's personhood. In Christian terms, this means to become more like Christ. After all, isn't that the on-going, absolutely fundamental principle, in our pilgrimage? To become more like him is to become more amenable to being agents of needful introduction by solid implication. So ministry is so obvious we have to work at it to avoid it!

Summary And Conclusion

In a way, taking necessary steps with the Father holding our hands is a simplified description of living the Christian life. At each crucial point in our development there is a step to take. We may find it to our liking. Likewise, we may discover we don't like it at all! Paul's friends had a step to take. Otherwise, they would remain thwarted in what was intended for them. This is so like our lives, isn't it? Hopefully, every step shows forward movement under the banner of Jesus Christ. We may be complimented for our goodness, only to learn it just isn't good enough for the eyes of one who is the only one who ultimately counts.

Dear friends, pause to give thanks for your lives. Do so because you know there is more to learn and celebrate, as you and others change to a greater good. There has to be that hunger in us that seeks to eat more solid meat and fewer potatoes. If we but listen attentively, the dear Lord will come to you directly or send someone to provide an opening for you to take the next step. Plateaus may be nice and comfortable but they are also debilitating. In time, as opportunities come and go, they can so erode that they won't support much of anything that is truly valuable. Don't allow the awful shame of such a predicament claim your place in God's kingdom. Stand tall or fall on your knees, whichever is required, and move forward in the spiritual life Christ intends. You will never lack opportunities. He continues to stand at the door and knock.

Getting It Straight

Introduction
What a colorful figure Paul must have been in flesh and blood! His individuality shows a man who refuses to be dominated by anything. For us to be able to experience his ministry, as he went about, would have been something that would have made an indelible imprint on us.

As he wove his life and ministry into his day and time the enemies were many. This was especially true among his Jewish brothers and sisters. Only by the grace of God was he able to fulfill what he had been called to do. The hatred could be intense and his very life was at stake. Nevertheless, as his letters say, he went about in a thankful mood.

One wonders how the Christian movement could ever have gotten off the ground without him. Much of the New Testament reflects his power, personality, and pen. His churches sometimes were battlegrounds but he stayed the course. He wanted his people to get things straight and gave himself totally to see this happen.

Our calling to the pastorate is much like that. We want our people to get things straight. Perhaps the momentous question that is always before us deals with our willingness to give our all. So much real success deals with exactly that matter, which invariably depends upon a deeply personal decision.

Focus
We cannot live our lives well in fragmentation.

Body

1. No one can indefinitely live a morally fractured life.

Sometimes in high places, especially in politics and religion, we watch in dismay and even disillusionment as our icons crumble. The list is long and there is nothing new, that is, if we survey the history of nations and the world. There is no need to name names. They are frequently in the news. Of course, we must be shrewd and perceptive enough to determine the reliability of the various forms of media. This is not easy. In fact, it can be downright difficult! Our temptation may be to point the finger at someone, who has betrayed some of the most basic criteria for living a healthy life. I believe this is only helpful after we take personal inventory.

We view and often experience morally fractured lives all about us. Appearances mislead us and we can be devastated. Never judge a book by its cover is long-standing and sound advice. To be honest, this state of affairs can also work in an opposite manner. Someone may have allegedly fallen and we learn this is only an allegation and is not provable. People deserve the benefit of the doubt — at least, the first or second time. If we don't like someone, it is easy to find him/her guilty and spread the word with glee. It is a quagmire in today's world. Sometimes we know so much and yet we know so little! We all tend to be morally fractured in some way.

To live one's life personally in one way and publicly quite another, certainly and simply calls for correction. We may like to think fornication and adultery are excusable between two consenting adults. It seems fashionable to seal off one's infidelities to a restricted area and claim they have no bearing on our public and vocational lives. I believe this trend increases our illness as a nation and jeopardizes the general welfare. We are intended to be whole human beings with morality at work in every sector of our precious lives. The dear Lord did not come to save us in fragments, leaving some untouched, especially those of our own choosing. We must be brave and brazen like Saint Paul.

Some say early on in their lives, either directly or indirectly, "This part of my life belongs to the Lord, this part belongs to me." In other words, lordship is denied in certain areas. Again, we must not be too judgmental. We all have the same tendency at work in us. It is as though humankind was born with it. Perhaps it illustrates the affliction of original sin! Such fragmentation always and eventually shows itself. The wounds come to the surface. The unforgiven sins become noticeable. The out and out hypocrisy exudes an odor that hardly anyone can miss. It is a sad and very trying time. Of course, the remedy is found in repentance and forgiveness with the promise to live a new life. Then, all aspects of our coming, going, and staying show wholeness. The world, believe it or not, is always looking for just such a person.

2. We are called to live in Christ as a distinctive human being.

To live in him is to be formed by him and that is not to make everyone look, more or less, exactly the same. To get things straight means we become human beings who stand out in the Lord. Yes, the body has many parts, and each of us is a special part. More in Pauline language, our bodies are temples of the Holy Spirit. Think what a magnificent quilt we are throughout the world! There are too many shades and sizes to count. We were all bought with a price and that adds immensely to our image. Christ died and arose for us. Now, we die and arise with him. We are a witness to the world.

Billions of dollars are spent each year in our country on our appearances. Let's ask a rather embarrassing question. Does that have anything to do with showing others we belong to Christ and he belongs to us? Suppose we shut down the industry for a year, except for certain basics like soap and water. Would this greatly hinder the cause of the Christian faith? Perhaps the chief argument would be that such a move would put numerous people out of work. Well, that becomes quite a dilemma, doesn't it? In complete seriousness, I wonder why it is essential for many Christians to do what they do in order to appear attractive. You may want to ask me what rock I crawled out from under, but hear me out. There is a requirement that we be sincerely holy people. In our depths, we know this is true and we are not bad people. Perhaps we have not yet gone far enough.

Our bodies are temples and that is awesomely spiritual. Each of us lives in a different body but we are all in temples. It is questionable if most Christians accept that and yet I do not want to be critical. My personal experience tells me quickly, and more directly than I like, there is much in my life — past and present — that needs to be washed by the blood of the Lamb of God. Those of us who have been given good health for many years can be too proud and ungrateful. Have you seriously thanked God today for health and financial resources? Always what we have is from God. Yes, what did you and I earn or create? Once in a while our singular greatness can blind us! If we are to be successfully retrieved, we are to remember we were bought with a price.

In the United States of America we are blessed with opportunities beyond the imaginations of millions living in other countries. Often they see our standard of living as something to acquire. In our inadequacy we tend to allow them to measure us in material success. How wrong this is! Perhaps this is where solid media emphasizing Christian unity and inter-religious dialogue come into play. Don't misunderstand me, some really good things are being done. More — much more — needs to be done. Christians flaunting their good fortune in terms of material success just isn't right! Getting things straight, really, is to trim the fat and live more healthy lives that exalt the Christ. Fractured moral lives that tend toward immorality then can be placed where they belong: the local trash heap. God is faithful to lead us to less meaning more for him.

3. Chastity may be unwelcome but it is the Christian's call.

Misuse of the body, especially in sexual activity, is one of the most pressing issues of our day and time. There are those who insist it ranks number one because it influences every area of society. Where can we begin with such a gargantuan problem? Good people who practice the Christian faith say they don't have the slightest idea! It is so complicated, and what is chastity anyway? Is it a simple refraining from actual intercourse between a man and a woman? May God the Father, Son, and Holy Spirit mercifully aid us as we attempt to work our way through this labyrinth of definitions. How can we teach our children and youth that sex is sacred?

Two becoming one flesh in a deeply religious sense is fodder for the late night comedians and comediennes. Shunning fornication would likely bring the biggest laugh! Saint Paul is deeply serious, as usual, and in tune with values that have consistently been a part of the Judeo-Christian tradition. I suspect many of us would be hard-pressed to come up with a person(s) who is prudish as we commonly understand it. Of course, that may not be all bad in view of the fact human nature after all is sinful and allowances for repentance and forgiveness are absolutely necessary. Surely we don't have to be caught between a rigid moral code that lacks compassion and a licentious lifestyle that preaches anything goes. We must pray daily for our young people to abstain from sexual activity until marriage becomes realizable.

In a Christian sense, how can the prospective bride and bridegroom prepare for the wedding vows, promising until death do they part? We might suggest for them to begin as new teenagers to promise to be chaste until they are married. Would the great bulk of those in our churches consider this a doable way of maturing? Those that I know would be serious and concerned but they would not go that far. Our Catholic friends can be of help here. They have a long-standing teaching of chastity and virginity. It has been there since the very early centuries and in a way is underlined by speaking of Jesus' mother as the blessed Virgin Mary. In addition, marriage is considered a sacrament. Yes, all of us can learn a great deal of practical idealism from them!

Then, there is this business of all situations being relative. This has been with us now officially for more than two generations. In reality I believe you can make a case for it beginning with Adam and Eve! Paul is not speaking of relativity in sexual matters as a way to live victoriously under the banner of Christ. Assuredly, he recognizes the curse of our first two parents and understands the tremendous harm that is done by sexual activity outside of the marriage vows. With all the relationships, divorces, and remarriages in our society how can we put Humpty Dumpty back together again? First, we must decide to practice total faithfulness in marriage with one wife or husband. Then, we must teach our children by precept and examples this way of life. Temptations are many and subtle today. In our weakness God's power is available.

4. Our bodies need our ongoing and loving attention.

It would be a mistake to spiritualize Paul's understanding of our bodies into making them ghostlike and non-biological in function. He is instructing us about what we can see and touch. Our arms, heads, hands, lungs, livers, feet, and all parts are his consideration. We are made in the image of God and therefore are to be stewards of what God, not ourselves, have created. To accept Christ as Savior and Lord does not mean we forsake or belittle our bodies for superior spiritual reasons! True, we eventually die and our bodies become dust but in the meantime we are to be good stewards. This means we neither abuse nor misuse what is entrusted to us.

The longer I live the more I am convinced there is an art to caring for our bodies. This art begins by our recognition of the gift coupled with the responsibility for it. Regardless of our sizes and shapes, beauty or lack of it, and physical prowess, it is ours and we are supposed to take care of it. That is not only a spiritual directive but common sense. Most of what is needed to apply this art can be learned, unless we run into major health problems or accidents. There is no need to make something difficult when, for the most part, it isn't. Money may or may not be needed. Physicians and other professionals may or may not be needed. God's gift is to be handled with tender loving care and at times that may mean strong medicines of discipline. Give thanks for our mortal bodies.

To be fruitful is to take good care of yourself. This is a reasonable expectation and has no bearing on a vain spirit, unless we make it so. Clergy too often try to go seven days and seven nights each week only to learn that is not the way we are made. We are guilty of attempts to please others that jeopardizes our health and in time it will show in our bodies, unless we make needed adjustments. We can feel good about ourselves — in the best and highest sense — provided we heed Paul's marvelous instruction. Every Christian is expected to produce fruit and the way we generally do this the best is by taking good care of ourselves. If we are excessively smoking and drinking alcohol, how can we be in top shape to do the Lord's work?

When our lives become fragments, especially the misuse of our bodies in a sexual way, look out! Case after case shows the apostle is on target. Someone rather elderly said to me that life is much more than sex and, of course, that is true. Yet, note the part it has played in our lives. What have we done about the devastating hurt that can potentially come from supposedly little missteps? Yes, Paul is right. We need to get it straight from the inspired rabbi. In our entirety, we are meant for the Lord. Anything short of that is not good enough. Ask God to save you from the misconception we can do his will and pay little attention to our bodies. Of course, the worst, unhealthy fiasco is to be caught in an adulterous relationship and to believe you can continue it and serve God. Likewise, prostitution is more than a lark. It is two becoming one flesh.

Summary And Conclusion

Saint Paul is the man of the hour in his instructive words to us. The world and especially those who claim Christ as Savior and Lord are to pay close attention. Living our lives in fragments is more than wrong; it is destructive to the brink of disaster. Our bodies, here and now, are created to be in full union with the Lord. Every part and portion is to belong to him. Stewardship is imperative. Sexual misdeeds, whatever form they take, must be labeled for what they are: a means to send our immortal souls to hell. Our bodies are not merely flesh and blood; they are temples of the Holy Spirit. Praises be to God for our precious bodies!

The sharpness and transparency of the text gives us reason to pause in silence and ponder its magnificent simplicity. In short, many of us will say these are difficult words out of step with our times but they bear a full gift of truth. The crux of the matter is at hand for those who profess the Father's Son. Will we believe wholeheartedly in the apostle's strong and firm advice or will we accommodate the pressures of living in a mostly secularized society? While many Christians must work in environments not at all conducive to such teaching being implemented, what shall we give in exchange for our immortal souls? Let us always allow for compassion and mercy. However, let us always be faithful to the revealed word of the living God. If we are now living our precious lives in morally destructive fragments, plead with God for help!

Being Single-minded

Introduction

The Second Coming of Christ was much in the thoughts of the ancient church. Saint Paul was no exception, as his letters often indicate. Time was growing short and soon the present form of this world would be passing away. The expectation must have been both thrilling and somewhat ominous for Christ's people.

There is a particularity about the events coming soon after our Lord's Ascension and the Day of Pentecost. A single-mindedness is virtually demanded. It all has to do with a single God/man they knew was the one in whom they found their salvation. He had given them more than hope. He had given them assurances of heaven with him.

In one sense, nothing has changed during those twenty centuries. We are to be centered on the one and only certain Savior of humankind, that little Jewish boy born of Mary. As he made his way as a lad and to maturity, including dying a terrible death and conquering the grave, anticipation filled the air. He was the Father's Son!

So, we are called to immerse ourselves completely in him, leaving no stone unturned. It is a radical invitation that begins and ends with him, and him alone. Perhaps we could use the cliché "the more things change, the more they are the same." Christ bids us to come both to die and arise with him.

Focus

We belong totally to Christ and no other.

Body

1. We are to believe in Christ for our salvation.

The radical and unequivocal nature of such a dogmatic stance has caused highly tensioned feelings in countless numbers. Yet, if we believe in the New Testament as the inspired word of God, both our choice and answer are clear. To live changed lives with the promise of heaven is our positive plight and all that entails. For those of us who have accepted Jesus Christ as the way, the truth, and the life we have, at least, an elementary understanding of the price we must pay. Also, by the grace of God, we have a built-in resource that refuses to be defeated. We don't always like what we are doing or refraining from doing but that is mostly irrelevant!

One's salvation is the most highly valued possession we have. It is who and what we are. To some extent, everyone has salvation or a set of beliefs and behavior patterns that manifest themselves. Even the cold and committed communist has this! Some follow and are absorbed by various ideologies but we must be very careful to stay the course with our Savior, who is Christ the Lord. Some say, almost derisively he/she finds identity only in his/her job. Well, I guess in a way that's we Christians! People and positions come and go in our lives but our true occupation or vocation remains the same. To live differently from this is to invite spiritual complications that only tend to muddle and postpone what (who) is intended for us.

The interreligious nature of today's world must be confronted and hopefully reconciled in ways helpful for all concerned. Arguments are seldom useful, especially if they are heated arguments before numbers of people. Our call is one to dialogue as peacefully as we can — in particular — among Jews and Muslims. Respect is always necessary. After all, aren't they also God's children? Yes, and do we presume to know all the ways God has and does deal with all of his dear children? Of real assistance along this line is a reading and pondering of Romans 9, 10, and 11. All three religions have Abraham for their father. Our call to radical living under the banner of Christ does not close the door to intelligent and dutiful dialogue.

Who has to have the greatest influence in our lives? Friends, this is a no-brainer! We are to be immersed in the healing waters of his love. It is a love that knows no bounds. It reasonably follows that such a style of living will rub off on others. In the Christian context, not to be fishers of men and women is a sad commentary and contradiction. To be sure, idealism is much at work here and we may try to be more than we are intended to be. Frankly, I don't think we should be overly worried about this. Remember, to pray that every day is successful in God's sight and not ours. This is a brilliant conditioner that allows us a kind of holy objectivity, which can immensely aid our spiritual growth. To live every day in his shadow is not to live in darkness but in light the world scoffs at and finds mostly meaningless. Christ beckons for us to be fully open to him.

2. All our bets are placed in Christ.

Casino gambling, as well as numerous other forms of gambling, seem to have become more and more popular in our nation. All of the reasons are well beyond me, but I do believe the one that comes quickly to the forefront is the chance for a winner to become independently wealthy and create an image of power in the recipient. Such a windfall brings immediate attention and both positive and negative recognition. It is a way of becoming somebody overnight and the realization that what was once out of reach financially, is no longer true. Christians take all we have and are; then we bet them on the belief Christ is the answer to our sins and incompleteness.

From the time we are small, some of us were taught not to put all of our eggs in one basket. Then, in a spiritual sense, that is exactly what we are inspired to do! Perhaps the thought occurs to us from time to time, that if we are wrong in our decision, we have lived a wasted life. It is a sobering thought. For the thinking person it makes perfectly good sense, even though it can be depressively destructive. To have lived and died in vain is perhaps the most horrendous thought a sane human being can have. It can send terrifying chills running up and down our backs. At its worst, urges to commit suicide come upon us. Paul would tell us confidently and firmly he hasn't changed his mind. All bets, not just some or most, are placed on the master, the man of Galilee. This is the way our lives are intended. There is no change on the horizon!

The gift we have and the grace provided to be encompassed by it is one that those with a mostly secular orientation to life will not understand. Some days I am not sure how much the dear Lord's disciples understood it! It is in our willing spirit and temperament of heart that we discover such magnificence to be worked out. It really isn't news but there is a genuine difference between Christ's people and the world. That does not mean we are to run away and hide for fear of contamination. However, it certainly does mean we have placed our bets on the Father's Son. We are risk takers, betting 100 percent on the authenticity of our salvation here and now and forever and ever. It is the right thing to do!

Are you satisfied with all of this? Would you rather it be some other way? Perhaps you would like to travel about the country or even the world, placing your bets in different casinos. Then, at least, you would have the chance of winning under various circumstances. The saying, "winning some and losing some" may be a more shrewd approach to what you understand life to be. Don't bet on it! Saint Paul is lurking around with compassion but a firm hand, telling you in no uncertain terms to get with the revealed program. It is difficult to imagine him humorous, except possibly to prove the point he lived and died by. If you want to squander some extra cash with a cult or new age guru, this could be quite an eye-opener and lead to betting everything on Christ. It could also put you on a demonic roller coaster that eventually runs with an outrageous and fatal ending.

3. Our destiny is tied to Christ.

We are a peculiar people. One extraordinary man was born into history who we say is God in the flesh. We worship him and call him several names but, in particular, Savior and Lord. Our revelation in the New Testament indicates without reservation he was with the Father from the beginning. Securely linked to this Son, we are locked into a unique relationship for all time and even when time is dissolved as a principle found in creation. Wow! Isn't

92

that mind-boggling? Indeed, we are a peculiar people. This is so much true we, at times, have laborious moments attempting to communicate with others the supposedly simple story of Jesus. It is hard to come up with all the superlatives!

It is as though we are owned by him and have become his slaves. Well, we were bought with a price and that was his precious and holy blood. To attempt to tell of our destiny separate and apart from this Jewish fellow, is most difficult — if not impossible. What we have to tell the world in joy and humility is the unparalleled satisfaction we have. If we go all the way with him, we have a peace that passes all understanding. That does not mean we are free from various kinds of pain or even, at times, serious doubts. It is more than a change of pace. It is joy unspeakable that remains calm in the face of the lovely becoming decidedly unlovely. Yes, it is likened to the man who searched the world over and found the pearl of great price, discarding gladly all the others.

Whenever the end comes, either with the Second Coming or our deaths, we are hopeful in ways foreign to those who do not have this Savior and Lord. Well, are we claiming too much? Is Paul pointing us in a direction that is never realized? Are we so peculiar we have our heads in the sand and could possibly be having hallucinations? My answer to this not uncommon inquiry is, "But, my dear friends, have you tried it?" As that answer is being given we must never assume power in our own strength. As Paul discovered, God's grace is sufficient because his power is made perfect in weakness. This is an imperative we must learn, hopefully early! We were bought with the supreme price of the Father's Son.

When the end for us comes in this life, are we prepared to have a glimpse of our funeral service and place of burial? Are the ushers and pallbearers the ones we have chosen? Will good and accurate things be said about us? Will our family and friends be present to bid us farewell? It is only human nature to ask such questions but aren't they all secondary? Some of us, more than anything else, want to hear our family and friends assuredly say he/she was a genuinely good person whose destiny was unquestionably tied to the ever-living Christ. The here and now meets eternity. Our witness is given and preserved because of his love for us and our response of giving ourselves unconditionally. Any artist would be hard-pressed to show this on a canvas or writer in a book. On our knees in silence or with heads high, shouting his praises, we are going to our real home.

4. We are to stay focused and live accordingly.

Anyone in the workaday world knows the importance of staying focused. Perhaps this has always been true but in the current era the demands are such that most would never hold a job for any length of time unfocused. The computer has much to do with this, and certainly the ever-increasing sophistication with intricate maneuvering is another. Our grandparents and even parents — depending on our age — would likely find few ways even to begin to comprehend what's going on in the workforce today. That is not in any way to cast aspersions. Since we were not at our peaks in their day, maybe we should note that their focusing may have been far more physically demanding.

The single-minded follower of Christ is different from the world at large. In the first place, we shut out the clamor of those who would rob us of our spiritually esteemed place. We do not necessarily devalue the world and its trimmings. After all, we certainly need it to survive! Our secret is in not allowing hurtful forces to take over our time, energy, and talents. In short, we stay focused on Christ and live accordingly. In the second place we never forget from whom our help comes. We do not save ourselves and we are not smart enough to provide the guidance essential for victorious living. We admit leaning on the everlasting arms is more than words set to music. A drummer different from that orchestrated by the world is continually at work. We love the angels singing.

The enemy of our souls has countless tools at his disposal. They come in shades and sizes we may or may not recognize. As some revivalists of yesteryear used to say, "Even the devil quotes scripture." To maintain there is no such evil force is to be blinded to the spiritual reality of our great leaders who paved the way for us. It seems the most persuasive person can be on the payroll of the one who tempted our Lord in the wilderness. You and I can readily recognize all of this at work, only to learn we are also at the brink of being duped! Note how easily we are led astray simply by getting us to focus in directions where Christ is not present.

Our lives tell stories. Others listen to them. Some watch them. We are on display! The Christian witness calls attention to itself in ways intended to be powerfully positive. We are being graded. That doesn't mean the teachers always know what they are talking about. It does mean they are either trying to tear down what they experience or desire what we have. We must not fail or if we do, quickly repent with forgiveness and continue our spiritual journey. So much is intended for all of us! The table is filled to overflowing with goodies. Praise God from whom all blessings flow. Friends, stay focused and live accordingly under the banner of Jesus Christ. While God is all-powerful, he still uses our hands, feet, minds, and hearts to carry the gospel of his Son. To whom do we belong? There is only one correct answer: Jesus Christ. All others are secondary.

Summary And Conclusion

Spiritually speaking, a scatter-brained person is in serious trouble! We cannot live our precious lives this way and that way, expecting to have the assurance of salvation. To wander across the fields of this and that provides only an unrest that may last a lifetime. Let the externals come and go. Let them be good times and bad times. Let friends come and go. Just be sure your interior life is in peaceful acceptance of Christ. Have we not heard? Jesus is primarily interested in our hearts. He wants to reside there permanently and do for us what we can never do for ourselves. Yes, we — at our very best — belong totally to Christ and no other. He provides a safety net for all of humanity. He continues to knock on the doors of those who have spurned his love, some for a lifetime.

The popularity of Second Coming publications is, at times, unbelievable. The hungry public in large numbers never seem to get their fill, and lots of money is made. Our call is not to be caught up in something we really have never known much about. In fact, our Lord tells us only the Father knows the day or night. Our major mode of living always has directly to do with the man born in a manger. If he returns right now, fine. If he returns, centuries from now, fine. We are to stay focused on to whom we belong. Not only that but rid ourselves of any competitor. Jesus will not tolerate others before him. In a way it is the restoration of one of the Ten Commandments. Be steadfast and of good cheer. Hold fast to that you know is satisfaction *par excellence!*

Looking Out For Others

Introduction

Being able to synthesize in such a way that harmony can be the outcome is among the many things the Apostle Paul does well. The often-pesky church at Corinth desperately needed such a skill, written and practiced in charity. To follow his inspired advice comes as a gift to all of us, 2,000 years ago or today.

The individualistic Christianity, largely the work of Protestants, has been and is both a bane and balm, for us. To do our own thing is commendable and perhaps essential but it can prove utterly destructive to those who cannot comprehend the diversity found in our faith. Think what great problems we have solved and yet left unsolved!

We are to look out for others, especially if we are more mature in the faith. However, this can be an open door to tragedy, unless we remember to keep a close eye on our imperfect lives. But Paul makes his point about as perfectly as it can be made. We walk away from it and discover Satan is staring us in the face.

Charity for one another is the way great and powerful congregations are built. It is also the way we as individuals become more than private disciples, ministering mostly to ourselves. The Pauline teaching does not disappoint unless we pay little real attention to it.

Focus

We are called spiritually to form others, as well as ourselves.

Body

1. Weak believers are always among us.

Even as we speak about the weakness of others, we are reminded of how weak we were initially in practicing the Christian faith. It seems to me we should be in a penitent mood every time we seek gently to correct others. They are where we were. But let's not be too quick to celebrate a permanent level of maturity. My experience is that even the saints from time to time fall from lofty and respected heights. The history of the church provides excellent examples. However, we do know those who went through such episodes became stronger. Even though they wept bitterly, as did Saint Peter, the powerful pain of it all enabled them not only to return to their former level but above it.

It is so important to practice what we preach before our weaker brothers and sisters. When can we ever say to them "don't do as I do, but do as I say"? The folly of lip service to the religion Christ gave to us is probably the most disastrous event in our lives in the long run. While this may sound harsh, pastors can be the most outlandishly guilty of all! We can preach tithing but do we tithe? We can preach praying constantly but do we do so? We can preach about daily study and pondering of the Holy Scriptures but do we practice this, except for Sunday preaching? We can preach about solid and ongoing relationships with other denominations but are we available to the pastor down the street?

For those content in their Christian living, it can be quite a jolt to learn there is a basic responsibility for others. We all know these lovely people, who are often prime movers or — at least — faithful to what they have been willing to accept. The proud and highly respected pastor or layperson may enjoy the attention and recognition so much he/she is unable to detect spiritual blindness. Some of us not only know such people but we have been there, haven't we? Experience teaches me there is a creative discontent in our lives that is not always welcome. We learn things we would just as soon not learn! Of course, we can all say we care for others but do we do so as the Holy Spirit has guided us?

There is what I call a grumbling syndrome among God's people. That can be at any level of the church or in any individual's life.

98

Hopefully, this is a means for the spiritually strong to enable the weak to become more like the crucified and resurrected Lord. Sometimes, even the most devoted soul perceives negatives and perhaps actual defeat, only to learn joyously we have passed through a phase lifting all of us higher. These are times of thanksgiving for what the Holy Spirit has been able to accomplish. Be alert to them because they certainly do happen! To grumble is not a sin in my opinion, unless it becomes an unquenchable thirst that is never satisfied. Sometimes those who are weak need something new and different in their lives virtually on a daily basis. Perhaps the news media has aided and abetted this!

2. Liberty in thought and action is intended to benefit others.

Isn't this what the United States of America is about? In our idealism — since the beginning — we have sought to make this a guiding principle. Sure, we attempted to improve ourselves individually but in doing so we likewise — at least at an idealistic level — wanted the same opportunities for others. We have always been a melting pot and continue to be. While at first this may not seem to have a direct bearing on Paul's teaching; it shows the influence of a definite belief in human rights. Truly, our nation has been a beacon to millions! Our Puritan fathers and mothers may not have understood this at first but there were forces that made them bend.

Isn't it a glorious sight to watch others grow in the faith? That's especially true if we have been a part of it. Oh, I don't mean we can document it! Mostly, our contributions don't come about that way. How fortunate we are because that means we cannot brag about it! Some Christian's are truly a work of art, as they go about being formed in the likeness of Christ. Their independence and sometimes brashness eventually becomes a gift for the wider body of believers. As experimentation comes and goes, the Holy Spirit synchronizes, harmonizes, and sometimes formalizes. Precious and essential spiritual formation glows for all to see, that is, those who are attentive. "Life, liberty, and the pursuit of happiness" are not necessarily secular terms.

The greats of our faith are those who have often reached out, creating high levels of frustration and more. They have also in some cases been those who have pulled back in order to bring others along that were weak in the faith. Perhaps the most notable personage is Pope John XXIII, who flung open the windows of the Catholic church but refused to abandon the revelation of the faith, as he understood it. While he has his critics, the Catholic church has never been the same and yet it is still the same! The widening and broadening of his pontificate made the Catholic church far more accessible to others, especially inquirers. Such beacons never made the mistake of Napoleon Bonaparte, who invaded Russia and moved too far from his supply lines!

The flow of religious and moral ideas across all lines is a major achievement for our time. To be sure, problems — some of them enormous — have been created. Yet, with the mind of Christ, rooted and grounded in the faith, we are able to discriminate among the uplifting and hurtful. In the cauldron of multicultural existence there is that momentous opportunity to grow more fully, totally, and completely into the likeness of Jesus Christ. Denominational lines often have come tumbling down. When they didn't, sometimes new forms for ministry were given birth. Shades of the Wesleys and the Church of England! So, let us give thanks for the wonders of our day and time, despite the very real potential for unimaginable holocausts. May the will of the Father be done!

3. We are to make a contribution to every life we touch.

Well, that sounds like a big order, doesn't it? There is a profound truth here that may not dawn on us until we are well along in years. Is it too much to expect? Definitely not, that is, if we seriously believe that all things are possible with God. As the Holy Spirit works through us, for us, and among us, each and every precious human being we touch can be benefited. In terms of prayerful extension many others can also be influenced for the good. To make a difference for good in another person's life is actually a reasonable expectation. To be flexible enough to enable others to see the Christ more completely is ministry, pure and simple.

Many of us — if not all — have wondered upon occasion about our positive presence. Not being able to sense growth in others tends to be a common experience. However, it is certainly true that when the most severe darkness comes, we are soon to witness the sun coming up. Perhaps for you that is not always the case, but frankly it has been true over and over again for me. Spiritual formation generally is not an easy matter. To move ahead of others and then be called to look back to their state and pick them up is not something many of us enjoy. After all, in our competitive world isn't it the American way to keep stretching ourselves and solidifying our positions? In spiritual dynamics we know this is not the way to go. The weak are to be treated with dignity and respect. God expects that of us!

Our prayers should be focused upon this very concept. We are to aid in forming others and not run away to some safe corner to sit in a rocking chair. Prayer remains the most powerful force in benefiting others. Of course, we are to keep in mind this may be a prelude to actual and open change. In others we set the table and before you know it, luscious food and drink appear to enhance our friends who are on the same pilgrimage. Being only a novice in spirituality, I do suspect the most telling battles of this world are fought in the prayers of righteous people. The prayers of the American people, as well as many others, have had to be colossal in their impact on history.

Some winsome people in my churches have worshiped most Sundays in the year and given generously of their money. As a pastor, when you ask about their prayer lives you hit a thud. It simply hasn't been developed! To participate in public worship and give our money are commendable. There is one more thing more commendable: prayer. Why? Because this is catching the ear of God and provides little or no statistical success. The success comes in relationship with the Father, Son, and Holy Spirit. Many have marveled at the prayers given by grandparents, parents, brothers/sisters, and others. While we have no overt proof in a scientific sense, how many of us were formed spiritually by them? Their contribution is more than we can repay, except in the obvious. We, too, can pray for those coming after us. They may or may not be relatives. Whoever they are, they need our prayers today and tomorrow.

4. Our lives are never lived in a vacuum.

Some appear to believe there is a space completely empty, except for them. Christianity is a relational faith. From the outset it assumed we would be in touch with others — laughing, crying, or celebrating. Our Lord's visits to secret places for prayer never became permanent. It must likewise be true for us. To build fences and walls around ourselves not only excludes others, but we are also excluded and do not receive the benefits intended. It is not always easy to let other people into our lives and there may be good reasons. Perhaps you have let a person into your life and been used. Perhaps you have confided in someone, only to learn the confidence was broken.

We have records of hermits who lived isolated lives and rarely saw anyone. This can be something quite different! There are those who take vows and spend years in seclusion on behalf of the kingdom of God. It is an extraordinary person who can do this. For you and me, plus virtually everyone we know, such an experience and way of life is foreign. Let us not magnify these isolated ways of living and call them the epitome of practical spirituality. Of course, we must not vilify such men and women that truly and wholesomely live a life of poverty, chastity, and obedience. For the average Mr. Church (man or woman) we are aware of our spiritual vocation to aid in spiritually forming others. As we benefit others, we benefit ourselves. All disciples committed to the Christ have known this at some level.

Christ also died for weak believers! Just because we may have more maturity, does not mean the crucifixion was more for us and somehow we are favored in the Father's eyes. Those words at first may hit you as strange and even humorous but take a moment or longer to test your depths. By our works and apparent successful living, are we better off spiritually than others? Am I seriously my brother's (sister's) keeper? It is an old question posed well before the Christian era. Are congregations guilty of separating into the haves and the have-nots? Had the pastor best be working with the haves in order to save time and cut down on his/her frustrations? In our souls there are times for whatever reasons we know this happens. Pastors, for the most part, learn early that the institution must be maintained at the corner of 10th and Elm!

God's patience saves the day for most of us, sometimes quoting our passage from Saint Paul back to us. There is this responsibility to look out for others and it doesn't go away. Those who get on our cracked nerves also belong to the family. They may be weak and — in our minds — a waste of time but that does not make them less a part of the family. Are they spiritually underprivileged because they just don't have the smarts? That is a terribly arrogant question and yet it must be asked. We cannot go our merry way and extricate ourselves from that which is difficult, trying our patience to the limits. We are all sinners saved by the grace of God. In our precious salvation the Father is merciful to both the weak and strong.

Summary And Conclusion

Knowledge can, in the Pauline sense, be a burden to us and produce an arrogance that alienates our brothers and sisters. We are reminded that love builds up and, sooner or later, everyone benefits. This is frequently not the way the world views people and things. The more degrees and professional experience we have, the more spiritually fruitful we are. Who are we trying to mislead? Love is what carries the day in good times and bad times. There are times Ph.D.s must learn from those who have never been to college or perhaps not even graduated from high school. Of course, we must not discount the possibility of academia and piety being an integral part of the same person. To tout ones ignorance and immaturity in childish ways is not what Saint Paul had in mind!

Our friend, Paul, is a brilliant teacher. He explains and challenges by turns. To get in a full-fledged argument with him must have been a powerfully painful experience! He strikes at the heart of the problem frequently present in our faith in the past and present. We can hear him saying love is patient and kind. It is also not jealous or boastful. You and I may need to test the waters of our real maturity again. We may need to have the cobwebs cleared from our hearts, so we can once again feel and understand we are to look out for others. This is not optional! Our trespasses are forgiven as we forgive others their trespasses. Regardless of your leadership role in the life of the church, covenant with the Father to be the person Christ desires you to be, with whomever you find yourself.

A Man For All Seasons

Introduction
The enigma of human relationships and how that relates to the living God is all about us. It always has been and likely will be. This is precisely what Saint Paul lifts up before us. We would like for all of this to be greatly simplified but it never is and so we continue to seek to live the Christian life as best we know how.

The history of the church is saturated with just what the apostle puts before us. In a way we are caught between two worlds and we have no choice. We live as well we can and hope for heaven. Sometimes our difficulties emerge because we fail to realize God is the God of both of them. The world may be corrupt and fallen but he has not abdicated his throne!

Our freedom, like Paul's, is one of countless dimensions and allows us to relate to precious people in ways we can hardly imagine. This is a privilege and a powerful dynamic, I dare say, many do not understand in the slightest degree. While the gospel is not for boasting, it is for proclamation and we must not fail to do so!

In a sense he is God's "secret weapon" in that he is able to stand with an unfulfilled Judaism and a promising religion evolving from it called Christianity. Perhaps no one in the ancient church was as well qualified and equipped. History bears this out in a remarkable fashion.

Focus
We are to be resilient for the sake of Christ.

Body

1. There are good politics and bad politics.

Politics — in the general sense — is inescapable in this life. To relate to other human beings, sooner or later, invariably becomes political. Every pastor of a local church, for example, is a politician! Does that cast doubt on the integrity of his/her leadership? I certainly hope not. As pastor and people live and work together, we know that management of time, talents, and money must take place. To think otherwise is unrealistic. To act otherwise is most likely to court disaster. Political science is an esteemed field of study, but the practical side of it takes it not only out of academia but out of the basic understanding of those connected to governmental processes.

To cast off concerns and issues as just being politics is to assume a negative aspect that is often not there. For example, every church and/or denomination has a polity. Simply stated, how else do we expect to function in this imperfect world? We can accuse others of playing politics, including Paul, but does that mean we are free and clear in our own less-than-ideal bailiwicks? This state of affairs has always been with us, regardless if we operated by episcopal, congregational, or presbyterial models. To get things done, even in the life of the churches, we frequently have to play politics in the highest and best sense of the term. This can be construed as being negative and below what Christ expects. However, do we really want to do his bidding?

Resiliency is not an option in our walk with others, yes, even in our churches. Survival in this sometimes obviously sinful world means to get the best answer or decision by the grace of God. Must we feel guilty because of this? Must we hang our heads in shame because we have failed to live up to the ideal? Frankly, and without reservation, I do not think so! Good politics means above all — sincerely calling upon the Father for guidance and letting the chips fall where they fall. We cannot flounder in a briar patch just because we refuse to make of it the best it can be under the circumstances. Of course, all veteran pastors and lay people deep down know this, often with a certain painful joy.

As our man for all seasons weaves his way through the necessary means of winning others, we experience a genius at work. All is done for the sake of the gospel and winning others to the cause of Christ. Perhaps it is seen as a method for him and not for us. Let us not be naive! The political machinations of this world are with us and that means in the honest to goodness lives of the people called Christians. But politics can be good, which can mean sacrificing our brilliance for the betterment of all involved. But, dear friends, never be a secularized politician, which is always self-seeking and devoid of the undergirding of prayer. Always look out for the spiritual interests of others and always bathe your means and ends in humble and sincere prayer. Otherwise, we could become an anathema!

2. We are called to be adjustable in the best sense of the word.

At first, our point may sound like we must be amenable to being tossed to-and-fro by others. Nothing could be further from the truth! For in the best sense none of us has all of the answers to anything or anyone. Think about all of the answers we don't even have about ourselves. In the United Methodist system of appointments — some would add disappointments — adjustments continually have to be made. The moving of one pastor generally means, at least, two others are moving as well. This involves negotiation with large amounts of patience by all concerned. My experience is that district superintendents really do attempt to make good appointments.

Anyone, lay or clergy, unable to adjust to new pastors and people are in serious trouble. This is true, regardless of the polity. Our needs sometimes simply have to go unmet for awhile. But this should never discourage us. Why? Because from every situation into which we are put, we can learn something valuable. That one truth is frequently the key to maturing in the faith for all of us. So, give thanks and be adjustable under the working of the Holy Spirit that blows wherever it chooses. What we are and become is for the sake of Christ and his one, holy, catholic, and apostolic church. Our walk with the Lord is sooner or later a learning experience. Stretching out to others and making the necessary adjustments should be — in time — a highly positive experience. Our spiritual muscles are always in need of growth!

One direction is not being promoted or recommended and that is what is popularly known as "going with the flow." There are times that we must stand our ground. This is especially true as we come into contact with those who are not interested in the church or may even be an enemy. If we are going with the flow, we must be as certain as possible such movement has the blessing of God and is being directed by the Holy Spirit. Disciples of Christ are exactly that. They have no other to worship and follow. The enemy, the devil, also has ways of putting us in places and positions that require adjustments fraught with serious — perhaps damning — consequences. Remember your childlikeness before the Father!

Conforming in our lives is both obvious and subtle. This is why changes in the life of congregations are to be made above board. For the pastor to slip one over on someone is no cause for jubilation. In fact, it may be the cause of much aggravation. To arrange or rearrange something for the good of the whole church, where adjustments are necessitated, calls for open discussion and a generous spirit. You may very well say such an approach is merely common sense and, yes, we do things that way. Don't be too sure! When we are in a hurry to meet a goal, we may cut some corners. Those empowered with responsibility and authority, lay and clergy, are to be keenly sensitive. This is not to imply everyone needs to know the number of paper clips in the secretary's desk on a given day in order to trust her.

3. To stretch in different directions in the Holy Spirit benefits all.

I am a great believer in stretching with the Holy Spirit as presence and guidance. That is not said in a way to become an annoyance or to become aggressive. It is to suggest we move forward in the faith by moving into new experiences. The progressive people tend to be continually exploring and seeking new opportunities for doing good. Those who remain stagnant seem always to be in the same places, unwilling to stretch into areas of promise. The attitude is much like the farmer, who was offered a new parcel of land. He was firm in saying, "I know what is here but I don't know what is over there." He said that in the face of the fact the parcel was adjacent to his!

Stretching assumes resiliency and that may very well be why some are so hesitant and reluctant. But if we are to imitate Paul, we, too, must become men and women of all seasons for the benefit of others. It can become a dull ordeal to live in a place that has twelve months of spring or summer or winter or fall. In Indiana, we never have to face that problem because we have, at least, four seasons and once in a while it seems like a dozen or more! Likewise, our churches and constituencies can be more or less suffocated by those who cannot seem to move from point A to B. If both pastor and lay leadership fall into this category, of what use are they to bringing the gospel to those pleading for an open spirit?

Try to put yourself in the place of Paul and all that was facing him. He was surrounded by powers who were disinterested in his message and — in some instances — threatened by it. Yet, it was his responsibility to be among them stretching here and there to present the gospel of his blessed Lord. He is even willing to become weak in order that he might win them. Except before the Lord, it must have been quite a task for him to become weak for the purpose of trying to win others. As some of his writings indicate, he was surrounded on every side by those who wanted to compromise or destroy his message. There were some who even sought to obliterate the message of Christ by killing all who faithfully followed him, and we hold back because its either too hot or too cold outside!

The many-sided Christian is the one in today's world who is most effective. That does not mean we compromise or water down our gift from the Lord. While our anchor must be safe and secure, that does not preclude moving in waters — deep or shallow — to influence others for Christ and the church. There are those who would view this as a fragmented and therefore unacceptable approach to presenting the gospel. Paul did not give up the gospel he was trying to promote! We don't need to do that, either. Ideally, we are strong enough in the faith, as we move about, to provide a certain spiritual aroma that causes others to want what we have.

The more we can relate to them in their patterns of living, the more apt we are to be successful in their conversion.

4. Rigidity is sometimes a means to stunt the spiritual growth of others.

Old First Church sat on the corner of High and Elm for so many years — rigidly, as the community viewed it — that it had to be torn down before it fell down! It didn't have to be that way. New life seemed to come and go but it could never stay long enough to make the essential changes. So, those longing to have more of the Lord's blessings mostly passed through. It was as though the Holy Spirit kept on grieving until finally it refuses to grieve any longer. It was sad and depressing, but did God take care of those who wanted to grow? Indeed, he did! They went elsewhere and found those who were open to change that Christ might be more fully glorified.

Are conservatives more rigid than liberals? That is not a simple question and there is no simple answer. We live in a world, the churches included, where name-calling is common place and frozen thought is typical. Both sides have their agendas. Some are liberals along certain lines and conservative along others. Liberals often picture conservatives as those "religious right" people who are so closed-minded that they have no clear view of what's happening in the world. Conservatives tend to measure liberals by their wayward morality and failure to interpret the constitution in a proper manner. Entire books have been written on this topic. The definition of terms and spins put on key words and ideas are there to see for the keen observer.

Is contemporary worship in its many forms rigid? A cry may be going up, of course, that has to be answered in the negative. In fact, contemporary worship is to avoid rigidity in worship. I must confess to those proponents that is not automatically the case. I am reminded, years ago, of the church we attended when I was a child, which prided itself on never using printed orders of service because they didn't want to get in the way of the Holy Spirit. Leaders mentioned with frequency how those formal churches shut out God by their insistence on following a printed order. Years later, in retrospect, I recalled how in our little church everything moved orderly and there was little deviation but, of course, we had no bulletins. Any form of worship can become rigid and do the very thing it says it doesn't! All in all, we are dependent both corporately and individually on being obedient to the Holy Spirit. This was Saint Paul's weapon. In whatever state he found himself he could be content because his resilient way of life in the Spirit was continually conquering evil that abounded. All is done for the sake of Christ. Can we do as well? Probably not but we can try in the strength that is promised and given to us. We are guilty of underestimating the power of our salvation and thereby stunt the growth of others. We sheepishly say — even emphasize — we can't do this or that. Our rigidity is held like some prize that requires constant vigil! In the meantime, events and happenings march on. Some people enter this world and others leave. Someone has need of your assistance.

Summary And Conclusion

The obligation of the apostle to proclaim the gospel is so deeply rooted he senses God will not hold him guiltless for refusing this call. His freedom and slave status are a paradox. In a way, it defies words to delineate it. Yet, towering in our New Testament is this remarkably unique man, who provides a witness for Christ and his church that never goes away. Perhaps our faith shall never again see such a positively resilient person going about doing the work of the Lord. His strength and spirit provide a model for us. We may discover ourselves far from this in practice. Nevertheless, the model is there and beckons us to come and learn from one of the geniuses of the faith.

Can we be too idealistic? Does the text suggest veering away from the purity of the gospel and making provision for an odious compromise? Of course, the answers must be yours. Humbly, I admit there may not be any crystal-clear answers. That only gently reminds me we are invariably living and ministering in an environment that contains mystery. A strictly rational approach to our salvation has always been filled with limitations. We have always, at one time or another, needed to take a leap of faith. So, dearest

Paul, we thank you for your insights that enable us to have hope in the conversion of a world, sinful and in desperate need of Christ. We also thank you for the hope that is engendered and gives us a look — imperfect and cloudy that it be — of our real home in heaven. We promise to work on in our little ways for now.

Plea For Discipline

Introduction

In a way, Christians are all in the Olympics! We are running the race that determines our eternal abode. We run to win and the prize is the most valuable we will ever seek. No money or property will purchase it. Only self-control under the banner of Christ grants a chance for winning.

The apostle is very clear and speaks to all who would enter the race that leads to everlasting life with the Father, Son, and Holy Spirit. It is an old/new teaching to whom all Christians for twenty centuries can relate. It is couched in terms both familiar and relevant.

For you and me, now early in the twenty-first century, it keeps us in touch with sublime revelation that remains at once practical and dependent on faith. As one ponders the brevity of one's life, the truth shines in all its splendor. This brief period of living on planet earth is but a dressing room for the main event.

God's grace allows and enables us to have this opportunity above all others to win the prize. The competition comes mostly from the evil one who does not want us to succeed and will do what's necessary to see that we don't. The track has numerous land mines and other devices, some very clever, either to make us fall and never get up or to quit the race altogether.

Focus

Self-control is imperative for authenticity.

Body

1. Freedom and self-discipline are not contradictory.

Many of us have a problem in keeping the two in harmony. On the surface, they certainly appear to be in contradiction, but we have as our guide Saint Paul who loved his freedom and yet preached and apparently practiced a rigid self-control. He shows us the way and builds his case convincingly. The wise men of the day might have a problem with living as he requires. Perhaps that is why he points out in different passages of his writings the need to rise above mere human wisdom. Christ leads us to higher heights and that is for the best and highest good: eternal life with the master.

I dare say free spirits are seldom seen as disciplined folks! They often are the most morally careless people on the face of this earth, delighting in shocking those about them. When you study the apostle's corpus of writings, you discover the two — freedom and discipline — existing side by side in creative tension. His understanding provides us with truth that transcends mere rules and regulations. It also gives us Christ's spirit which maintains all things are possible with God in the winds and sometimes hailstorms of the Holy Spirit. To debate this matter endlessly, much like predestination and free will, is fruitless and leads most likely to where we were never intended to go. Aren't we privileged to have a Savior and Lord who will victoriously see us through?

For us to become weak in order to be strong is cause for consternation and perhaps humiliation among some of us. Our disciplines will only take us just so far in our walk with the Lord, but they are essential. To admit to the need of self-control is a step all of us must take. To acknowledge the mystery of our freedom in this ongoing environment provides a way for peace that can pass the best of human understanding. Experience shows us that even the most dramatic of instantaneous conversions will cool off and lose their effectiveness, unless discipline is implemented. Our relationship with God is always a covenental one that is perhaps best described as a divine/human contract. God forbid that we ever view this as equals negotiating!

Our call is to faithfulness. People must be able to see authenticity in it, not only on Sunday mornings but at all times we are being observed. Every day of our lives we are being watched by others and being graded on whether or not we are *bona fide*. Generally, Christians live out our lives in fish bowls! To slip can be costly, even though in our hearts we are not wrongly motivated and before God have not sinned. But human nature, being what it is, does not allow us the luxury of letting our disciplines become so loosened others are given reason to say negative things about us and our faith. From that viewpoint, ours is seldom an easy life and the sooner we learn the devil is for real, the better off we are. We can never please everyone and that — lest we forget — is not our purpose.

2. Aimless wandering can be the loss of precious time.

The apostle would have us to understand we must be fixed on Christ and his requirements. There is a certain time consciousness built into his lesson for us. Our days and nights have a timekeeper. We call him the Father of us all. The cliché that we have just so much time may be something boring but it is good and important that we be reminded. Our waste of it is more than impractical, but if it persists, sinful, jeopardizing our eternal souls. Not only must we settle in on that which is absolutely basic to our well-being, we must do so with genuineness. There is to be much more than New Year's Eve's resolutions that diminish and die!

Remember a significant part of the word to us is that after we have proclaimed the gospel, we should not be disqualified. It is a sobering thought and indirectly pleads with us to make spiritually good use of our time. Wandering about, after telling others about the good news, can cause pastors painful grief. To tell your people about the Savior and then allow yourself to become an unsettled wayfarer is to invite an infectious attitude of loose living. Regardless of likes or dislikes, our parishioners do count on us to show them the way. Our most persistent critics sometimes will look to us in a pleading fashion to help them. Yes, the ordained pastor is in a special place before God and his/her people to be an example of right living and that means authentic self-discipline.

The plea for discipline is done in a framework most any person can understand. A race has time limitations. Measurements and judgments are made. The longer we delay running the race, the less time we have to compete. Procrastination, for whatever reason, lessens our chances of winning. How can you win, unless you enter the race? In the athletic world, professional or amateur, the facts are at hand. If you want to be a good runner, boxer, baseball player, or member of any other sports team, you can't wait until you are forty years old! Precious time has gone and it is gone forever in this life. Honest people, as they begin to get old, will occasionally share with us they have missed many opportunities. One blatant fact is time has not been treated with stewardship.

Enslaving our bodies may sound as though we are wrestling with sexual temptation. That may very well be but it also refers to all aspects of our lives that must be under discipline for the cause of Christ. Punishing our bodies for the cause of him who is the way, the truth, and the life is a noble effort. It is not *sadomasochism!* In reading the lives of the saints we discover fairly quickly this was a concern in their midst. What some of them underwent to be more completely servants of their Lord is a challenge to us. They understood their bodies were temples and to be treated with care and honor. Such treatment in their minds and hearts involved developing and maintaining authentic disciplines. This was accomplished not solely for their benefit but for the world to which they were mandated to minister.

3. Spiritual formation requires a disciplined heart and mind.

The two working together harmoniously gives us a willing spirit that seeks, above all, to do spiritual formation. Now, we are onto what makes glowing Christians, whose lives remind us of a well-oiled spiritual machine casting beneficial sunshine to others. Perhaps nothing provides greater salesmanship for the gospel of Jesus Christ. A miracle is at work that inspires other miracles in the lives of those needy human beings searching for something (someone) for which to live and die. It is a beautiful sight to behold, much like a lovely array of flowers that are perfectly blended with a fragrance which is captivating. Does this actually happen? Some of us can attest to it! We are to remind ourselves, daily if need be, that our chief function and goal is to be an instrument in forming others after the likeness of him who died for us and arose again. This is accomplished only by disciplined living under the guidance of the Holy Spirit. Authenticity is at the core and is not to be negotiated away. This is no place for manipulation and intimidation. Falsification is an abomination. We are expected to hold up under verification every day of our lives. Praise God from whom all blessings flow! We have been given much and much is expected of us. While failure may have to be tolerated, it is never acceptable. Praise him all creatures here below!

Some of us know what it means for the heart and mind to be working in different directions. Even Saint Paul knew the experience of doing the very thing he hated because his mind was not up to the task of providing discipline. Spiritual heartbreak can be the result and more than oneself may be injured. Heartaches are born in such a milieu. At their worst, heart attacks wreak havoc on others, especially God's people. In the clergy we witness this as some fall morally, usually in succumbing to sexual misdeeds or handling money in suspicious ways. The heart is good but the mind is tested in attacking temptation and fails. Fantasies are allowed to grow, even encouraged, and Satan has his way. Clergy always are in need of our prayers.

Our Lord, as he neared the time of his crucifixion, gives us a splendid example of perfect submission to the will of the Father. The struggle has been there for all of us to read for centuries. His human will was tempted to weaken and find a way out. It was strong enough to do what the Father required. Who among us can even imagine the self-control necessary? Furthermore, who can even begin to imagine what would have transpired had his discipline failed. Would he have fled to another country? Would he have compromised with the Jewish and Roman authorities, so his life would have been spared? We can develop more scenarios. His discipline gloriously provided for the sacrifice for our sins and the salvation of humankind. In a matter of hours, saying, "Yes," to

God the Father and, "No," to his human nature changed the world forever and ever.

4. Disqualification for God's kingdom is always a tragedy.

Our text concludes with the realism of which Paul was typically capable. What a shame to go about telling others about the good news and its requirements, only to become disqualified yourself! Christ emphasizes not to judge others and God will not judge us. Yet, over a period of years and in different parishes, it indeed seems to happen. Once in a while, there is a shocker with a pillar of the church coming unglued and crashing down in most every way. We never want to dwell on these negative happenings but let's admit the possibility is continually present.

Letting down our guard in a spiritual sense lays the groundwork for problems, big and small. Evil forces will slip under our radar and eat away at the finest teaching we know. Now and then Christians decide to go on a questionable lark. What is anticipated as being fun, relaxation, and enjoyment is found to be significant slippage in our life in Christ. We have to be recuperated and refreshed but there are right and wholesome ways of this occurring. It can't be done by breaking the Ten Commandments, just to test their validity! Vacations are not vacations from God. We can't stop running the race and then take up where we left off two or three weeks earlier. When we do our observations of others and ourselves, don't we usually find the erosion is little by little? The monster who desires our soul is generally a timid little shrewd fellow.

The Judas Iscariots of this world are among us. We identify them not to pronounce judgment but to solidify our defense. A division into sheep and goats is the Lord's business, not ours. Thank goodness for that spiritual detail because it shows us there is a kind of holy objectivity that translates into perfect justice. The Father in his providence has made room for all of us to be judged on his terms, so that his will is always ultimately done. My suspicion is that only a few of us have known a Judas who would knowingly and deliberately betray the Christ. As we survey the field of those who may very well have disowned our Lord in open and clandestine ways, we are firmly reminded of even our possible disqualification. We are to be forgiven as we forgive others.

For some in today's world — even professing Christians — it is so hard to make them consider something with a strong negative aspect. The standard attitude is that if you are going to open your mouth, say something that makes me feel good! We hear and see so much negativism in the workaday world; we don't want to hear it in the church. All well and good, except the gospel demands that the truth be told and all Saint Paul is doing is telling the truth. Our allegiance to Christ and the church cries out for the teachings of our faith to be disseminated, as nearly as humanly possible, in all fairness. We can never provide perfect interpretations but we are not supposed to. Yet, the spirit of the law is available and it does not take a brilliant theologian to lay before us all of the help desired. The Father's mercy abounds!

Summary And Conclusion

It is imperative there is authenticity in our self-control. We can celebrate our freedom with Paul but can we also lift up the need for discipline in our lives? Time is not on our side, in fact, it is on no one's side! Again and again we discover from others and ourselves we are to be formed in the image of Christ. Our goodness and hope of heaven are directly related to the matter placed before us: We are to be a disciplined people. Furthermore, we are running a race like no other and one that has eternal consequences beyond anything else. To be possibly disqualified should make us pause in deep thought, penetrating both heart and mind.

Our life/death task is before us! Physical prowess may have little — if anything — to do with it. Superior mental capacity, while potentially providing greater dedication and service, may be a detriment. To recite all the books of the Bible and quote theology endlessly may only be an exercise in damaging pride. The big and little, handsome and not so handsome, wealthy and poor, are to be self-controlled with the living Christ in charge of our lives. Are you and I up to this demanding assignment? An old preacher once told me that for the sake of our immortal souls we had better be!

But we are not supposed to cry out how hard the road is. We are to give thanks for the opportunity. Remember, millions still have never heard about our Savior and Lord. So, the rewards of our sometimes arduous journey or race are beyond any of our imaginations.

Gift Of Positive Thinking

Introduction

For generations the "power of positive thinking" has been touted throughout our land. It is among the most popular and utilized thoughts and themes we have ever known. Cutting across all strata of social and economic patterns it is generally a principle espoused.

While the influence generated is obvious, secular and less than desirable ways of life have utilized it. It is frequently taken from a Christian basis and becomes a means to achieve ends that at a minimum are questionable. Of course, there are those who would find this line of thought simply narrow.

Saint Paul wants you and me to know and be convinced there is an idea and person far more profound than the common understanding of the "power of positive thinking." There is this gift of our Savior that makes our lives "Yes" under his lordship, always. Ultimately, there are no negatives.

Our conversion and faithful living provide a blessed safety in a sanctuary most people will not likely see. For regardless of what happens to us, the answer remains, "Yes," to all of God's promises. It is a gift far surpassing anything worldly philosophers can provide. It is always a cause and call for personal celebration with a humble spirit.

Focus

Jesus Christ alone conquers negatives.

121

Body

1. There is remarkable — even miraculous — power in our saying, "Yes," to Jesus.

Isn't it intriguing how some people seem to miss a victorious life in Christ by an eyelash? They never quite say the "Amen" necessary to close the deal! Yes, we have our part to play and our own free will comes in to play. With the gift being offered we are put to a test. Will we accept it or not? Our blessed Lord's arms are outstretched and some way is found to elude them. Is it a matter of a dear one deluding himself/herself? Spiritually, all pieces were in place and every butterfly was flying in formation. Failure.

My experience teaches me to begin every day with affirmations and positives that come primarily from Holy Scripture. This none-too-pleasant business of repenting of our sins of commission and omission are a required ingredient. It is a moment of setting the tone for the Lord's gift to become fully operative. What can be perceived as negatives in reality become positives. Why? Because of an exceptional power of the one who loves us far beyond our own comprehension. Even in pain of the previous day(s) we sense God is still in control and will see us through all circumstances. Again, we must accept the gift and understand it is not a tool or instrument for us to seek self-aggrandizement. If we yield to that temptation, our ministries become plighted with poisonous debris.

The gift of Christ, indeed, conquers negatives, especially as we are totally co-operative. An abundant life is there for the taking. It all sounds so easy. The best way to overcome such an easy attitude, regardless of our good spirit, is to visualize in graphic form the price that was paid for it. Only through the heinous method of crucifixion was the present of all presents granted. He was and is the propitiation for the sins of humanity, specifically you and me. What an unbelievable affront to the Savior not to accept it! The promises of the eons come together in God the Father's Son. Really, we are to do more than give thanks. We are to fall on our knees and admit none of what was and is bestowed upon us was deserved. So humility precedes thanksgiving!

It takes plenty of spiritual power in today's world to survive. Perhaps it always has. At the same time think about how in our times things can change not only quickly but radically. Who cares about yesterday's headlines? Who cares about yesterday's newspapers and magazines? There is a fluidity in persons, places, and things that stretch the imagination and often make predictions mostly nonsensical. This is why, more than ever, we must find a permanent "Yes" and cling to it at all costs. Otherwise, we keep bouncing around in ways that do not add to the quality of our spiritual lives and frequently seriously disrupt the good that is there. It may be these are spiritually the best of times and the worst of times. Our Lord wants to make the negatives positive and it can happen, praise God!

2. Life is filled with opportunities to enhance yourself and others.

Of course, this must be understood and practiced in the living stream of abundant living Saint Paul proclaims. Self-enhancement programs that must surely exist in the hundreds may lack any significant attachment to the cause of the Christian religion or the Judeo-Christian ethical system. The harm they may do is found in the reality of their goal, which is solely to produce that kind of a person who can cope in a secularized environment. As long as we live we are coping but how we do this is crucial. The apostle's message is fundamentally for those already in the fold. Yet, we must not deny its appeal to the unconverted.

In a way, there is a chasm between using and utilizing. The first is often understood as a means to get what you want, regardless of the methods employed. The second is ministering in the context of God's love and aiming for a win-win outcome. "To utilize" is to bring others into potential successes. It is to affirm one's personhood under the banner of Christ, always saying, "Yes," to him and his ways. People who feel used are seldom those who will contribute significantly to the greater good. In a sense, who can blame them, even if it happens under the auspices of the Christian faith? Much care must be taken for the sake of Christ and his church to practice the ministry of "Yes," as so graciously given to us by Paul. Anything less will cause unneeded negative sparks to fly!

Our opportunities are intended for the upbuilding of our Savior and Lord. In doing so we grow in the faith and take others with

us. That is not to imply the path is free and easy or even uncomplicated. It is to maintain, and rightfully so, that Christ — in time
with our obedience — conquers negatives. What a truly beautiful
picture this is! The angels in heaven must be overjoyed every time
they witness this happening on planet earth. Yes, and who may
participate? Of course, all of Christ's sons and daughters are full
partners. There are happy days (and nights) in this approach to
Christian living. But be reminded, the tempter roams around, sometimes roaring like a lion, seeking to subvert our best ideas.

Is there anything in your life that is never in some way an opportunity? Perhaps, as one dear lady said, always try to make lem-
onade out of lemons. The worst situations that appear so bleak can
become made over by the God of all of us. Since the inception of the
ancient church we have seen this happen over and over. Death and
destruction were present. Perhaps both occurred but who became
the victor? This precious earliest of churches received the body and
blood of their Lord. Then, they prepared to give their bodies and
blood for the cause of Christ. Frequently, they gave their all and
proved to the world the "Yes" was still valid and the faith would
never be destroyed, not even temporarily. How blessed we are to
have such an unrivaled heritage. Yes, all of life is one colossal opportunity and we are called to be tremendously grateful.

3. Pray that every day will be successful in God's sight.

The closing prepositional phrase in this point makes all the
difference in the world, doesn't it? We are taken out of the need to
have our will done. We move decisively away from setting an
agenda that appeals to us. We are put in a frame of mind that opens
the door to understand what God wants. In short, we remove ourselves from the center of things and events. We no longer see ourselves as the arbiter of good and bad, or right and wrong. When we
pray this way in sincerity and humility, the best of all situations is
born in this world. In the Pauline sense both "Yes" and "Amen"
are moved to the forefront!

So why don't we pray along these lines more often? There
may be as many reasons as there are personalities. Yet, there is one
that tends to strike a loud chord and stick out most noticeably. We

are uncomfortable — even afraid — to let loose of our will and let God be God. It is a circumstance that is not unusual. Perhaps it is best illustrated by the little boy who prays (with his hands behind his back and fingers crossed) for the good of his playmate! We know the problem, clergy and laity are summoned to keep working at it until we do better — much better. The coming of the kingdom in many lives is thwarted by those who, knowingly or unknowingly, have their crossed fingers behind their backs. "Thy kingdom come, thy will be done" awaits our humble co-operation.

We can never see things the way God does and, yet, let us not be too hasty. We do have an inkling, don't we? Sometimes we have a lot more than that, and we are surprised — even shocked — to learn what he blatantly points out to us. We admit he does not measure success the way we do. But let's don't be too hard on ourselves. When we say "Yes" to life and death, a newness in the way we perceive things and people comes about. Every day is potentially successful in God's sight. It may or may not have to do with the stock market. It may or may not have to do with promotion in one's chosen field of endeavor. It may or may not have to do with your fiancé saying the wedding is off. It may or may not have to do with your child making better grades. Just trust the Lord of all!

The gift of positive thinking is so wide-ranging it is a distinguished part of our salvation. Through our dear Lord's crucifixion and resurrection we are given the possibility of every 24 hours being successful, that is, in God's sight. As we shove our groans and grumbles aside, the glory of this stupendous way glistens like the stars in heaven. As we learn to think in certain ways, the cornucopia intended for the Father's children is at hand. Do I hear there is a celebration in order? If there isn't, there should be. Our God's vision is total and complete. Prayers born and implemented with providential perfection in our spiritual makeup enables us to participate in the greatest of all adventures: the *will* of God. What more could we possibly ask?

4. Success and failure are in the eyes of the human beholder.

As we go through life, we learn the dividing line between success and failure can become thin to the place of non-existence. It is a memorable discovery in that we dare not forget the pearl we have found! From a spiritual viewpoint this can be a major turning point in the way we view events and, in particular, people. It finally dawns on us that God decides what is success or failure. While it is humbling, there is a solid positive for all who claim Christ as Savior and Lord. For one thing, we don't have to succeed or fail on our terms. Our vision and information are so limited. For another thing we sense a profound security. It is cause for joy.

It is not easy to accept the idea that Christ conquers negatives and in doing so can make of our perceived failures an experience in success. Our Lord reminds us again and again his kingdom is not of this world; that has to do precisely with our topic at hand. At the same moment his wisdom is such that our perception of success may very well be failure which must receive the healing touch of the Master's hand. So, we hopefully cross into an arena that facilitates our every action and reaction into a great big beautiful "Yes!" Serious spirituality, I believe, is given birth by such illumination. Then, the gift of positive thinking glows in magnificence even on our bad days. Indeed, how shall anyone escape who neglects so great a salvation? Our only really conclusive failure is the rejection of Christ and the Holy Spirit on a permanent basis.

We acknowledge goals must be set and evaluations done in this world. The sometimes harsh actuality of these processes may very well send us into tantrums or to hospital beds or spur us to greater energy and focus. On the other hand, it may produce a genuine sense of success or perhaps lift us into glorious clouds of euphoria. In any event, God still loves us and will have compassion, provided we are receptive. Most of us have found ourselves in such a quandary. We have felt like asking where the presence of God is. Hopefully, it is here our cherished gift of positive thinking comes into play. Hopefully, it is also a time that we plead to God for patience, allowing neither worldly success nor failure to take the place of the here and now and eternal "Yes."

There is no substitute for the eyes of faith. Truly, it is how we see things and people that make the decisive difference in the way we live. There are different types of blindness. The spiritual kind is the worst and eventually the most influential in determining both how we live and die. Encouragement among our brothers and sisters may be the best contribution we can make to, and for, them. Please, let me help you see and, at least, partially understand God has not forsaken you. Please allow me to suggest what God may have for you. Whatever it is, he always seeks your betterment. A suggestion: refrain from saying, "I know exactly how you feel and here is God's will for you!" Our need to help and please people we love may tend to drive us in that direction.

Summary And Conclusion

To realize and fully accept our gift is a major turning point in every life that trusts in Christ's salvation. For some it may be "the" major one. More than sheer happiness is a result. One's life and death become wonderfully significant. We know beyond a doubt we have entered into that most blessed of relationships. We become established, knowing whatever happens to us, shall be well with our souls. A fulfillment, foreign to the world, is present. Our attunement with the Holy Spirit assures us we are going to touch others in a meaningful way for Christ and his church. Hurtful and unnecessary negatives are drowned in the deepest waters of the oceans. Every day will be okay because God says so!

It seems many — if not most — followers of Christ ease up to this profound truth, only to step back a pace or two. Then, in time, we bump into it again, debating whether or not to accept the gift. Such ongoing opportunity and refusal to enter into this blessed bond may well be the story of one's spiritual existence on this earth! This is not a shout for human judgment. It is a clarion call for those of us, who have accepted the gift and live by it, continually to provide ways for others to come aboard. The more we know spiritually, the more responsible we become. Away with negatives that soil our lives and those of other precious human beings! Many have been in the batter's circle too long and need to step up to the plate. To strike out or hit a home run probably does not matter. The crucial thing is we are at bat.

Making Disciples

Introduction
The fruit or lack of it in our ministries is ever before us. The truth is seen among both clergy and laity. Over a period of time it is there for others to observe and most likely evaluate. Actually, generations and centuries speak to what we have done or not done for Christ and his body, the church — visible and invisible.

Paul is inspirationally confident in the product he has labored to bring about. His work evidences a writing on their hearts, not written in ink but with the Spirit of the Living God. The proof is there. All anyone needs to do is look carefully. Those he has influenced are wonderfully valuable *letters* to the world.

It should be obvious that those professing Christ as Savior and Lord are desirous in making disciples for him. Sadly, it is not always that obvious! For reasons, known only by God for the most part, we too often provide a surface approach in our evangelistic efforts. Our lack of fruit produces a dampening expression.

Praise God, there is nothing quite like others showing the world Christ has come in their lives and we are, at least, somewhat responsible! Our concern over making our mark for the furtherance of the gospel slips into oblivion. The smallest and most colorless fruit that is genuine, changes a dreary day into something beautiful.

Focus
It is imperative to understand the proof is in the pudding.

Body

1. False advertising is an ever-present malady.

As some have maintained, anything or anyone can be made to look very good or very bad, depending upon the skill of a given promoter. I have a strong suspicion we view this happening everyday in some form or another. Of course, there is nothing new about such phenomenon, as Saint Paul recognizes. We wished it weren't true in our churches but frankly, it is seen with regularity. Sometimes repentance is needed. Some of our brothers and sisters just simply were not honest. Perhaps the purpose was to protect someone and then we learn a bit late the Lord desires the truth in love. How would the creatures in our culture go on without clever exaggeration?

It is here that clergy are summoned to take a closer look. Our own résumés may contain misleading — if not outright — misrepresentation and they are circulating! We confront a common and sometimes agonizing dilemma: Are we really that good or have we yielded to the temptation of dishonest presentation? Our competence is from God and requires thanksgiving for who and what we are, as best we can truthfully assess that. To advertise ourselves in ways we suspect or know Christ condemns is simply stupidity or close to it. Why should we even want a church or position that pragmatically calls for a problematic view of who and what we are? Of course, if we don't know who and what we are, that is a bigger problem!

At times we just promise more than we can deliver. Deep down we really and justifiably want something beneficial to come into being. What do we do? We go off the deep end and make promises out of line with the Holy Spirit. We have not actually consulted with him and therefore, have evaded the essential provision of harmony. We like to think we are doing the will of God but we are in a hurry to prove something to someone and that person is not God! We have all been there and have learned we can reap rotting fruit or even a whirlwind. Call or label it what we want, we have entered the odious field of false advertising. In a turnabout, we might not want to see the proof in the pudding!

Some of us have watched and experienced this desperation for nearly a half century. Forms come and go. Media expands in quality and quantity. We genuinely want good things to happen but we forget about imperative consultation with the Spirit of the Living God. Sophistication has tended to put space between those we want to help and ourselves. Clergy and laity do not need to face those for whom their message is directed, at least, not nearly to the extent we once did. In bygone days we were frequently kept honest by our close pastoral relationships. This was true in some of the largest churches. For a generation or longer there has been a tendency to remove pastors from the so-called firing line. Conditions have changed enough that accountability is most certainly a big problem. The spirit of the law is so widened and deepened we can hardly be recognized from some secular institutions!

2. The Holy Spirit has a will and ways that hopefully permeate our beings.

The history of the church shows we have gone through periods where the Holy Spirit is mostly defined as something ethereal. When the manifestation did occur, a miracle or outstanding sign of some kind seemed to be the result. Praise God, we have passed through some truly powerful times of experiencing him daily in the lives of people. It is my prayer and that of others we continue to do so! The awesomeness and beauty of the Holy Spirit in our day and time is almost more than we can handle. It is like another Day of Pentecost has come upon us. We have witnessed some glorious proof in the pudding!

Saint Paul and his co-workers knew first hand that the Spirit gives life. Disciples are made as this wonder of wonders works in the daily lives of precious people. It is indispensable in our ministries to convert others that we be permeated or at least profoundly influenced by this Spirit. As we get more and more acquainted with this force, we are sold on the authenticity that emerges for all of us to witness. We can be surprised or astounded. We can shed tears of joy or laugh out loud. This sometimes hidden and sometimes open manifestation is so moving because we know disciples are being created or being improved in their walk with the Lord.

Paul absolutely knew what he was talking about! The delightful dove moves about, providing demonstrations of day breaks.

How can we be sure we are saturated by the Spirit of the Living God? That's a tough question, isn't it? Some who claim to be led seem all too often fumbling and stumbling with little to show in a factual sense. Efforts are made, perhaps with sacrifice, and all appears to be in near perfect order. Then something or someone moves out of kilter, at least, in our assessment and our balloon bursts with an embarrassing bang. We become encouraged, only after we discover, the moment is simply a means to where the Spirit desires to take us. Our faith is tried and then days, perhaps weeks or months later, we rather sheepishly admit our myopia! There is a holy fascination about this that should greet and grip us as we give thanks.

Understanding moving at different levels aids us, doesn't it? To be honest, many of us never quite know the level we are experiencing. Yet, think how often thoroughly committed Christians come out at the same place. We are not quite sure how we got there but we got there! Our wisdom is shown for what it usually is: limited and restricted. As we accept the reality of all this, why don't we just succumb into a blessed period of positive inertia that allows for the Holy Spirit to have free reign? Really, there are moments when our best actions are no actions! We are to relax in the arms of the all-knowing and ever faithful Father of our Savior and Lord, Jesus Christ. Yes, disciples can be made this way. The Spirit will not be confined by our insistence on controlling events and assuming we are the only ones knowing God's will.

3. Discipleship is verified eventually only in flesh and blood.

So, how do we go about measuring this? That can be a problem — perhaps insurmountable — to those unsympathetic with our religion or crusty personalities who insist little or no change is probable, even in the realm of salvation. Again the eyes of faith are what make the difference. Those of us who have seen this inspirational event occur again and again do not need selling or even coaching. We have witnessed tablets of stone become tablets written on human hearts. In this case, experience is the best teacher. When we relate to a new being in flesh and blood, there can be no denial!

We all know of stories about people steeped in doctrine, who have memorized the creeds and much scripture. Unfortunately, there are examples of their hearts below the surface never being anything but stone! It suggests their practice of our precious religion is only done with their heads. It is all a matter of the brain. Our blessed Lord surely would view such a state of affairs as unhealthy and even deadly. Rules, regulations, and memorizations are means and not ends. Salvation means flesh and blood. Our Savior was not in combat with a debating society. He was showing a needy humanity he would especially give his heart for all of us. Had Jesus given us only a set of rules to follow, we would have only another philosophical system. We have infinitely more than that and an open door to heaven.

My respect for the scientific realm is considerable. In fact, let's admit science and religion are no longer mortal enemies trying to destroy one another. They haven't been for quite some time. A case in point is the part prayer plays in diseases, accidents, and the like. Studies show where prayer is seriously practiced the improvement rate is definitely higher. Throughout the health care industry there are examples galore where the two have worked together to the benefit of patients. Wholeness and holiness are frequently accepted in a context showing science and religion are partners. The strides we have made here, especially in the last two generations, have been remarkable. After all, God is the God of both!

The warmth and contentment of the Father's boys and girls — regardless of their ages — has no real substitute. We can at times see salvation in the faces of others. Our spirit bears witness to their spirit. There is a sense of both peace and vibrancy that involves heart and mind — in particular, the heart. Some would label this subjectivity and even worse. Yet, we know in the Christian religion this is paramount and gives us the proof we seek. Can we be fooled occasionally? Of course, we can. Is this reason to shy away from the Spirit that gives life and offers sermons that mostly walk and seldom talk? Yes, unquestionably yes, persons who change internally and live differently outwardly can be spotted. They can also be known and deeply appreciated by those who celebrate the oneness found in the visible and invisible church.

4. Ideally, we are an open book for others.

A bishop in the United Methodist church told his clergy that his life was an open book. Having made his trip from the militant church to the triumph church some years ago, does not lessen his testimonial. How high he would rate among our bishops would be difficult — if not impossible — to determine. Yes, and whose criteria would we use? His openness for a few of us remains intact. There was every reason to believe he was exactly that: an open book. That didn't mean he shared all the confidential material about pastors! It did mean, as a man and bishop, his life was there for all to explore. His words are like a sturdy lighthouse that refuses to go down in stormy weather.

The vulnerability of the apostle is well known. Many Jews hated him and some Christians didn't trust him. To one group he was a turncoat and to the other someone who didn't fit well at all. Nevertheless, as he persistently laid his life on the line, he must have hid nothing. He belonged first and foremost to Christ and his business was to make disciples for his Master. It was a ministry that wrote on their hearts, "Jesus Christ is Savior and Lord." He and his colleagues were ministers of a new covenant, unique and powerful for living a victorious existence here and now and forever and ever. Apparently, he liked to show and tell. You want to meet a Christian? Come and I will introduce you to one! Should we imitate him? Definitely. Can we imitate him? Yes, but be prepared to die to yourself.

For many it is increasingly problematic to sustain one's life as an open book. What we have to remember is we are dealing in spiritual matters. By its very nature, the secular world works against being fully open to anything or anyone. The disreputable are legion and trust without conditions is virtually nonexistent. Now, we are brought to terms with an essential for living as we ought to be in our day and time. In short, as nearly as possible, our vulnerable lives must be kept among those in the household of faith. That may sound like retreating from a world that desperately needs us. I don't believe it is. Even passages in our Lord's teaching convey to us we must be careful in our dealings with those who do not share our commitment.

We are not competent of ourselves and survive only by the grace of God. However, our free access is tempered by a spiritual shrewdness we had best learn to practice. As some sidewalk evangelist reminds: have a loving and open spirit but don't be stupid! We may resemble Saint Paul but we are not him and his colleagues. We do not live in the same culture. Disciples are made by common sense as well as martyr — like methodology. Being wise as serpents comes from our favorite rabbi! Yes, the proof is in the pudding but we have to be around to sample the pudding. Ideals push us forward and upward in our spiritual questing. That is good, right, proper, and beneficial. We must never lose sight of them. Ask the Lord to keep you as open as he wants you to be.

Summary And Conclusion

It is exciting to know you and I are colleagues in the making of disciples! We are all in the same boat, so to speak, in that our strength and competence are decidedly limited. But make disciples we must. Noting that our product is always found in flesh and blood should be a regular reminder. To be internally encased in steel and externally mouthing the greatness of the gospel is not acceptable. In the long run, we cannot gain others for Christ by neglecting and downplaying our need for spiritual enrichment and guidance. The call to loosen the Holy Spirit among us and live lives that invite others to become like the Master is a key task and never completely goes away.

What does it take to get our spiritual batteries charged and keep them charged? Most importantly, a humble spirit saturated by the Holy Spirit is imperative. Is there some reason to wait, perhaps because of a theological difference? In the name of God, I hope that is not the case! Always keep a vision of greeting someone in heaven because you were faithful to the Spirit of the Living God. We must not fail, dear friends, and we are so privileged just to have the opportunity at all. For countless years, pagans came and went looking for the Son of God to appear. We have no waiting to do. The opportunities are at hand. We virtually have to close our eyes not to see them. We can do better — in fact — much better in union with the Spirit. We know where the proof is.

The Transfiguration Of Our Lord
(Last Sunday After Epiphany)
2 Corinthians 4:3-6

Proclaiming Jesus Christ

Introduction

It is not easy to promote someone else. Human nature rises up against it. If we believe in our self-worth and capabilities, why should we try to sell someone else? Yes, and why should we seek to gain acceptance of a religious leader, who will eventually cause us trouble. For example, Jesus for some was not only an irritant; he was an anathema as well.

As usual, Saint Paul is not much interested in whether you like or accept him as a person. His driving mission is to proclaim Jesus Christ as Lord. He and his colleagues were slaves for the sake of Jesus. Some would call him very brave and courageous. Others would see him as a man who was ignorant — even stupid.

Unbelievers are blinded by the machinations and subtleties of this world. The light of the gospel is hidden. Paul is called to a most difficult task. He must be an agent for light to shine out of darkness. In doing so, one and only one person is to stand out. His name is Jesus Christ. Probably no one envied his assignment!

There was total commitment. If death came, so be it. For him it would be approaching a welcome exit to spend eternity with the Father's Son. Are such people around and visible today? The answer to that is up to you.

Focus

Our real mission is to make known the Christ.

137

Body

1. We are to rise above personal egotism for Christ's sake.

Church history tells many opportunities for conversion have been lost because a religious leader refused to enable Christ to become the center of things. He/she tragically could not give up the need to be number one. It is as though they refuse to get out from under the spotlight because that would dim their role as the one solely responsible for converting others. For those who are natural-born achievers, who crave recognition, the casualty may be quite high. Nevertheless we are not intelligent enough to know why God calls some specifically to win others, who really would rather not have the job!

Actually, whether we are low-key or quite the reverse our mission is the same. Light must shine out of darkness and we are the agents to make this happen. Our salesmanship only becomes truly successful as we sell someone other than ourselves. The whole precious program is out of line for those determined to make a name for themselves apart from the Master. Some days, even those who have accepted the slave status of servanthood discover themselves to be in revolt. It is so against our natural inclinations the best disciples struggle to be at peace with their real mission. Where you and I find ourselves is crucial to our continuing in the faith and being fruitful in spreading the light to others.

The temptation is not to tell the old, old story of Jesus and his love but to tell our story in an effort to secure status. Recall our Lord's temptations in the desert. Pastors — in particular — are vulnerable. A human personality, rich in goodness, has a natural attraction. It is a little like the layperson who talks about wanting to go and hear *so and so* preach. That sounds so innocent and complimentary, until we note the preacher seems to be in first place and worshiping God in second place or lower. Christ is intended to be proclaimed, not the best and most likable preacher in a nearby city. Is that a bit of a stretch? My experience says popular preachers are to be on guard. The proclamation of our Savior and Lord is the one and only top priority.

The really big battles pastors face are almost always internal. The wars are sometimes fierce, as we labor to keep ourselves out of the limelight. The shrewdness of Satan, let's face it, outwits us and there we are with our names in bold letters, just above "Proclaiming the Christ!" It's funny and yet it isn't because so much is at stake. Pastors cannot — strictly speaking — win others to themselves, establishing a following, and expect to do the will of God. We are instruments and means. We are not the ends of much of anything because of a simple fact: we are mortal, being created and not the creator. To be sure, for those of us who have been in ministry this is common ground. Yet, how quickly we can yield to the temptation of placing ourselves first. We are called to be on guard.

2. We are to take slave status that provides a clear image of the Christ.

How can cherished human beings in the sight of God see, unless we are obedient and work to remove dangerous and even deadly cataracts? Spiritual eyesight, when it is faulty, gives birth to distortions that lead others in wrong directions. Not only do they arrive at dead ends, they take others with them. Correctives are amazing in some cases. Why? Because Christians are willing to walk the second mile in helping others see better, hopefully a spiritual 20/20! As we cooperate with the Holy Spirit, we recognize the strength given to us by the one who has all the strength there ever was, is, and shall be. Our full cooperation can give truly amazing results.

Slavery can take on a purely negative connotation. That must never happen under the lordship of our Savior and Lord! It is noteworthy some thinkers have insisted we will be a slave of someone or something. Frequently it is our self-will and righteousness. For others it may be full commitment to a political, economic, or social ideology. Some intellectuals throughout recorded history have led countless people in directions far from the salvation of God's Son. Witness the catastrophic effects of communism that often espoused atheism. Some started off in the right direction, only to depart and relegate the Christian religion to a miscellaneous place in life. Obviously, the kingdom of God they proclaimed was not at all like that of our Christ. Praise God, you and I have a blessed slavery.

In a profound sense, we are also slaves for others. Just like our Good Shepherd, we are to lay down our lives for lost sheep. Perhaps we have not seen that much at work in our lifetimes. It is far more connected with the ancient church and those martyred witnesses that have been in all ages, including the present. In the foreign mission fields there are true stories that are heartbreaking. Even an elementary understanding of human rights is cast aside. The killing and prior suffering are almost beyond comprehension. How can this happen in a world that is supposed to be civilized? Our answer is not difficult. Whenever we get totally serious about Jesus Christ in some cultures all hell breaks loose!

Saint Paul was such a strange fellow. He found full meaning to his life and death in the blessedness of Christlike slavery! His mission, painfully human as it was, never seemed to deviate from making Christ known. While there are others in the gallery of the saints who may have a more prominent place, we may want to look carefully. Some might even compare him to a good terrorist ready, willing, and able to be blown up in order to remove barriers that get in the way of receiving Christ. Perhaps that moves beyond our best sensitivities, but think about it a while. To be sure it is suicidal, but martyrdom has always been seen in some people's eyes as unneeded and a way to die bravely because the person did not want to go on living. Problematic? Yes, but it may be an avenue of opening dialogue with radical Muslims.

3. We are to lose ourselves in Christ for his cause.

When we begin to lose ourselves in anything, we tend to fight back. That's true eventually even in the jobs we love or the movement we are convinced is right, true, and just. Regardless of the great love our Savior bestows upon us, there is fear and apprehension of losing ourselves. The scriptures tell us that to lose ourselves for the purpose of finding ourselves is imperative. Still, our tendency is to revolt and I suspect — if the truth were known — that is exactly what happens in most cases. Of course, the saints in their words and actions make abundantly clear that the most completely powerful way to proclaim Christ is by being absorbed by his love that knows no bounds.

When we examine our lives with full honesty, we probably make a discovery that brings a sense of failure. We want Christ as Savior and Lord with all our hearts, minds, and souls but are unable or mostly unwilling to move beyond that. The way things are is just fine. Others note our exemplary lives and we feel fulfilled. When we are making an obvious contribution on behalf of Christ and the church, why grow anymore? Some even say that if it isn't broke, why fix it? Common sense and pride say to leave well enough alone. So, our proclamation rates above the average in our biased inspections. When I already have all of this, why should I want more? The apostle says it isn't enough, until our proclamation is fully unfettered.

Are we moving along lines that are not all that important? No. Why? Because the purpose is to proclaim Jesus Christ and that is only supremely done by losing ourselves in him. Is there room for compromise? Of course and there always is. You and I may very well choose that broad pathway like countless others. If we do, let's admit to ourselves what we have done and not claim the opportunity was never presented. Full commitment and spiritual success go hand-in-hand. Being lost in Christ is full commitment. In college we used to joke about being a "B" or "C" student and not to take the trouble of striving for an "A." Who needs the increased dedication and hard work? Employers are not looking for intellectuals who have no practical judgment, so let's play it safe. Just who are we attempting to fool?

The Christian is to be in a growth pattern all of his/her life. Our real mission of making Christ known can be perfected, until the day the death angel greets us. While we know this is true, there is invariably the temptation to avoid and evade by methods both subtle and not so subtle. The aim is never a better place in heaven. However, some of us who strive to be fully in Christ are accused of that very thing. We can even be described as holier-than-thou disciples who want to outdo others and wear a more expensive crown! They are annoyed by us and sometimes will deliberately stay away from us. This happens not only among laity but among the ordained clergy as well. Sometimes the negative politics of the clergy can be demonic, as pastors are pushed into patterns which do not proclaim Jesus Christ.

141

4. We are to give thanks for the part we can play.

Thanksgiving is built into Saint Paul's writings, perhaps like no other's in Holy Scripture. Is there ever a place in our lives with Christ that giving thanks is unneeded or perhaps out of order? For me that answer is a firm, "No." To live in Christ, proclaiming him with every facet of our being, means if everything has not turned out right, it ultimately will. The saints have maintained and lived by this, regardless of the situations in which they found themselves. Greatness glistens before our eyes, as Christ is proclaimed, in ways that are frequently miraculous and beyond human understanding. Sorry to say, in our often partially dedicated lives, we are thankful when most things are going right for us!

The corpus of Pauline writing shows a man so thankful that some probably inquired about his sanity. How can anyone go through what he did and continually give thanks just to be a vessel for promoting someone else? The normal attitude is to insist that if we are going to do the hard work and suffering, then we are going to get the credit. After all, isn't that the only really fair way to handle one's life? Well, it does certainly sound equitable for all concerned, that is, until we seriously come to terms with our Savior and Lord. He wants all of us — today, tomorrow, and forever! He calls us to come and die to ourselves that the Lord may be fully proclaimed through our lives. It is asking a lot and only a little because to be held in his embrace is the apex of happiness.

For the Christian, every minute of every day ought to be filled with thanksgiving. The chief reason is the promise God will never leave us or forsake us. International figures with military power and so much money they can't count it find themselves excluded from such security. There is a value system here that confounds the world and always has. Indeed, how can anyone lose himself and find himself? The only sense it makes to the world is the failure to actualize oneself into his/her own authority figure that gains the respect of secular society. If one gets lost and loses control of life, what is left but a series of failed attempts to be somebody — as defined by worldly values? No wonder we people who totally commit ourselves to Christ appear to be a bunch of idiots!

Nothing quite paves and prepares the way for accepting Christ as an unbridled attitude of gratitude. Aren't the people in your church, who really inspire and motivate you, filled with gratitude? To be one of spiritual depth and ungrateful is a contradiction. Of the thousands of parishioners I have known over many years — to my mind — there are no exceptions. Disciples of Christ are naturally and spontaneously thankful. Take another look at your church and tell me what you find. Okay, take a careful not a cursory look! All days are for thanksgiving, especially in the life of the one, holy, catholic, and apostolic church. The knowledge of the glory of God in the face of our redeemer is also our glory as our faces shine like stars in a troubled universe. Brothers and sisters we have a privileged place!

Summary And Conclusion

Every person in life has a mission, spoken or unspoken. It is doubtful some even recognize it, until their later years. Nevertheless, there it is and for a few more than one mission makes up their lives, depending on their age and conditions. As disciples of Jesus Christ we know where we stand. The questions are all answered about this matter. Day in and day out we proclaim him. It is part of the air we breathe. In joys and sorrows, failures and successes, thanksgivings prevail as we shout or whisper his name. It becomes our chief reason for being and communicates to others how we see our lives and deaths. Our driving duty is to let light shine out of darkness.

Praises be to God who comes to us as Father, Son, and Holy Spirit, doubts are settled and we are grateful for the challenge we have accepted. Friends, if you have delayed in accepting the only mission that ultimately counts, please reconsider. If need be, retrace your steps and try to discover where you refused to accept this awesome adventure. Review, as long as you need to, your life. Then come to terms with the invitation that is still being given. My experience is the dear Lord comes to us with a holy pressure, uncomfortable though it be which is always for our benefit. So, as all prophets and evangelists have persistently declared: today is the day of salvation. Indeed, today is just right — if you have not done so — to promise the Father all the rest of your days will be spent proclaiming Jesus Christ, as Savior and Lord. We Christians are so fortunate. In the long run we are never losers!

Sermons On The Second Readings

For Sundays In
Lent And Easter

Faith As Alternating Current

John T. Ball

Selling Sin
In A Celebrative Age

Dialing the number of a large, well-known metropolitan church, the caller asked, "What time is your Sunday worship service?" A booming voice replied, "We don't have worship around here, we have celebration at 11 a.m.!" Today the "C" word is in. Celebration drives the gathering of the people of God. Praise singers warm up the congregation in the opening moments and the mood is laboriously upbeat. Worship in most of our congregations exudes the positive mood. We live in a celebrative age, where mention of anything negative, like sin, is out of bounds.

In liberal or conservative churches, Lent is something of an embarrassment. Focusing on our need for repentance and making amends is something we avoid, instead centering on the forgiving love of God, the sustaining power of the Holy Spirit, and the positive elements of Christian faith. Selling a good look at sin is a struggle, even on Ash Wednesday. Sin does not sell well in our celebrative age.

A contemporary Ash Wednesday service makes the point. After some scriptures and prayers of confession, the congregation came down the aisle to receive the mark of ashes on the forehead. After this, the worshipers took a couple of steps and stood in front of a large bowl of water. There the pastor dampened a cloth in the water and wiped off the ashen smudge from each worshiper, who returned to the pews. All told, only a few seconds were given to ponder the fact of sin. Absolution and forgiveness were quickly invoked as if we cannot manage a serious conviction of sin.

It seems that positive thinking has become the dominant feature of our culture, including the church, so that we are sheltered from wrestling with the fact of sin — personal and social. We may be thankful that we are delivered from many of the narrow traditions of Grandpa's and Grandma's Christianity. However, their staunch seriousness about the faith puts our soft spirituality to shame.

Here we are on Ash Wednesday, smack dab in the middle of Lenten considerations of sin, repentance, and making amends, but without any enthusiasm for such disturbing realities. Instead, we strain toward the glories of Easter and one more rendition of the "Hallelujah Chorus." Can modern Christians in affluent America with our culture of success and positive thinking find our way back to a sturdy experience of Ash Wednesday and Lent? If so, we may have to begin with some history of this tradition.

Ash Wednesday Begins The Season Of Lent

The early Christians had no sentimentalities about sin. They knew that the real human issue is our deliberate disregard of God in favor of our own preferences. Some people in our time are not so certain about the centrality of sin. They tell us that sin is only one of the great enslavements from which we need deliverance. One New Testament scholar says that our captivity by structural oppression and our alienation from a sense of life's purpose and meaning are both as destructive as sin. Certainly the New Testament speaks of both these enslavements and of our need to be delivered from their destructive effects on our lives. However, oppression and alienation are assaults from the outside. Sin is the enslavement we have chosen and in which we continue to participate, not the result of things over which we have little control. Our real spiritual dilemma is that we choose our own desires rather than God's wishes for us. Here is the real issue.

When the early Christians began to mark the forty days before Easter, minus Sundays, they were not thinking about their oppression under the Empire, nor were they paying much attention to any alienation from a victorious life. Rather, they focused on their sin — the condition of inner resistance to the grace of

God, a resistance often stronger than any desire to live the holy, godly life. Thus they created a holy space where they came to worship, considering their deliberate denial of God in their lives. They took these forty days before Easter and remembered Jesus' forty days in the wilderness, putting their lives over against the stern realities of Christian cross bearing. They had no illusions about their ability to avoid the failures of discipleship. They knew it would be no significant triumph if they came to church on Easter Sunday, having omitted the walk through the hard honesty of Lent. They shunned any self-congratulations and prayed for God's grace to forgive their sin. They pleaded for the empowerment to live beyond their natural ungodliness. Only from a somber Lent did they think they might celebrate the joy of Easter.

Sin Is A Personal Malady

Let's attempt, if only for a very small moment, to detach ourselves from our excessively self-affirming culture and inquire about the radical wrong within us. This will be difficult for there is not much around us that caters to a critical assessment of the waywardness of the human heart. We are so convinced of our right to baptize every natural desire and inclination, that anyone or any circumstance that might bring our sin into clear focus is hustled out of sight and mind. And if our exclusionary tactics will not suffice, we will haul out the psychobabble and declare that any negative thoughts about our supposed innate worth and dignity are dangerous and bordering on the pathological.

It's a long shot, but in a serious Lent, we moderns could yet find ourselves hearing the Word of God about our human condition. We could start by remembering the garden story, which, by being on the first pages of scripture, ought to tell us something. Some of us have taken comfort in knowing that this story is not history as Grandpa and Grandma believed. Yet we seldom listen when they go on to say that this story's point does not hang on history, but on what is called its existential point — this is how life is for us before God and one another. The story says there is something within us resisting the ways of God, and any saving trust in God's mercy and grace.

Lent could be a moment when we face the fact that we are the Adam and the Eve in that garden, spoiling the only essential life-giving relationship we know. We could recognize that we are the ones then, living east of Eden, outside the grace and mercy of God, with our inner malady compounding itself in anxious, devious, and destructive living. An old African-American gospel chorus runs the list of needy sinners: brother, sister, preacher, deacon, before asserting, "It's me, it's me, it's me, O Lord, standin' in the need of prayer." This could be our Lenten anthem, much more pertinent than the sentimental and evasive stuff we often sing.

Miracles for us moderns are not interruptions of the flow of nature, or unexpected historical occurrences. For us, a miracle would be concluding that sin is an inescapable reality in which we resort to all sorts of diversionary strategies, lest we find ourselves having to come to terms with it. For too long, moderns have supposed that an earlier generation's anguish about personal sin was something from which we have been delivered through our modernness. We have come to believe that there is something horrid about confessing that we are sinners, desperately in need of God's grace and forgiveness. There is no guarantee that Lent will change all of this, but we must not rule out the ability of God to confront us during these forty days. The cure for us is like chemotherapy for the soul — it nearly kills us before we become healthy once again. If this should happen, Easter would be as no other we have ever experienced.

The Malady Takes On Structural Proportions

In a pastor's meeting, one passionate brother stood up to speak to the needs of the church and the world. He acknowledged all the racism, the plight of the poor and the oppressed, HIV, terrorism, corporate corruption, and the church's terminal timidity. Then he offered his remedy, "We just need to love one another!" It was like a pointless speech by another pastor during the heyday of the civil rights controversies. He said that all the racial tensions would ease if blacks and whites would offer courteous greetings.

These sentimental suggestions fail because the church neglects the truth that the structures of human existence reflect our sinfulness. Family, government, economy, educational and medical institutions, cultural activities — all perpetuate injustice, favoritism, and bestow inordinate awards and favors upon those few. Love and kindness are not going to check the entrenchment of sinful institutional injustice.

Langdon Gilkey's father was the dean of the chapel at the University of Chicago in the 1930s and a friend of the young Reinhold Niebuhr. Gilkey tells of his father bursting out of his study yelling, "Reinie's gone crazy!" He then said he was reading Niebuhr's recent book, *Moral Man and Immoral Society*. "He's written this book," said the elder Gilkey, "and I don't understand at all why he has done it or what's he's saying — and neither does Harry." (Harry Emerson Fosdick, pastor of Riverside Church in New York City.) Both Gilkey and Fosdick later acknowledged the wisdom of Niebuhr's writing that social structures and institutions often move with crushing injustice in spite of the morality and good intentions of persons who maintain these structures.

Abraham Lincoln found himself at the center of unimaginable violence in an effort to quell a political rebellion and end the national tribulation of American slavery. Lincoln seemed aware of his compromised position so that neither self-righteousness nor vindictiveness became part of his outlook. He believed the violence and death on the battlefields made it impossible to speak confidently of the theological meanings of the war or of any moral posturing. The guilt of slavery was widespread and the ways of correcting it became filled with moral complications. Our refusal of God's ways entangles itself with our corporate lives, becoming a disruptive assault on human happiness and fairness for all.

This means that the church needs deliverance from any sentimental voicing about making our public world a godly place. This hope will not come with a simple call to love. Righteousness is difficult enough on the level of personal relationships. It is infinitely more complex when we seek to attack the evil ingrained in our public institutions. This may be why many mainstream and evangelical churches have domesticated the gospel, limiting it to religious and spiritual needs of our personal faith and lives. We recognize that the great public needs, dominated as they are by institutions and systems, are complicated and so resistant to change

151

that we become discouraged and frustrated. So we specialize in prayer, Bible study, evangelism, healing ministries, feeding the poor, and sending out missionaries. All of these ministries are vital and necessary, yet their dominance of the agenda of the church shows that we are largely incapable of imagining a prophetic ministry over against the dominant systems of our day.

If somehow during Lent we could consider the issue of sin as it plagues our necessary systems and institutions, the church might take on a new vitality and mission beyond the present passion for church growth. Sin is a hard sell in our time. It means owning up to the sins in our hearts and minds. Sin is at the heart of the injustices and oppressions by which we organize life together. Social sin is even more difficult to manage than our personal transgressions. However, the weeks of Lent might be an opportunity for us to consider the difficulty of its mission, just as its Lord sensed the difficulty of his mission. We can struggle with personal and corporate ministry issues during this forty-day wilderness moment.

Listening To Minority Voices

The endurance of humanity and even the whole cosmos could depend upon giving a serious listening of minority voices. British historian, Arnold Toynbee, has written about the question of humanity's future in sober terms. Toynbee calculated that of 26 known civilizations, sixteen are dead, nine are at the point of death, and our present worldwide civilization is very much in question. Our future might depend upon on listening to the disturbing, but salving minority voices.

We cannot heed all those minority voices that vie for attention. Some minority voices are blatantly self-serving or filled with suicidal destructiveness, like those that called for the Jews to rebel against Rome in 70 C.E. This foolishness resulted in a crushing defeat and the dispersal of the Jews from their homeland. It is clear that unwise radical minority voices pushed the American South into secession after the election of Abraham Lincoln in 1860.

Carl Sandburg tells about the dangerous minority voice of William Lowdnes Yancey, of Alabama. Yancey, with his inflammatory oratory urged the South toward disunion. Sandburg writes, "His living voice had magnetized many a barbecue audience and led men to clutch imaginary weapons and spring forward to meet a fancied foe." Oblivious of neither the political nor the moral consequences of secession, Yancey was for revolution. Sandburg continues, "He had said so often that a hurricane is healthy for cleaning out scum and miasma. He took to the floor (at the Alabama secessionist convention) ... to declare the election and inauguration of Abraham Lincoln an insult and a menace. Even though the convention found his words excessive and dangerous, they were sentiments long declared by the minority voices of southern Yanceys that moved even the moderates into the death-dealing resolve to secede."

If Sandburg is not your cup of tea, then take it from Margaret Mitchell's novel and movie, *Gone With The Wind*. Mitchell was no academic historian, but she recognized that there were hosts of careless minority voices in the South driving the nation into the horrors of the Civil War.

Biblical Tradition And Dangerous Minority Voices

We can see this same thing in the biblical story as it struggled with dangerous minority voices. Some of these were present at the time of Jesus. Some minority voices declared that holiness before God meant separation from the common life. So the Essenes opted for celibacy and withdrawal, going to the desert to await God's intervention. This guaranteed their demise. They weren't concerned about future renewal, since God was about to act. This style of holiness possessed no possibility for future and self-renewal. Other minority voices in the first century defined holiness as separation through moral purity and cultic emphasis. But this option was available only to the few who could financially adopt this restrictive holiness. Certainly the Pharisees do not always get a fair shake in the New Testament. However, their minority voice became a possibility only for the affluent, often resulting in an unattractive self-righteousness. Jesus, holding a more inclusive sense of holiness, resisted their claim. These minority voices never captured the interest or attention of Jesus.

The ministry and message of Paul also rejected the minority voices offering dangerous promises. Paul disassociated himself and his converts from the seductive minority voices of his Greco-Roman world. We can easily list the minority voices he rejected — the restrictive version of Torah Christianity, gnostic world-denial, charismatic confusion, the cult of personality, and ecclesiastical elitism. Any one of these minority voices invited disaster to the gospel and they continue to do so in our own time, too.

154

Many current Christians find the early creeds of the church to be a nightmarish mix of biblical urgency and Greek philosophy. Yet these creeds molded a unity of Christian conviction that preserved the church against dissolution. The creeds set themselves against minority voices poised to render the church nice, but irrelevant. Rejecting the minority voices surrounding the formation of our early creeds may have saved the gospel as a serious voice in human history. Today we need to be aware of the dangerous minority voices lurking within and around the Christian life and faith.

There Are Godly Minority Voices That Invite Our Attention

On this first Sunday of Lent, we have this passage from 1 Peter before us, a call to suffer for the truth of God revealed in Jesus Christ. Christians always need this voice. Dietrich Bonhoeffer, one of the great heroic Christian spirits standing against the evils of Nazi Germany in the 1930s and 1940s, said when Christ puts his claim on us "he calls us to come and die." For Bonhoeffer, laying aside his pacifist credo and taking part in a plot to assassinate Adolf Hitler was of great and ultimately mortal risk. His voice was a minority one. Most German Christians joined their faith to Hitler's cause. Only a few, like Bonhoeffer, were willing to speak and accept the suffering that inevitably came with voicing the minority protest. Speaking this minority voice cost Bonhoeffer his life — hung by his Nazi captors only a few days before the war was over. Suffering, intentionally assumed for Christ, is always a voice we need to hear.

However, there is another voice in this text, a minority one. The text says that after the cross and the resurrection, Jesus "went and made a proclamation to the spirits in prison." This means the early Christians reflected on what happened between Jesus' crucifixion and his resurrection. In this interim they daringly proclaimed that Jesus went into the central precincts of hell and offered salvation to the damned.

Immediately, we recognize the minority status of this voice. The dominant Christian voice of God's offer of salvation in Christ shouts, "There is salvation in no one else, for there is no other name under heaven among mortals by which we must be saved" (Acts 4:12). This slams the door shut on proclaiming a more generous view of God's grace. This exclusive majority voice is what drove the early church's evangelistic thrust. This is what undergirded the nineteenth-century missionary enterprise of the Protestant church.

A biography of the great missionary, David Livingston, tells how he went fearlessly into the unknowns of central Africa, burdened by the thought that millions of Africans would perish without Christ. Such self-sacrificing commitment was commonplace in those times. It is often repeated by many of the conservative evangelical traditions. One older Christian told how she, being a third-generation child of American Baptist missionaries to India, at nine years of age, was put on a ship taking her to America for schooling. We of our child-centered families can hardly imagine such a painful separating decision. However, it was done repeatedly in those times because the missionary work had a stern mood about it commanding that missionary parents be willing to hurl their young children off to the care of their homeland church. If there is no salvation outside a confession of Christ then this makes impeccable logic and is the reluctant but imperative outcome of the missionary enterprise.

However, occasionally there are minority voices challenging the dominant, majority voice on this issue. Chryostom of Alexandria was one challenger in the fifth century. The New England Universalists of the 1800s made the same claim — God's grace can overcome all human ignorance or resistance to God's love, here or in the hereafter. In the modern church, some have ventured this minority voice in what the hymn calls, "the wideness of God's mercy." Prominent twentieth-century theologian, Emil Brunner, declared that the grace of God in Jesus Christ saves all humanity. The difference between Christians and non-Christians is not that Christians are saved and all others are not. The Christian difference is that we know that salvation is granted to all.

Reinhold Niebuhr once said that people are "charmed" into faith, not by terror, self-seeking, or by logic. Our times and our world call for the church to listen to this minority voice, too. The glad, good news of Christ is our best and only lasting evangelistic possibility.

Other Minority Voices Needing A Hearing

History is rough on wrapping the gospel in a comfortable package called, "the faith once and for all delivered to the saints." There is a proper understanding of such a statement meaning that our faith in the reality of God's grace in Christ is constant and unwavering. However, the "once and for all" element is not a guarantee that our statements of the faith in human words and images will never call for modification, revamping, and sometimes the abandonment of certain elements. As we move through history, circumstances and insights change, so that yesterday's faith package becomes a burden and shoves us into irrelevance. We must listen carefully to the minority voices that speak through our struggles and witness to the faith. Often these bring fresh and more meaningful understandings of the gospel and what God wants from us.

A young theological student journeyed to the Graduate Theological Union surrounding the campus of the University of California at Berkeley to work toward a Ph.D. His advisor was Claude Welch, one of the founders of GTU. Welch's career centered on the history of modern Protestant theology. The student learned that some Protestant thinkers were listening to an array of minority voices of that time. Some of these voices were critical of traditional biblical understanding, Darwinian natural science, the witness of non-Christian religions, and of the dominant economic and political arrangements. Welch's saga indicates his paying significant attention to the minority voices of that era, has saved the gospel for the modern world. It linked itself to modern secular truth claims, while pointing out many invalid and debatable axioms of traditions and modernity.

Our Lenten pilgrimage can be a serious listening to the minority voices from our own time. Biblically, one of these voices might be Amos' insistence that only justice and righteousness count with God. For Jesus, we need to listen to his minority voice that success with God is being the servant of others. Paul's minority voice to us could be his insistence that we are embedded in a Christ-love from

157

which we cannot fall. In addition, the minority voice of Revelation needing a constant hearing, is its voice declaring God — everlastingly set against worldly oppression and might.

Other minority voices in our Christian tradition meriting a Lenten hearing might be from Martin Luther. He insisted that the godly life is always a risk in faith, never a comfortable certainty. Catherine of Sienna's minority voice gets it right in telling us that neighbor need trumps our worship and devotional commitments. John Wesley becomes a minority Lenten voice reminding us that the Christian life is inextricably social and connected to others, never a private matter. Cardinal John Henry Newman's great hymn, "Lead Kindly Light" needs our hearing, too. In it, Newman points to those moments when the kindly light allows us only the next step, and not a certainty of the way or the conclusion. Walter Rauschenbush has a vital minority voice when he said that our social structures need saving, just as much as our personal hearts. Elizabeth Cady Stanton and Susan B. Anthony came together as a single minority voice saying political and civil rights are gender blind. Albert Schweitzer became a saving minority voice as he lived out the truth that worldly blessedness implies caring for that less favored by worldly arrangements.

Eleanor Roosevelt's minority voice calls us to committing ourselves to using political and economic power to assuage the suffering of the poor and needy. The minority voice of Reinhold Niebuhr has cleared out illusions about our easy ability to live the Christian life and to infuse justice into our social and political structures. Dag Hammarskjold has become a minority voice affirming that real mystical moments drive us into the heart of neighbor service. Mother Teresa's minority voice holds up a checklist for Christian living by asking us how much we dare to side with the sick and dying have-nots. Pope John XXIII became a minority voice when he reminded us that God has disciples in the quest for a peaceful world that will never make a personal Christian confession of faith. Episcopal Bishop James Robinson is a newer minority voice tellingly declaring that loving, committed, and faithful sexual relationships leap over the dominant traditional voices of what marriage means.

The book of Hebrews says a great cloud of witnesses surrounds Christians. Hebrews implies that these witnesses are mainly minority voices. We must listen to them carefully, lest none of us hear them at all. However, if in Lent we could once again hear these voices, we would experience a salvation that is worldly and everlasting, painful yet joyful, and becoming for us the wonderful gift of God. This can make our Lenten journey a very special moment. Lent could be a time for this discovery.

Abraham: The Near Death
Of God's Promise

Since Dr. Raymond Moody published his book, *Life After Life,* we have heard a lot about what are called, "Near Death Experiences," often dubbed NDEs. These experiences result from having come near to death from illness, surgery, or accidents. The anecdotal material from Near Death Experiences varies widely, yet has some common elements: separation from the self, moving through a tunnel, powerful emotions, flashing lights, a sense of dying too soon, meeting loves ones, a life review, having cosmic knowledge, and a decision to return to the body.

Most of these NDE moments seem blissful and encouraging to the goodness and meaning of life. Interestingly, believers and atheists alike report their NDE moments. We have no scientific agreement on the cause of NDEs. For many they ground a belief in life after death. Others suspect that NDEs may have something to do with the origin of the world's religions and their founding figures.

It is quite interesting that many experiencing an NDE report euphoria coupled with a sense of being chosen. Other NDE experiencers want to ponder these moments by a temporary withdrawal. Perhaps Jesus and Abraham come to mind. Both of them felt they were chosen, and Lent begins with remembering the reports of Jesus going into the solitary wilderness.

Abraham's Near Death Experience
Today Abraham, some fifteen centuries before Paul, is cited in chapter 4 of his letter to the Romans. Here Paul argues for his doctrine of justification by faith through grace. Paul writes to testify

how we are reconciled to God, given our sin and waywardness. The crucial concern is how this disruption may be healed. One old answer said ritual, prayer, and ceremony could do the trick. But Paul and his Jewish tradition had long abandoned this. It appeared magical and proved ineffective.

But another impressive theory arose, a significant advance over the rites and ceremonies answer. This newer answer, while not completely abandoning ritual, prayer, and ceremony, called people to live out the ethical parts of the Hebrew Bible. Doing this was believed to bring individuals and society into a reunification with God, creating the blessings of peace, joy, and just social arrangements. This was a magnificent answer and even after Paul rejected this answer, we can find much truth in it for our private and public lives before God and one another. It can serve to tell us how to live after our reconciliation.

What Paul is contending for in recalling the story of Abraham in this passage from the letter to the Romans, is that the way of faith in God's mercy is older than the ethical law of the Torah. Paul says it was three centuries after Abraham before the Torah began to take shape. Before Moses, Abraham was living out the grace and promise of God.

Yet Paul says that this was not easy for Abraham. God promised that he would make a great nation of him and his descendents. Being chosen by God for this was sheer gift. It was not because Abraham was such a wonderful person — someone honest and just to the core, nor because of his vast intelligence. Abraham was chosen simply because he was chosen; it was all graciousness on God's part, not from something which qualified Abraham to this role. But discouragingly, Abraham and Sarah had no children. How could a great nation come from them and from their descendents? This holy couple was advanced in years, far beyond the normal years of having children. Paul says,

> *Hoping against hope, he believed that he would be "the father of many nations,"... he did not weaken in faith when he considered his own body, which was already as good as dead.* — Paul 4:18-19

The wonderful promise of God was given, even though Abraham was having an NDE.

The Fragility Of God's Grace

God's goodness is always threatened. Abraham and Sarah feared they would have no children, dying with God's promise unfulfilled. Paul cites Abraham for his trust in the face of such a threat. But this underscores the truth that God's grace is so often challenged by our personal and public evils. Alfred North Whitehead cited "the perpetual perishing" of all our dreams and values making this one of the great obstacles to believing in the goodness of God and life.

We want democracy for the entire world. We believe that democracy is the best way for people to live out their public lives. Of course democracy is not perfect. Winston Churchill said it is the worst form of government — except all the rest! But democracy comes close to the biblical dream of the kingdom of God on earth. Our nation and others have used the violence of war to impose democracy in Iraq and Afghanistan. Yet, democracy in these places is a fragile sort of blessing. It remains to be seen if true democracy can overcome the democracy imposed by military might, and it remains to be seen if democracy can long endure, to use Lincoln's phrase from his Gettysburg Address.

In this Lenten season we are pressed to consider how God's promise nearly dies in our own lives. There was a time when God's grace awakened in us the possibility of the Christian life. We felt called to a life of love and caring, paying more attention to the needs of others than to ourselves. We hoped to become someone who was gentle with the sins of others, and quick to acknowledge our own waywardness. Even if this hope was only a faint cry within, its promise became the center of our life and living.

We soon discovered how such a dream and hope are at the mercies of evil. Many historians tell us that Hitler and his Nazis were doomed in fighting a two-front war. Their armies were engaged in Western Europe trying to check the advances of the Allies in North Africa and later in France. At the same time their armies were also fighting the Russians in Eastern Europe. The strains of a double-front war proved their demise.

In God's dream for us we face a two-front struggle, too. One front is the continual impact of our culture and society. We are urged to choose the values of our consumer society — a high position job with a triple digit salary, a bigger home in an upscale neighborhood, a luxury car, vacations in exotic places, membership in a country club, and the means to send our children to a high-prestige private school. These materialistic gods and idols urge us to place our security and self-esteem in them. When we get caught up in these, God's dream for us nearly dies.

The second front in our personal struggle to keep faith with God's dream is within. At some point we understand that we can fake personal godliness — fooling others and ourselves. We know that we can pretend to love others when we don't really care about them. Learning of the good fortune of a friend or colleague, we may exhibit all the graciousness required, saying that we are so pleased that this has come to her or to him. But inwardly, we feel we are more deserving. We begrudge our friend's good fortune. More devastating for us to admit, tearing apart our facade of Christian gracefulness toward others, is our inner glee when someone stumbles into bad fortune. Our delight about this happenstance prompts us to share the story of their fall; it drives us to constantly be on the hunt for similar stories, making us feel better about ourselves because it lessens the competition to our own self-worth.

So What?

A pastor once said, "Every sermon should have a 'So What?'"
Folks in the pews have often longed for a "So What?" to lots of sermons inflicted upon you. You have wished for the preacher to come to grips with a serious "So What?" before shuffling together her or his notes and waiting for the closing hymn. So here is a feeble try at "So What?" It comes in two parts.

First, the fragility of the promise of God in our social structures, or in our private lives often wins out over the powerful odds against them. This is Paul's point. Writing to Christians distressed

164

that the 2004 presidential election seemed to be a victory for those advantages to the wealthy over against the needy and oppressed, Peter Story expressed some heartening words. Story is a retired Methodist bishop who, with Archbishop Desmond Tutu, challenged the system of Apartheid in South Africa. He wrote,

> *In our four decades of almost despair in South Africa, it was important to remember that while God prefers to work with enlightened, committed, and compassionate servants of the people, God has extensive experience of advancing the Kingdom in spite of the arrogant and shallow people we often get instead.*[1]

Perhaps we should pay less attention to the biblical miracles that seem so questionable to modern Christians and focus instead on this miracle: God brings life out of those godly realities that seem so doomed outwardly and inwardly. It is these miracles, enlivening our faith rather than fussing over the miracles that strain our scientific credulity.

But we have not yet fully responded to the prompting of our text. We must admit that sometimes Abraham and Sarah die. God's dream and theirs dies with them. Also, often God's public concerns die while the rewards to the rich and powerful continue. Not only this, but it seems likely that billions of years out into the future the whole cosmos will burn up or freeze all life to death. Then certainly all things will die short of what God would want so that everything will go down to oblivion — or does it?

In Lent we are driving toward Easter. Our celebration of Easter will hinge on our willingness to confront the fragility of God's dream, how all life and reality are headed toward death. Then Easter — happening more than the Sunday after Good Friday — goes beyond our being left only with what Bertrand Russell called "yielding despair." Even if Abraham and Sarah go down before the birth of Isaac, God's dream and love are still working. At Easter we will be permitted to sense that God's dream is larger than this life, death, or the dissolution of all this is, and out of such faith we are enabled to live this life with courage, with goals and dreams for provisional social and personal improvement, and with a joy that is incomprehensible.

---

1. *Social Questions Bulletin, The Methodist Federation for Social Action*, January-February, 2005, p. 5.

Finding Our Salvation
In Today's World

One of Louis Armstrong's vocal hits went like this:

> *I see skies of blue, and clouds of white,*
> *The bright blessed day, dark sacred night,*
> *And I think to myself, what a wonderful world.*
>
> *I hear babies crying, I watch them grow,*
> *They'll learn much more, than I'll ever know,*
> *And I think to myself, what a wonderful world.*
>
> *Yes, I think to myself, what a wonderful world.*
> *Oh yeah.*

We know what he means. We have all felt like this. Life and the world seem wonderful and joyful. We rejoice in the wonders of nature, the achievements of humanity, the inspiration of music and poetry, we cherish our loved ones near and far, and we are thankful for food, rest, and creative work to do. We "think to ourselves, what a wonderful world."

Our Sense Of Lostness

Biblical religion calls us to believe in this wonderful world and the reality creating it. The opening passage of scripture says repeatedly as God shapes the universe, the world, and humanity, "God saw that it was good." Human existence is intended to be

167

good and life is to be filled with meaning, purpose, and joy. Biblical religion asserts that within all existence is a *lover* who loves us. This *lover* prompts Armstrong's song, "Yes, I think to myself, what a wonderful world."

However, we also have moments when we do not feel this way. A loved one dies and we are plunged into grief. We find feelings of hate and destruction within. Suddenly we lose our job, or the doctor tells us we have a terrible disease. We are saddened that much of the world's population lives with constant hunger, AIDS, poverty, and political oppression. We discover the most distressing fact of all — we are inwardly skewed toward selfishness — securing our own survival or our comforts at the expense of others. Then the "wonderful world" becomes "the frightening world."

The Bible knows about this, too. It recounts that early biblical story about a first man and woman living in a wonderful and happy paradise. The story is really a story about ancients and moderns alike. There comes a moment when we are forced out of our safe, happy garden into a world of fright, terror, violence, and self-destruction. Yet we long to return to our safe, happy paradise, but we can't for the gates are closed. The Bible calls this experience the Fall. We tumble down from our highest happiness and delight, finding ourselves scrambling to fashion some security against the inner and outer threats of the world into which we have fallen. We begin to despair; thinking there is nothing good about the world, about life and even about ourselves. We fall into despair.

There is a church in Atlanta, Georgia, that does not try to cover the pain of those who gather there on Sunday morning worship. The service does not begin with traditional, majestic hymns of praise to God. They do not have singers in the chancel, gyrating behind microphones, offering chirpy little ditties thrown up on a huge screen behind them. Instead, this church begins with words and songs of lament like so many of the psalms of scripture. The congregation gathers to sing songs of lament about the pain in their lives and the life of the world. So, worship might begin with the cry of Psalm 13:

168

How long, O Lord will you forget me forever?
How long will you hide your face from me?
How long must I bear pain in my soul,
And have sorrow in my heart all day long?
— Psalm 13:1-2a

These words focus on the pains and difficulties of life. They confess with honesty that we bring to worship our hurts, our pains, our disappointments, and our despair in finding any significant goodness in the world or in ourselves. If we are ever to sing any of the songs of happy praise, we must begin with admitting the many things that challenge any serious optimism about the world and ourselves.

Some Unsaving Options

Our search for a rescue from our despair is a search for salvation. In our lection this morning, Paul says there are two significant ways we are frustrated in recovering our sense of the wonderful experience of life. One of them he calls "the way of the Greeks." The Greek way tries to discover a basic wisdom about life that will enable one to manage a serene life in the midst of its pain and suffering. It says we can reason ourselves toward mastering the destructive powers, and find happiness in spite of life's precariousness. The Greek way offers that if we really know the right way to live, we will inevitably choose that way. In short, human reason and knowledge imply the ability to live in ways that bring us happiness.

Of course, Paul does not believe that. He calls it foolishness. In his early life Paul poured over the 613 commandments in the Torah, the Jewish Law. In the Law he found the wisdom for a happy and prosperous life. However, Paul discovered that knowing how to live does not empower us to decide for it. Paul even said that the ability to choose between the right and the wrong way to live is weighted toward choosing the wrong thing.

Paul seems to be right. Our ancient and modern optimism — either the ethics of the Greeks or the ways of the Law — seems unsupported in the human record. Many point out Germany in the late 1800s and the early 1900s as the unquestioned center of human knowledge and learning. Anyone who wanted the best in graduate education went to study in Germany. The highest educational experience in those times was found in the German universities.

However, in 1914, when Germany rushed the world into the slaughter on the battlefields of France and Belgium, many questioned that knowledge and learning delivers us from violence and self-destruction. A young Swiss pastor, Karl Barth, educated in the finest theological schools in Germany, listening to the pounding of artillery guns during that war, became disillusioned with the prevailing notion that human knowledge saves us from despair. He agonized that many of his German theological professors easily endorsed the war aims of Kaiser Wilhelm and his military advisors. Barth began preaching and writing in the mood of Paul, saying that wisdom is no way out of our dilemma.

In our morning's lection, Paul says that his own Jewish tradition is equally foolish in searching for unquestionable faith through great historical events or in mystical experiences of God. To Paul, the Jews are trying to find convincing events or personal moments that will ground their faith in a wonderful world. Paul says this is foolishness, too. There are no revealing events in history, not even the Exodus, compelling absolute faith. We may believe that the hand of God was in the escape from Egypt; but this does not create faith or godly living. We may believe that God has healed us from a dreadful disease; but this belief does not produce a certainty that life is ultimately good, filled with joy and meaning.

Nor do those moments when we sense the presence of God. Religious experience is not totally convincing. We can always doubt these experiences. Our sense of God's presence comes and goes. In the eighteenth-century revival in Great Britain and America, John and Charles Wesley preached an experience of God's saving grace for all. They told their hearers they could feel the mercy of God within, creating a rock-solid certainty. However, there is a coded letter to Charles in John's *Journal* long after both their converting moments. In that letter, John confessed he no longer had the inner feelings of God's presence and wondered if the Methodists should quit preaching such a doctrine. Religious experience is not the unassailable foundation of a vital faith in the goodness of life, either.

Christ And Salvation

So where does this leave us? If neither human intelligence nor religious experience can enable us to sing, "What A Wonderful World" what are we to do? If we are perishing because neither our human smarts nor our religious experiences do save us, then what can save us? Paul's answer is "the cross of Christ."

Too often we think the saving power of the cross of Christ only as something that happened when Jesus was crucified during that Passover around 20 C.E. We have devised all sorts of explanations why the death of Jesus on the cross has become the salvation point for us. All of them are inadequate and many of them are incredulous. Many moderns opt out of the faith because some of the doctrines of the cross are unbelievable in our day. For instance, we are told that Jesus' death on the cross defeated the forces of evil that keep us from God and joyful living. In another explanation, we say that Jesus' death at Calvary satisfied God's sense of justice regarding human sin. In a magical way, the cross becomes the means of overcoming our separation from the goodness of life, and cures our inability to find an ultimate goodness in human existence. Today, for many Christians and non-Christians, these understandings of the cross are insufficient.

However, what if Paul's proclamation of the cross of Christ is much more? Sometimes Paul suggests that he understands the cross in ways that are unacceptable. In his late letter to the Roman Christians, he takes great pains to indicate how the death of Jesus overcame the chasm between God and ourselves, empowering us to trust in the goodness of life. However, this is not how Paul best understood the cross.

The cross for Paul is often a shorthand statement for the full range of Jesus' life, teaching, death, and resurrection. The cross symbolizes the manner in which Jesus lived his life — literally giving it away toward the needs of others. The cross reminds us of the teachings of Jesus telling us the way to real, joyful, and meaningful life is to recklessly care about others through personal

171

concern, especially those who have little of the world's goods and opportunities. Some modern theologians have characterized Jesus as "the man for others." For them the cross is the inspiring culmination of the way Jesus lived and taught. The cross expresses Jesus' willingness to die, preaching that the way to find God's love and joy beyond all the pains and sufferings is to "be for others." Jesus' cross is our invitation to a life of suffering love as the way to the grace of God, saving us from despair and death.

For Paul, salvation is not something that we can figure out with our reason and intellect. This Greek way is bankrupt and always fails. We cannot find life in events and moments that display a certainty that the love of God is within and beyond our sufferings and trials. This Jewish way is also inadequate, for it fails to compel obedience or trust. For the Jesus way of salvation enables us to sing, "What A Wonderful World." In caring for others, our troubles and sufferings do not go away. They might increase. However, we will come to know a power, bigger than any personal sufferings, filling us with a joyful trust that these pains are no match for the love of God. Let us pay serious attention to Paul's claim: "For the message of the cross is foolishness to those who are perishing, but to us who are being saved it is the power of God."

Goodness — A Way Of Life

Traditionally, the letter to the Ephesians was thought to be another one of Paul's New Testament writings. It even says so at the top of the text: "The Letter of Paul to the Ephesians." But in the last couple of centuries, we have trained our literary and history skills on the scriptures with the result that some of our traditional assumptions have been modified. For instance, we no longer believe Moses wrote the first five books of the Old Testament — Genesis, Exodus, Leviticus, Numbers, and Deuteronomy, and though the headings of many of the psalms say that King David wrote them, it does not seem likely. Nor do we feel comfortable any longer with thinking that the gospels, Matthew, Mark, Luke, and John, are the work of Jesus' original disciples.

Our lection today claims to be authored by Paul. Yet we now believe that Ephesians, written by an unknown author and inspired by the writings of Paul, used many of Paul's ideas and thoughts. This unknown author did as many ancient authors; he claimed the authorship of Paul to remind others of the great apostle and to give his own writing significance and authority. There was no intention to deceive. It was an accepted and common practice in the ancient world.

We do this today. An author may claim that someone else inspired his or her book. One of the early books by John Cobb, a contemporary professor of theology, *A Christian Natural Theology*, makes clear that his book is an effort to think about the Christian faith based on the philosophy of Alfred North Whitehead. Cobb is clear that Whitehead did not write his book, and that he does not

173

agree in every detail with Whitehead's thinking. However, he is quite up front with the fact that Whitehead inspired his thinking, and that he uses Whitehead's thoughts to fashion his own.

The letter to the Ephesians is likely from some anonymous author. It doesn't really matter who wrote the letter to the Ephesians, for the rich treasure of the work stands, regardless. A modern take on Ephesians concludes it is from an unknown person using much of the wisdom of Paul to write his own letter. Of course, this is a tentative conclusion. Someday we might find that our modern conclusions about scripture need revision over our present opinions. Plausibility is all we have in all our knowledge.

Salvation Is For Today

Ephesians is a work of praise for what has occurred in Christ: God is bringing all humanity together and the best place where this can be seen is the church. While the separations plaguing humanity are all too obvious in nature's havoc and in the trampling of history, in the church there is an intense manifestation of the uniting work of God through Christ. The church is the avant-garde expression of the purposes of God. The church is a preview of things to come. Fancy talk would say the church is "proleptic" — it reveals what is on its way through the love of God in Christ. In the first chapter, the Ephesians' author says that Christ, known in the church, is the announcement of "a plan for the fullness of time, to gather up all things in him, things in heaven and things on earth." Such words are a wakeup call when we allow church to become a placid, folksy, place where we focus on our own petty needs and are encouraged to make our peace with a tragically divided humanity. A serious reading of scripture, especially like Ephesians, announces the great truth of Christ not only promising wondrous things to come, but acting as a challenge to the status quo, calling us to live out in all the world, the meanings of this radical vision of Christ and the church.

Therefore, in our lection for today, the Ephesians' author gets around to making this point. He says the reconciliation that God reveals in Christ, through the church — a reconciliation intended by God from the beginning of creation — is both present and yet to come. "For we are what he has made us, created in Christ Jesus for good works, which God prepared beforehand to be our way of life." We are called to live out the reconciling work of Christ in our everyday lives, and in all the systems of culture, politics, and economics through which we organize our lives together.

Ephesians, like most of scripture, will not let us reduce our response of faith to waiting for the next life. The biblical tradition across the centuries came to believe that life does not cease when we quit breathing and when our brain waves flatten out. As difficult as this teaching is for moderns, our take on God's love drives us to believe that it never ends, meaning we are on a pilgrimage to eternity. Again, this is hard to believe in our scientific age where truth is reduced to what we can observe and measure in scientific terms. Nor, according to the standards of science, is there any certainty in the "near death" experiences reported by many people. Yet, believing in life beyond this life has always been difficult; it is never a matter of solid certainty, guaranteed by Jesus' resurrection. But if we do not allow truth to be limited by scientific limitations, then we can believe with Paul that "death cannot separate us from the love of Christ," known and experienced in the church.

Nothing releases us from doing the reconciling work of Christ now. The popular "Left Behind" books portray faith as something mainly for the next life, and are dismissive of the call of God in this world. One also might charge them with a crass and unloving mood as they casually write off those who have not become believers. On the one hand, we can be pleased that religion is a serious quest by the people who write and read such books, even though we express serious reservations about their take on the faith.

Similarly, we can rejoice that many churches are growing in numbers in our time. However, some of them are so fixed on locking up their personal salvation and readying themselves for the next life that they dismiss God's call in Christ to do God's work in this life. They do not see that scriptures such as Ephesians do not allow us this comfortable luxury. Instead, Ephesians and other biblical writings call us to plunge into the suffering and misery of private and public life, bringing the reconciling love of Christ to people and systems. When the church is really the church this is

175

the message proclaimed. Turning our back on this world is not the solid faith of our scriptures.

A High Calling For The Church

In the earlier days of Paul's ministry, he and others hoped that Christ would return shortly to inaugurate the kingdom of God and renew earth and heaven. This expectation was part of Paul's own messages written to the church. His first letter to the Thessalonians is his initial attempt to express the Christian faith to the little church there. Part of that message deals with the prevailing expectation that they were living in the last days of history. It rejoiced in the belief that Jesus was returning soon. The fulfillment of all their hopes and dreams of God's new reality of earthly peace, justice, plenty, and freedom from disease and death was about to happen. Paul and the early Christians learned this hope from their experience of Jesus. He proclaimed this "good news" against the face of human misery, hoping this act of God would come soon and suddenly: "For you yourselves know very well that the day of the Lord will come like a thief in the night" (1 Thessalonians 5:2).

However, Paul continually told the folks in his little churches that they should not sit around and wait for the wondrous return of Jesus. They are to begin to love one another, offer reconciliation, and struggle for justice right now. Paul's writings are filled with encouragements to hope for the great day, and at the same time care for one another as they would someday in the full reality of the kingdom. Yet, he insisted that the interval between the present and the return of Jesus was short.

By the time we get to the letter to the Ephesians there is a considerable lessening of emphasis on the near return of Jesus. Consequently, the author of Ephesians has shifted from believing humanity was living in the last day before the kingdom to thinking that the return of Jesus might be delayed for a long time. The second- and third-generation Christians began to feel that it might be a long, long time before this great event occurred. In the meantime, Christians needed to anticipate that great day by the quality of their lives.

Later, when the Emperor abandoned his empire in the west, the church accepted political responsibility for the civil duties of order and justice in their world. Christians were charged to live as if God's kingdom in Jesus had already come. This meant there was a great need to learn the ways of the kingdom. The church now became a place to develop the skills and attitudes of kingdom living. In addition to being a place where people dreamed of the full realization of God's renewal of heaven and earth, it also became a center of training for anticipatory living in this kingdom. Occasionally we speak of a "High Church" congregation, meaning a church rich in elaborate liturgy and pious actions. But another meaning of "High Church" is held up in the letter to the Ephesians. A "High Church" is to be a place to encourage and train people in Christian living, and to encourage the impact of Christian values on the structures of society. What a high and exciting vision of the purpose of the church!

Realistically, we say that we are often disappointed when the church fails to be this wonderful place where we are inspired to keep the dream of God's kingdom alive, and to train ourselves in what God wants from us. We know that the church can be petty, vicious, and lacking in any high vision for itself. Some of the New Testament was written because the church experienced a falling away from its great calling. Writing to the Corinthians, Paul said that when they met together they often did more harm than good. All of us know moments when we want walk away from the church because it seems ten percent divine and ninety percent human.

A friend's granddaughters play high school basketball. They have many inborn abilities for the game, but they do not just show up for their games, pull on their jerseys, and hustle out to play. Before that they need a place to learn the skills of the game. This place is a gym filled with teammates, lockers, and racks of basketballs, backboards, and skillful coaches. They couldn't play with any sort of skill by trotting out before the cheering crowd unless they had such a place. They need a location where they can learn the skills of basketball.

If we are to fulfill the good works for which we have been created in Christ Jesus, we need a place to sustain our hopes and to learn how to live like the people of God in the world. As we go along in Lent, we can find ourselves recovering the great significance of the church as God's gift through which we can learn to act out the Christ as God's promise of the kingdom to come. The really good news is that this can bring us a joy that is immune to all the pains and sufferings our church life demands. A later New Testament author says that Jesus, "for the same of the joy that was set before him endured the cross, [disregarded] its shame, and [took] his seat at the right hand of the throne of God" (Hebrews 12:2b). Perhaps this becomes a strange reward to the world, but it is of infinite worth to the faithful. Ephesians tells all about it.

Mediating The Grace Of God

God is always mediated to us. God never comes to us directly and immediately. This is a good thing. If we experienced God in all of God's full glory, power, and love, we would be overwhelmed. This is why the story of Moses on the mountain with God, says Moses could see only God's backside, never fully face to face.

We must find our relationship with God through something else — particular events, personal experiences, holy books, prayer and worship, and through people. We need to remember that all truth is mediated and never comes directly. Truth mediated through people is a common experience. The truth of medicine comes to us through doctors and those involved in the medical professions. The truth of modern science is mediated, as is the truth of music and the arts. The gift of the arts comes through musicians, dancers, actors, composers, playwrights, painters, and sculptors. The great things coming to us through them bless us.

Religion, including biblical religion has its mediators who put people in touch with a redeeming and sustaining God. We call them priests. Priests preside over worship services, counsel with people in crisis, conduct initiatory rites like baptism, offer prayers and blessings at times of marriage or death, teach the traditions of the faith, visit and encourage the sick, and have a deep concern for the sufferings of the poor and helpless.

Lately, priests in our Christian tradition have been at the center of attention in modern America. Some priests have been charged with sexual molestation of young children and teens. Their ecclesiastical superiors have often disregarded their offenses and failed to take seriously the gravity of this charge. In some Christian denominations, there is great controversy over the insistence that women be ordained as priests and pastors, while other denominations have lately openly received women as priests. Still more controversial has been one tradition's consecration of a bishop who is openly gay and in a committed partnership with another man. These are issues that invite our serious attention.

Lost in all this controversy is the abiding place of priests who humbly put us in touch with the mercies and mandates of God. Years ago, Bing Crosby played the part of a young priest in the movie *Going My Way*. In this sentimental idealization of parish life, this young priest teamed with the elderly senior parish priest, played by Barry Fitzgerald. It was a soothing and comforting portrayal of the lives and struggles of the priesthood and pastoral clergy. Yet it depicted a powerful illustration of priestly concern — the young priest [Crosby] made God a redeeming force for a gang of rebellious juveniles.

In the New Testament letter to the Hebrews, Jesus is portrayed as the priest above all other priests putting us in touch with God. Hebrews gives us a vision of Jesus who sets the example for all priests in the biblical tradition. In the fifth chapter of Hebrews, the author says Jesus is the ideal priest because: 1) he did not glorify himself, 2) he knew our human moments of feeling abandoned by God, 3) he turned his suffering into inspiring obedience, and 4) by implication, he called us to become priests putting others in touch with God.

On Not Getting In The Way Of God

Jesus is the ideal priest because he got himself out of the way, putting us in touch with the grace and power of God. In our text, "Christ did not glorify himself in becoming a high priest," hints at the subtle temptation for lay or clerical priests to make themselves the center of attention. When we are a priest to someone who is pouring out their anguish to us, rehearsing their guilt, or simply voicing their personal despair, it is easy to center the exchange on us. We become interested in using this person's plight to bolster our self-esteem and our need to be known for having wonderful

180

abilities. Some of us may even think that a telling of an instance of our being a priest to someone would make a good story in our next book.

One of the best things happening in the education of priests and pastors is clinical pastoral training. Using the insights of our religious heritage linked with the knowledge of modern psychology and psychiatry, present and future pastors are taught how to get their egos out of the way and become more helpful to those who come to them. Pastoral clinical training is often set in a hospital environment where the students work directly with people who are there because of fate or their self-destructive ways. Under the supervision of a trained chaplain or other leader, priests learn to listen to the pain and confusion of others, thereby helping them discover or rediscover the presence of God in their lives.

Perhaps the most important task of lay priests is to keep their clergy humble. The church has often glorified its ordained clergy and pastors to the point of their becoming unbearably arrogant and delighted to be the recipients of their congregation's attention and applause. Soon the life of the congregation centers on the promotion of the fame and abilities of their pastor. Then the ordained leader becomes corrupted and full of himself or herself instead of full of the humble Spirit of Jesus. This promotion of priestly and pastoral glorification eventually destroys the priest and pastor along with the congregation.

Years ago a talented young tenor, Mario Lanza, burst on the popular music scene. When he sang, "O Be My Love," with his strong tenor voice, millions listened enraptured. He sang all the ballads of the day and he was a sensation in movies and on the entertainment circuit. His close friends and companions fed him high-blown estimates of his popularity until he lost any critical ability to put their self-serving praise into perspective. He gave himself over to self-glorification and it destroyed him.

Somewhere there is the story of the pastor who asked his wife, "How many great preachers do you think there are in America?" With little hesitation she answered, "One less than you think!" Gifted pastors need congregations who "priest" them by calling attention to any hint of undue adulation or of basking in personal glory. This priest/pastor focus does not sell well with discerning people, and it is an obstacle to any real mediation of God to others. Thus, Jesus sets the standard for the priesthood of laypersons and the clergy alike.

Our Seasons Of Abandonment

A second reason our text gives for depicting Jesus as an ideal priest is his sense of abandonment by God. Calling up the memory of Jesus' prayers in the Garden of Gethsemane, Hebrews says, "Jesus offered up prayers and supplications, with loud cries and tears." Suffering standing at the edge of unbelief is a strong qualification for putting others in touch with God's salvation. A pastor once asked the Christian literacy advocate, Frank Laubach, if he could come and join his team. Laubach sensed that this man came from a comfortable, suburban parish where he preached to a rapidly growing congregation. He was filled with the American idols of success and security, shielding much of the world's suffering. Laubach told him, "Take a trip around the world and have your heart broken by what you see. Then come and offer your services." Most of us need something like that to enable us to broker the grace of God to others.

Henri Nouwen, that perceptive spirit of our time, said only the "wounded" can heal the wounded. He didn't mean that we ought to go out and attempt to get our spirit broken by the pains and sufferings of life. We don't usually need to do this. Even our comfortable pastor wanting to join Laubach's mission could find much to break his spirit all around him. He could find people who were struggling with grief and sorrow. He could discover many experiencing abuse in their formative years, resulting in emotionally and psychologically crippling distress. Some nearby would be terrified by severe physical illness. Others would suffer the lack of a mature theology helping them to mesh with their modern world. Others could easily be found who are dragging around loads of guilt for breaking their marriage vows. Some could be seen coming face-to-face with the disturbing reality that their chase after success and security is a fraud. A few he could find might be in pain from taking a courageous stand for social injustice and for the cause of the poor, the racial minorities, or the sexually different. And even his upscale congregation would be hurting because they were victims of these same social ills. These human hurts on his doorstep could qualify him to minister to those like Jesus, who feel abandoned by God.

One of the wonderful organizations in our world is Alcoholics Anonymous. It was founded on the conviction that those who have suffered the terrible anguish of alcoholism are the best qualified to help other alcoholics into sobriety. Their success bears out our point. Those who have been to the depths of life's despair and returned have an unusual skill for saving others from destruction.

New Testament scholarship reports that Jesus' words were the earliest collection of the memories of Jesus. His immediate followers remembered what he said about God's love and how they could find hope for their lives and for human destiny. For a time, it was enough to remember and ponder these words, but later, even these wonderful words weren't enough and so they began to recall the agony of those last days in Jerusalem. They remembered Jesus sensed the powers of Pilate and the high religious officials were closing in on him. It was apparent to him that he was on a trajectory toward death. Even more painful than this, his close followers began to show signs that they might desert him, which they eventually did. Memories of his desire to escape his fate were written down. While they were not around at the cross, they thought he must have uttered the opening words of Psalm 22 as life was slipping away from him, "My God! My God! Why have you forsaken me?" In reconstructing these moments, some from memory and some from creative imagination, the disciples authored the Passion story in a way that had the strange power of putting them into a saving relationship with God. This is why we reenact those terrible moments in our worship for Holy Week as Lent draws to a close. Jesus' suffering joined to our suffering for others becomes our qualification for mediating the redeeming feature of God to others.

We Owe Our Life To Others

We close this Lenten sermon by gathering up all that we have said by affirming our indebtedness for our salvation to others. This is the meaning of, "Christ died for our sins." Even though we may have great difficulty with this statement in its unnuanced, simplistic form, it is utterly true. Salvation comes to us from outside us. Salvation is not self-generated, coming out of our own powers and wisdom. We must not imply that Christ's death is only to bring forgiveness and mercy. This is a part of what is meant. But Christ's death means more than this. When we say, "Christ died for our sins," we are confessing that our remembrance of his giving up his life for us, breaks up inward sin that keeps us from wanting to love God and live the godly life of caring. This sin, as Paul describes it, is like a computer virus, rendering us incapable of having the strength to get beyond our despair about humanity and ourselves.

Moderns are often resistant to this admission. Our culture seductively tells us our destiny and salvation is within our immediate grasp. Our cultural ideal is the self-sufficient person, the mythic hero of the American western cowboy lore. The late movie actor, John Wayne, lived out such an image for us. He made us feel that we could muster up the strength and courage to overcome anything. We have been made to believe that accepting help expresses weakness and tarnishes our self-esteem. We are the three-year-old who suddenly pushes our parent away, preferring to take full charge of zipping up our jacket. We don't want anyone to help us. Or recall an old television commercial where the exasperated housewife shouts at her mother who was trying to help her on one of those bad hair days, "Please, mother, I'd rather do it myself!" To accept help at the vital center of our life's struggles often comes off as weakness and helplessness.

We, who ponder the sufferings of Jesus during that last fateful week of his life, already know that we are quite deficient in saving ourselves. The Prayer of General Confession forced the worshipers to confess, "There is no health in us." The shallow optimists resist this claim. Yet, our Christian tradition may be both more realistic and more effective in delivering us from the death-dealing despair that comes with the normal and the extraordinary pains of life. A little reflection on the sufferings of Jesus can become a saving moment for us — not just once and for all — but in repeated doses. Jesus' priesting is a continuously saving event. The unknown author of the letter to the Hebrews had it right: "He became the source of eternal salvation to all who obey him," to all who let the mediated salvation of God take over.

Palm/Passion Sunday
And Today's Faith

In the slaughter of World War I, 1914-1918, a whole generation of European men went to their deaths. The victors were France, Great Britain, and Italy. Together with the United States, they gathered in Paris to shape a peace treaty. Europeans sensed that the intervention of the United States encouraged by President Woodrow Wilson provided the victory. When President Wilson went to Paris to hammer out the peace in 1919, millions of Europeans hailed him as their savior. Huge crowds turned out to cheer him everywhere he went. They shouted, "Vive, le Wilson," and they hung banners in his honor wherever he traveled. For them, Wilson had been the driving force urging America to join in the crucial struggle toward the armistice. They also sensed that Wilson had a vision for a lasting peace, where all wars would end. To them he was a savior.

We remember this as we focus on "Passion Sunday," the day Jesus entered Jerusalem like Wilson in the cities of Europe, with shouts and cheers. We are not certain why Jesus went up to Jerusalem at that particular time. Nor do we know who joined in those cheers, scattering palm branches along his way. New Testament scholarship is hesitant to be certain on all of this; nor do we know what was in the heart of Jesus as he entered the city. What we do know is how the New Testament gospel tradition felt about it.

The gospels say Jesus entered Jerusalem because he believed his going to his death fulfilled God's plan for the salvation of the world. Today we're not certain that he had a definite reason for going up to Jerusalem that particular Passover. What seems

187

certain is that after his crucifixion and resurrection, many believed his death was a crucial element of his mission and message. After all, the crucifixion shocked the early Christians so profoundly, provoking them to believe he was still with them, meaning his dream of a kingdom of God on earth was still on God's table. It is likely that the New Testament accounts of Passion/Palm Sunday are more about how that event affected his early followers, than what really happened.

Nor are we confident that huge crowds acclaiming him to be the Messiah, is solid history. Some feel his disciples had no sense that Jesus was any sort of Messiah, triumphantly entering the city to go to the cross and be resurrected. That the gospel accounts say his closest followers fled when he was arrested makes us wonder. If they knew, from Jesus, that he was the Messiah, claiming a special relationship with God's imminent kingdom, why did they panic and flee to the safety of Galilee?

The Positive Side Of Critical Bible Study

Where does this leave us? Some think such conclusions from modern critical Bible study cut the ground from under any vital faith. If the New Testament accounts of the life, death, and resurrection of Jesus are not reliable history then all we have is pleasant, but meaningless, fiction about Jesus. Christians who call themselves fundamentalists feel this way. For them, if the New Testament and the gospels are not solid history, then there is no reason for trusting God who brings us to salvation through Jesus.

A seminary student who came from a fundamentalist background was put into a spiritual crisis when his biblical studies class began to question his uncritical biblical heritage. The critical Bible studies so devastated him he walked the floor at night in his apartment, trying to internalize this challenge to his faith. He never really got over this crisis. He drifted out of ordained ministry, saw his marriage crumble, agonized over a handicapped son, the violent death of another son, and never maintained a durable intimate relationship with another person. There have been numerous casualties of our modern critical approaches to the scriptures.

188

But like all things, there are two sides to this story. While our newer understandings of scripture have devastated the faith of many, it has also opened the possibility of serious belief to other modern people. Bishop John Shelby Spong describes his personal journey out of the fundamentalist culture in the American South. Along the way, this spiritual heritage became, for him, a hindrance to his Christian faith. He could not continue to hold a literal approach to scripture as he moved toward his adult years. He admits he is grateful for this basic grounding in a non-critical fundamentalist approach to scripture in his formative years. But as he moved out of the narrow world of his childhood and youth, he could not honestly express his faith in those terms and styles any longer. The experience of being forced to move on to a more critical, liberal faith became his central mission as an Episcopal priest, as a bishop of that tradition, and in retirement.

Spong is sensitive to those who cannot mesh their childhood faith with the modern world of science, critical historical research, and the increasing presence of other faith traditions. He has devoted his life to helping such people leave their confining spiritual moorings and move through the difficult, but rewarding effort toward a faith that joyfully embraces the truth of both past and present.

Jesus: A New Image Of God

Something that impressed the close followers of Jesus, something that they later said gave them a new understanding of God, was Jesus' willingness to put himself at risk. When Jesus told them he was planning to go up to Jerusalem, his disciples tried to warn him how dangerous that would be. Jerusalem at Passover would be filled with thousands of people. The possibility of a crowd disturbance by religious fanatics or violent revolutionaries would put Pilate and his security forces on "high alert." His followers may have sensed that Jesus' message of the coming kingdom of God could be easily misinterpreted by Pilate; Pilate was always suspicious of anything that might challenge his duty to keep order. Again, the high religious leaders of the Jews, those with a comfortable arrangement with Rome allowing them to keep their religious power and authority, would certainly be hostile to anyone who offered an alternative.

This may be the basis of the gospel stories where Jesus tells his friends that he felt compelled to go up to Jerusalem. These stories come to us many years after Jesus' death, reflecting later faith and understanding of what Jesus meant to them; but they may have a solid core of historical veracity about them. They ring true where Peter protests that Jesus should not do that: "And Peter took him aside and began to rebuke him, saying, 'God forbid it, Lord! This must not happen to you' " (Matthew 16:22). It was evident to Peter and the disciples that this was a very risky decision.

Of course, Jesus is not dissuaded by their fears. Luke puts his strong commitment to going to Jerusalem in the face of danger and risk: "He set his face to go to Jerusalem" (Luke 9:51b). Concern for his personal safety could not keep him away from Passover. He must have been eager to preach, teach, and heal amid the large audiences there. Later reflections say this was part of God's plan — giving himself up for us in a shattering, violent death. Certainly, his death provoked the radical claim of God upon the lives of many, but we need not theologize about Jesus taking this risky venture. His courage in proclaiming the kingdom of God was inspiring, for he and his disciples knew the high odds against his survival. Jesus became a profound source of inspiration simply because he was willing to put his life up as a witness to the saving truth which it contained.

We can understand this today. In politics the candidate for national office who has a valorous war record gains devotion and affirmation over another candidate who has none. Many Americans believe that the Vietnam conflict was a tragic mistake, a mar on the image of our country. The great national outrage and dissent over our involvement in Vietnam made this clear. Many Vietnam veterans were sensitive to the massive anti-war movements, feeling the protests to the war's dubious goals and shameful violence made them anti-heroes. While not withdrawing our objections, we have come to a high admiration for those who responded to the call of their country. Likewise. we have an admiration for Jesus who put himself at risk for others.

A God Who Suffers With Us

All this brings us to our lection from Paul's letter to the Christians at Philippi. How well this scripture fits our observance of Passion/Palm Sunday. In Philippi there was opposition to Paul from those whose self-interests were challenged. We do not know the specifics of this opposition. Some may have come from outside the church and some of it may have been from petty jealousies from within that congregation. Regardless, this opposition made Christian discipleship difficult and dangerous. Even if the gospel didn't put everyone in danger of their lives, certainly living out the sort of life that Paul demanded put them at odds with those who were at the level of narrowness, self-aggrandizement, and those who put security before anything else. Dealing with this would not be easy. Folks like this are always disruptive and in responding to them, one's time and energy are diverted from more central matters. They steal life from us.

An old observation given to a young person heading out to their first pastorate was, "Well, as you are called to feed the lambs in your congregation, be warned that you will find a few old rams." Living out the Christian life takes its inevitable toll. Let no one tell us that suffering for Christ is soothed over by mystic moments, by glorying in the resurrection, having someone who tells us that the Christian way is the way to an easy and successful life. But when we live this dangerous, risky, self-giving life it can be wonderfully attractive to others.

Paul reaches out to quote a hymn sung in his little churches. Its poetic lines speak of the effect of that risky caring for others — the same risky caring prompting Jesus to go up to Jerusalem:

> *Who, though he was in the form of God,*
> *Did not regard equality with God as something to be*
>   *exploited,*
> *But emptied himself, taking the form of a slave*
> *Being born in human likeness.*
> *And being found in human form, he humbled himself,*
> *And become obedient to the point of death —*
> *Even death on a cross.*
> — Philippians 2:6-8

191

Then Paul drives home his point:

> *Therefore God also highly exalted him and gave him the name*
> *That is above every name, so that at the name of Jesus*
> *Every knee should bend, in heaven and on earth and under the earth,*
> *And every tongue should confess that Jesus Christ is Lord,*
> *To the glory of God the Father.*
>
> — Philippians 2:9-11

Passion Sunday calls us to receive this truth — for the first, or for the umpteenth time. Easter's joy will come soon enough. In the meantime, let us resist the rush toward Easter and hustle up to some Jerusalem that calls us. Then, like Jesus, we will be ready for Easter.

Dave, Tell Me About The Cross

Dave, having just finished seminary, and before leaving for doctoral studies on the west coast, drove down to see his grandfather. Grandfather, in his early nineties and still with an inquisitive mind, took Dave out for lunch. During the meal Dave's grandfather leaned over and said, "Now Dave, tell me about the cross."

Dave's grandfather was a retired public school teacher and administrator. He was a faithful member of the church. He and his wife reared their children in the church, and when his son, Dave's father, became an ordained minister, both grandfather and grandmother were quite proud. Grandfather taught a Sunday school class, served on many boards and committees in the local church, and for many years was a member of a regional judicatory. Books on religion were scattered about the house and grandfather's comments and his underlinings were on many of their pages.

So the question becomes, "Why does Grandfather feel the need to understand the cross after his long involvement in church and the Christian life?" It could be that his church never said much about the cross. Mainstream churches are often accused by more conservative, evangelical traditions of neglecting the cross. This is hardly the case with Grandfather. He lived in small, midwestern towns and while the life of those churches was certainly not the "blood of Jesus" sort, he certainly heard many sermons about the cross, and sang the well-known hymns about the death of Jesus.

More likely Grandfather wanted to both review the meaning of the cross and pump his grandson for some new understandings. Even though his physical body was deteriorating, and he had recently buried his wife, Grandfather had a continuing curiosity about the cross. Perhaps grandson Dave could help him. The best Christian theology says we are on a spiritual journey toward God. Paul put it plainly: "We are being saved" (1 Corinthians 1:18b), telling us we never arrive. Spirituality is a process, a continuing process keeping us from arrogance and promising wonders yet to come. So Grandfather requested, "Tell me about the cross." There was still something more for him.

Meanings Of The Cross

Lent and Holy Week's agendas are to rehearse yet one more time the meaning of Jesus' cross. Last week we observed Passion/Palm Sunday being careful to avoid wrestling with the cross and leaping into Easter prematurely. We must first walk though, through our involvement in the crucifixion narratives, lest Easters become a bogus triumph coming at the avoidance of dealing with the pain and suffering of Jesus, and by implication, our pain and that of the whole world. Lent and Holy Week are a "reality check," not always pleasant, but offering the only healing and salvation available. Older preachers had a slogan for it, "no cross — no crown."

So what might we say about the cross as we attempt to grasp its saving meaning to commend it to others? Immediately we recall the traditional understandings of the cross. As previous generations, we will find much that is helpful in these, for they have nourished Christian life and witness over the centuries. Occasionally we will notice that these traditional cross meanings may need to be repackaged to better fit our own time and day. We should not hesitate to do this; nor should we feel it is disrespectful to these traditions. It is clear that a serious look at cross traditions shows us a process of revision and updating. We will attempt to lift up five ways of expressing the meaning of the cross.

A couple of things need to be said before we begin. First, when we speak of the cross we are speaking of the entire life and teaching of Jesus, not simply what happened on Golgotha Hill. Second, these cross witnesses are not always in agreement. They are like the contradictory explanations of light by modern physicists. As with the light theory, the cross story has explanations that cannot be reconciled with all the others. Third, there is no story of the meaning of the cross that will exhaust all its mystery. Spiritual truth is always beyond our capacity to explain. It is like love, or cosmic wonder, or the ecstasy of childbirth, or of the full meaning and story of anyone's life. Fourth, the meanings of the cross have always been eschatological. This big Greek word for — "at the end" — simply means that God's work in Christ through the cross is yet to be completed. The cross pushes out beyond life, beyond time and space, and out into the fullness of eternity. Therefore, we must be content with partially satisfying understandings of the cross. Here are five very brief hints of what Jesus' cross might mean:

1. The cross calls us to trust in God's present and future victory over human, natural, and historical evil. Historically, the cross of Jesus brokered the rich religious heritage of the Jews who proclaimed a God who seeks us out in love and mercy. Paul and others used the cross to focus on the love and mercy of God in Jesus, available to all humanity. The ministry of Paul centered on the cross. He struggled to present Jesus and his cross, free of any limiting particularities from its Jewish religious and cultural setting. He believed Jesus and his cross were for all people, a spiritual heritage for everyone.

2. The cross spells out the power of Jesus' sacrifice, his giving up his life, and calling our attention to the self-giving and suffering love of God. Hardly anything jolts us spiritually alive like one who gives up their life to bless others. Jesus, Stephen, Peter, Paul, and most of the original disciples paid with their lives for sharing the message of Jesus. Since their time we have many martyrs, and today — people like Dietrich Bonhoeffer, Archbishop Romero of El Salvador, and Martin Luther King, Jr. All these challenge the shallowness of our lives inviting us to reflect that this is the way the eternal God continually gives us peace and joy, joining us in our pains and sufferings.

3. The cross tells about Jesus, who in refusing to accuse his executioners, acts out the mercy of God with his own love. On his cross he prays, "Father, forgive them for they do not know what

they do." If we can trust that such a response from Jesus re-presents the never ending love of God, then we will rejoice, knowing that we are acquitted of our deepest sins, known and unknown.

4. The cross of Jesus described as his taking the rap for our sins, calls us stand in the place of sinners, substituting ourselves for their transgressions and freeing them from self-destruction. In our individualistic culture we are wary of any suggestion that we are obligated to anyone but ourselves for our rescue from troubles and moral foolishness. Certainly Mel Gibson's movie, *The Passion Of The Christ*, makes a simplistic and unsuitable form of this tradition. But he does make a point: our salvation is always a gift from someone else. Objections from more sophisticated circles miss the cross point. These objections fail to move beyond the Gibson-types or confessing that someone else always pays for goodness.

All along, others have stood in our place and we have survived because of their caring for us. Our parents took upon themselves the burdening demands of seeing us into adulthood. Parents became temporary substitutes for us. In our youth and adult years, persons other than our parents have placed themselves between the consequences of our immaturity, occasional destructive willfulness, or our disregard of our call to care for others. In an extreme instance, ask the parents of someone convicted of a terrible crime. Those parents take upon themselves the shame and pain of their wayward child. Similarly, Jesus stands in place of the full consequences of our rejection of love for God and neighbor, making our confession and repentance possible and leading to a more godly way of life.

5. The cross of Jesus becomes an inspiring example allowing us the power to melt down our soft or hard rebellion to the ways of God, and encouraging us to express a similar love to those around us as a way of thanking God for such unearned love. Stories of other people can be inspiring. Evil often has its way here, for some stories inspire us to rebel against God and neighbor. Many times those who model a life of violence and hate inspire us. But inspiration can go in a good direction, too. It is the witness of the New Testament and Christian tradition that the example of Jesus' cross has the power to urge us to give ourselves in unsparing ways to the

196

needs of others. Jesus was constantly saying that such self-giving is the way to real life and living: "Those who lose their life for my sake, and for the sake of the gospel, will save it" (Mark 8:35b). Several years ago, a young Christian doctor gave up his life for the raw needs of the people of Southeast Asia. Tom Dooley continued his work long after he was diagnosed with terminal cancer. Tom Dooley's self-giving example, like Jesus, is an inspiring reality in our time. As we recall how Jesus trudged up to his death surrounded by a jeering crowd, and hemmed in by Roman executioners, we find it calling us to a similar life, where our self-giving is transformed into glory and peace. Later, Paul would speak of this as "the peace of God, which surpasses all understanding" (Philippians 4:7).

The Cross As Saving Truth

Small wonder that the cross became the focal moment out of which we tell the full story of God's saving love in Jesus. In addition, as a visual center in our churches, pinned to the lapels of jackets or dangling from necklaces, the cross is very much part of our personal and collective world. One can understand some contemporary religious styles that play down the cross in their sanctuaries, or even remove it altogether. They are right in wanting to take away any obstacle that might come in the way of those who are alienated from the church by symbols, sermons, hymns, or prayers that mention the cross. We know that many are put off by what we must call their misunderstanding about the cross. But sooner or later, the church will have to present the cross simply because it is the vital center of any valid Christian faith. When, where, or how this is done is a matter of wisdom. Eventually the cross will have to have its moments with us. Perhaps those of us who have dared to risk the negative response of some moderns will be enabled to discover how to present the cross in ways that enable faith to flourish. Today's sermon is a hopeful attempt at this task.

A closing disclaimer may help. We live in a day when the partial implications of our various religious traditions become clear. Christians respond to the cross of Christ — in its full presentation of the life and teachings of Jesus — as a means where we are saved to a life full of meaning, purpose, and hope. Yet we believe that such saving traditions also lie beyond our Christian story. This makes us glad because it means that God's self-revealing is not limited to just a portion of humanity. It also makes us humble because we know that we have no right to press down our cross story on those from other spiritual traditions, insisting that our version of the love of God in Jesus, is the only one. We live in a day and time when we can rejoice in our various traditions, sharing them and receiving other versions in respect and gratitude.

We need not switch traditions, nor do we need to invite others to switch to ours saying that ours is the only true tradition. Of course, we may change our commitment from one salvation story to another, but this must be done because we find it more meaningful than our previous tradition, not that we were formerly wrong. Truth, in all its forms contains much that is subjective and shaped by our partial and limited perspectives and personal experiences. Religious truth is the most subjective of all human truth systems. In addition, we should make allowance for this, because not only are we enriched by the various God stories of other religious traditions, but the survival of humanity may depend on this humble recognition. We cannot allow the violence flowing from a "one size fits all" religion. Yet even with the necessary disclaimers, Christians reverence the cross of Christ and continue to find in it offering saving truth, power, and hope.

True Resurrections

Today, Easter is the central festival of the church, out of which comes two derivative festivals, Christmas and Pentecost. Christmas yearns for Easter and the ability to trust that violence and contingency do not have the last word, and the empowerment of Pentecost comes only after Easter's victory is already in place. Of course in our economy, Christmas has something of a popular edge because it is more marketable, and Pentecost comes and goes in churches high and low without fanfare. In an earlier time, one British pastor got it right. He selected one of the Easter hymns for his congregation to sing every single Sunday of the year.

Without Easter, there would be no ministry of Jesus to celebrate, in which we find godly wisdom and saving hope. Without Easter, there would be no continuing message and mission of Jesus to the entire world. Sunday morning regulars are aware of this. Yet, it must be true for all you folks who crowd into our churches on Easter Sunday. Many who are not among those finding the church a regular place for nourishment and faith, seem to sense that the Easter message and experience holds life and hope together.

As regular and casual worshipers are together here today, we sense that Easter goes to the center of the most troubling question life presents — is there any enduring hope? This troubled the great twentieth-century philosopher, Alfred North Whitehead, who called this human anguish the "perpetual perishing" nature of life. His sensitivity certainly came in losing a son in the slaughter of World War I. Yet, even without that terrible loss, there was for him and for us, the constant loss of persons, experiences, and significant values. Leaving childhood and moving into our teen and adult years we are confronted by painful losses. Nothing seems to last. The happy moment, the giddiness of romantic love, the constancy of many friendships, the beauties of nature, styles of speech or moods of culture, bodily strength and agility of mind, the certainties of science and philosophical arguments, nations and entire cultures, political arrangements, great moments of faith and conviction, the total mastering of our sins and ungodly thoughts and actions — all these change and pass away.

Death is the great trauma standing over all of these. Early or late, we are forced to deal with mortality — our own and that of others. Some say moderns do not face death with the same intensity and constancy of earlier times. Pointing out that before modern medicine, infant mortality was rampant; families considered themselves fortunate if half their children survived childhood. Go to some old cemetery and note the birth and death dates chiseled into the headstones. They will read something like this: "James Andrew Greenwood, born February 10, 1846, died August 22, 1849." And for adults of those days, disease cut many of them down in their early years. Tuberculosis and pneumonia were two main culprits. Someone has said, "If your husband, aged 43, contracted pneumonia, you began to make plans for his funeral." Calling those times a "death culture" was quite correct. They would agree with Edwin Arlington Robinson's line on Eden Flood who knew "that all things break," especially our human lives.

The Sad, Transient Nature Of Life

A few can face the passing away of all good things — people, music, love, human joys, nature, and even the cosmos itself. They are among the finest people we know. We count some of them as friends and allies, together promoting and sustaining personal and collective values we jointly cherish. They do not give themselves over to a desperate attempt to grasp some provisional meaning and joy, like the beer commercial urging us to live with gusto and self-regard for "we only go around once." No, these people living under the melancholy sense of the ultimate perishing of all things, including themselves and their loved ones, are strange witnesses to righteousness. They stand out as people of courage, trustworthiness, selfless to a fault, planning for a better world, even though it all comes to nothingness. Sometimes the quality of their lives puts believers to shame. Measured against believers, who sometimes exhibit less than the virtues of high-minded unbelievers, we can understand the person who said, "I prefer the company of a good atheist over a wimpish, selfish Christian."

Yet, we can sometimes sense beneath many of our admired unbelievers; a sadness and futility taking a high toll on their days and nights. In words that follow our lection this morning, Paul says, "If for this life only we have hoped in Christ, we are of all people most to be pitied" (1 Corinthians 15:19). We know this because we have gone through times when belief and trust in God's restoration of life to all things has left our feelings and our reasoning. We need to be honest about our faith in this way, for none of us knows uninterrupted moments of trust and faith. In the journals of the early American Methodist Bishop, Francis Asbury, he wrote of times when he was "tempted to atheism." We have times like this, too, and when this happens we find it difficult to believe that life has the final word over death. Then we fall into despair making all our present life troubled and difficult. "Whenever I feel afraid, I whistle a happy tune" sings Anna, the schoolteacher in Rogers and Hammerstein's *The King and I*. But whistling a happy tune may not brace us for facing the ultimate bleakness of life, nor can it erase the crippling sadness.

One of the reasons for the power of Christianity in the Greco-Roman world was its insistence that there was a glorious hope beyond death. Paul speaks of this central conviction in our lection from the New Testament letters for today. He grounds this hope by citing the resurrection of Jesus. When the crucifixion seemed to end the mission and message of Jesus, Jesus came alive to them in ways that we will never completely understand. Paul speaks of Jesus returning to power and influence among them through visions and appearances: "He was raised on the third day ... he appeared to Cephas, then to the twelve. Then he appeared to more than 500 brothers and sisters ... Then he appeared to James, then to all the apostles. Last of all ... he appeared to me."

Death was just as troubling to those of Paul's world as today, even when we cover up our despair with a frantic pace, numbing it with drugs and alcohol. For generations, the biblical people had no such hope. They felt themselves part of God's special relationship to Israel, meaning their individual lives were subordinate to this reality. All they felt possible was a long and happy life in this world, the best that God could give them. Later, several centuries before Christ, they anguished over the fate of the young sons slain in the Maccabean wars. It troubled them that these valiant defenders of Israel had gone down to death long before the fullness of their years. Some biblical people began to think that for these young men, the justice of God implied a life beyond this one. So they began to speak of a resurrection for all the dead. By this time, Jesus' life was for many, part of the faith of Israel.

Paul, too, was hopeful about all this. The philosopher Plato, in the classical Greek philosophical tradition has already formed his doctrine of immortality, an affirmation that the essential person could not be touched by death. For many, this became a consolation that enabled them to live beyond crippling sadness and hopelessness. Yet these philosophical consolations were limited mostly to the people of education and status. The poor, the slaves, and the common people had no such hopes. Life for them was grim, difficult, painful, and filled with suffering and death. These were the folks to whom Paul took his message of the resurrection. It was part of Paul's version of the good news of Jesus, welcomed by people who became part of the early churches beyond the Jewish homeland.

However, this trust of God's restoration of life beyond death has never been easy. It certainly was not so in Paul's time. Part of the reason, he wrote in 1 Corinthians 15, was because some had doubts about the resurrection. They felt that it was too good to be true. So Paul begins writing, "Now I would remind you, brothers and sisters, of the good news that I proclaimed to you...." Easter is our own moment to be reminded of this difficult but happy trust.

Resurrection Built Into All Of Life

We need to make clear that our faith in the resurrection is a matter of faith not an absolute certainty. Neither the Bible, nor the philosophers, nor "near death experiences," nor beliefs from other religions, nor science will answer all our possible doubts. We will still have our moments when we feel, as Freud charged, that believing in immortality is the result of our inability to live courageously with the sobering truth that everything dies — the whole universe and us someday.

But we can live out of what the poet, T. S. Eliot once called, "hints and guesses." Eliot wants us to understand "hints and guesses" are all we have; yet they can bring us to the point where we are willing to take the plunge of faith and trust. Modern scientists speak of "top down thinking" contrasted with "bottom-up thinking." The resurrection urges us to do "top down thinking." The wondrous fact of Christ's resurrection means that we can trust that it is God's gift to us, too.

Yet, many moderns may find this way closed to us. If we are going to trust in the resurrection we will first have to do "bottom-up thinking." We will need to discover common, everyday experiences of resurrection that help us to move toward the resurrection as a wondrous expression of God's love for all of humanity and the universe. This is the gist of a book by a British Christian, H. A. Williams. In *True Resurrection*, he says most of us must begin where we are right now, with some everyday, experiential considerations.

Williams wants us to see resurrection in the lives of people all around us. He writes of the dissolute person who suddenly makes a radical turn in their life and begins to be sober and responsible. He calls us to ponder marriages that are going nowhere, then something happens that turns the marriage into a meaningful relationship. A scientist's career failure opens into a new and better wisdom. He tells of when, after a friend's bitter betrayal, we may discover within us the power to forgive and resume our friendship.

Williams says that these are legitimate experiences of resurrection. They are all around us. They happen all the time. They are not spooky or weird. They are believable and they renew this present life with joy and meaning. Many of us have been at the end of our rope when we found that we were enabled to carry on with courage. Many of us have overcome addictions that were squeezing the life from us, finding that we no longer had to be captive to these death-dealing forces. Many of us have discovered in moments of terrible loss and suffering, what Paul called "the peace that goes beyond all understanding." Many of us have found our hopes and dreams smashed and broken, only to discover out of the broken pieces we have been able to fashion more enduring dreams and hopes.

Williams says we live in the midst of resurrection every moment of our lives. If this is true, can it be so difficult to believe that the power and presence of Jesus survived the cross and empowered his followers to carry on his mission? If this is true, can we also believe that our common, everyday resurrections hint that we, too, may rise up from death and enter the glorious mystery of eternity?

Coming to trust this, we can believe in Christ's resurrection and ours. And, if we can trust in this great possibility, we may find that the crippling despair and sadness as we experience "perpetual perishing" is taken away. The medieval poet, Alighieri Dante wrote his great poem about human destiny, *The Divine Comedy*. He called our life circumstance a comedy, not because it was something silly and hilarious. He called our journey a comedy because finally it was not tragic; it did not end in nothingness, but in the wonderful eternity of God, forever and ever. Is it so strange that the word commonly attached to our Easter greetings is "Happy"?

On Having A Good Church Fight

Today's scripture from 1 John is one of the treasures of all the New Testament. John writes, "This is the message we have heard from him and declare to you, that God is light and in him is no darkness at all. If we walk in the light as he is in the light, we have fellowship with one another, and the blood of Jesus his Son cleanses us from all sin."

Worship leaders often use this passage for a scriptural call to worship. It is one of the superlative positive statements in the New Testament, affirming that God, the ultimate reality is like a light that illuminates our darkness; and if we follow in this light we find our waywardness swallowed up in the forgiveness that flows from Jesus. These words could only be received with glad and joyful hearts.

Interestingly, these comforting and strengthening words came out of a church fight somewhere late in the second century, C.E. Some separated themselves from the church because they held different views. These separatists were unable to accept the church's teaching that Jesus was divine as well as human. They could not believe that divinity could be resident in humans, since humans were transient and perishable. Others thought they were perfect and incapable of sin, because the Spirit made them above the temptations to sin. This second group went two different ways: one part of them believed that anything fleshly or bodily, was an invitation to the devil. Another part felt they were above any possibility of sin, even when they violated the law and commandments.

The church was in turmoil. Before they left they argued and fussed among themselves. When this occurs, the church becomes an unhappy place. In John's world, Christians experienced the brokenness of the loving fellowship of the church. Even more distressing, was the result that outsiders would form a very negative opinion of the church. A conflicted church forfeits its claim that the gospel of Jesus Christ is a reconciling reality for all humanity. People tentatively attracted to the church would become alienated from all that the church stood for.

Yet wonderfully, out of this mess came these great words of 1 John. We would not have John's rich testimony if the church had not fallen into distress. While this is no endorsement to provoke or sustain a serious church fight, we might think of other instances when some meaningful witness to the truth of Christ has come from a painful rupture of the peace and love in the church. We might even consider that division in the church does not enhance the attractiveness of the faith. Our scripture passage prompts us to do some wrestling with these considerations.

Some Wonderful Church Fusses

One example is not too far to find. Shortly after the death and resurrection of Jesus, those who believed Jesus was the fulfillment of Israel's hopes caused a disruption in the life of the synagogue. This conviction clashed with traditional Jewish beliefs and caused much dissension. Soon, the Jesus people were expelled from the synagogues and forced to become a separate religious tradition. At that time co-existence was impossible and thus the church was formed. The church was born out of a bitter struggle within the synagogue.

The church became a gift to the whole world out of this painful parting. Had this not happened, Israel's faith would be confined to the small minority. A fracture of the peace of the synagogue then gave the traditions of Israel's faith to the world through the story of Jesus. Out of such pain and disruption came the church.

The Protestant Reformation is another example of a blessed church spat. Long before Martin Luther unwittingly provoked an uproar in the church, by his 95 complaints about the state of the church, there were other disputes running through the church. Many of these were humble members of the church, sensing that the church was far from the Spirit of Jesus. Usually their voices were not heard. Others daringly shook the peace of the church. John Huss, many years before Luther, began calling for church reforms. He so threatened the church he was convicted of heresy and burned at the stake. John Ball was a Lollard priest in England; he felt compelled to join with English peasants who were protesting the oppression of the wealthy landowners. He was hung and quartered. William Tyndall challenged the church's ban on translating the scriptures into the vernacular languages, and like Huss, it cost him his life. Yet, in the cumulative force of these protests, something better in the life of the church was eventually born.

Luther's challenge to the church proved too much for the church, launching the Protestant Reformation. Even though we cannot be pleased with all that followed the disruption in the church caused by Luther, there has been much serving to strengthen and purify the witness of the church since. Out of the Reformation has come the church's insistence that risky faith, not comfortable certainty, is our basic response to the gospel. Out of the Reformation has come an insistence the scriptures are the primary witness to our faith. Out of the Reformation has come an objection to the claim of the clergy for prestige and unquestionable authority. Again, out of this disturbing struggle in the life of the church has come much that both Protestants and Roman Catholics now embrace as true and strengthening.

Likewise, in modern times, the church has been troubled by those who insist that we can discover even greater meanings in scripture through using our critical powers of literary and historical investigation. Today, before we can receive the Bible as the sacred word of God, moderns must first approach the Bible as a human work coming out of our struggle to be people of faith and hope. Many moderns are unable to consider the Bible as something coming directly from God, showing no trace of human input. This claim is troubling to many. To them it seems to make the scriptures a human book without holy or sacred meaning. For at least two centuries denominations and local churches continued to fight over this issue; the call to sort out the human elements of scripture before listening for its godly voice has seriously divided the church. New denominations, seminaries, and colleges have their origin in this church fight because some Christians think the modern approach to scripture is a denial of the scripture as the Word of God. In America, the classic example of this struggle came when Harry Emerson Fosdick was forced from the pulpit of the First Presbyterian Church in New York City, since he embraced the newer approaches to the Bible. About the same time, John Scopes, a high school biology teacher in Dayton, Tennessee, was tried for teaching evolution to his high school students. Publicity over the trial made this issue known to the entire nation.

But serious reflection suggests that if the Christian witness is going to have a serious engagement to the modern world, it will have to present the gospel in the historical-critical fashion disturbing to many in today's church. One church leader titles his book, *Why the Church Must Change or Die*, arguing that the sacredness of scripture's message is enhanced by this new disturbing approach to the Bible, not diminished. He also claims that the gospel presented in this modern, non-traditional way is the wave of the future for the church's witness. Otherwise, the church will soon cease to have a serious hearing in our modern world. So here again, a troubled, fractious church points the way toward a significant proclamation of the gospel in today's world. Franklin Littell once said that an indispensable atmosphere in the church was its cultivation of "raging dialogue." For out of this "rage" may come a more credible sense of the biblical faith.

Godly Tensions In The Church

If these considerations are close to the truth, then it follows that the peace of the church is not always a good indication that it is really being the church. A young pastor wrote to his bishop asking if his superior would offer a "Quiet Hour" in his congregation. The bishop replied that the pastor's congregation, needed a tornado not a Quiet Hour! The truth of Christ may often be judged by how disruptive the life is of the congregation. Methodist founder, John Wesley, gathered his preachers annually to hear reports on their work. First, he asked each one if he had led anyone to Christ. If the preacher answered, "No," Wesley's next question was, "Well, did you make anyone angry?"

Psychologist, Eric Berne, once classified the psychological games we play. These are "games" we use to manipulate others to our own advantage. He called one game, "Uproar." We play the game of "Uproar," bringing disruption into the family, or in a marriage, or at the office so that we can hide our shortcomings in the din of uproarious distraction. Teenagers are skilled at Uproar; however, many adults continue the game far into their mature years. No Christian engages in the "Uproar" game simply out one's personal agenda, but Christian witness could call for a little "Uproar" in the life of the church because it has become too comfortable and complacent. Without some positive "Uproar" the church loses its critical edge for challenging present ills and dangers.

A layperson played "Uproar" in his congregation in the 1930s. A woman of the congregation felt called to preach. However, the pastor resisted because he felt the scriptures prohibited such a practice. The layman along with another from the congregation believed Christian common sense trumped any Bible teaching to the contrary. So they drove to the district judicatory official's office and successfully pleaded her case. She was granted the privilege to preach the gospel, becoming a well-known evangelist in the judicatory. Of course, this caused serious tension between these two laypeople and their pastor and a few sided with the pastor. It was not a comfortable time for that congregation. Yet, they were making a strong statement about the equality Christ brings. This equality was stated by Paul in his famous passage from Galatians: "There is no longer Jew or Greek, there is no longer slave or free, there is no longer male and female; for all of you are one in Christ Jesus" (3:28). Is this perhaps the meaning of Jesus' comment on his ministry, "I have not come to bring peace, but a sword"? (Matthew 10:34b).

A recent movie about the life and witness of Dietrich Bonhoeffer gives us another point. He and others disrupted the life of the German church when it opted for Adolf Hitler's agenda for a

German-dominated Europe. Bonhoeffer joined with the minority of German Christians who understood that Hitler's goal for the church was to make it a baptism of plans for aggression against nearby nations and for the elimination of the Jews. Many German Christians objected to this challenge by Bonhoeffer and others to the peace of the church. But the witness of Bonhoeffer and his colleagues has blessed the church and the world by an example of gospel courage and a powerful clarity about the claims of Christ. Out of this painful moment of disruption in the church has come such a godly gift, agreeing with our morning scripture's context, that the love and mercy of God often rides in on the troubling times of conflict within the church. This witness surely applies to both our traditions, our denominations, and to our local congregations. It is well worth pondering that quiet, peaceful congregations and denominations may not be the places where one can hear and live out the gospel as in more turbulent, conflicted ones.

Salvation Is A Journey, Not An Arrival

In this Information Age, we find summaries of the news helpful. Without the time or energy to read through loads of material, or listen to in-depth reports of current events, we rely on brief summaries of what is happening around the world. There is danger in relying too heavily on these brief reports, however, for they can be misleading. Even those who bring us the daily newscasts understand this. The evening newscasters will be the first to tell us they wish that their news reports were lengthier. However, as rough indications, these summaries orient us and give some sense of the direction things are taking.

Similarly, the scriptures have summaries of faith and practice that help us retain our direction before God and one another. The Hebrew Bible offers the *Schema*, a great summary of faith: "Hear, O Israel, the Lord our God is one. And you shall love the Lord your God with all your heart, and with all your might and with all your strength." This has long been a guide for us of biblical faith. Another favorite summary is from the Prophet Micah. In summarizing what God wants from us, he writes, "And what does the Lord require of us, but to do justice, to love kindness, and to walk humbly with our God?" (Micah 6:8).

Paul gives an excellent summary of the Christian experience when he says, "So if anyone is in Christ, there is a new creation: everything old has passed away; see, everything has become new!" (2 Corinthians 5:17). In another place, Paul summarized the things God's grace calls out of us, "And now faith, hope, and love abide, these three; and the greatest of these is love" (1 Corinthians 13:13).

211

Perhaps the best known New Testament summary of Christian faith comes from the Gospel of John: "For God so loved the world that he gave his only Son, so that everyone who believes in him may not perish but may have eternal life" (3:16). Today we have a wonderful, but lesser known, summary coming out of the first letter of John: "Beloved, we are God's children now; what we will be has not been revealed. What we do know is this: when he is revealed, we shall be like him ... And all who have this hope in him purify themselves, just as he is pure." In three brief verses, John summarizes our Christian existence as a present reality, yet one that is still to be completed, and something that creates in us godly living.

Salvation As Present

How true is John when he says, "We are God's children now," for something of the redeeming love of God has already happened in our lives. We have experienced the gift of knowing we belong to God in the present tense — right now! In reading the gospels we constantly see that part of the attraction of Jesus was that he gave people a present sense of being within the forgiving and empowering love of God. Jesus made real, right now, our gracious standing before God.

This present experience of God's redeeming love, and the call to witness to the coming kingdom has often revived the church across the centuries. Periodically, the church descends to presenting the faith as believing doctrines, or holding orthodox opinions. Certainly we should not shy away from bringing all our powers of reason and intellect to the task of expressing our Christian faith. In our era we have failed to engage in this difficult and exhausting task. All too often we have avoided the work of expressing the faith in ways that cohere our modern understandings, and with our grasp of history and the structures of science. The church seems to believe that unnuanced of "old-time religion" is good enough for today. It would be easy to think that these theological travesties are confined to the conservative-fundamentalist segments of the church. But sadly, all these judgments are observed in the mainstream churches. Today, one can hear in most mainstream churches this statement following any reading of scripture: "The word of God for the people of God," giving no indication that such a statement cannot honestly endorse all lections without qualification. The modern church, conservative and liberal, has failed to speak the faith in the language and understandings of modern people. We need a moment of confession, a *mea culpa*, here.

Mark A. Noll's *America's God*, makes the case for the inability of Abraham Lincoln to find the current theologies of his time, liberal and conservative, adequate for coming to terms with the horrors of the Civil War. Noll says this tragic event in our nation's history demanded fresh, new theological thinking; but none were undertaking this demand. Contemporary theologian, John R. Cobb, works over this issue in his book, *Becoming a Thinking Christian*. Christianity and all the other religious traditions are under the heavy burden of presenting their faith in ways that modern people can understand and to which they may respond. We can only hope that this call will be taken seriously.

The other danger always lurking near the church is reducing our faith to an ethic. Christ is offered as a way of life, a wisdom, or a supreme truth about how to live. Who can quarrel with the importance of wise and godly living? Yet in our time, Jesus and Christian faith are presented in much this way. Jesus is the teacher of God's wisdom, portrayed by many contemporary New Testament scholars.

These scholars rely on what is called "Q," an assumed collection of the sayings of Jesus. Furthermore, no one has found Q, but these scholars conclude the Q material goes back to the oldest remembrances of Jesus, older than the Passion stories, telling us how Jesus went up to Jerusalem, was crucified, and rose from the dead. Believing in Q settles a lot of mysteries of the gospels. We are grateful for what Q tells us about the mission and ministry of Jesus, but it is questionable that Q is the only remembrance of Jesus for faithful living then and now. Yet scholars say Q is the primitive remembrances, telling us that the fundamental good news of Jesus centers on a way of living and acting. In short, the gospel becomes an ethic, a collection of wise images and illustrations of godly, saving living.

Of course, we need wisdom for the godly living to which Jesus calls us. But we need more than an ethic. This is the weakness of the ancient Greek assumption that knowing goodness is sufficient. Socrates believed being informed about truth carries with it the ability to live the truth. In contrast, the biblical experience says that our anxieties and self-concerns are so intense that we resist wanting to do the truth. More seriously, we discover that we are not capable of finding the power to live by the truth we affirm. Paul makes this clear in the New Testament, and much modern psychology makes this same point. One Christian noted this by speaking the "grandeur and misery" of our human situation. Our grandeur is that we can envision the truth of how we ought to live. Our misery is that we lack the power to live out the truth.

The Christian witness in First John insists that we are "children of God" right now. He proclaims that in Christ we experience the desire and power to live in ways that are pleasing to God right now. The gospel is neither a correct set of thoughts and ideas about the ways of God, nor is it an ethic, an illustration of how to live the righteous life. Instead, as John says, the gospel is an experience of God through Christ, beyond doctrine and ethic: "Beloved, we are God's children now."

Salvation As Deferred

John goes on to say that this gift of God's presence and power is "not yet." The gift calls us into a future fulfillment of the gift. He says, "What we will be has not yet been revealed." Our life in Christ is a progressive pilgrimage toward God and God's saving activity in our lives, both personal and collective. It is important for us to sense the meaning of this "not yet," calling us to a continual playing out of the presence and power of God.

Much of the glory of the Bible is here. Someone says life is understood in three ways: The first way depicts life as a "treadmill." Here we feel that life "is just one damn thing after another." There is no larger meaning to life. Life is a treadmill when we keep plodding on without any goal or purpose. Sadly, millions of people feel this way. It does not take great insight to understand much of the senseless, destructive ways so many treadmill people live, for

214

treadmill living is the difficult struggle within the bleak sameness of yesterday, today, and tomorrow. Treadmill living drains us of any vital purpose, like that well-known image of Shakespeare's, "Full of sound and fury, signifying nothing."

The second way of understanding life is describing it as "saga." Saga living heroically responds to the gift of life, by celebrating our human strengths and abilities, pitting us against the demonic forces that constantly threaten. Homer's great epic, *The Iliad*, is a witness to life as saga. Achilles and other saga heroes and heroines become inspiring incarnations of human greatness against the evils that threaten human dignity and meaning. However, saga living is ultimately doomed; for as inspiring as the stories of these lives are, the destructive power of transience and death finally prevail. Human achievement and human hope are ultimately crushed.

A third image of life is pilgrimage. Life becomes our heading toward some great and lasting conclusion. First John offers us this image when he writes, "What we shall be has not yet been revealed." Pilgrimage is life lived as a journey toward a consummation with God. It overcomes the despair that hovers over treadmill or saga living. Pilgrim living is the joyful experience of empowerment given in Christ. Pilgrim living helps us to find light and meaning for the present. It also offers us the hope that we are on our way toward that great day when all things shall be wrapped within God's eternal love — we, those we love, those we dislike, and all the present and past values of life and history.

Biblical Examples Of "Not Yet" Salvation

First John is not alone to announce this goodness yet to come in fullness. In the service of the Lord's Supper we say, "Christ has come, Christ has risen, Christ will come again." This as an affirmation, beyond any literal form, urging us to believe and hope that God is bringing all of us into an eternal consummation. This is what the New Testament teaching of the Second Coming of Christ is all about. We trust Robert Browning's line, "the best is yet to come."

Paul also, describes our salvation as a dynamic process: "[We] who are being saved" (1 Corinthians 1:18b). He delivers us from the danger of feeling that salvation is already a fully accomplished fact in our life or world. Those who make such a claim of salvation do not have the signs that corroborate their confession, and it does not take any serious reading of the morning paper or watching of the evening television, to conclude that salvation is a distant hope in our present world. But Paul's testimony agrees with First John. Both know that we are far from where we wish us to be. The good news is — we are on our way.

Perhaps the letter to the Hebrews catches this issue as well as any. The Hebrews author cites the biblical men and women of the past who looked forward to a better and lasting reality. "They confessed that they were strangers and foreigners on earth ... They desired[ed] a better country, that is a heavenly one" (11:13:b). Another time he writes, "For here we have no lasting city, but we are looking for the city that is to come" (13:14). There is a real danger that we might misunderstand such grand words, thinking they are a call to give up on the present world and ourselves.

Hebrews, Paul, and First John are not among those who allow present pains and difficulties, of the evils and disappointments of this world to count against faith. They do not recommend rejection of the world or gritty endurance. No, their sense of journey and fulfillment enables them to rejoice in the provisional joys and meanings of this present life. More than this, they believed that responding to life as "not yet" means setting themselves against the ungodliness in themselves as well as unjust and oppressive structures of the world's collective systems. Pilgrim living gives birth to caring for the sick, supporting schools and learning, acting politically and challenging the social evils as they impact the poor and powerless. Jesus, however we understand his vision of the kingdom, had this in mind when he challenged his followers to live out God's kingdom right now. This was possible because Jesus, the author of Hebrews, Paul, and so many others held fast to their conviction that life, the world, and they are heading toward God.

Faith As Alternating Current

Some troublesome things about the Christian life are its mood swings. These are not the common mood swings of everyday life, nor are they the mood swings indicating some psychological condition. They are the distressing oscillations between radiant and joyful faith, and times when we are unable to have any sense of God's sustaining presence. The early pioneers in the development of electricity assumed that electrical current ran constantly without interruption through the wires. Edison held this view. The difficulty was that direct current could not be sustained over long distances. Providing electricity across long distances required cumbersome boosters at short intervals. Then George Eastman proposed that the current be sent in an different fashion, alternating from positive to negative. This proved to be more useful and it enabled electrical power to be sent over long distances.

Our Christian life is inevitably like that of alternating current. No matter the claims otherwise; we do not have an uninterrupted experience of faith and peace. Instead we know swings of emotion and faith that brings us times where doubt and a troubled spirit prevails. Our morning lection from First John understands this: "... We will know that we are [accepted by God] ... and [our faithfulness in loving] will reassure our hearts before him whenever our hearts condemn us" (3:18-20a). Here is an honest confession of those moments when our hearts are uncertain about the love of God; yet it says that our steadiness in living the life of love will bring us calm and peace beyond our dark times.

Many Christians today and in the past have witnessed that the spiritual life is more like alternating than direct current. Christians experience low moments when the glowing warmth of faith has almost been extinguished. A professor of pastoral care, training seminarians to minister to people in grief, said that when his wife died, he was so helpless that he could hardly manage toasting the bread for his breakfast. Another has written that we may be filled with admirable faith and trust, but when we stand at the grave of our spouse, we are filled with grief and sorrow. There are times when we lament and have "a broken and contrite spirit." When this occurs we have no capacity to speak or hear chirpy and misleading comments about the glorious joys of Christian existence.

The Gospel's Ultimate Promise Of Joy

Let us consider first of all, that the ultimate promise of the gospel is one of joy and sustaining power. This is the witness of those experiencing the resurrection faith. The early Christians were filled with the glad news that in Christ, God overcomes our sin, our struggles with fate, and the prospect of our mortality. They not only believed in this good news; the New Testament reports that they experienced it. This experience changed their lives. The resurrected Christ brought them this felt conviction in a powerful way. They felt it in their days and nights.

When August Comte was proposing a fully rational religion replacing Christianity, he believed the ancient faith was no longer valid for the modern world. He asked a friend how he could get his new faith to be inspiring and attractive. His friend said to kill the central figure in his new religion, raise him from the dead, and he would have no difficulty offering his secular faith to humanity. Christianity and all religious traditions are grounded in the personal experience of their followers. John Knox, of modern New Testament scholarship, said in Jesus the love of God ceased to be an idea and became an experienced reality. Here we may locate the power of Christian faith, then and now.

Christianity's attractive power comes as a saving experience, not as a proposition to be intellectually accepted. Evangelistically, we can urge people to accept the saving grace of God in Christ, but this will not be effective unless people have an experiential sense that they really are well within the grace of God. We need not abandon the intellectual and reasoned thinking about the gospel we proclaim. This has always been essential. In many cases today, this will be vital before people can hear the gospel in ways that are intellectually sound to them, bringing them out from an understanding of faith that has become unacceptable to them. In Samuel Miller's inaugural address in becoming dean of the Harvard Divinity School, he insisted that intellectual soundness was absolutely crucial for Christian witness in our own time. He warned that simple good intentions, devoid of intellectual bite would not deliver the gospel in today's world. We agree.

Yet we need to go beyond a clear, reasonable argument for becoming or staying a Christian. Faithfulness must have an experiential power in our lives. In the 1700s, John Wesley led a renewal of faith that evangelized the lower classes of Great Britain and the American colonies. The Church of England was offering a respectable faith grounded in the enlightenment, the age of reason. Many excellent statements of a reasonable Christian faith came from the English clergy and Christian laypersons. They rightly sensed that the faith must engage the new standards of reason and the growing power of science. Wesley himself was indebted to much of their work.

However, these intellectual endeavors could not speak to the full experiences of people; they did not get to the emotions and the everyday experiences. Wesley recognized that faith must also speak to the heart, to the common experience of common people. In the Wesleyan revival people came to experience the love of God. This experience enabled them to live lives of righteousness, having a high moral quality. Wesley's message was never one that abandoned itself to intellectually undisciplined emotion. He tells us that when he began to use laypeople as full-time preachers, he insisted they become acquainted with the sturdy theological thinking in historical Christianity in its best and most cogent interpreters. His gospel and his own preaching were far from being an emotional bath in the blood of Christ. He was critical of those he called, "the blood of Christ" preachers. Yet the final conclusion on Wesley is

219

that he enabled people to experience the love of God, becoming a saving experience for them in this life, and a joyful hope for the world to come. Faith begins in such experiences.

Yet Faith And A Troubled Spirit Alternate

Still, our faith waxes and wanes. Faith is an alternating current — strong for a while and sometimes weak and indistinguishable at times. When faith's radiance and strength have fallen flat, we are caught in one of the most difficult and dangerous times in our Christian lives. Our text speaks of those moments when "our hearts condemn us." Yes, John Wesley's preaching and teaching brought many into the saving experience of God's forgiveness and mercy. They became people filled with the joys of those redeemed in Christ. Wesley made real the New Testament promise that we can have an inner witness that we are children of God. His brother, Charles, wrote texts to hymns that celebrated this experience. One of the best of those hymns calls us to sing, "Hear him ye deaf, his praise ye dumb, your loosened tongues employ, ye blind behold your master come, and leap ye lame for joy." Beneath such lyrics is an affirmation of the high mood of Christian joy and deliverance.

Francis J. McConnell's biography of Wesley tells of Wesley's confession of his down times, times when "his heart condemned him." Many of these occurred long after he became the dynamic leader of the Methodist revival. Bishop McConnell quotes from a letter, Wesley wrote to his brother, Charles. In this letter Wesley poured out his distress at losing his sense of joy and faith in Christ. Writing in a code that he devised to hide his openness, Wesley wrote:

> *I do not feel the wrath of God abiding on me, nor can I believe it does. And yet (this is the mystery) (I do not love God. I never did.) There (I never) believed in the Christian sense of the word ... (I have no) direct witness, I do not say that (I am a child of God).*

Here is an example of how even those who proclaim the saving experience of God's salvation in Christ, know also that the experience alternates rather than remaining a steady constant. For

220

the Christian who has newly discovered the inner witness of Christ's presence, such moments are devastating. And, for the Christian of long standing, suddenly falling into such moments can also be a time of great distress. Christians are not exempt from these times and we must find ways to deal with them, or face the terrible prospect of concluding our experience of God's love has been a cruel hoax.

Borne Along In Our Empty Moments

Both Wesley and our text give us a clue on how we might handle this. Wesley's revealing letter to his brother goes on to say, "And yet I dare not preach otherwise than I do, either concerning faith, or love, or justification, or perfection. And yet I find rather an increase than a decrease of zeal for the whole work of God and every part of it. I am ... [borne along], I only know that I can't stand still."

Wesley reports that even though momentarily he does not have a great sense of inner faith and conviction, he feels "borne along" by his commitment to preaching the conviction of God's love through Christ. He tells of a "zeal" to continue his work regardless of how he feels at the moment. Here is how our such times of low spirit can be managed: if we keep doing the deeds of love and caring to which Christ has called us, we discover that we are given a reason for life and meaning larger than any temporary emptiness of our souls. Like Wesley, we may find that our "zeal for the whole work of God" increases rather than diminishes in such moments.

In reading the gospels, we can sometimes sense what is not stated — a reading between the lines. We can surmise that Jesus' mood began to move toward such an inward crisis as he set his face to go up to Jerusalem. From his high moments of preaching, teaching, and healing in the safety of Galilee, he now begins to deal with the possibility of death. His heart becomes filled with the anxiety. His rebuke to the disciples trying to dissuade him from going to Jerusalem, his clash with the officers of the temple, his solemn words in the upper room, the prayer in Gethsemane's garden, down to the cry from the cross — all imply that his heart and inward experience were not filled with glowing faith or a steady sense of God. If this was true for Jesus, should we expect anything different in our Christian experience? However, we can expect, like Wesley, to be carried on by a power beyond our sparse and barren faith.

First John comes to the same conclusion regarding such times — when our spirits alternate between strong faith and joy, and moments of depression and anxiety. First John writes that these are the times when we must "love, not in word or speech, but in truth and action." We continue to do the works of love to which Christ has called us, and in this we will discover a filling and a strengthening, giving an ability to do the works of love and caring even when we do not have the inner gladness of Christian witness. The real experience of Christ is the power to deal with what life brings — highs and lows, successes or failures, mountaintops or painful valleys. To have the Spirit of Christ is not some constant Pentecostal "high" as some suggest. It is to be possessed by a power that enables faithfulness even when all is falling apart around us.

We can see the truth of this when look at the serious, godly commitment we make. Two people fall in love. Their days and nights are filled with the feelings of love and romance, creating songs and poems. Life seems a great and wonderful joy based on the affection they feel for one another. Then comes the commitment of civil union, or marriage as two people give their lives to one another. Over the years, such moments are subdued in the working out the meaning of their love and responsibility for each other. Some can't handle the inevitable necessity of the inner glow changing to a concern for the needs of each other, displacing much of the rapture that first attended their coming together. But again, is this a loss that must be revived else the relationship proves false?

Some think so. Tons of books and magazine articles are written informing us how to put romance back into our marriage; yet this wisdom can deceive one into believing the rapture of the initial commitment can be revived in a significant way. Truthfully, marriages and civil unions across any length of time demand a power to continue in faithfulness, of finding a zeal for expressing love and care for one another, surprisingly proving to be much more of a delight and meaning than our earlier high moments of romance.

If this is true in the relationship of committed love between two people, we can believe that it is also true for our relationship to Christ. Beyond our loss of the initial glow of faith, we may move to a deeper experience, the experience of being carried along by God's love. This happens as we continue our acts of love for others — including those we dislike — regardless of how we feel at the moment. So, "little children, let us love, not in word or speech, but in truth and action. And by this we will know that we are from the truth and will reassure our hearts before him, whenever our hearts condemn us."

---

1. Francis J. McConnell, *John Wesley* (New York: Abingdon Press, 1939), p. 210.

Love — The Only
Absolute Commandment

Love is central to the New Testament message. Jesus called his followers to practice love. Paul said love is the single indispensable ingredient of the Christian life. That great theological summary of the gospel in the work of John declares, "God so loved the world that he sent his only Son into the world so that whoever believes in him should not perish but have eternal life" (John 3:16). Similarly, our text from 1 John joins in this call to love, for love is the vital matter of Christian life and living.

Yet, love is a difficult way to live. Jesus on the cross makes this clear. Serious Christians conclude quickly that love is not an easy thing. There is an organization helping parents dealing with difficult sons and daughters called, "Tough Love." Tough Love helps these parents who have children bent on destroying themselves and all that love them. Instead of rescuing these sons and daughters from the results of their destructive behavior, they love in a "tough" way. Tough Love parents will not allow a drug-addicted child to return to the family circle until they change their behavior. Tough Love parents will not bail their children out of jail. Tough Love does not loan money to abusive children nor allow them to con their siblings into assisting their destructive ways. All this approach goes against the normal sense of how parents act. Tough Love joins with other parents in similar situations to find the strength to love in this way. While something of a last resort, this strange way of loving is effective with many at-risk sons and daughters. It is tough — but it is love.

However, Tough Love is not really a new way to love. Love is always tough. Christian love deceives if it is presented as a lovely and successful way to live. Whatever truth there is in "gentle Jesus, meek and mild," it must also be said that the Jesus way of love involves us in pain and suffering. In what ways is the love to which Christ calls us so tough?

Love Is Tough Because Of Our Inward Resistance

Greeting her congregation at the close of the service, a pastor was confronted by a distraught worshiper. He was distressed because Psalm 137, used in the service that morning, closed with these terrible lines,

> *O daughter Babylon, you devastator! Happy shall they*
> *be who pay you back for what you have done to us!*
> *Happy shall they be who take your little ones and dash*
> *them against the rock!* — Psalm 137:8-9

John Wesley and others have said that these words are not fit for the mouths of Christian congregations. If love means wanting the best for those who hurt and abuse us, then we cannot wish to inflict the pain of vengeance upon them.

One of the best parts of the Hebrew Bible is the book of Jonah. Its meaning is not that Jonah is swallowed by the great fish. The word of God in Jonah is in reflecting how often we, like Jonah, refuse to love as God loves. Jonah did not want to offer God's mercy to Ninevites, pouting when they responded to their deliverance. Jonah's story challenges those with a too narrow vision of God's compassion. Jonah speaks to our own time over this same issue.

Why do we resist the life of love? It is because we believe we cannot love without denying our own needs, interests, and securities. This is why so many find marriage too high a price to pay, for it means subordinating ourselves to the other person. Marriage exacts from us the need to care for our spouse or partner in ways that interfere with our own needs. When children enter a relationship, the demand of living for others becomes a burden many cannot handle. The resistance increases when it becomes clear that

226

the spouse or partner or the children have selfish agendas that tangle up the relationships. Our Christian faith tells us of love's difficulties, but we prefer to listen to a more comfortable message from our culture, telling us that our personal happiness is the point of marriage. The result is disaster. Love is tough because inwardly we resist its demands.

Love Is Tough Because Others Are So Unlovable

British pastor, Donald Soper, spent Sunday afternoon in Hyde Park Square. There he debated with people of all political, economic, or religious persuasions, as he stood on a small platform and challenged their take on various issues. He delighted in arguing for Christian faith before the doubters and scoffers. Soper was also the pastor of British Central Hall, headquarters of British Methodism across from Westminster Abbey. He worked in Central Hall's ministry to the poor and indigent. One day a woman came to him and said, "Dr. Soper, how wonderfully you care for those unfortunate people. It must be a great joy to you." In a moment of dispensing realism, Soper replied, "No, often it's not a great joy at all. Time and again I find myself working with people who are dirty, unappreciative, and often quite unlovable."

A judicatory official that worked with matching up pastors and congregations was talking about the problems of his ministry. He admitted that he often found great satisfaction in his work. Then he went on to say, "Sometimes it's terribly difficult. We have so many pastors that are just no damn good!" His work was no cinch because the ineptness of many of the pastors made them unlovable and so problematic.

One cannot read the New Testament letters of Paul without sensing that he was working with persons who often were unlovable, putting his love for them to the test. They fought over food at their common meals. Some of them were involved in illicit sexual relationships. Others inside and outside the church stirred up his converts with strange doctrines and burdensome restrictions. Some of the leading women were fussing with each other (and probably the men too, but that would be lost as the New Testament was written and edited by men). They idolized some of their leaders

227

over against others. Some decided that since Jesus was returning soon they could just laze around. Paul's coworker, John Mark, bugged out midway on an important missionary journey, and Peter waffled on freedom from the law when important Jews came around.

If we hear the call of love, we will need to be relieved of the notion that it is a life of ease and calm. Loving others is tough because they can be unlovable.

Love Is Tough Because Life Is So Complicated

In the life of the congregations, its Bible study, worship, and sermons, we sometimes get the notion that the call to the life of love is altogether personal and simple. Thinking of the love relationships as one-to-one, eyeball-to-eyeball, we find its claim upon us to be rather simple. We reduce the claim of loving to our spouse and children, the members of the congregation, the pastor and the church leaders, and our next-door neighbor, even if they are not part of the congregation.

Then one day we are jolted out of this comfortable and narrow view of love's claim. We begin to ask if love has any meaning in the larger world of people and nature. We wonder if love has relevance to world peace, hunger, justice for minorities, economic systems, medical research, sexual orientation, or political structures? Some large mega-churches insist that the church must stay out of these matters, denying that love has any larger meanings to these issues. One has a hunch that such a denial is based on protecting their large memberships. Perhaps they wisely understand that the call of love in these larger arenas would create controversy, affecting their attendance and financial support.

It is true that there is little outright New Testament concern to make a witness of love in the larger world. Paul, and the early church, believed God would soon intervene in history, convene the day of judgment, and inaugurate God's kingdom of peace, justice, well-being, and eternal life.

Wise Christians soon realize that the call to love in the larger world must be translated into the quest for justice. Justice is the name of love for the world. However, it remains tough, for justice answers and strategies are complicated and controversial in themselves. Yet the cross keeps reminding us that difficulty is no excuse for refusal. Loving the world is tough, but Christ calls us to its task.

Love Is Tough Because It's So Often Disappointing
Finally, love is difficult because it does not always work. The prodigal sons' father must have been a loving father to his sons; their unloving decisions did not come from a lack of love from their father. The younger son broke his father's heart when he left home, possibly never to return. His older son was a deep disappointment because he was so judgmental and harsh. The father invested a lifetime in loving both his sons. Instead of returning such love they broke with that love causing the father anguish and heart-sickness.

The prologue, the beginning words of John's Gospel, tells of God's disappointment over the world's refusal of Jesus: "He came to what was his own, and his own people did not accept him." Much of the biblical story is right here. At this point, the gospel clashes with our American myth. We Americans are told that success is always within our grasp. We falsify the real truth that contradicts this myth. Frantically, we insist that success always comes to those who persist, but the real truth is that most of us are doomed to significant failure by circumstances over which we have little control. The result is despair, disappointment, and a sense of guilt at not having succeeded. Christians have no right to insist that love is the sure-fire way to peace of mind, spiritual, and/or economic prosperity, the admiration of others, and improvements in handling the great issues of our day. Rather, love is always tough, and in many ways, it is terribly disappointing.

So what is a church for? A nice place to meet friends, a place to hear great music and inspiring preaching, for handing the Christian heritage on to children, a center for celebrating birth, marriage, and death, an opportunity to share and discuss great life issues or an alternative voice for our success oriented culture? Yes, the church should be all these things. Blessed are we when we are able to become part of a church like that. Yet, beyond all these things, the church is a place where we confess that love is a most difficult calling. In church, we can share our hurts, disappointments, and failures in the tough business of love. At church, we find the strength once again to make the effort to love — tough as it is, but joyfully accepted by God.

The Commandments Are Not Burdensome

In the Exodus story, Moses leads the Israelites out of Egyptian captivity and takes them to the mountain in Sinai. There he calls them into a commitment to Yahweh, the mountain and sky God who secured their freedom. Knowing that raw freedom would prove to be a disaster, Moses and Yahweh work out ways they must live. We know these rules as the Law, one of the scriptural glories, blessing all that walk in the heritage of the Hebrew experience. The Law for them and for us today, is one of the gifts of God, for it tells us that reality is structured so that living by these commandments brings life and joy in our faithfulness to the Law.

Yet it is clear that the Law is also troublesome; for we would rather disregard it, choosing to live on our own terms, and according to our own desires. A young adolescent, living with her grandparents, became behaviorly impossible. She was abusive to her grandparents, who offered her a home away from the troubled marriage of her parents. However, she crossed the line of their generosity when she told them, "I don't care how anyone tells me how to live my life. I'm not going to listen to any of your advice, either!" The grandparents shipped the granddaughter back to her mother and father. It was clear that this young woman was out of touch with reality, for living as we please is courting serious disaster.

Reality Is God-shaped
The Bible declares that reality shapes itself around the purposes of God. These God-shaped purposes are built into the way

231

things really are. They are not up to referendum or recall, as if we could decide which laws are operative, or not. Like our inescapable drive to concede our need for food, sleep, and exercise — these godly structures are there, regardless of the way we feel about them, something our granddaughter has not yet admitted.

Modern science insists that certain realities exist apart from our knowledge or submission to them. Folks in Dayton, Ohio, are familiar with the story of two of its most famous citizens — Orville and Wilbur Wright. Early on, the Wright brothers wanted to discover the means of powered flight. They built gliders trying to understand the inexorable givens that would enable them to fly. They poured over the information gathered from the experiments of others. Their most important breakthrough came in discovering how to "warp" the wings of their gliders so that they could stabilize their craft in the air, and when they added an engine to their glider on an early December day at Kitty Hawk, North Carolina, in 1903, they flew. Their struggle was mastering the given realities of aerodynamics. Their dream of flying forced them to take into account these physical realities. In the process, they did better than all the others who shared their same dream.

The Bible tells us there are also spiritual realities driven by the purposes of God. Humanity takes no poll on our preferring such realities or our rejection of them. God has ordained them without asking if we would find these congenial. Saint Augustine's famous line says we are made for God and we are troubled until we make our peace with this. Following Augustine, we can say that we are made for love, for justice, and for peace. A lot of evidence confirms our love-shaped existence. Modern psychiatry tells us that psychological well-being is grounded in our ability to love, meaning that we must live beyond our own immediate needs and comforts. Finding the richness of life means that we put ourselves out for someone else. Structured for justice, we organize our larger life together in our families, in society, and in the world. Things are right when we see that a rough fairness determines the way we live together. In addition, who in our violent world will seriously question the inescapable godly demand for peace? Domestic violence and political violence both cry out that we live in a peace-determined universe, not its violent counterpart.

But All This Seems So Burdensome

The biblical record and human history tell us that we are a bit like that granddaughter we mentioned. Living according to these godly givens is burdensome. So often we want to be free of the realities that seem to be unpleasant restraints. "Do your own thing" was part of the youth rebellion. However, the young people were only uttering what is in all our hearts. We want to be left alone. Today, many protest the burdens and obligations of government. Others today are unhappy about making marriage commitments, caring for neighbors, or other obligations. For many, burdens of obligation seem be a heavy load.

However, it is not long before we make the painful discovery that denial of the spiritual realities of godliness, or of the rightful claims of others upon us brings far greater burdens. Jacob offers us an example from the Hebrew Bible. Jacob desired the blessings that belonged to his brother, Esau. He contrived with help from his mother and his own cunning to deceive his father into giving him that blessing. Soon the burden of his deceit was greater than conceding the blessing rightfully belonged to Esau. Understandably, Jacob became fearful of Esau, and it troubled his days and nights. He fled the country and lived with his Uncle Laban in another country. Even there his ambition for wealth entangled him with his uncle. In short, the burden of wanting his selfish way became difficult. Finally, this heavy judgment drove Jacob to risk returning to his family and attempting reconciliation with Esau. Lesson: refusing to follow the ways of God is always more troubling than the burdens themselves.

If we read between the lines of the Zacchaeus story in the New Testament, we find the same thing. Zacchaeus wanted to secure his life by becoming rich at the expense of his own people. Taking the job of collecting taxes for Rome, he learned the art of increasing the taxes owed, and putting the difference into his own pocket. He grew wealthy from this larceny but it pushed him away from those from whom he collected the taxes. We can assume that his burden of inner discontent made him climb up into that tree to catch a glimpse of Jesus who had just come to town. When Jesus invited himself to Zacchaeus' home for lunch, it became an opportunity for Zacchaeus to shed his heavy burden. Under the righteous aura of Jesus, he confessed his sin and declared he was ready to make restoration of any wealth gained by fraud. Jesus then pronounced Zacchaeus among the saved — meaning that Zacchaeus' inner burden of guilt and unease lifted.

The prophets of Israel had the same message but on a larger scale. Their message was that in allowing injustice and unrighteousness they were poisoning the life of the whole nation. The burden was taking a toll on the nation. The prophets warned this would bring the judgments of God upon themselves. They said there would come a day when the wrath of God would descend upon them and destroy their national existence. Living as a people against the ways of God would bring them terrible consequences. Their sense that the ways of God were too burdensome for them, made the prophets insist that their present discomfort would be nothing compared to the painful and shattering day of God's judgment.

Today our nation must listen to this prophetic message. All too easily, we neglect the needs of the poor and the powerless. Quality schools are denied to those caught in the poverty of our inner cities or in many rural areas. Adequate health care is nonexistent for many at the lower end of the socio-economic scale. Our justice system puts a heavier burden on minorities and those with little means for arguing their case before the courts, and filling our prisons with many of those same people. Extravagant salaries and benefits go to a minority of managers in our corporations while most employees struggle in meeting their basic needs. Political office has become the prerogative of the wealthy while common people cannot afford its costs. Armies comprised of men and women of poor or modest means fight our foreign wars. The tax code favors the rich over and against those in the middle- and lower-economic brackets. Minorities of race, gender, and sexual orientation face the denial of basic rights, sometimes embedded in a legal system, or sometimes in official policy. Our media provides escapist entertainment of sports, mindless sit-coms, ethical free sexuality, violence, all consumer driven values — without a glance at the moral traditions of Western society.

Our national unease comes from our disregard for the reality of God's justice and righteousness. Today, America, for all our wealth and power, is not a happy place. We have opted for an irresponsible freedom and a frantic chase after the gods of security, wealth, individualism, and immediate satisfactions. We abuse the environment without any sense of violation. In those prophetic words, we have "sown the wind and reaped the whirlwind ..." (Hosea 8:7). We are likely to experience later what a terrifying price we have paid for abusing the ways of God.

The Commandments Are Not Burdensome

Now we are ready for our text: "The commandments are not burdensome." Well, of course they are at one level. We cannot eliminate all those words about cross bearing from the New Testament. "Take up your cross and follow me," Jesus tells us. Following the ways of God in the pattern of Jesus does demand something from us — we must agree to suffer. We suffer as we care about those we love in our immediate family and among our friends. When difficult times come to others we are not only pained, but we also sense a call to help them through difficult moments. This places a burden and a demand on our time, our energy, and our inner calm. These things cover up our placid "chirpiness" about our wonderful life, and how happy we are as Christians. Instead, we sense that a heavy load comes down upon us.

Alternatively, if we give ourselves to work for justice, against hunger, for better schools, or for protecting the environment, we discover that we suffer two distinct burdens. One is the personal cost. Our own private agenda must step aside in significant proportions to our larger task. This is a burden. The other one is how many will not understand our passion for these matters. Some will wonder, or even ridicule our drive to care for something other than our own ease and enjoyment of life. This, too, is a burden.

Yet after all of this, the text is correct — "the commandments are not burdensome." Perhaps it is something like the distance runners who tell us that at the point where they think they can no longer stay in the race, they get their "second wind." Out of their costly investment of effort, they are empowered to complete the race. Running is no longer a burden for it now has become a flow of energy. We might understand this in thinking of a concert pianist. Our pianist devotes hours and hours of burdensome practice of scales and exercises. They take upon themselves a high price and burden. However, in their concert they experience a moment when this entire burden becomes the gift of spontaneous freedom as they play the music of the composer for the benefit of the audience. Artists and athletes often call this gifted experience as performing in a "zone." In a zone, the artist or athlete performs with a marvelous flair, so that it doesn't seem like playing as much as a freedom to exhibit the God-given powers of human witness to realities of music or a sport. Everything moves from effort to an effortless moment.

Our text suggests something like this. When we give ourselves over to the ways of God and dare to take upon ourselves all the demands that this will put upon us, we discover that suddenly they cease from being burdensome. The Jew claims the Torah, the Laws of God, to be such a blessing beyond their burdensomeness, becoming a deep joy and delight. A couple of very familiar scriptures will bear us out. Jesus said that when we take up the cross and follow him, we would find our lives. The burdens of cross bearing become our deep sense of really being alive. The other scripture is from Paul who speaks of a peace of God, which goes beyond all understanding. Paul says that in all our sufferings for Christ, we will find an inner peace of joy and feeling like a sense of well being, canceling out all the trouble and pain we endure in our commitment to Christ and his ways. Our challenge is to discover as 1 John says, "The commandments are not burdensome."

All That Goes Down
Must Go Up

We are now almost fifty days after Easter, days that were filled with the immediate presence of the resurrected Jesus. These were times when Jesus' followers believed that these experiences would go on forever. Then came a time when this immediate presence of Jesus faded like all great moments. If we go to the concert hall and hear the orchestra perform one of those powerful symphonies of Mahler, we leave the concert hall, and for a few hours the magnificent music surrounds us. Eventually it fades, like the presence of Jesus, and we are back to our common, ordinary days. Jesus, like Mahler, is gone.

Yet, for the disciples and early Christians this was not the end of the story. They began to claim that Jesus ascended up into the heavens where God vindicated his life and death. Jesus, for them, became the spiritual Lord of all humanity. Our text supports: "This Jesus God raised up, and of that all of us are witnesses. Being therefore exalted at the right hand of God, and having received from the Father the promise of the Holy Spirit, he has poured out this that you both see and hear" (Ephesians 2:32-33). Our lection today comes from the letter to the Ephesians. The passage asserts, "God put this power to work in Christ when he raised him from the dead and seated him at his right hand in the heavenly places, far above all rule and authority and power and dominion, and above every name that is named, not only in this age but also in the age to come" (1:20-21). Quite extraordinary claims about the crucified and risen Jesus!

237

Moderns need to handle these Ascension statements carefully. Because the ancients thought differently than we, we may not be comfortable with this story — Jesus ascending from earth to heaven. But we will miss the meaning of the story if we understand it only this way. The Ascension is not about Jesus rising through physical space; it is about Jesus rising from his apparent defeat and death to a place where he commands our devotion and commitment. The Ascension is about Jesus, whose earthly life in coming down to the physical and spiritual needs of others, quite forgetful of himself to the point of death, is finally given a place of honor by God.

Ascension reveals one of the most important spiritual laws of life. This law is the reverse of the law of physical gravity — "All that goes up must come down." In God's spiritual kingdom, "all that comes down must go up." This means our deeds of unselfish caring will be honored by God, lifting them up to where they become an inspiration to others. This notion will be what guides our celebration of Ascension Sunday today.

Jesus Came Down To The Needs Of Others

Moderns must not casually reject the great creeds of the church, particularly where the significance of Jesus is put into the terminology of Greek philosophy. Even though the nuance and form of ancient languages distances themselves from our time, it is still worth our effort to understand what earlier Christians and their creeds were expressing about Jesus. Similarly, modern astronomers have a much different take on the cosmos; yet the earlier theories of Ptolemy's understanding of the heavenly bodies can be appreciated for their conviction that the universe was orderly and wondrous in ways.

Yet, we need images and assessments of Jesus that are consistent with our modern understandings. We find some speaking of Jesus as "The Man for Others." Throughout the gospel narratives, we find Jesus living and acting as "The Man for Others." He instinctively went to the poor, the moral outcasts, those suffering from illness or the sorrow of death, to lepers who were alienated from family and society, to women who had little secure place in those times, and to children for whom survival was often a great risk. Jesus even crossed the ethnic lines to minister to Samaritans, Syrophonecians, and even officers of the Roman oppressors. In all of this, he disappointed those who hoped for a vengeful Messiah. They yearned for deliverance from the powers holding Israel's future captive, wishing that they were cast aside making possible their nation's return to its previous glory and prestige.

Jesus gave them a startling, alternative illustration of deliverance coming through living for others. Some think that Judas' betrayal came because he could not accept the way of godly suffering and caring. He may have wanted a powerful display of destruction for all that opposed Israel. Jesus did not stop at living out this mission for others. He demanded it for those who would join him. Once, when his disciples were arguing about what made for status in God's kingdom, Jesus told them that kingdom greatness would come in this same way. "Whoever wishes to become great among you must be your servant, and whoever wishes to be first among you must be slave of all" (Mark 10:43-44).

But Jesus was no sentimental optimist. He knew that the way of caring was a struggle against the powers that were ingrained in the world. In those times there were many scenarios of the world under the control of evil, perhaps a figure like Satan. Consequently, the ways of God had to contend against these evil forces. Some felt these forces were ultimately doomed because God was going to prevail. In the meantime, caring and centering on the needs of others, not on ourselves, became risky ventures.

The world then and now often seems to prefer the views of Frederich Neitzsche who proclaimed the virtues of power and strength. Caring and suffering love for Neitzsche were "slave virtues," and real humans struggle to clear out all enemies. Some think that this claim of violence helped fuel the barbaric rise of the National Socialists in Germany after 1918. Hitler and the Nazis affirmed the destiny of the German people to rule in worldly strength, dominating by the sword, leaving death and destruction in their wake.

We should be suspicious of contemporary calls to love ourselves. In some instances, a person's psychological health may originate in a lack of proper self-love. In other situations, the admonition to love oneself can play into a neglect of a life of caring because caring demands so much of our time, our energy, and our money. It is deceptively easy to make the case for loving ourselves in ways that never get around to extending costly love to others. Human nature is too flawed for us to carelessly sling around a call to self-love. We usually don't need this encouragement, for we are masters of self-love as a screen against the needs of others. It is interesting that Jesus said very little, if anything, about the importance of loving oneself. He did not spend much time thinking self-love was high on the list of priorities. Perhaps he felt that if we really gave ourselves over to the needs of others, any lack of self-love would take care of itself.

Jesus Has Inspired Others To Join Him In Coming Down

Ephesians says the power of God is at work in the world, even though there remains a terrible struggle between God and us. This is reflected in our own modern times in those joining Jesus in caring for others. Little Mother Teresa, a Hungarian nun, gave herself to care for the sick and dying in India. She and her convent sisters would roam the streets of Calcutta, taking the ill and dying back to the convent to bathe, feed, and give them medical care. Many of these poor people were beyond the point of recovery, meaning there could be no possible reward to Mother Teresa and her companions for their outpouring of love. Yet Mother Teresa became a powerful modern example of Jesus' love coming down to the raw needs of others.

Angelo Roncalli became Pope John the XXIII in 1958. Advanced in years, many thought his tenure would be brief, lasting only until a more dominant Pope emerged. Much to the surprise of all, John focused on the need to reform the liturgical practices and theological thinking, alienating many faithful moderns from the church. He called a great council of the church together, Vatican II, and out of this came the rendering of the Mass in the vernacular, and many theological and ethical revisions that expressed the faith in provocative contemporary concepts.

Vatican II disavowed earlier statements condemning the Jews as being responsible for the death of Christ. In one of his finest moments, John issued an encyclical on world peace, *Pacem in Terris.* Boldly he addressed it not just to Roman Catholics or other Christians, but also "to all men of good will." John could have excused himself from these efforts to reform the church, thereby avoiding much abuse from the ultra-conservatives. He could have enjoyed his last years in pomp, splendor, and the adoration of the faithful. However, he chose to care for those for whom the message of Christ could not be heard. He came down to the needs of the world as it stood before the church.

Almost everyone knows of Martin Luther King, Jr. He was a son of the parsonage, intellectually bright, an excellent preacher, and held a Ph.D. from a major mainstream theological school. Martin answered a call to become the pastor of an African-American Baptist church in Montgomery, Alabama. He hoped to become the dean of a seminary to pursue a teaching career. Marking time as the pastor of Dexter Avenue Baptist Church, Martin became involved in the Montgomery bus boycott. The African-American pastors taking the lead in organizing the boycott quickly asked Martin to be their leader. This was a crisis moment for him, for he really wanted the life of a Christian intellectual. Becoming the leader of the boycott would mean that he would have to give up all those dreams. He faced what a line in the "Wesley Covenant Service" points out:

> *Christ has many services to be done.*
> *Some are more easy and honorable,*
> *Others are more difficult and disgraceful.*
> *Some are suited to our inclinations and interests,*
> *Others are contrary to both.*
> *In some we may please Christ and please ourselves.*
> *But then there are other works where we cannot please*
>   *Christ*
> *Except by denying ourselves.*

Martin came down to the needs of African-American people to be able to ride the public transportation of Montgomery, and to sit in whatever seats that were open in spite of the segregation laws of that time. There is no doubt that Martin Luther King, Jr., was inspired by the example of Jesus to the point that he put himself out in vulnerable situations, ultimately losing his own life.

All That Comes Down Must Go Up

God's own power determines that all that comes down in our caring love, goes up to be honored by God, and all perceptive humans. For a time it seemed that, all these examples we have cited were doomed to failure and forgetfulness. Jesus was hung up on a cross by Pilate's soldiers and died like any common criminal. Even with the resurrection, his witness might have been lost when the inevitable experiences of his presence faded over the days and weeks to his followers. However, Ascension declares that God lifted Jesus up to a high place where he holds an inspiring and challenging claim upon the values to which men and women give their lives. We may choose the life of self-concern and self-indulgence. However, the Ascension whispers that we cannot be free of the troubling inner voice condemning our choice. Moreover, those of us who choose to come down to lives of caring, especially for those who cannot ever repay our love, will know the blessing of the joys of the godly.

Albert Schweitzer was a young German Christian intellectual who, in 1908, wrote a very controversial book about the historical Jesus. He challenged the standard, liberal interpretation of Jesus that was the dominant view of that day. Yet, for all his startling dismantling of the current view of the message and mission of Jesus, he closed his book with words that read almost like words of scripture:

> *As one unknown and nameless, He comes to us, just as on the shore of the lake He approached those men who knew not who He was. His words are the same: "Follow thou Me!" And He puts us to the tasks which He has to carry out in our age. He commands. And to those who obey, be they wise or simple, He will reveal Himself through all that they are privileged to experience in His fellowship of peace and activity, of struggle and*

242

*suffering, till they come to know, as an inexpressible
secret, Who He is.*[1]

You may know that later Schweitzer came down from his intellectual career and became a medical doctor in tropical Africa. Today he is one of the great Christian inspirations in the whole world. Do we need any more insistence that all that comes down must go up?

---

1. Albert Schweitzer, *The Quest of the Historical Jesus — A Critical Study of its Progress from Reimarus to Wrede* (1st German edition *VonRemarus zu Wrede*, 1906) (Great Britain: A & C Black, Ltd., 1910 [English translation]). The complete book is available online at <http:www.earlychristianwritings.com/ schweitzer/>.

The Blessings Of Writing

I write these things to you....   — 1 John 5:13

One of the blessings of God is the gift of writing, of putting our thoughts and observations on clay tablets or jars, on parchment, or on paper. Scholars are not certain when humans first began to write. Many think it happened in Samaria, the civilization between the Tigris and Euphrates, now modern-day Iraq. It may have happened about 3000 B.C.E. Nor is there a consensus on how writing was first used. It may have come from Shamans using it to pass on their skills and secrets. Or writing could have originated as a means to inventory the goods of merchants. Whatever, writing has enhanced the human quest for a richer spiritual and material life.

In our text for today, 1 John says he writes this letter so that readers and hearers would be filled with the great theological convictions that drive his work. He tells us, "I write these things to you who believe in the name of the Son of God, so that you may know that you have eternal life" (v. 13). Writing became the instrument for communicating the good news of the gospel. This God-given skill is one of humanity's most cherished possessions.

Writings Blessing Our Worship

Writing is central to our gathering in the sanctuary. Worship often begins by voicing the words written by the Psalmist, "This is the day the Lord has made. Let us rejoice and be glad in it." These words were written centuries ago and they bless us still. Next we might stand to sing a hymn of praise. Perhaps it is that great hymn, "Now Thank We All Our God," reminding us to rejoice that "from our mother's arms [God] has blessed us on our way." Alternatively, we might sing the stanza, "I'll praise my God who lends me breath; and when my voice is lost in death, praise shall employ my nobler powers." These magnificent words are from the hymn, "I'll Praise My Maker While I've Breath." With such stirring words, we cannot but be elevated into strong affirmation. While the tunes to these hymns are an important part of their impact, the words are at the heart of their impact.

After our hymn, we usually move to confess that our lives have fallen short of the will of God. Sometimes we join in the prayer, "Almighty and merciful God, we have erred and strayed from thy ways like lost sheep. We have followed too much the devices and desires of our own hearts. We have left undone those things which we ought to have done." These words from an earlier time invite us to become honest before God, the first step in opening ourselves to God's mercy and forgiveness. These words, again, are a gift enabling our repentance, coming from long ago. Other traditional words that are part of our worship treasure come from Archbishop Cranmer of the English Reformation. He invites us to pray, "Cleanse the thoughts of our hearts by the inspiration of thy Holy Spirit, that we may perfectly love thee and worthily magnify thy holy Name." The continuing power of such ancient language challenges our modern prejudice that only contemporary language can carry powerful meaning and significance. In fact, the age of flowing language may enhance its sense of gift to our worship.

The scriptures are vital to our worship. Scriptures are an indispensable part of our written treasure. The effort to collect, edit, and translate the scriptures is a great story, often filled with deep devotion. A bestseller, *God's Secretaries*, relates the efforts of the scholars who translated the King James Version of the Bible in 1611. Few would deny that this translation has shaped both the English language and the faith of English-speaking Christians since. It is unmatched in its rhythmic flow of language, often missing in some of our contemporary translations. So many contemporary translations are deficient in beat and cadence. They are flat like the language of *Newsweek* or *Time*. Lutheran theologian, Joseph Sittler, said when we suppress the rhythm and cadence of speech in our writings, we miss the sense of the holy. Perhaps this is why contemporary translations keep appearing one after another: their flat writing soon goes listless and we await the next attempt. The Revised Standard Version of the Bible wisely retains the flowing cadences of the original King James Version, combining clear meaning with poetic mystery. This great writing has blessed us.

After the preaching and the prayers, we might gather for one of the great creeds of the church. Again, we are indebted to those who put these strong faith statements into writing; the most well-known creed attributed to the early apostles. When we drive toward its closing phrases, "I believe in the Holy Spirit, the holy catholic church, the communion of saints, the forgiveness of sins, the resurrection of the body, and the life everlasting," we affirm a realm of trust and confidence that nothing can shake. Written words convey deep and abiding meanings. Sometimes our worship receives an infant, a child, a youth, or an adult for baptism. Who can fail to respond to these words as the pastor opens the baptismal service?

Brothers and sisters in Christ:
Through the Sacrament of Baptism
We are initiated into Christ's holy church.
We are incorporated into God's mighty acts of salvation
And given new birth through water and the Spirit.
All this is God's gift, offered to us without price.

Such words force us to consider the great occasion of God's grace through baptism. And when we celebrate the Lord's Supper, we often pray these words as the service closes:

Eternal, God, we give you thanks for this holy mystery
In which you have given yourself to us.
Grant that we may go into the world
In the strength of your Spirit,
To give ourselves for others,
In the name of Jesus Christ our Lord.

Such language is a gift, moving us to live out the faith in our common life. These words keep us from enjoying a private, personal faith, allowing us to go untouched by the needs and sufferings of the world, and thereby effectively denying Christ.

Great Writings That Have Blessed Us

Other great writings have blessed us and we must give God thanks for them. For instance, the plays of William Shakespeare — *Hamlet* and *Macbeth*, the histories of Henry IV and Henry V, the comedies of *As You Like It* or *All's Well That Ends Well*, and certainly the Sonnets. Shakespeare, writing near the same time as the translators of The King James Version of the Bible, bathes us with rich Elizabethan English. Moderns need a good dose of Shakespeare from time to time, so that our flattened prose can rise from its unimaginative plodding and fill us with awe and wonder.

Great poets have also blessed us. John Milton, Keats and Shelley, and Robert Browning and his wife, Elizabeth Barrett Browning, dispense poetic treasures that provoke and enchant. In our own day the somber verse of T. S. Eliot, or American poets like Carl Sandburg and Robert Frost rescue us from the ordinary writings and speech of our time. They deliver us from writings that seem not to understand both the misery and grandeur of human existence. These are part of the rich spiritual blessing that the gift of writing has given us.

We are also indebted to the writings of historians, writing about the human story and sort out its meaning. In a popular vein, Will Durant and his wife have gifted us with their masterful multi-volume work, *The Story of Civilization*. British author, Arnold Toynbee, did us a great favor when he reviewed the history of humanity, trying to find the clue why civilizations have come to birth, flourished, and then perished. His insights are both a judgment and a promise for the future of our world. One American history that has blessed us is Carl Sandburg's, *Abraham Lincoln*. With the deft skill of a poet and of a deeply sympathetic author, Sandburg has captured the inspiring story of this president from humble beginnings through his presidency and tragic death. Both our major and minor historians bless us, bringing light to the past, and help us move into the future.

Some others have blessed us with their writings. For instance, Charles Darwin in *Origin of Species* shattered the simplicity of our understanding of the development of life. He concluded that biological life has risen through an evolutionary way becoming the standard for modern science. Some have resisted Darwin's insights because they feel that Darwin's ideas are incompatible with belief in a creating and sustaining God. Other religious folks find Darwin both reasonable as well as compatible with their religious convictions, filling them with wonder and awe at the processes that have brought us life.

Sigmund Freud is another writer who has blessed our modern understandings. Without endorsing all he wrote, or his own world view, Freud has made aware of what he called "the subconscious," a place within where drives, motives, fears, ambitions, and irrational forces lurk, often determining our lives. Freud wrote that the subconscious explains why we sometimes experience troubling emotions, or act in ways that shame or confuse us. To him, mind is much deeper than the consciousness through which we experience our world in everyday life. Coming to responsible maturity means recognizing our subconscious before it destroys us in the process. Many have sensed that Freud and Paul would come together at this point. Paul, too, believed that we are in the grip of an inner flaw determining our actions and thoughts, leading us to destruction. We can be grateful to the writings of Freud for he opens for us the possibility of hearing Paul all over again in a new and powerful way.

Celebrating The Gift Of Writing

Winston Churchill had a sharp wit, especially in responding to his detractors. Once in reviewing a critic's book he said, "The Almighty, having deprived this author of the gift of thinking, has nevertheless endowed him with the ability of writing." None of the sources we have cited, authors and translators of scripture, hymns, prayers, creeds, liturgical statements, dramatists, poets, historians, biologists, psychiatrists, or economists are faulted in this way. All of these bring something of the truth of God, enriching our lives and calling us into the continuing work of God in our world.

Therefore, it was a holy moment when an ancient Sumerian took a crude tool and made some markings on a clay tablet. Out of such a modest act has come the wonderful gift of human writing. This gift has freed humans to communicate and preserve their thoughts, decisions, and memories of the past. Even more, the gift of writing enables humans to express their hopes and dreams for the future, blessing untold generations after them. One wonders if this was in the mind of 1 John when he put down these words, "I write these things to you who believe in the name of the Son of God, so that you may know that you have eternal life" (1 John 5:13).

Sermons On The Second Readings

For Sundays
After Pentecost
(First Third)

Birthpangs Of The New Age

Maurice A. Fetty

Dedicated to my grandchildren:

Sarah Friend Melton
Emily Elizabeth Melton
Louis Allen Jannetty
John Matthew Jannetty
Sara Marie Jannetty
Jack Stanley Montgomery
John Stanley Melton
Samuel Walker Montgomery
Elyce Jane Bayat
Cassidy Khristopher Loux
Carson Carol Loux

and to other grandchildren
who may be born after this printing!

Preface

Pentecost is the sometimes neglected and oft-forgotten festival of the church year. Everyone knows Christmas and Easter, but Pentecost often is crowded out by Memorial Day parades and celebrations or by the rituals associated with the beginning of summer, such as beaches, boats, and cottages.

Nevertheless, if Christianity was born on Easter, the Christian church was born on Pentecost. Just as Jesus was raised from the dead by the power of the Spirit of God, so too, the believing disciples were raised to new life by the empowering gift of the Holy Spirit.

If out of the birthpangs of the tomb Jesus was born to life eternal, so too, out of the birthpangs of the old age, the church was born into the life of the New Age. If the disciples looked back in memory of sacred events, they now, with the gift of the Holy Spirit, looked forward to the future God had in store for them and for the whole world.

It was and is Pentecost, when with the sound of a mighty, rushing wind, and with tongues of fire, and with the gift of the Holy Spirit, we experience again and again the birthpangs of the New Age coming to birth in each generation.

Maurice A. Fetty

The Day Of Pentecost
Romans 8:22-23

Birthpangs Of The New Age

It may surprise you to know that from time to time, ministers get complaints. Would it further surprise you to know ministers get complaints about hymns that are sung in church? Most people want to sing the old, familiar hymns which are about ten in number. However, from time to time, we get complaints from people griping that we always sing the same old hymns.

One such complaint was registered last Easter. After a triumphant, spirit-lifting service, a lady in a dour mood greeting the minister saying, "I'm never coming back to this church again." Taken aback, the minister maintained his composure and diplomatically asked, "And why won't you be coming back? Was something wrong with the service? Did someone offend you?"

She replied, "I'm not coming back because every time I come, all you do is sing the same old hymns." "Oh, really?" replied the minister, "and what hymns do we always sing when you come?" he asked. She replied, "O Little Town Of Bethlehem" and "Christ The Lord Is Risen Today."

Most ministers have gotten used to CE Christians: Christmas and Easter Christians. We have even gotten used to the parishioner who comes occasionally saying to themselves:

Every time I pass a church
I stop in for a little visit,
So when at last I'm carried in,
The Lord won't say, "Who is it?"

255

So while every church has some of those, and while every church has CE Christians, not many churches have CEP Christians. That's right, there are very few Christians who make a point of coming on Pentecost, because Pentecost, the birthday of the church, is the forgotten festival day.

Often coinciding with Memorial weekend, or the beginning of warmer days when June is busting out all over, Pentecost frequently is obscured by patriotic parades and pilgrimages to the beach or summer place (not to mention golf courses and boats). And yet, Pentecost is one of the most important celebrations of the church — the time when the Holy Spirit of God was given in a new way to signal the beginnings of a new age and a new people.

Christians often see Pentecost pre-figured in the lectionary reading for this Sunday from the Prophet Ezekiel. Ezekiel, that unique and sometimes almost bizarre visionary, saw a valley filled with dry, bleached, human skeletons, and as he sees the pathetic sight, God asks, "Can these bones live?" Dealing with God, Ezekiel is smart enough to say, "Thou knowest, Lord."

The bones were symbolic of the Judeans who lost their lives when the Babylonians (ancestors of the Iraqis) conquered and exiled them in 587 B.C. The terrible defeat of the Judean armies, the death and decay of the Judean nation, were symbolized by the valley of dry bones.

Then in the vision, Ezekiel saw an amazing thing. The Spirit of the Lord came upon the bones, brought them together with a loud voice, put sinew and flesh on them and then breathed into them the breath of life as God did with Adam at creation. God, said Ezekiel, was going to restore the dead nation of Judah in that way, breathing new life and hope into them. And he did, returning them to their homeland in 538 B.C.

Pentecost also celebrates the coming of God's Spirit into a so-called "dead" people, to breathe new life and hope into them, and thereby to create not an old Judah or Israel, but a new Israel, a new people of God. So the Spirit of God came mightily upon Jesus' disciples in Jerusalem in 30 A.D., coming upon them and empowering them for the New Age.

That same Spirit of God came upon Saul of Tarsus, changing him into the great Apostle Paul, champion of the cause of Christ and harbinger of the New Age. The Spirit, says Paul, is always working to bring in the New Age, both corporately and individually. We are always in the birthpangs of the New Age.

I

Notice first the birthpangs of the New Age for the individual.

It is a strange paradox that Paul speaks of, the promise of the new in the face of the power of the old; he talks of liberation in the context of bondage; and he alludes to the fullness of health in the midst of suffering.

In Paul's view, the individual is caught in a no-win situation. Paul earlier had been brought to despair about his own powerlessness to become the person he wanted to become. Born with an impeccable pedigree, prestigiously educated, and energetically brilliant, Paul despaired nevertheless that he would never become the person he wanted to become — that is, until he was empowered by the Spirit of the living Christ.

Paul had come to see the futility of a giddy optimism on the one hand, and on the other, the despair and emptiness of a negative pessimism. He would have agreed with theologian Karl Barth that "Art, science, and morality display the passionate longing of men for infinity." And yet he knew with Barth that, "Even the greatest genius is born, dies and lives as we do."[1]

But when Paul experienced the Spirit of the living Christ, he tells us he became a new being, a new creation. It was as if he were born again into a new reality, into a new self-understanding, into a new way of seeing. It was as if the Spirit of God had come amongst the dry bones of his pessimism and despair, and had breathed a new and vital Spirit with him.

In his excellent book, *True Resurrection*, Harry Williams talks about the dramatic experiences of people closer to our own time. Consider for example, Ludwig van Beethoven. As most people know, this great composer, at age thirty, began to suffer from deafness, which would be the equivalent of an artist beginning to suffer from blindness. Beethoven did not know when his piano was out of tune and sometimes, when playing for friends, he touched the piano keys so lightly no sound came out, but he did not know.

He was lonely and often in love, but remained a bachelor. At age 31, he wrote, "You can scarcely imagine how lonely and sad my life has been during the past two years. My weak hearing haunted me everywhere, and I ran away from people and was forced to appear like a misanthrope, though that is far from my character."

Beethoven goes on to say that at one time he was at the point of suicide, but instead of suicide, came the miracle of the resurrection. He then wrote, "You will see me as happy as my lot can be here below ... I will seize fate by the throat. It shall never wholly overcome me. How beautiful life is." So this great composer — musical "father" to Wagner and Brahms, completed his famous *Ninth Symphony* with its great and triumphant "Ode To Joy." And when he finished conducting it for the first time, the musicians had to turn him to face the audience to see the thunderous applause which he could not hear. Suffering was the birthpangs of the new Beethoven, the Beethoven of the new age, "a suffering made triumphant by the Spirit of God."

It has been my friend's high privilege to visit Florence, Italy, a couple of times, and each time he made it a priority to visit the Academia di Belle Arte not only to see Michelangelo's famous *David*, but also to view his four sculptures leading up to the *David*. They look unfinished. The human figures are emerging from the rough stone as though they were tearing themselves out of it with tremendous effort and anguish and pain.

The figures are, of course, us, our potential selves, struggling to be actualized, to be drawn out of the stone bondage of past fixities into the liberation of true selfhood. And yes, it is the hammer blows of suffering, the chiseling of experience which help shape us. Out of the hard blows and knocks of life, God, the great sculptor, is attempting to sculpt us into our true self, our real self, the next self that is always waiting to come to be, no matter what our age.

I suppose if we could speak to all the eight-month-old fetuses in the wombs of the millions of pregnant women, to ask them if they wanted to be born, they would probably all vote "No." They would say, "We're comfortable, warm, well-fed, protected, and content. Who wants to take chances in separation, in cold and loneliness, in independence and risk and possible conflict? No thanks, we'll stay right here."

At each stage of our life, whether eighteen or eighty, we are, as it were, in a womb, being developed for a new selfhood. It is the living Spirit of God which calls us forth, which lures us through the travail of labor to become the "new you." It calls us to be the more complete person we are destined to be, and on this Pentecost, if we are open to him, God is ready to bring us into a new age of selfhood.

II

But if that is true of the individual, it is also true of the church. God is ready to bring the church into a new age.

In 1966, Harvard Divinity School theologian, Harvey Cox, wrote a book which became a surprising best-seller. In the book, titled *The Secular City*, Dr. Cox predicted, along with many others, that religion would die out to be replaced by the "secular man," the "man come-of-age," the person who would "do it on his own." He would need no religion as a crutch to lean on, no imagined heavenly Father to save him in his dilemmas.

About the same time, many theologians across the country were speaking of the "death of God." *Time* magazine ran a bold cover story which asked, "Is God Dead?" "Yes," said many theologians, "God is dying" and so is religion, hinted Cox in his book, *The Secular City*.[2] But in his new book, *Fire From Heaven*, Harvard's Dr. Cox says bluntly, "I was wrong" and the death-of-God theologians were wrong, dead wrong.[3]

Religion is extremely alive and well in the world, says Cox, and in many places it is growing like wildfire. It is not, as popularly believed, Islam, which is the world's fastest growing religion, no, not Islam or Buddhism, but Christianity. It is not mainline Christianity like Methodists, Episcopalians, Presbyterians, and Congregationalists, which is growing rapidly; it is Pentecostal Christianity growing like wildfire especially among the Third World countries and among the poor and dispossessed of richer countries.

259

Pentecostalists get their name from the festival we celebrate today, and just as the Spirit of God descended on the first Christians in Jerusalem, empowering them, converting them, giving them the ability to speak in tongues, transferring them into a kind of religious ecstasy, so Pentecostalists of our time claim a similar kind of experience.

American Pentecostalism had its beginnings in 1906, in the Azuza Street Church in Los Angeles, in a building that had once been a livery stable. At once interracial, non-denominational, and with no attention to class distinctions, people at the Azuza Street Church claimed to have a powerful experience of the Holy Spirit — so powerful that people would swoon in trances, or babble ecstatically in unknown languages, which was called "the speaking in tongues" just like that which happened on the original day of Pentecost. Some people possessed by the Spirit of God, would roll in the aisles in ecstatic happiness, and thus gained for the group the often derogatory name "Holy Rollers." Others would jerk or shout or sing praises to God in highly emotional services that were shocking and distasteful even then to the more sedate and refined and reserved Christians of America.

But Pentecostal Christianity, not to be equated with fundamentalism, grew and grew and leapt across racial and national and ethnic and class and religious boundaries. The disenfranchised, the poor, the oppressed, the outcasts, the wretched of the earth were, and are, experiencing the overwhelming affirmation of the empowering and enabling Spirit of God. In South Korea, for example, the largest Christian church in the world and in history, is the Yoido Full Gospel (Pentecostal) Church with 800,000 members. Once a Buddhist country, South Korea is rapidly on its way to becoming a majority Christian country, and Pentecostalists are leading the way, because, as they tell us, they are open to experiencing anew the Spirit of God, whereas many mainline churches are not.

In his book, Harvey Cox quotes the song of British rock star, Sting, which says:

You could say I lost my faith in science and progress.
You could say I lost my belief with the holy church.
You could say I lost my sense of direction.

Dr. Cox suggests the rock singer's song typifies many people today. In the last two or three centuries two contending forces have slugged it out, claiming to be the ultimate source of meaning and value, says Cox. One force was traditional religion and the other was scientific modernity, and now, like two tired boxers they have reached an exhausted stalemate, says Cox.[4]

People today remain somewhat intrigued with conventional religion, but use it only as a kind of toolbox to get at spiritual values. People are no longer concerned with "one dimensional modernity or with stagnant religious practices," says Cox. People are more into intuition, immediacy, participation, and practicality. Traditional clergy or correct doctrines or professional theologians have little authority. People weary of dull religion and empty scientism, want to *experience* the divine, not just *talk* about it, or point to somebody else's experiences of the divine in some distant past. Rather than rehearse a previous generation's peak religious experiences many people today want to have their *own* — that is, if they are not afraid.

But when we become educated, successful, well-to-do, gentrified, skeptical, stratified in ethnic, class, and socio-economic groups and neighborhoods, we tend to shut out the empowering, transforming, uniting power of the Spirit of God. David Halberstam, in his book, *The Next Century*, quotes a Japanese intellectual worried about the effect of prosperity on his people. The intellectual says, "For thousands of years God and poverty kept man disciplined. Now, in the modern age, God is dead and poverty is disappearing. How will we be disciplined?"[5] How indeed!

The answer is to be found in Pentecost, in an openness to the Spirit of God, in a willingness to be born anew in a way that overpowers our defensiveness, our fortress mentalities, our rigidities, our presumptions that the past experiences of this church were better than the present or future can ever be, our unwillingness to inquire of the mind of Christ as to the kind of church he would have us be, rather than presume we are to be a replication of the past, however glorious.

Perhaps there is waiting here in the womb of time a new church ready to be born, a church willing to learn some new hymns rather than rigidly insisting on singing only old ones; a church willing to consider that its organization and institutional procedures are deadening and counterproductive and out-of-date; a church ready to concede more time for feeling and less for formality; a church willing to humble itself before God, instead of presuming it knows what God's will is for it in this time; a church willing to experiment with new forms of worship and learning; a church willing to consider the priority of the faith over the so-called securities of wealth or success or fame or the fixities of an outdated churchmanship; a church open to the ecstatic and the new; a church that is willing to say that whatever else happens, God will be first in our lives, even before Sunday morning sports; a church willing to be inclusive, to reach out across class and racial and ethnic boundaries to experience the oneness of the original Pentecost.

"Can these bones live?" a coy God asks Ezekiel. An equally coy Ezekiel replies humbly, "Thou knowest, Lord," for he knew as Jesus knew, that with God, nothing is impossible. And the valley of dry bones became alive and vital and vibrant with the empowering Spirit of God.

Can we become the new people and the new church we are destined to be? "Thou knowest, Lord." But already, says Paul, we have been given God's Holy Spirit. That urging we feel within, that longing, that hope, that expectation, that dream on the verge of fulfillment — they all are the birthpangs of the new age — the new age of you, the new age of your marriage, your career, your family, your faith, the new age of the church, the new age of the world.

For as Paul says, "If the Spirit of him who raised Jesus from the dead dwells in you, he who raised Christ Jesus from the dead will give life to your mortal bodies through his Spirit which dwells in you" (Romans 8:10-11).

And that, dear friends, is Pentecost over and over again for individuals and for the church. May it be so with us.

---

1. Karl Barth, *The Epistle to the Romans* (London: Oxford University Press, 1922), pp. 311-312.

2. Harvey Cox, *The Secular City* (New York: Macmillan Co., 1966).

3. Harvey Cox, *Fire From Heaven* (New York: Addison-Wesley, 1995).

4. *Ibid.*, p. 299.

5. David Halberstam, *The Next Century* (New York: Morrow, 1991), p. 117.

From Father Failure
To Divine Father

One of the most significant steps in our growth as human beings is the discovery that our earthly parents, contrary to our childish notions, are imperfect. A friend remembered well an incident in that process of discovery in his own life. He always thought his father was the perfect driver and that he was absolutely safe riding with him until one day he almost hit the side of a bridge. His father was a very good driver, but he was not, he was discovering, perfect.

Eventually, the discovery of the imperfections of our fathers goes much deeper than driving. We begin to see they lust after other women, are influenced by greed, are not always wise in their counsel, can make poor decisions, and can exhibit weakness both in body and character.

Freud, and other psychologists, suggest it is at this time we begin to project a heavenly Father, a perfect, divine Father, who will never exhibit weakness and who will never fail us. This heavenly Father, created out of our childish need and adolescent discovery of the imperfections of the adult world, becomes omnipotent, omniscient, and omnipresent; an infallible father-figure upon whom we can lean and from whom we can draw meaning and strength.

This projected father, created out of our emptiness and weakness and sense of dependency, is basically an illusion, say many psychologists. It is the Father-God of our wish-dreams similar to the ideal king or president of our wish-dreams who will solve all our problems. Thus, not only is our projected heavenly Father a self-created illusion; he is a symbol of our unwillingness to accept responsibility for ourselves and for the world.

Therefore, in this view, religion functions as a way of sustaining childishness and dependent adolescence in the human race rather than producing maturity and responsibility. Religion serves then as a prop, as a crutch, as a way of escaping from the harsh realities of life. In this view, religion becomes a way of evading the truth about ourselves and the world, and causes people to avoid responsibility for the world by saving souls out of the world and by hoping for the end of the world as soon as possible.

As people who are more or less religious, how shall we react to this critique of a fundamental religious concept?

I

One reaction is to agree with the critics that religion is basically illusion and that the God and Father of our Lord Jesus Christ is primarily a wish-dream, a Father-figure created out of the Jewish-Christian community to satisfy our needs and longings for a perfect father wherein meaning and strength and life and purpose ultimately can be found. As such we can claim it is as good an illusion as the world has going and that it produces some remarkable results.

Think alone of the music, art, and literature this illusion has produced for the world, not to mention the businesses, churches, scholars, publications, colleges, seminaries, hospitals, orphanages, and so on.

Another reaction to the charge that God is illusion, a creation of our needs, is to agree but also to point out to the critics that they themselves live by other illusions which function as God. For example, Marx and Lenin once provided the ultimate source of meaning for some people.

One time, a lady was standing outside a Christian meeting handing out tracts that said Lenin was the light of the world. Revolutionaries through the centuries have claimed an ultimacy for their special brand of political ideology. Do not these people and ideas serve as illusions, as crutches, as perfectionist patterns for a world without failure? Theologian Paul Tillich has suggested that each person has an ultimate concern and that that ultimate concern can function as a god, but that ultimate concern may be illusion.

Other people elevate psychologists and psychoanalysts to the position of perfect father, the one who explains all and provides the necessary and meaningful answers to reality. Freud held sway as an authoritarian figure for many years. Indeed, the Christian idea of God had to be subjected to Freudian psychoanalysis to see if it was acceptable. God, said some of the Freudians authoritatively, was illusion. God was out and Freud was in.

When the God of our Christian illusions is deposed, people do not then live in a vacuum without a source of meaning and sustenance. Instead, something else is drawn in as a source of meaning — family, sports, career, nation, pleasure seeking, and of course, the most persistent of all substitute gods — money.

Who is it that lives without a support system of some sort? Who is it that is truly independent, truly self-made, truly self-reliant? We all are dependent to some degree, but the religious question has to do with the nature of our dependency. What kinds of dependency and independency are there?

II

Consider, for example, abnormal dependency. As we have seen, discovery of the weakness and failure of the earthly father may lead us then to project an ideal heavenly Father who has no weakness, who never fails, and who takes care of everything for us so our lives will be problem-free. While this might be an apt description of God it may prove an infantile conception on our part, enabling us to continue to be spiritual thumbsuckers.

We have all known religious people who insist they turn everything over to God — all their decisions, all their thinking, all their responsibility for living. In other words, they want to remain spiritual infants, dependent, afraid, infantile, childish, and irresponsible. In their view whatever happens, therefore, is the will of God. And God gets all the praise or blame, and the individual thus absolves himself or herself of all guilt. What at first glance seems to be complete religious devotion turns out to be infantile, irresponsible dependency of a soul that refuses to grow up.

It was somewhat in that context that Dietrich Bonhoeffer liked to speak of man come of age and the God who abandons us so we can come of age. Just as a wise parent knows that the time must come for a child to sink or swim on his own, so, too, Bonhoeffer suggested, the time comes when God must withdraw himself to enable the spiritual self to grow up. Consequently, human beings often go through dry spells of faith when God seems distant and remote. People speak then of the silence of God or even of the death of God as we did a few years ago.

Bonhoeffer suggested that humankind, in our time, had come of age, and that it must be weaned from dependency upon the divine Father and take responsibility for itself. And, just as an infant feels rejected in being weaned, or just as an adolescent feels rejected in coming of age, so too humankind, in our time, has felt rejected by God. God is silent. God is indifferent. God is dead.

The other side of abnormal dependency is *abnormal independency*. This is the characteristic behavior of adolescent rebelliousness and self-assertiveness. The emerging adolescent must establish his or her identity and sense of independence over and against the father or mother.

Adolescents at this stage frequently avoid their parents, will not go to the cottage or boat with them. They often are ashamed of their parents and are reluctant to introduce them to friends, fearing their friends will see what they see — namely, old fogies from a lost generation of the distant past. Like the ancient priest Melchizadek, adolescents like to claim they are without father or mother and that they just appeared full blown into the world. If this attitude continues into adulthood, they maintain themselves as self-made men or women, refusing to acknowledge dependency upon the human community of teachers, ministers, doctors, business and government people, and so on.

Abnormal independency proceeds to distorted pride, to the classic hubris, to the elevation of the self, and the claim that we need no one at all. We can do everything by ourselves, thank you.

This attitude often leads, as it did in the 1960s, to the idea of the secular man, the man come of age, who needed neither earthly father nor heavenly Father. It was man's world, his age, his life, and he would handle it himself. In its best form, this led to secular humanism, so widely disdained by the religious right today. In its worst form, it led to Nazism and other totalitarian ideologies. It led to Nietzsche's "Superman" and the horrendous distortions of human nature that manifest themselves in hedonism, materialism, greed, narcissism, and eventually, in holocaust.

But there is a center position of normal dependency and independency. While it is important that we be weaned spiritually and that we grow out of spiritual adolescence, it is foolhardy to deny we have no spiritual ancestors or to claim we came into the spiritual or material world by ourselves. We are, in fact, dependent on countless people even though we may be mature and adult. As Plato observed, we often like city life because we can depend on so many other people to do things for us — provide food and transportation, make clothing and shelter. We depend on thousands for education, entertainment, business, and so on. There is nothing immature about that. It is a sign of maturity to recognize we cannot provide for our own needs.

But there is yet a deeper sense of dependency of which the philosopher Friedrich Schleiermacher spoke — a sense of absolute dependence upon the universe, upon God. It is the sense that we did not make ourselves, that we have come from higher life and intelligence. The awe and wonder evoked by the beauty and order of the universe, the remarkable symmetry and complexity of our bodies lead us to acknowledge a mysterious dependency upon the forces that have brought us into being, forces that have given us life and consciousness, forces that sustain us, powers from which we draw meaning and significance.

This sense of absolute dependence, this feeling of having come from someone greater than ourselves, forms the base of the religious attitude, says Schleiermacher. Just as it is a sign of adulthood and maturity to acknowledge dependence on others, so it is a sign of higher maturity to acknowledge ultimate dependence upon the universe, upon God. Therefore, thanksgiving for life and love and thought is a fundamental act of worship.

However, mature dependence does not mean, as we have seen, a retreat to infantilism, to childishness, to thumbsucking, and

269

breastfeeding. As the writer of Hebrews says, there is a time when we must move on from spiritual milk to solid food. God did not intend to make the world a perpetual nursery. Instead, he made it a place for soul-making, where human beings, with their unique capacity of freedom, rise up to take responsibility for the world and for themselves. It is not responsibility over *against* God, but responsibility *with* God.

To take responsibility for the world *with* God is to accept some of the praise as well as some of the blame. You remember the old story of the minister who said to the gardener, that's a nice garden you and the Lord have there. Yes, said the gardener, but you should have seen it when the Lord had it all by himself! God provides the basic life forces and reproductive miracle, but man shapes, cultivates, and organizes the life. That is true in gardens, in literature, music, art, politics, and religion. The world is a cooperative effort between man and God. Man, in false pride, takes all the credit, or in false humility, takes none of the credit. Each is incorrect, but to take credit together for all the beauty and achievements of and in the world is an act of celebration. Worship includes that.

Likewise, man and God must share the blame for the world. God has to accept responsibility for the evil and suffering, the pain and heartache, the disease and death. After all, he created a world where such things are possible.

But responsible man, man beyond thumbsucking and adolescence, will also take some of the blame for the world. Just as an individual must someday stop blaming his parents for his behavior and thus excusing himself from self-responsibility, so humankind must stop blaming its behavior on heredity or environment, upon God or fate or determinism, and thus take responsibility for itself.

In his freedom, man has introduced war and slaughter, exploitation and oppression. By his own design he has maimed, killed, destroyed, and threatened his own kind with extinction. And for this, the proper religious attitude is contrition, confession, and change.

270

III

Therefore, in our worship, in our religious activity, it is our desire to be, as Paul says, led by God's Spirit to become his children, rather than children of the flesh.

This is to say we will stop blaming our parents for our failures, even though they may be worthy of blame. We come to worship to be released from the childishness of being forever locked into the regret and despair of hereditary and environmental deficiency. We come to worship, to be released from our fleshly habit of excusing ourselves for our behavior, always justifying our weaknesses and misdeeds by those of our parents and grandparents.

By the same token, we come to worship, to be released from the tendency to project nation or president or celebrity into God. The ancient Celts, for example, projected their king into divinity, and then when he failed to perform divinely, they ritually murdered him. Americans often project presidents into divine roles, but then either actually or psychologically assassinate them when they fail to be the perfect cult father, the perfect hero, and father substitute.

In a similar way, contemporaries of Jesus projected him as an ideal king or messiah who would solve all their problems. When he disappointed them and failed to bring in their ideal kingdom they crucified him and began to search for a new ideal king.

But God raised him from the dead, exalted him as Lord and King, and handed him back to us as Messiah, forcing us to accept responsibility for his murder. In so doing, we take our place before this exalted Lord who ironically helps us confess our escapism and vain, idealistic self-projections. Paradoxically, once we accept responsibility for ourselves and for the world, God, as divine Father, shares responsibility with us and cooperates with us for good.

Therefore, as children of God, we cease blaming our ancestors for our behavior and we refrain from projecting our ideal of God unto God. Instead, we commit ourselves to God, who by his grace accepts us into his family of love, ever beseeching us to become new persons.

As children of God, we come not to resign ourselves to the dreary repetition of past generations. As children of the Spirit,

271

through confession and repentance, we resist the downward, earthward, deterministic pull of heredity and habit, to write new agendas for career and family life. We come to worship to be released from self-defeating self-images inherited from past family and sibling relationships.

As children of the Spirit, we accept into ourselves the failure of father and mother and thereby our failure, and by accepting failure into ourselves we accept death and confess our powerlessness before it. But through such radical humility and courage, we prepare ourselves for the Spirit of God which is life and life-giving.

Instead of projecting a divine Father that is an idealized, infallible version of the earthly, failing father, children of the Spirit receive instead the true image of the heavenly Father that calls them neither to infantile dependency nor to grotesque superman or superwoman self-images, but to healthy, mature, cooperative relationship with their spiritual Father.

We come, therefore, to take responsibility with God for the self and for the world, a responsibility that ultimately requires love and thus the willingness to suffer. In a world where God and man are free, anything can happen, evil or good. And, often the good requires the suffering of hard work, patience, determination, forbearance, forgiveness, and sometimes even pain and death.

Thus as Paul suggests, we suffer along with God for the wholeness of the world, being neither rebellious against father failure nor infantile in projection to divine Father, but cooperators for good with those who love God and are called according to his purpose. For we believe that by suffering with him we shall also be glorified with him.

Proper 4
Pentecost 2
Ordinary Time 9
2 Corinthians 4:5-12

Parades And Crosses —
The Challenge Of Ministry

He had grown up in a fashionable suburb of a large American city, a cosmopolitan area of considerable size and sophistication. He was a winner from the time he was born; you know, one of those babies that comes into the world with a smile and a confident air that life is friendly and meant for success. Oh, yes, he did his share of crying, and as an infant and pre-schooler, he had his share of sickness. But all in all, he was the kind of boy you would expect to see in a prize-winning television commercial.

In elementary school he was always liked by his teachers, although with his healthy, all boy personality, he steadfastly avoided giving any appearance of being a teacher's pet. He knew the turbulence of the teenage years, but that didn't stop him from excellence in that rare combination of athletics and academics.

In a way, he was the kind of son every parent dreams of. He was bright, but not conceited; handsome, but not stuck on himself; well-groomed, but not fastidious; polite, but not obsequious; well organized, but just easy and mischievous enough to make him the life of most any party. Although he was full of passion and a favorite of the girls, his upbringing and his Christian convictions kept his passion under control.

In fact, it was his Christian convictions that had his father a little bit worried. His father was a supporter of the church and had even served a term as a deacon. He attended regularly, spoke favorably of the church, and generally encouraged his son's participation in church activities, although he freely acknowledged that it was the boy's mother who was really the religious one in the family.

273

Although the son was a leader in school in every way, he was also active in church. He rarely missed youth meetings, sang in the choir, and even attended an early morning Bible study. One summer he went on a youth work camp to the Appalachians to help build a community center for the poor mountain folk, and one time the minister had asked him to preach the sermon on Youth Sunday. He received a lot of compliments. A lot of people told him he would make a good minister.

It was his senior year in high school and he was more active than ever as a leading athlete, president of his class, and as one of the best students academically. He scored very high on his S.A.T.s. And he kept active in church. The youth leaders asked him to lead some Bible studies for the middle school group. Once again, almost by popular demand, he was asked to preach on Youth Sunday. Once again, the compliments came rolling in. You should be a minister, said one of the dear saints of the church. An older gentleman, one of the patriarchs of the church, said he had a gift for preaching. Perhaps he ought to consider the ministry. The boy smiled and thanked him.

I

It all happened deep in January after the father had been on an extended, but very successful, business trip. The father had already been very successful, reaping a handsome income that provided a fine home and cottage, with skiing in Aspen and surfing in Hawaii. If shortages of cash flow was a preoccupation of some families in their neighborhood, such was not the case in this family. They were careful not to flout their wealth like the *nouveau riche* nor to live ostentatiously like the psychologically insecure, but neither were they secretive nor miserly. They had and enjoyed the good things of life.

Flying back from his trip, the father looked forward to sharing all the good news of his success with his family. In fact, he already was planning a family trip to celebrate the sizeable increase in income. But perhaps more than that, he was dreaming about his son. To be sure, he had his ups and downs with him like most fathers. But all in all, he was immensely proud of his boy as was almost

274

everyone else. Now he was dreaming of the day when his son might come into the business with him and take it to even greater heights. Of course, first there would be college and hopefully a master's degree in business administration from Harvard, and it might be good experience for him to work for someone else for a while. But eventually, he dreamed of the day his son would join him in the business.

He knew his son had the ability to do almost anything with his high grades and positive, hard-working attitude. The son had spoken some of medicine and law. He had the rare ability to excel in both science and literature. The father contented himself with the thought the son might enter one of the professions. But beyond all that, he longed for the day the son would be a full-fledged partner with him in his successful business.

However, as I was saying, it all happened deep in January after the father returned from his extended and highly successful business trip. It was one of those rare evenings in upper-middle-class life when everyone planned to be home. The mother had prepared a wonderful, welcome-home dinner in the dining room with leisurely dessert scheduled for the living room beside the fireplace.

It was then, by the fireplace, that it happened. The family and father had enjoyed animated conversation throughout dinner, and now by the fire, everyone was on the third cup of coffee. There was a lull in the conversation, and the son spoke up and said, "Dad, I've got something to tell you." "Yes?" "Well, Dad, I think I've finally decided what I want to do with my life." "Oh, well, really? Sounds great! Let's hear about it." "Well, Dad, I've been doing a lot of thinking lately, and I've about decided I'd like to study for the ministry."

The son, who had been looking at the dancing flames was about to continue, when he glanced at his father to see a puzzled, bewildered, unbelieving, crestfallen countenance, rolled together in one frightening, unforgettable expression. The father, in turn seeing his son's surprise and grimace, quickly regained his composure, looked into the fire, then at his wife, and then sipped long and hard on his coffee. There was a long and awkward silence.

275

II

"So," said the father, regaining a bit of composure, "so, what makes you think you want to enter the ministry? I thought you were headed for law or medicine or better yet, for a business career with me. We could do extremely well together you know. You would start out light years ahead of where I was at your age."

"I know, Dad. I have thought of medicine and law and being in business with you. It would be great fun to do that with you, but I am feeling more and more I should go into the ministry."

"Well, son, those are noble ideas and the ministry is a high calling. But, really now, have you considered what kind of a life that would be? Ministers are about the lowest paid professionals in the country. They go through seven or eight or more years of higher education only to drive secondhand cars and live in a parsonage decorated by a committee."

"Besides, I was reading in the paper the other day that the average minister in America makes only a modest amount a year, and that includes housing allowance and fringe benefits. Son, I make ten to twenty times that amount even in a bad year. Why would any intelligent, high achiever like you want to enter a profession that would pay you in later life what most lawyers start out with right out of law school? What kind of a future is that? How could you really enjoy the good things in life with that kind of income? How would you put your kids through college? How could you support a family anywhere near your accustomed lifestyle?"

"I know, Dad," said the son. "The low pay of ministers does bother me. It seems to me that many churches do exploit their ministers. But I was talking with our minister about that and he showed me our annual report and pointed out that he was considerably better paid than the average."

"Sure, son," said the father, "but look where he is, in an exceptional church. And I have no doubt you would end up in a similar church, but I still make four or five times as much as our minister, easily, and so could you. No minister dares make much more than the average salary of his congregation, no matter how good he is. You remember the old trustees prayer which goes like this: 'Lord, you arrange to keep our minister humble, and we'll arrange to keep him poor.' People are funny that way. For some reason they think money and ministry are incompatible. You'll have no financial future in the ministry, my son."

"I know, Dad. It seems strange to me that it is okay for lay Christians to make a lot of money, but not okay for Christian ministers. But, Dad, I'm really not going into the ministry for money. That's obvious, I guess. Of course I would like to make a good living for my family, and I sure don't want to take the vow of poverty, but my feeling for the ministry is deeper than that."

III

His father asked for a fourth cup of coffee, and then ventured the obvious question. "You say you have deeper feeling for the ministry. What do you mean?"

The son was a bit encouraged. He had thought by this time his father might be in a complete rage. And even though he knew his father was suffering from deep disappointment, he was, nevertheless, earnestly trying to understand his son's feelings for he knew the son thought things out pretty well before he made a decision.

"Well, Dad, I guess the feelings have grown on me gradually. But this past year when I was leading the Bible study with the middle school kids, something clicked inside me. I knew they admired me as an athlete and leader, but when I talked with them about Jesus and God and how they should commit their lives to them, they responded in a new way. I mean, it was like I touched a dimension of their lives nothing else and no one else could touch. You know I really love sports and get a great thrill out of winning and being popular. But when I talked with these kids, I seemed to be touching them in ways sports could not. It was like I was filling an emptiness or void in their lives. I was giving them a reason for life or a purpose they all could share, even if they couldn't achieve in academics or sports. Some of those kids now come to talk with me about their problems and I seem to be able to help them. It really gives me a deep sense of satisfaction."

"Well," said his father, "you could do that as a youth sponsor while you were in business with me. You could be a deacon and teacher and all that and still not enter the professional ministry."

"That's true," said the son as he shifted his weight and leaned forward in his chair. "But I had a similar feeling when our minister let me preach those two Youth Sundays. I felt good, almost natural up there. I felt as if people were really listening, really listening for a special kind of word they don't hear anywhere else. Besides, I got a lot of compliments!"

"I understand, I think," said the father. "You did do a fine job up there, and I was mighty proud of you, as always. But let me play the devil's advocate for a minute. It's only natural for people to compliment you and encourage you as a young man. But think how little esteem most people have for a sermon. No one wants to be preached to or to hear a sermon. And you know we have one of the better preachers around. When I was on the board of deacons, you should have heard the complaints if our minister preached beyond the hour. He was reminded again that the head can only absorb as much as the bottom can endure.

"Frankly, I don't think most people, even church people, respect preaching much these days. If anything, they prefer a ten or twelve minute talk about how to get along a little better in life. If they miss getting ahead of the brunch line at the club, they suffer an acute attack of apoplexy!

"To tell you the truth, my son, even though I love the church and our minister, I just don't think preaching and teaching in the church is where the action is. People look to professors and scientists, commentators, doctors, opinion-makers, and best-selling authors for their authority. They think religion is important, but a bit quaint and irrelevant, and a little bit off to the side of life. Preaching and worship and religious processions may seem a little glamorous, but I think the deeper truth is that people do not respect it in our day. And that's a cross you would have to bear if you went into the ministry."

The son sat back in his chair and thought a bit. He looked at his mother who, by the gentle expression and radiant glow in her eyes, encouraged him to go on. "The trouble is, Dad, I think you may be right. I know what a lot of my friends and their families think of the church and the ministry. Sometimes they exhibit a kind of subtle mockery. One of my buddies has a kind of odd minister. He says his dad calls him the third sex.

"Nevertheless, while you were away, I spent a lot of time talking with our minister. He agreed that the ministry was not at the center of life like it used to be. The minister once was one of the few educated people around, that no longer is the case. He no longer has that automatic authority either from education or position. Many people think the minister is unacquainted with the rough and tumble world and really cannot speak to it with authority."

"Right," said the father. "I think that's the way it is. If you really want to influence society and change things, go into something else, maybe law and politics."

"I raised that very question with our minister," said the son. "He said we certainly do need good Christians in all vocations, but he reminded me that I needed to take a long look at history. The Bible and the church have been around a long time, he said, longer than any nation or political or economic system. He said there have been other times in history when preachers and preaching have been ignored, even ridiculed, persecuted, and killed. He mentioned William Tyndale and John Huss, who were burned at the stake. He pointed out the threat on Martin Luther's life and the fact that Polycarp was burned at the stake. Then, of course, he mentioned the Apostle Paul and Jesus himself.

"In the long sweep of history, he said preaching has often been very difficult. And right now, it is out of fashion in Western culture. Fads and fashions come and go, but the gospel of Christ and the Bible and the church will remain forever. He said that, as a minister, I would be serving a higher calling whose reward might not be realized in this life, but that I would be enlisting people in the cause of Christ, nurturing them, helping them, praying for them, attempting to aid them to be good disciples of Christ. I guess that's the deeper feeling I get when I teach those young kids and when I preach. I get the feeling I'm participating in something eternal and ageless, something that really satisfies and makes sense.

"Our minister said an old veteran minister once told him he should stay out of the ministry unless he just couldn't help himself. I'm feeling more and more that way, that I would make a mistake if I stayed out. Our minister said that perhaps God was calling me into the ministry.

"He said many churches don't take their share of responsibility for recruiting young people for the ministry. He said he knew of one large church that had, in its many years, recruited only one person for the ministry. He said they were really dependent on other churches who had taken their responsibility more seriously.

"I told him I hadn't heard any voices or seen any visions. He said that didn't matter, and that perhaps God was calling me through these experiences and people. I hope you won't be angry at me, Dad, but I guess that is how I'm feeling."

IV

Well, what is a father to do? This one thought deeply as he sipped his coffee. Despite his personal heartache, he had a deepening respect for his son whom he loved and admired so much. He realized as he spoke that his own deep feelings about the church and the ministry were being exposed. Yet, he felt he owed it to himself and to his son to express his honest objections.

"Well, son, I have to admire your convictions. But I still have lots of questions and hesitations. I remember one lady on our deacon board who said she wouldn't want to be a minister because of all the problem people in the church, and I chuckled to myself, because if ever our minister had a problem, she was it."

"I know. I talked about that with our minister, too. He was very open. He said, sure, there are problem people in the church. But he said for every problem person there are ten absolutely wonderful people, so devoted, so committed, so involved, and self-giving that it makes everything worthwhile. Church people often sense they are a part of a grand scheme, participants in something lasting and eternal. Our minister said he felt highly honored and privileged to lead people in such a high calling. Besides, he said it was his privilege to minister to people in times of celebration like baptisms, confirmations, and weddings, and to minister to them in times of trouble and sorrow, sometimes all in the same day. He said he loved being able to help people like that."

"But doesn't it seem a waste of brains and talent to use it in the ministry?" his father blurted out in desperation, not really thinking.

The son smiled, "Did you hear what you just said, Dad? Did you hear what you just said about Christ and the Bible and the church?" The father blushed with the knowledge of the truth about his real feelings.

The son went on. "Our minister said that Jesus' own family thought he was crazy when he left the family business to go into the public ministry. They once came to get him to take him home. Perhaps they were afraid of what might happen to him. There can be a lot of glamour and prestige and excitement in ministry. There are speeches and crowds, processions and parades. But, said our minister, there are crosses too, sometimes several crosses. That's how it was with Jesus on Palm Sunday — all trumpets and shouts and fanfares, and then there was Good Friday."

"That's what I'm afraid of son, Good Friday. That's what I'm afraid of."

"So am I, Dad. But then, there's always Easter. Isn't there?"

Looking To The Unseen

It once was reported on the news that one of our Mariner space-craft was expected to make a new discovery. Billions of miles away on the borders of our solar system, the Mariner was expected to discover a new planet or star or even a black hole. Astronomers have long speculated about the existence of another planet in our solar system to explain the irregularity of the orbit of planet Uranus. It seems to be lured by the pull of the gravity of another body, the lure of the unseen.

In the winter, while walking his dog, my friend was always amazed at an unusual phenomenon. All the windows and doors of houses were closed. He was walking silently and his dog was noise-less, yet dogs in the houses appeared at windows to bark as he passed by. Apparently, they were responding to the power of some unseen force, the power of high pitched sound, inaudible to us, but very real to dogs.

I read recently of birds who respond to the power of the unseen. First, the birds call to each other and sing to each other in songs audible to human ears. But then, observers tell us, they seem to move into a song pitched above the human capacity to hear. The whole world is full of instances where what is seen or readily heard is only part of the reality. Whether we speak of sound or the spectrum of light or the migratory instincts of birds or life instincts of animals or radio waves or gamma rays or the universe itself, there is evidence of the reality of the unseen.

Indeed, some of our most cherished experiences are not readily visible. Watch a teenage girl spend hours preparing for her big date,

283

or watch a young man groom himself meticulously for his beloved, or observe the touch of a married couple endeared to each other for fifty years, and we witness the power of the unseen.

It was the experience of the power of unseen realities which led Paul to assert, "We look not to the things that are seen, but to the things that are unseen; for the things that are seen are transient, but the things that are unseen are eternal" (2 Corinthians 4:18). If Paul as a Jew had first experienced the seen things of power, recognition, success, a sense of achievement and widespread acclamation, he now was experiencing, as a Christian, the seen things of mockery, shipwreck, persecution, imprisonment, and flogging. If once he seemed on a clear path to success and acclaim, he now seemed to be on a path of hardship and suffering. If once his career was well-plotted and well-admired, now he met the scorn of enemies and the ridicule of friends, and yet Paul asserted he looked to things unseen rather than things seen, for seen things are temporal, but unseen things are eternal.

What then are some of the eternal unseen things to which we should look?

I

For one thing, we would assert with Paul that the mystery of God is greater and more real than the apparent realities of the temporal world.

This is not to say that the physical, material world is unreal and unimportant. It is rather to say that it is not of ultimate importance. This is not to say that what we see is total illusion. It is rather to say that it is transient compared to the abiding reality of the mystery of God.

The late scientist, Jacob Bronowski, wrote that earlier in the twentieth century when scientists had primarily a materialistic, mechanistic view of the universe, they presumed they were about to discover the basic particle of existence and thereby explain the ultimate mystery. But each time they approached, said Bronowski, reality, which seemed within their grasp, lurched away into infinity. Once again, said Bronowski, they were on the edge of mystery.

By mystery, we do not mean something that is unknowable, but something that cannot be possessed. By mystery, we do not mean a reality that can never be experienced; we mean instead, a reality that leads us always into larger and larger spheres of understanding. Mystery is something like the shores of the ocean. We touch the reality but never embrace or encompass it. Like the call of the sea to the adventurer, mystery calls us into the adventure of discovery and learning.

Consequently, when Paul was opened up again to the mystery of God, he could never again embrace his narrow creeds and content himself with his self-righteous dogmatisms. As a result, Paul had a new openness about him. He was no longer rigid and unbending. Released from the role of obnoxious, religious snob, Paul now emitted warmth and humanity and humility that made him an agent of the very mystery that lured him on toward the unseen but real.

Following in Paul's footsteps we too look to the unseen mystery of God that beckons us from our stuffy rooms wherein we enclose ourselves. The mystery of God lures us from pride and arrogance and deflates our presumption and snobbery and makes us more human and approachable. By acknowledging the mystery of God we are released from the pretense of having all the answers to become fellow pilgrims in pursuit of a deeper understanding of life and the purposes of God. Such is the lure of the unseen.

II

By looking to the unseen we are reminded that spiritual reality is greater than material reality.

The prophets of old have asserted this truth time and again. Humankind, they said, looks at external, material things, but God looks on the heart. We are impressed with fortunes and political power, but nations are to God like a drop in the bucket, says Isaiah, and princes are a delusion, says the psalmist.

Jesus asserted the same truth. A man's life does not consist in the abundance of his possessions. What shall it profit a man if he gain the world and lose his soul? We more or less give assent to our Lord's words, but as a matter of fact too often give almost our total energy to the acquisition of this world's goods. We tend to judge a man by his net worth and speak cynically of buying and selling those with less money than ourselves.

If, in the 1960s, the youth of our nation raised seriously the questions of the meaning of life, the youth of the 1980s were most intent on knocking down the big dollars. If from time to time we are led into serious consideration of our spiritual health and destiny, we often beat a hasty retreat to the security of a materialistic self-understanding of life.

In the second century A.D., the writer of First Timothy advised: "As for the rich in this world, charge them not to be haughty, nor to set their hopes on uncertain riches but on God who richly furnishes us with everything to enjoy." He goes on to say that "they are to do good, to be rich in good deeds, liberal and generous, thus laying up for themselves a good foundation for the future, so that they may take hold of the life which is life indeed" (1 Timothy 6:17-19).

Yet, on the practical level, our schools and colleges put most all their emphasis on intellect and hardly any on character. They stress the importance of academic achievement, but seem to care little if young people are sexually immoral or over-indulgent in alcohol. Preparation for success in business or profession is uppermost while the development of an adequate philosophy of life tends to be ignored.

Consider the practical level in marriage and family. Many couples, newly married, expend extraordinary amounts of energy to acquire material success and physical comfort. But at the same time they frequently neglect each other on the spiritual, emotional, personal level. Many a marriage has long since become empty and boring because husbands and wives, in pursuit of the external accoutrements of success, have neglected each other. They have affirmed the physical dimension but denied the spiritual.

Yet, it is precisely in the unseen spiritual depths of the human personality wherein we find the uniqueness and mystery that entice us and lead us toward richer relationships and deeper self-understanding. The materialists are forever killing to dissect, hoping to find the secret of life and love by destroying it, but the people of faith are lured by the unseen mystery of life itself to say with poet William Blake:

He who binds to himself a joy
Does the winged life destroy;
But he who kisses the joy as it flies
Lives in eternity's sunrise.

Or as Jesus put it, "He who saves his life loses it, but be who loses his life for my sake and the gospel's, finds it" (Mark 8:35).

III

Lastly, the lure of the unseen suggests that eternal, spiritual life is more real than temporal, physical life. Most of humanity has for centuries believed in some sort of immortality, some sort of life after death. There has been the deep feeling that there is something more, that temporal physical existence does not explain the deep yearnings within the human heart and mind. In our own time numerous people have written books about out-of-body experiences and the experiences of those who have died clinically and have been brought back to life. George Gallup, the pollster, published a book attesting to the overwhelming numbers of people who have had these experiences, and are convinced that there is indeed life after death.

Nevertheless, many of us live as though this life were it and that we had better squeeze every ounce of pleasure out of it while we can. Consequently, we have many people rushing headlong into hedonism, into narcissism, into the mentality of "I've-got-to-do-my-thing-while-I-have-a-chance."

But, the pursuit of pleasure for pleasure's sake is often disappointing. Philosopher John Stuart Mill once observed that pleasure and happiness are often a by-product of devotion to a higher cause. The melancholy preacher of Ecclesiastes tried every pleasure he could think of and concluded it was vanity.

The great British preacher of the nineteenth century, F. W. Robertson, observed, "There is a strange penalty which God annexes to a life of pleasure: everything appears to the worldly man as a tangled web a maze to which there is no clue." If such a man says there is nothing new under the sun, it is a result, says Robertson, of his determination to live only for excitement and pleasure. "His heart becomes so jaded by excitement that the world contains nothing for him which can awaken fresh or new emotions."

It seems many college young people today live just such a life. Many of their weekends are spent in heavy indulgence in alcohol. A typical party consists in heavy and excessive drinking coupled with the smoking of pot and the use of cocaine.

Sexual looseness and immorality are commonplace. Fueled by affluence and protected by privilege, many young people are rushing frantically toward spiritual death. Empty, bored, without deep inward purpose, they give themselves compulsively to the stimulation of every nerve ending believing therein they have life and love. Grasping desperately the seen, clutching anxiously to every physical pleasure and stimulation, the unseen and deeper realities elude them and life does indeed become vain. A sense of futility haunts them and boredom and depression begin to hold sway.

But not so with Paul. Instead, we have, he says, treasure in earthen vessels. We have within us the hope for life eternal, vouchsafed to us by the gift of God's Spirit and grace. Convinced that life was more than the body and love greater than excited nerve endings, Paul was able to endure even suffering, sometimes unbearable suffering.

Paul said, "We are afflicted in every way, but not crushed; perplexed, but not driven to despair; persecuted, but not forsaken; struck down, but not destroyed ... So we do not lose heart. Though our outer nature is wasting away, our inner nature is being renewed every day" (2 Corinthians 4:8-9, 16).

Likewise with us. When we seek first the kingdom of God and its righteousness, when we arrange properly our priorities, then other things fall into proper perspective. When we place our faith and hope in the unseen God, the seen dimensions of life are infused with new richness and satisfaction. When we give ourselves to the development of character and spiritual depth, then we enter into new realities and receive the contentment of God's Spirit and grace.

Therefore we can say with Paul, "We look not to the things that are seen but to the things that are unseen; for the things that are seen are transient, but the things that are unseen are eternal."

288

No-fault Religion

It happened in a church parking lot, and my friend saw it happen. A lady, backing out of her parking space, rammed my friend's car, causing considerable damage. My friend was able to talk to the woman before she drove away. She was distraught and he was distraught. But, after exchanging the appropriate information, they departed to leave it in the hands of the insurance people.

When it got into the hands of the insurance people, the no-fault insurance clause went into effect. Yes, the woman's insurance company agreed to pay the damages — but only up to a point. My friend had an older car. The repairs would cost more than the car is worth, they told my friend. Therefore, we are only going to pay you a fraction of the repair costs.

My friend went to small claims court to try to collect the full amount of the repair from the insurance company or from the woman, but he lost. He lost, he told me, because of the no-fault provision. Shaking his head in disgust and disbelief, he grumbled about no-fault insurance. "People should be held accountable for their actions," he said. "If they are wrong they should take the blame and pay the consequences."

Another friend of mine went through a painful divorce. However, long before the painful divorce, his wife had begun having an affair with another man. The affair became intense, so much so, that my friend's wife actually moved in with the other man. In time, that cooled, and my friend and his wife reconciled and she moved back home, only soon to be gone again.

289

Eventually, my friend's wife sued him for divorce. In time, she walked off with half the assets including the house and half of his business assets. It was a case of no-fault divorce, even though she was the adulteress, even though she walked out on him, and even though he was willing to reconcile after her affair, she still got half of everything.

My friend described the situation in terms unrepeatable here, but suffice it to say he felt he got a raw deal from the so-called no-fault divorce system. "Shouldn't the person who violates the marriage contract somehow be held accountable?" he asked. He was not that keen on no-fault divorce.

So why then, you might ask, would we discuss a topic like no-fault religion. At first glance, it would appear that a no-fault religion would be one where "anything goes." At the very least it would be a watered-down, *Reader's Digest* condensed, abridged religion of the Ten Suggestions, the Golden Hint, and the Last Brunch. At the most, it would be a religion of relativism where your idea is as right as mine, and your conduct as good as any. It would be the religion typified by the wall plaque which reads:

> *There is so much good in the worst of us,*
> *and so much bad in the best of us,*
> *that it ill behooves us to judge any of us.*

Presumably, in no-fault religion God would abide by the same slogan. No one would be held accountable, no one would be blamed, no one would be guilty, no one would be responsible, and even though everything might be wrong in the world, everyone would be regarded as right.

In this no-fault religion, criticism would be left to unreconstructed curmudgeons and judgment would be dismissed as the disposition of the perpetually dyspeptic. Values would be only matters of taste and principles would be regarded as rationalizations of the way we prefer to behave. In short, no-fault religion would condone anything and condemn nothing, and God would look amusingly like a senile grandfather with the grin of a benign Cheshire cat.

No-fault religion? Is this what Paul had in mind in this text where he says God does not hold our faults against us? Hardly. What then does he have in mind?

I

Strangely and ironically, the no-fault religion Paul has in mind is one that gives us courage to face up to our faults and to accept responsibility for them. He gives us the courage for disclosure. Biblical scholar, R. H. Strachan, in his excellent study of Paul's Second Letter to the Corinthians, says that Paul emphasizes God's attention to humanity and his involvement with humanity. When Paul preached to the Epicurean and Stoic philosophers on the Aereopagus in Athens, just below the Parthenon, they scoffed at the idea of God being intimately involved in humanity — indeed if God even existed. And for some of the Stoics, life might be best lived by withdrawing into a tortoise shell existence so as to not be hurt.

But this was not the God Paul had experienced through Jesus Christ. Quite the contrary. Here was a God who was indeed transcendent, holy, and powerful, but a God who was also intimately involved in humanity, manifesting himself in human flesh, and making himself known personally in time and space in Jesus Christ.

We humans may choose our independence and go our own way. We may choose to ignore God, but God does not choose to ignore us. And God's judgment of us is a manifestation of his incapacity to be morally indifferent and to let evil alone, says Dr. Strachan. "Divine love is also divine goodness. No love can be called good which lacks the capacity for instinctive repulsion in the presence of the mean and the base," says Strachan.[1]

If it does not really matter to God what we do and who we are, we are hardly more than insects and worms. The cynics and skeptics would be right. If God doesn't care, if there is no moral order, if there is no right and wrong, if there are no ultimates of good and beauty and truth, then in the end it is all chaos and futility.

But it is precisely not that kind of religion which Paul suggests in his no-fault religion, rather, it is the religion that encourages us to face up to our faults and wrongs precisely because there *is* meaning in a universe where God is God.

Consequently, one of the first tasks of this kind of religion is disclosure, says the late Daniel Day Williams of Union Theological Seminary. In his excellent book, *The Spirit and the Forms of Love*, Dr. Williams points out how important it is to admit the conflict and disorder in our human living. And, he adds, "Nothing is more common in human relationships, both for individuals and groups, than the belief that *we* are men of good will and all the ill will lies in the *other*."

Dr. Williams continues, "The history of human pretenses, self-deception, and failure to see our hostility and resentment of the other is a constant theme of the world's literature, and its consequences are strewn throughout history in politics, revolution, and all the tragedies of human hatred."[2]

Therefore, one of the painful works of love is that of disclosure — disclosure not so much of somebody else's wrongs, but of our own. And Paul's no-fault religion is one that assures us that "behind a frowning providence, [God] hides a smiling face." We are able to face up to our wrongs, because we have the confidence that underneath there is a right, a truth, a justice, and a love that will prevail.

We can make ourselves vulnerable to the judgment of God believing his mercy will prevail. We can open ourselves to his holy scrutiny, believing that in the end he will not reject us and cast us out, but accept us and include us as his own, as did the father of the prodigal in Jesus' famous story.

No-fault religion does not mean the universe is indifferent and there is no fault anywhere. Instead, it means God cares infinitely about us, and because of that he gives us the courage to confess our faults, so that they will not be held against us. Isn't that good news!

II

If Paul's no-fault religion gives us courage for self-disclosure, it also gives us hope for reconciliation.

Theologian Paul Tillich got his start in Germany as the son of a Lutheran pastor. A brilliant student, he excelled in his studies and soon was advancing to significant teaching posts in Germany. But when Nazism threatened both his life and his career, Tillich, with the help of Reinhold Niebuhr and others, immigrated to this country to teach at Union Theological Seminary in New York City.

Tillich soon attracted national attention and ascended to became one of the world's leading Protestant theologians. Although his personal moral conduct often left much to be desired, he was a very popular lecturer and preacher. Whenever he preached in James Chapel at Union Seminary, the place would be packed not only with seminarians, but also with students and faculty from Columbia and Barnard across the street.

Tillich liked to preach about reconciliation, a reunion with oneself, with one's community and with God, and reconciliation is possible, said Tillich, because of forgiveness and acceptance. "He who is accepted ultimately can also accept himself. Being forgiven and being able to accept oneself are one and the same thing," said Tillich. "No one can accept himself who does not feel that he is accepted by the power of acceptance which is greater than he, greater than his friends and counselors and psychological helpers."[3]

And this forgiveness we receive is unconditional. "There is," says Tillich, "no condition whatsoever in man which would make him worthy of forgiveness. If forgiveness were conditional, conditioned by man, no one could be accepted and no one could accept himself."[4] We always want to bring something, a gift, a good deed, something to show we have earned it. Just as many of us have difficulty accepting gifts graciously from one another, (perhaps because we think there may be strings and obligations attached), so we have difficulty accepting the gift of forgiveness from God. "We want to contribute something," says Tillich, "and if we have learned that we cannot contribute anything positive, then we at least try to contribute something negative: the pain of self-accusation and self-rejection."[5]

Human communities set up severe requirements for belonging, for being included, for being accepted. A friend of mine, a distinguished professional, told me of his application to an exclusive private club. The professional was well established in his career, was a veteran of several highly placed relationships and groups, and was regarded as a leader in his field.

Nevertheless, he was required to submit numerous letters of recommendation from club members as to his worthiness, qualifications, and suitability. He then was subjected to casual, but rather stuffy, scrutiny as the membership committee sniffed him out at a reception for potential new members. He made it, but later quoted Groucho Marx's self-deprecating line that he wasn't sure he wanted to belong to a club that would have him for a member!

Private clubs need to have their membership rules, of course, but belonging to the people of God is quite different. God doesn't sniff out our qualifications, scrutinize our credentials, review our accomplishments, or weigh our merits. He includes us not on the basis of our merits, but on the basis of his grace.

We can be reconciled to God and therefore to one another, not because we are without fault, not because we are without sin, not even because we might in our anxiety, claim to have impeccable credentials. No, not because of all that, but because God was in the world reconciling us to himself, not holding our faults against us.

III

The no-fault religion of which Paul speaks promises the power of re-creation. "If any person is in Christ, he is a new creation, a new being," says Paul (2 Corinthians 5:17).

Very often when people are in a pessimistic mood they will ask. "Do you think it is possible for people to change?" And from time to time when we are weary and perhaps in a pessimistic, cynical mood ourselves, we ask the very same question, "Is it possible for people to change?"

To be sure, over the years we have developed a mild skepticism toward those who say with their mouths they have changed, but whose actions say they have not. If the general public complains about the hypocrites in the churches, ministers could probably complain even more — ministers who have been the targets of vicious and vociferous attacks by their own parishioners who profess to have had their lives changed by Christ.

Nevertheless, despite all that, I believe people do change and sometimes radically. Probably the twelve-step groups experience radical change as much as any in contemporary society. And in some of the more conservative, Evangelical churches, radical conversion and change often are witnessed. In our more staid mainline churches, we are reluctant to allow the fact that God might change someone rather suddenly and dramatically, instead of through a long process. But whether as a seed changing into a flower, or as a self-centered, spoiled, rich kid in a former church of mine, who overnight became generous and kind and thoughtful, because of conversion, I do believe people change. They can become, as Paul said, a new creation, a new being.

And why is that so? It is because in God's no-fault religion our past is not held against us. After all, it was Paul himself, who in his arrogant legalism, persecuted Christians, locking them up and consenting to their murder. "I was the chief of sinners, because I persecuted the Church of God," he confessed in his writings. Yet God did not hold his past against him. Instead, he made him the vibrant, vital, ambassador of grace and renewal throughout the Greco-Roman world.

But it is the power of God that does it, says Paul. And M. Scott Peck, the psychiatrist says the same thing. In his book, *The Road Less Traveled*, which has been on the best-seller list for many years, Dr. Peck says, "God's grace and God's love can help people change and grow." He says, "There is a powerful force external to their consciousness which operates through the agency of loving persons other than their parents, and through additional ways which we do not understand." Then Peck adds, "It is because of grace that it is possible for people to transcend the traumas of loveless parenting and become themselves, loving individuals who have risen far above their parents...."[6] To experience this grace is to know God and to know tranquility and peace, says Peck.

That's it exactly, said Saint Paul nineteen centuries before Peck. Anyone who has experienced the renewing grace of Christ is a new creation, a new being. The old has passed away. All has become new. It was the grace former slave trader, John Newton, experienced when Christ touched him, and he gave up his terrible work, and wrote the familiar hymn, "Amazing Grace."

No-fault religion is not morally ambiguous or ethically indifferent, nor is it without rules and standards and principles. Rather, it is a religion that says that it is precisely because God is principled and involved, forgiving and loving, we can say, God was in Christ, reconciling us to himself, making us new persons, not holding our faults against us. And that, dear friends, is the gospel, the good news.

---

1. R. H. Strachan, Second Corinthians, *Moffatt Bible Commentary* (New York and London: Harper & Brothers, 1948), p. 117.

2. Daniel Day Williams, *The Spirit and the Forms of Love* (New York: Harper & Row, 1968).

3. Paul Tillich, *The New Being* (New York: Charles Scribner's Sons, 1999), p. 12.

4. *Ibid.*, p. 12.

5. *Ibid.*, p. 8.

6. M. Scott Peck, *The Road Less Traveled* (New York: Touchstone Div. of Simon & Schuster, 1978), p. 300.

Proper 7
Pentecost 5
Ordinary Time 12
2 Corinthians 6:1-13

The Acceptable Time

When Paul arrived at the city of Corinth, Greece, the middle of the first century A.D., he knew he had a challenge on his hands. Located on the isthmus between the Gulf of Corinth and the Saronic Gulf, Corinth was a prosperous port city where boats were transported overland from the Aegean to the Adriatic, thereby cutting many dangerous miles off their voyage. The marketplace abounded with goods and traders from many lands. Though never known as a center of learning, traveling philosophers and teachers attempted to gain a hearing and earn a living. But Corinth was a place of commerce, and the speculative life common to Athens was more difficult to find in Corinth.

There was religion at Corinth, however, plenty of it. Years earlier the city had boasted its giant temple to Aphrodite, fertility goddess of the Greco-Roman world. Situated atop the rocky mountain behind the city, the temple enjoyed a commanding view of the harbor and the city. Hundreds of sacred prostitutes were kept busy by the endless flow of traders, businessmen, and worshipers. Indeed, Corinth still had, in Paul's day, a reputation for being a wide open town where one could enjoy most every sin known to man.

Following his usual custom, Paul made his way to the synagogue and there began his message — the message that the long-awaited New Age had arrived. The Messiah has come, he announced to his skeptical audience. Citing the prophecies of the Old Testament, he attempted to show that they had been fulfilled in Jesus of Nazareth.

Noting the expressions of disbelief on the faces of his hearers, Paul acknowledged that he, too, had once been skeptical and unbelieving. In fact, he had even persecuted the followers of Jesus, hoping to put an end to the troublesome heresy. Once he had regarded Jesus from a human point of view, but he regarded him as such no longer. A radical change had occurred in his life. The living Christ had appeared to him and had commissioned him to preach the good news that the New Age had come, that the kingdom of God had arrived. And since that time he had become a new creation; the old had passed away, the new had come.

Paul soon found himself thrown out of the synagogue, but he continued his preaching in the house of Titius Justus where he converted Crispus, ruler of the synagogue. But a year and a half later the Jews brought charges against Paul and he was brought to the tribunal to stand trial before Gallio, proconsul of Achaia.

Most of the people of Corinth did not believe Paul. They were not aware they were listening to a man who was changing history. Engrossed in the activities of the day, engaged in business and commerce, indulging themselves in pleasure, they, like Jerusalem before them, were not aware of the hour of their visitation. Consequently, Paul kept reminding the Corinthian Christians that *now* is the acceptable time to believe the gospel of the New Age.

Paul's message to them was not just one more of the many philosophical or theological ideas floating around at the time. Instead, the God of whom he spoke was the God of the universe who had acted in time, within the realm of history, to change forever the course of history. His message was not just one of many to think about or be entertained with. Instead it was the message of urgency. The acceptable time, the crucial time of salvation had arrived.

I

This is the acceptable time to believe the gospel, because we have the time now. Tomorrow may not be ours.

We know from our own experience how easy it is to procrastinate, how easy it is to put off important decisions, how easy it is to neglect significant opportunities. People involved in business and investments know the importance of timing. How many of us have regretted we did not invest in a certain piece of real estate a few years ago? Or how many of us bought at the top of a bull market and sold at the bottom of a bear market? Hindsight, as we all know, is 20/20 vision.

Think of opportunities missed. Here is a young man just out of college. He passes up a good career opportunity holding out for something just a little bit better. Here is a woman, who in her eighties, confided she passed up the opportunity to marry the man she loved and ended up years later with someone who was really second choice. The time for her opportunity came and went.

In Shakespeare's *Julius Caesar* (Act IV, scene 3), we have the immortal words we know to be true:

> *There is a tide in the affairs of men,*
> *Which, taken at the flood, leads on to fortune;*
> *Omitted, all the voyage of their life*
> *Is bound in shallows and in miseries:*
> *And we must take the current when it serves,*
> *Or lose our ventures.*

Shakespeare was writing very much in the mood of Paul and the prophets. Now is the time. Today is the day of salvation.

If today the Spirit of God is speaking to us, let us open up and hear his voice. If today we feel the winds of God in our beings, let them cleanse us of apathy and refresh us with their power and energy. We *have* today. Tomorrow may not be ours. *This* is the acceptable time.

II

This is the acceptable time, because if we wait for the perfect time, the perfect minister, and the perfect church, we will wait forever.

Paul had a lot of critics, even in the Corinthian church, who challenged his authority as an apostle, who questioned his methods, and who disputed his teachings. The critics notwithstanding, Paul pointed out how he and his associates had not put any obstacles in their way for believing.

299

He had undergone shipwreck, imprisonment, mockery, beatings, hunger, afflictions, hardships, and many sleepless nights to bring them the gospel. The suffering, the deprivations, and self-sacrifice should have convinced them of their sincerity. Unlike many traveling teachers and philosophers of Paul's day who were out to entertain, Paul was out to save.

In addition to his sufferings, Paul said they came among the Corinthians with integrity, kindness, forbearance, truthful speech, the power of God, and genuine love. Unlike many would-be leaders of the day who fleeced their flock whenever they could, Paul and his associates *gave* everything they could.

Paul knew the waywardness and fickleness of the human heart. Many in Corinth were making excuses for themselves, saying Paul's letters were strong but his personal sermons weak, therefore they would not heed them. Looking for a flaw in Paul and his style of approach, they neglected the time of their salvation.

People haven't changed much. In one church, a lady could never really hear her minister because he didn't dress quite according to her standard. In another church, a woman ignored the minister's essential message because he mispronounced a word. In another church, a man would not really listen to the minister because he had not gone to an acceptable seminary. Of course, ministers should dress properly, use good diction, and be well-educated. But the message they bring is more important than that.

Some people say they some day will come to church, some day change their ways, and some day really get involved as soon as the church packages its program in a better way. Other people say they would come to the church more if they really knew what was happening. Do you read the bulletin, they were asked? Everything is printed there. Well sometimes, but we need more information. So in an effort to inform people, the church sent out brochures, letters, and flyers. And what do you think people said then? They said, why are you sending out all those mailings? Doesn't it cost a lot of money?

People continue to make excuses. If the church would do this or not do that, we would come. If the minister would say this and not that, we would respond to the message. If religion would just have this emphasis rather than that one. If the church just had a better music program, or youth program, or education program, or woman's program, or preaching program — if it just had something better, we would respond with commitment in time and money. But many churches could say with Paul, we put no obstacle in any woman's way. True, we are not perfect. We have this treasure in *earthen* vessels, not perfect heavenly ones. Yet, we are bearers of the treasure, agents of the message of salvation, and if you are hearing the word, *now* is the acceptable time of salvation. If you wait for the minister or church or program to be perfect, you will wait forever. After all, if it were a perfect church, could you get in? Today is the day.

III

Lastly Paul says, our mouths are open to you; therefore widen your hearts to us. We have given everything for your sake. Now it is time for you to respond in generosity and love, says Paul.

The ministry was not easy for Paul. Highly competent himself, he saw people of far less ability and stature receive all he had to offer, and use it to their advantage, and give nothing in return. Having denied for himself the things that make for worldly prestige, he often was treated as a nobody by those who owed their very souls to him. Devoted to the high calling of the kingdom of God and its righteousness, he witnessed the ongoing self-indulgence and immorality among those who professed faith but did little about it. In another place he speaks sarcastically of the Corinthians growing rich and powerful and pompous while at the same time snubbing their noses at Paul and his associates who had served them to the point of exhaustion.

Even yet many people do not want their children to enter the ministry because they do not hold the office in respect. People will use the good graces of a minister to win acceptance in a church and then ignore him. Many want to receive all that the church and ministry offer, but will not contribute a son or daughter to full-time Christian work. Speak of sending the brightest son or daughter into the ministry, and the prospects of long hours, low pay, and exploitation of dedication send many parents into convulsions of apoplexy. Others say, that if their son or daughter is going to get involved in church politics, he or she might as well get involved in politics that really matter, where real power and money are involved.

This is the acceptable time to believe and to respond to the grace and generosity of the gospel and the church. And that is not the message of Paul alone, but the message of the church of the ages. Think of the church's approach to us through art and architecture, through literature and philosophy, through theology and service, through helpfulness and compassion, through music. The history of the church and its ministry is one of openness and generosity. We are beneficiaries of an enormous inheritance, and now is the time for us to open up in gratitude and faithfulness, in obedience and service. Now is the opportunity for the new day. This *is* the acceptable time.

Are You A Taker Or A Giver?

It was quite a picture — on the front of the *New York Times* magazine. There were the "Little Big People" as the cover article names them — "little big people" who are precocious, even out of control, with affluent parents who have only themselves to blame. The picture shows a yuppie- dressed eight- or nine-year-old boy, stylish, cool with his own cellular phone in hand. In the center is a modishly over-dressed twelve- or thirteen-year-old girl, stylish, sexy, and eating high priced Chinese take-out food. On the right is a blasé, cool ten-year-old boy, attired in the latest pseudo-athletic styles, holding his tiny personal portable television beside his baseball cap. These are the children who have had it all, says Lucinda Franks in her cover article.

Herself a mother of a nine-year-old, Franks says her generation of parents has tended to give their children everything. They wanted their own children to have the childhood they never had — empowering them with all the rights and honesty of feelings and independence they never had. But then she asks, "Will our independent children thank us for making them the center of the universe, or have we robbed them of a childhood they never can regain?"[1]

Franks describes third graders discussing suing the teacher because of her disciplinary action. She relates the story of a seven-year-old boy who told his female classmate she was "so yucky you must have sex with Nazis." Franks tells about upper west side Manhattan sexually precocious fourth graders who had a dating party to which their parents delivered them, no questions asked, as the little girls bounced in with their halter tops and bicycle shorts.

Members of my generation, says author Franks, have given new meaning to the cult of child worship. We have given them so much with their lives crammed full of gymnastics and tennis and French lessons. Instead of playing creative games of fantasy, today's little child may be playing a substitute game on his Nintendo screen. "He is," says Franks, "a computer whiz, a little philosopher, and a tiny lawyer, bursting with opinions on the president, on the best museums, the best vacation spots, and the college he thinks he will attend."[2] But you will note there is nothing about religious beliefs or spiritual values or the idea of sharing with those in need.

A social psychologist, speaking recently to a church group, spoke of the fantastic materialistic over-indulgence of children today. She related the story of her own child's friend's birthday party. No simple balloons, soda, and ice cream like the old days. Now it's a trip to the favorite restaurant with a group of 25, then on to the movies or beach or game room with presents galore, or even an excursion to Disney World. Each parent then tries to outdo the other in the lavishness of the child's party, so that by the time the child is 25, he will need something like Malcolm Forbes' several-million-dollar birthday bash in Morocco to make him think he had been to a party.

If there has been extraordinary materialistic indulgence, there has also been an indulgence of authority. Some parents, says Franks, are always asking their children if it's "okay," asking their permission. A ten-year-old boy told the author, "Trust me, I know some kids who are guilty of parent abuse." He continues, "They feel like they own their parents and that they could just take all their parents' money out of the their bank account and run away if they wanted." One family therapist commented, "Sometimes I think I'm too old-fashioned to practice in today's world. Half the time the children act like adults and the adults behave like children."[3]

Are we getting the picture? It starts at birth — cared-for, coddled, diapers-changed, sucking at the breast for as much and as long as we want, continuing to suck, to demand, to exploit, to expect, and to insist we get what we want when we want it well into childhood, then into adolescence and into early, even late adulthood. So many of us become professionals at taking and taking and taking; but did we ever, do we ever, really give? Who are you? A giver or a taker?

I

Let's think about our times of poverty. Are we a giver or taker in poverty, in times when we have little?

A friend of mine remembered a little of the Great Depression. But he remembered its effects and the tremendous impact it had on his parents and those of their generation. They recounted story after story of how difficult were the times, of how there was little money for anything. Fortunately, they were living on the farm at that time, and could grow most of their food and butcher their own meat. Nevertheless, difficult as the times were, there always seemed to be enough, for social gatherings and church suppers. There always seemed to be enough, because even in their extreme poverty, people shared.

Our text of today alludes to a similar economic situation in the first century A.D. Because of a famine and other adverse economic circumstances, Jewish Christians in Judea were suffering badly. Perhaps some of their suffering was also due to their earlier experiment in communal living where they sold all their property and pooled all their resources.

When the Lord's Second Coming was delayed, and thus the end of history, their resources ran out. Add to that the drought and famine and we see their plight. Even if they still had their land, they would not be able to grow food. It was for those Judean Jewish Christians a time not unlike our Great Depression.

Consequently, Paul and Titus set out to collect money to help the famished, poverty-stricken Judeans. And guess where they go for help? They go to another area of the world which at that time, as far as Christians were concerned, was also poverty-stricken. They went to Macedonia, home territory of Alexander the Great. They went to the churches in Berea, Thessalonica, and Philippi — to Philippi, named after Alexander's father, Philip; to Philippi, a great retirement center for Roman nobility and military personnel.

But this was also the Philippi where, due to the efforts of Paul, Christianity first started in Europe; Philippi where Christianity was born in the home of Paul's jailor; Philippi, the mustard seed beginning of the faith that was to sprout and bear fruit in cathedrals, churches, universities, hospitals, missionaries, musicians, scholars, literature, and millions upon millions of lives made new. This was Philippi, a city church with a generous heart from the beginning, one of the few churches from which Paul received financial support for his work.

Perhaps for that reason — their reputation for generosity — Paul and Titus ask them again for financial contribution, not for themselves, but for the poor Christians in Judea, hundreds of Roman miles away. And here is the beautiful thing; Paul notes that even though they were "down and out poor" in Philippi, the Philippian Christians even begged for the chance to help out the suffering brothers and sisters in Judea.

The Romans probably were partly responsible for their poverty, because they had stripped the land of much of its timber, minerals, and salt, and may have left many Christians unemployed. Added to that hardship had been some kind of persecution of the Christians. Yet, as Paul says, "in a severe test of affliction, their abundance of joy and their extreme poverty have overflowed in a wealth of liberality on their part" (2 Corinthians 8:2).

It is a strange anomaly, but often the poor are better givers than the rich. Sometimes poverty breeds more generosity than wealth. The poor often are remarkably kind to neighbors in trouble, in part because they know what it is to suffer, and in part perhaps because their sympathies are not deadened by abundance.

The poor tend to out give the rich on the larger scale also, at least as far as churches go. It is a known fact that the typically poorer American denominations give more to their churches per capita than the typically rich, sometimes three or four times as much.

But, back to the Depression generation — whose nature it was to give and give generously even in times of relative poverty during the Great Depression! My friend tells the story of his father who was ushering in church one Sunday when they had a guest preacher. In that time, it was the custom to take a collection to pay the expenses and honorarium of the guest preacher. After the offering plates had passed through the entire congregation his dad and a fellow usher discovered they were completely empty. So his dad pulled out his last five dollars and put it in so the preacher could buy gas to get home.

Like the Philippian Christians of Macedonia long ago, his dad was a giver — even out of his poverty. How about you in your poverty? Are you a taker or giver?

II

Let's move away from poverty and affliction to affluence and abundance. Are we, in times of affluence, takers or givers?

Affluence can do strange things to people. If my friend's parents' generation assumed the reality of poverty and the fear of the Great Depression just around the corner, our children's generation assumes the reality of affluence, and the next economic boom just around the corner. Any recession is seen only as a temporary blip on the ever-ascending graph of higher and higher expectations. In every day in every way they expect to become more prosperous. But, will they become more generous? Will they take more and more or will they give more and more?

It is a strange irony, that the more we make, the less percentage of it we share for worthy causes like the work of the church. J.C. Penney, the founder of the Penney Department Stores, knew something of the temptation of that strange phenomenon.

Mr. Penney, from his earliest years, had practiced tithing — that is, he gave ten percent of his earnings to the church. When his stores grew and grew and he began to make really big money, the question was raised whether he would continue to tithe. After all, ten percent of $25,000 is only $2,500, but ten percent of $2,500,000 is another matter. $250,000 to the church, he asked himself? That's a lot of money and I could do a lot with it. But, so could the Lord, came the answer, and so J.C. Penney, multi-millionaire many times over, continued to tithe, to give ten percent out of his affluence as well as out of his earlier relative poverty.

Charles Wesley, founder of the United Methodist church, used to lament the growing affluence of the members of his denomination. When church members are relatively poor, they tend to depend more on the Lord and upon one another, said Wesley, and they tend to be generous with the church. But when they become well-to-do, they tend to shift their affections from the Lord to money. Fairly well off and financially comfortable, they tend, said Wesley, to forsake the church, to trust in the pleasures and comforts, the clubs and vacations and social associations money can buy.

Perhaps he was reflecting what Jesus observed centuries ago, that it is difficult for many to handle money well, to keep it in perspective, to use it for good, to possess it rather than have it possess you. How hard it is for a rich man to enter heaven, said Jesus. It's easier for a camel to squeeze through that narrow needle-eye gate to the city than for a rich man to enter heaven.

Why? Because in a strange irony, affluence, wealth, and abundance often produce a compulsive greed for more rather than a generous heart for sharing. It's a strange truth that the poor widows of the world often give a greater percentage of their wealth to the work of the church than do the rich widows and the rich business and professional people and celebrities. In your relative affluence and abundance, are you a taker or giver?

We return now to the children of affluence who were the focus of our attention at the beginning. Why to the children? Because the life of taking is typical of the childish life. The childish life is one that starts sucking at the breast and then never stops sucking at the resources of society and the economy without ever giving back.

The childish life is insistent, demanding, highly expectant, self-centered, greedy, ready always to take and take and take with no sense of responsibility to give and give and give. The childish life wants everything and everybody to revolve around its needs and desires and demands. Typically, the childish person is always a taker, never a giver.

The Christians of Corinth, Greece, to whom our text is addressed, had now moved beyond their earlier childish behavior Paul had addressed in his first letter to them. Now, they are, to his great relief, excelling in everything — in faith, in utterance, in knowledge and earnestness, and especially in their love for Paul and Titus and the church.

It seems that unlike the Macedonians, the Corinthians were also excelling financially. So out of their abundance he urges generosity. Give liberally to help your fellow Christians in Judea as God has given liberally to you, he urges them, and they do! Out of their affluence, they move beyond the childishness of taking, taking, taking to the maturity of giving and giving and giving. And when they did, they had no lack.

My friend used to joke with his children that he would know when they had become adults, because they would then take him out to dinner and pick up the check, rather than vice versa. Thankfully, he said, that has happened with all the children. Regularly, they pick up the check. And what a treat it is. It is now their nature to give, to be adult, to be responsible.

Are you a taker or a giver? Perhaps now it is time for you, either out of poverty or affluence, to step up to the challenge, to "pick up the check" for the work of the church in this place and in the world.

---

1. Lucinda Franks, "Little Big People," *New York Times* magazine, 10/10/93.

2. *Ibid.*

3. *Ibid.*

Proper 9
Pentecost 7
Ordinary Time 14
2 Corinthians 12:2-10

The Paradoxical
Power Of Weakness

There are people who speak to us more powerfully out of their weakness than out of their strength. Brian Piccolo was a powerful, professional football player who entertained thousands with his feats of muscular strength and stamina. But cancer attacked, and out of weakness he spoke more powerfully than before. Whenever they show the movie, *Brian's Song*, we think of him and his faith and courage.

Paul experienced a similar fall from glory. He had seen powerful visions of God, had entered into the third heaven to be filled with spiritual ecstasy. Nevertheless, he experienced a severe weakness, a sort of Achilles' heel, a dent in his shining armor that he called his "thorn in the flesh." What it was we do not know. Epilepsy perhaps, or semi-blindness, malaria, or uncontrollable stuttering.

Whatever it was, it embarrassed him and brought humiliation and disgust. It made him appear weak, and he asked the Lord to remove it, but was refused. Paul says he learned that this was God's way of keeping him humble. Furthermore, Paul noted that he discovered that through his handicap, through his weakness, God was made strong. "My grace is all you need; power comes to its full strength in weakness," said the Lord. Consequently Paul said, "I shall therefore prefer to find my joy and pride in the very things that are my weakness; and, then the power of Christ will come and rest upon me" (2 Corinthians 12:9). Strange, the paradoxical power of weakness.

Other writers had been aware of that truth. Pliny said, "We are best when we are weak." Seneca observed that "calamity is the occasion of all virtue." Paul saw further the power of weakness in the church. "Not many of you were powerful ...; God chose what is weak in the world to shame the strong, ... so that no human being might boast in the presence of God" (1 Corinthians 1:26-29).

Paul knew the tragic hero often trusted in his own strength, overestimating his capabilities, thus coming to ruin in his hubris, his pride, because he was not able to see his inadequacies.

I

Thus, one step to new power is to confess our weakness and inadequacy. This is difficult, of course, for as Danish Theologian Soren Kierkegaard has observed: "The worshiper is the weak man; so he must appear to all the others; and this is the humiliating part."[1]

Consider the experience of the musician who attains considerable success in a remote city. When he appears in concerts, people come from miles around. They arrive to pay tribute to his talent and ability. He grows from strength to strength. Even local music critics are dropping their customary reserve to extend considerable praise.

The musician is stimulated and encouraged to go further. He goes to New York to study under a world-famous teacher. Do you see his adjustment? Strong in the remote city, he became weak in New York. Proud in the west, he was humiliated in the east. Provincially acclaimed, he was disregarded nationally.

However, despite the disappointment of his former fans and the indignation of his supporters over his humiliation, the musician was a wise man. He knew that in his humiliation before the great teacher, he was being exalted into great musicianship. By confessing his weaknesses he was gaining strength. Through acknowledgment of his provincialism, he was released more and more into the universalism of great music. Rather than defy the great teacher in envy, he acquiesced to the master in admiration. Aware of the limits of his own knowledge, he drew upon the boundless reserves of his mentor. Paradoxically, in his weakness, he became strong.

Consider the opposite. Would not defiance of the great teacher be based on the pride of a small, provincial reputation? If the musician had been closed to the strength of the master, would he not have been relying on the weakness of his limited past? If he had relied on his own knowledge, would he not in fact, have been closing himself off in ignorance? If he had avoided the humiliation of criticism by the great teacher, would he not have been curtailing his growth by congratulating himself on his mediocrity? Paradoxically, insistence on his own power would have made him weak, whereas confession of his weakness made him stronger and stronger and stronger. The more he acknowledged his faults, the more perfect he became. The more he owned up to his smallness, the bigger he became. Strange power — weakness.

How correct Soren Kierkegaard was when he remarked: "Consider how poor a man would be if he could pass his whole life without ever having lost himself in worship through marveling at God!" He then added profoundly, "One can worship only by becoming oneself weak, thy weakness is essentially worship; woe to the presumptuous man who in his presumptive strength would be audacious enough as a strong man to worship God! The true God," said Kierkegaard, "can be worshiped only in spirit and in truth — but precisely this is the truth, that thou art entirely weak."[2]

Do we not, in our strength, deride the man, who in his weakness, worships God? Do we not heap scorn on the man who needs a crutch, who admits to a flaw in his character, who acknowledges unsureness, a frailty? Are we not impressed with the man who, with complete bravado assures us everything is all right?

A friend of mine lived in Indiana. As you may know, Indiana is tornado prone. My friend lived near an old creek bed that seemed to provide a natural path for tornados. One day during a threatening storm, my friend tried to reassure his little boy who always was terrified by bad weather. With considerable bravado he took his boy to the window, pointed to the creek bed now surrounded with houses, and showed him the storm, reassuring him they were quite safe in the house, that there was nothing to be afraid of, that everything was going to be all right. No sooner had he gotten the words out of his mouth than a tornado swirled up the creek bed, chewing up everything in its path including several houses. In one unforgettable moment the little boy knew the weakness of false bravado.

A healthy self-confidence is indeed an admirable thing, but over-confidence and swaggering bravado are quite another. I am reminded of the mosquito who rode across a bridge on the back of an elephant. The bridge creaked and groaned and swayed. Once across the mosquito said to the elephant, "Boy, we sure strained that bridge didn't we!" The mosquito needed an honest reappraisal of the weight he was carrying.

So do men. Like the father of that terrified child, we need to acknowledge our weakness in the face of great powers and forces and issues that are beyond our control. It will not do to pretend our power adequate for all the powers of life. Like the salty old mariner we need to pray, "Help Lord, for thy sea is so great and my boat is so small."

If we humble ourselves, we are exalted. If we acknowledge our weakness, we will find strength. If we confess our ignorance, we shall be enlightened. If we admit our fear, we shall find courage. If we accede our partiality, we shall be prepared to experience universal truths. And as the musician goes from weakness to strength with his teacher, so shall we go from weakness to strength with God.

II

Another paradox is to see the power of handicap and innocence.

In Edmond Rostand's delightful play, *Cyrano De Bergerac*, we have a memorable example of the paradoxical power of weakness. Cyrano's weakness is not physical, mental, or emotional. It is his appearance. Otherwise handsome and dashing, his "thorn in the flesh" is his nose. It is overwhelmingly large and ugly. Rather than retire to defeated obscurity, Cyrano decides to take the offensive. His weakness thus becomes his strength; his nose attracts attention, enabling him to make cutting insights into the foibles and hypocrisies of polite society. Disadvantaged by physical appearance, he uses his weakness to develop and to exercise his powerful wit to great advantage.

Thus in defense he could say,

I carry my adornments on my soul.
I do not dress up like a popinjay:
But inwardly, I keep my daintiness ...
I go caparisoned in gems unseen,
Trailing white plumes of freedom ...
— Edmond Rostand, *Cyrano De Bergerac* (Act 1)

Cyrano understood the weakness of powerful appearance, its charade, its vanity and hypocrisy. He saw the power of weakness, the honor of humiliation, the honesty of being despised.

Think of Helen Keller, blind and deaf. Yet out of her weakness she became strong — strong enough to speak to the whole world. Think of Beethoven going deaf, yet pounding out the triumphant strains of the *Ninth Symphony.* Call to mind Livingston in Africa, so weak, so few converts, yet so strong in the continuing effect of his work.

Consider the power of a baby's weakness. I have seen grown men, powerful men, crawl around the floor on their knees in front of their babies, entertaining them, getting them to coo and smile. Many of the wives of those same men have been trying to get their husbands on their knees for years — and to no avail! Many competitors — powerful and clever — have been attempting, with all their might, to get these men on their knees, to have them grovel at their feet — but with little result.

But a weak, innocent, charming baby, in all his/her frailty gets the almighty one on his knees. For the baby's benefit he will stand on his head, make funny faces, strike the most undignified poses, and even bark like a dog. Paradoxically, in his/her weakness, the baby has great power. But the wife and the competitors in all their power, really are quite weak.

Of course, some of you are likely to object, saying the baby posed no threat to the father. Therefore, he could let down his guard. His little child appealed to his love of life, rather than to his competitive instincts; stimulated his true humanity, penetrated to his heart of love; and called forth his sense of wonder and mystery and his joy over the miracle of life.

And you are right. By his/her weakness, his little baby conquered more than that baby ever will know.

III

But notice something even more profound. God himself comes to us in weakness. Martin Luther used to marvel every Christmas at the humility of God coming to us as a baby. Imagine the risk, the weakness, the vulnerability. The *Almighty* manifests himself in a manger.

But even more profoundly, we marvel at something even more remarkable — the paradox of the cross. Think of it, the unique Son of God allows himself to be crucified, humiliated on a cross. Where was his power? The crowds were looking for strength, but when he seemed to be weak they turned against him. The disciples were looking for violent revolution, but when he allowed himself to be arrested, they forsook him. Pilate expected him to be shrewd enough to defend himself with clever half-truths, but washed his hands of him when he persisted in the powerlessness of silence.

And yet, despite all that weakness and powerlessness and silence, Christ has spoken powerfully to millions upon millions for centuries and centuries. Paradoxically, the impotent man has become potent; the scorned man has become an object of worship; the ridiculed fool, the recipient of our wisest esteem. Why this paradoxical power of weakness?

The answer is to be found in the very nature of God himself. Very often we are prone to think of God in his magisterial power. We remember the writer of Hebrews speaks of him as "a consuming fire." The prophets warn us of his anger and wrath and his inscrutable judgments. Consequently we are well advised to worship him in reverence and awe. And so we should, for God is truly to be feared. He plays for keeps.

Nevertheless, if God spoke to us only out of his all-powerfulness, his omnipotence, who of us could stand? If the explosion of an atomic bomb is just one little sample of the power of God who controls the energy of all atoms, how could we possibly exist if God addressed us in the majesty of his power?

Rather he comes to us in the power of his weakness, the majesty of his humility, the victory of his suffering. He addresses us in the omnipotence of his love, calling us into relationship with himself, luring us into the openness of weakness rather than the smugness of power. As Kierkegaard sagely observed, "If God were only the Almighty, there would be no reciprocal relationship, inasmuch as for the Almighty the creation is nothing. But for love it is something. Incomprehensible omnipotence of love!"[3]

Sometimes people will say to me, "Why doesn't God, in his great power, just compel every one to believe, to love, and to live in peace?" or "Why doesn't God just wipe us all out and start over again?" And I reply very quickly, "Don't tempt him!" But the point is, God does not deal with us according to his love of power, but according to his power of love. There is judgment there. Let us be sure of that powerful judgment. Beyond that there is mercy, loving forgiveness, powers of reconciliation demonstrated in the weakness of the cross. The unique Son of God, who deserved more than anyone to be exalted, humbled himself, suffered humiliation, so that he might win our love.

Harry Emerson Fosdick tells the story of seventeenth-century humanist scholar, Muretus. A fugitive from France, he became ill in Lombardy. Haggard and ragged he asked the doctors for help. Thinking he was an ignorant beggar, they discussed his case in Latin, the language of the educated. *"Faciamus experimentum in anima vili,"* they said. "Let us try an experiment with this worthless creature." And to their astonishment, Muretus replied in Latin, *"Vilem animan appellas pro qua Christus non dedignatus est moni?"* "Will you call worthless one for whom Christ did not disdain to die?"

Fosdick then adds, "When a king stoops to pick up something, it must have value. When Christ dies for someone, there must be something in him worth dying for.... The cross," says Fosdick, "where man is at his worst [crucifying the Son of God], has, more than any other influence, made man believe in his best."[4] Ironically and paradoxically, the ugly weakness of the crucified Christ becomes the beautiful demonstration of God's love. In his omnipotence of love, God is willing to let his one true Son die, so that by

317

his weakness and suffering he might woo our hearts from selfishness and pride to love of himself. God allows himself to fail in power politics in order to succeed in the politics of the heart. He allows himself to be pierced with spears of hate in order to send forth arrows of love and forgiveness. Overwhelmed and beaten down, derided and spit upon in bitter hostility, his blood and bruises became a balm for our wounds of strife, our gashes of hatred. Oh, the paradoxical power of weakness.

When I survey the wondrous cross
on which the Prince of Glory died;
my richest gain I count but loss,
and pour contempt on all my pride.

Were the whole realm of nature mine,
that were a present far too small;
love so amazing, so divine,
demands my soul, my life, my all.
— "When I Survey The Wondrous Cross" (vv. 1, 4)
by Isaac Watts (1674-1748)

---

1. Soren Kierkegaard, *Christian Discourses* (London: Oxford University Press, 1961), p. 137.

2. *Ibid.*, p. 139.

3. *Ibid.*, p. 132.

4. Harry E. Fosdick, *Riverside Sermons* (New York: Harper, 1958), p. 320.

Proper 10
Pentecost 8
Ordinary Time 15
Ephesians 1:3-14

A Time For Us

In the musical, *West Side Story*, Leonard Bernstein's modern paraphrase of *Romeo and Juliet*, Tony and Maria, the two lovers, confidently sing that there will be "a time for us," a time when their day for true love will arrive, a time when all the pieces will fit together, a time when the fulfillment they dream of will be realized, a time when human life will make sense, a time when the mysteries and questions will be resolved, a time when they will have the confidence they have not lived and loved in vain.

Many of us loved the musical, because like *Romeo and Juliet*, it spoke to some of our deepest human longings and needs. We labor and toil, make love and fight, strive and endure, because we think some day it will all come together like the finale of some grand symphony. Someday, we think the cold gray of January will melt into a perpetual June, busting out all over with flowers of success and blossoms of happiness. Somewhere, someday, there will be a time for us, a time when our career will come to its zenith, a time when the children will fulfill our expectations and hopes for them, a time when financial security will arrive, and we will not have to worry so much about the end of the month, or the end of the year. How we long for that time.

And yet, how quickly time passes us by, even the young sense it. Middle school students wonder where the time goes. Older people who used to have time on their hands, now wonder if they have any time at all. One businessman remarked that weeks seem like days. Time seems to pass so quickly.

The Bible is full of the awareness of time. The writer of Ecclesiastes says, God "has made everything beautiful in its time," and that there is a right time for everything (Ecclesiastes 3). The prophets speak of the appointed time of the Lord, the time for judgment and destruction, or the time for mercy and salvation. John the Baptist began his preaching with an urgent sense of time, saying "the time is fulfilled, and the kingdom of God is at hand; repent and believe the gospel" (Mark 1:15). Jesus and Paul speak repeatedly about the importance of time, as do most writers of the New Testament.

It will not do to say all time is alike, that one age is exactly the same as another, or that one life has exactly the same timing as another. There is a tide in the affairs of men, says Shakespeare, which needs to be taken at the flood, else it may not return again for our benefit. There are the significant days, the opportune moments, of which we need to make the most, when timing is everything. There can be a time for us.

And yet, we need to see the time from the perspective of biblical writers. The writer of Psalm 90 urges us to count our days, to get a heart of wisdom. Paul, in the Ephesian letter, suggests we redeem the time, that we make the most of the time, because the days are evil.

We wonder, will there be a time for us? How shall we make the most of the time? How shall we understand time?

I

There is first the adolescent sense of time.

It is characteristic of children and youth to be oblivious to time. To a young child, a day can be an eternity, especially if it is the day before Christmas. To a preschooler, a week is very long and a year unimaginable. Preschoolers live from one moment to the next, from one cookie to the next; from one television program, one hug and nighttime prayer by daddy, or one trip to the ice cream store to the next. In their innocence, they know night and day, and summer and winter, but they have little sense of the transitory state of time.

Adolescence frequently is an extension of the child's nonchalance about time. Thankfully youth often are optimistic, even if superficially and blithely so. They have a way of expecting their time to come. Many believe theirs will be a better world, that things will be improved when they have their day, and they tend to live in the present as if there were plenty of time for what they want to do. Many think they are immortal, as you can tell from the way they ride their bikes or drive their cars. For most youth, the future is open, and the present is to be enjoyed.

Institutions and nations also can have an adolescent sense of time. Churches often have to grow up. Many young churches go through the naiveté and willful childishness of children. Cities often go through stages of unbounded optimism, mature reflection, and old age despair. Our nation seems now to have advanced beyond the boundless optimism of its youth, to the pensiveness and self-doubt of middle-age.

The western world itself has been obsessed with a belief in inevitable progress. After accepting the theory of biological evolution, whose higher life develops out of lower, we adopted a theory of social evolution, wherein higher social life evolved out of lower. There was a naive belief in the gradual, but certain, ascent, not descent, but ascent, of the human race. Every day in every way, things were getting better and better.

"Will there be a time for us?" we ask. "Of course," the world responded. "There will be a time for everybody," we said in the adolescent enthusiasm of the enlightenment and the youthful optimism of the late nineteenth century. Our time is coming.

II

But the adolescent sense of time is only part of the story. There is also the middle-age sense of time.

It is difficult to define middle-age chronologically. I find increasingly that many people push the definition of middle-age to a higher and higher age bracket. (It's a floating definition, much like the definition of young.) If the adolescent sense of time can extend into the thirties, the middle-age sense of time can at least come down to pervade the forties.

There are many signs of middle-age. For example, the adolescent has no children, but has all the advice on how to raise them.

321

The middle-aged person may have six children and very little advice. The adolescent presumes to have most of the answers to life, whereas the middle-aged person is more and more perplexed with the tough questions, and has fewer and fewer real answers. The adolescent goes full steam ahead in profession or career, asking few questions as to why or where. The middle-ager looks longer now at days past and days to come, lingers over questions of meaning and destiny, and wonders if his time will ever come.

It is difficult to define middle-age, but we can say it is a time when boundless optimism gives way to careful reflection. It is a time where carefree exuberance bows to cautious planning. Middle-age knows the truth of the old saying, "Life is uncertain, eat dessert first!" Middle-age is the realization that we are not immortal, that our presumed security is not so secure after all.

Consequently, the middle-age mentality often succumbs to the temptations mentioned in Ephesians. Aware that time is passing us by, we begin to use time frantically, attempting to create significant moments. Conscious that our time has not come, we often resort to hedonism. Newly conscious of the guilt of the past and our fear of continued failure, we resort to age-old attempts at ecstasy. In facing the transitory state of life, we are tempted to grasp things and persons, pleasures and pastimes, to give us security and significance.

Like the prophet Jeremiah we lament, "The harvest now is over, the summer days are gone, and yet no power cometh to help us" (Jeremiah 8:20). The children are born and nearly grown, the career is well launched and plateaued, and yet no power seems to have come to help us, to give us a sense of significance and fulfillment. Will time pass us by?

Institutions and nations face middle-age also. Our great land struggles now with its identity corporately, as we do individually. As philosopher William Barrett says in his book, *Time Of Need*, "Contrary to the confidence in our powers of technology and information, the prevailing image of man we find in modern art is one of impotence, uncertainty and self-doubt."[1] Barrett goes on to comment about the middle-age of our nation, saying, "the discontent that now creeps through modern culture is the self-doubt of a civilization that has lost faith in its own value. This doubt," says Barrett, "has even shaken our confidence in progress which was once an unquestionable article of faith."[2]

The days can be evil. Some of us find personal fulfillment in history; some of us do not. Some of us are happily married; some of us are not. Some of us are enjoying the sweet fruits of success; some of us are not. Some of us are fulfilling our potential, actualizing the full extent of our powers; some of us are not. Some of us can look back on our lives with satisfaction and contentment; some of us cannot. Some of us are proud of our children; some are not. Some of us have fulfilled our dreams and ideals; some have not.

Paul urges us not to despair the times, but to make the most of them. Use every opportunity you have, but do not expect you will climb every mountain and at last find your dream. Some enchanted evening you may see a stranger across a crowded room, and make her your own; but then again, you may not.

Paul says that the days can be evil. Do not expect everything to go well just because you think yourself good or righteous. Trouble comes to the just and the unjust. Evil attacks the righteous and unrighteous. If through providence and chance your time really comes, thank God and be glad. But if not, know that the times of God go beyond history, and that his destiny is to bring us all into unity with himself; which will be the ultimate time beyond time.

III

This brings us to the time of old age.

I am reminded of the older couple who lived close to a church whose bells rang out the hour of the day. At two in the morning the bells went crazy. Instead of ringing twice to denote 2 a.m., they kept ringing up to 100 times. The man nudged his wife in bed and said, "We'd better get up, dear. It's later than it's ever been before!" Probably many older people feel that way.

The time of old age is well known in the Bible. Job says, "Man born of woman lives but a few days." Every older person agrees with James who observes, "What is your life? For you are a mist that appears for a little time and then vanishes" (James 4:14). The writer of Psalm 90 says we are like a watch in the night. We are

323

awakened for our turn to stand guard, and then we are gone, forgotten. Or we are like the grass, which in the morning is fresh and vigorous, but in the evening, after the heat of the day, withers and dies.

Our life is seventy years, or eighty at the most, says the psalmist. Yet, their pride is but toil and disappointment, for it is soon gone, and we pass away. Every older person, lonely at home or bored at a nursing home, knows something about this melancholy mood, this transitory state of life. With the writer of Ecclesiastes, they wonder if life is not ashes to ashes, dust to dust. In the weariness and loss of strength and independence, in the aches and pains of old age, it is easy to wonder if it all was for naught. The seventy, eighty, or ninety years that are unimaginable to the adolescent or distant to the mature woman, are but as nothing to those who have reached them, the years flying away as a bird we can neither capture nor follow.

Will there be a time for us? Yes, but not simply or naively or easily. For Psalm 90 teaches we are subject to tragedy. The psalm teaches us what all great tragedies teach — that the best and the brightest, the most noble and heroic, the most beautiful and powerful and brilliant are subject to judgment and death. "The tragedies," said theologian Paul Tillich, "reveal the tragic situation before the divine. Even the tragic hero who becomes great and proud and tries to touch the Divine sphere, comes to despair and destruction."[3]

Thus the tragic heroes in our day rise and fall. Jack Kennedy, a symbol of a new jet-setting nobility, who presumably knew how to handle power, was assassinated. Martin Luther King, Jr., the great civil rights reformer, was gunned down by a sniper's bullet. Rock stars literally are shooting stars, which flash across the headlines, and then burn out in their own atmosphere of drugs, sex, and desperate narcissism. Celebrities rise and fall, and we rise and fall with them, searching for that special time for us, at least vicariously. Even *West Side Story*'s youthful Tony and Maria do not survive to fulfill their dreamed-of time, just as Romeo and Juliet did not survive. Their time did not come as they hoped.

So the psalmist urges us to count our days to get a heart of wisdom. "The wise heart," said Paul Tillich, "is the heart which

324

does not try to hide this from itself, which does not try to escape into a false security or a false cynicism. The wise heart is the heart which can stand this knowledge courageously, with dignity, humility, and fortitude."[4]

The time of old age should teach us that although we may be close to dust, we are more than dust. Though like the animals we go down into the earth, we know there is something within that is more than earth. The entire Bible speaks of hope superseding tragedy. Because of God's unending love, the cycle of dust to dust is broken. Because of the grace of Christ, the great numbers of us who really never find our place in the sun, who suffer disease and poverty, oppression and death, and who really never come into their own time, will be given their time beyond time.

There is a time for us. There is a time for you. For some, this year will be a fulfilling, satisfying time. Some will achieve and enjoy success and happiness. But for some, this may not be that time. The real time is beyond time, in hope, in resurrection, in the eternal life of God, which is a gift and not an achievement. We are destined, says Paul in Ephesians, to be full of love and eventually to be united with God in the ecstasy and joy, which are beyond time.

As Robert Browning put it in his famous poem, *Rabbi Ben Ezra*:

> *Grow old along with me!*
> *The best is yet to be,*
> *The last of life, for which the first was made;*
> *Our times are in His hand*
> *Who saith, "A whole I planned,*
> *Youth shows but half; trust God: see all, nor be afraid."*

Let us live then, young or old, with the confidence that whatever happens, God is for us, that nothing can separate us from his love for us, that our times are in his hands, that we are his.

1. William Barrett, *Time of Need* (New York: Harper & Row, 1972), p. 6.

2. *Ibid.*, p. 364.

3. Paul Tillich, *The Shaking of the Foundations* (UK: Pelican, 1964), p. 72.

4. *Ibid.*, p. 73.

Modeling A Necessary Future

It was the custom in my friend's church for many years to have a week of family camp in the summer. Families by the dozens packed their cars, vans, and SUVs and made their way to the camp for a week of fun, exercise, and inspiration.

There were matins, a hearty camp breakfast, stimulating lectures and discussions, and lots of sports, crafts, and recreational activities. In the evening, appetites were ravenous and vespers were inspirational as they ascended the hill singing, "We Are Climbing Jacob's Ladder." Evening programs, talent shows, and communion services were engaging. In the afternoons, the brave of heart even went swimming in the pond which, because of its color, was aptly named "Prune Dip." My friend never went!

And yes, as I said, there was matins, which means morning prayers and devotions, at the camp flagpole. It was at matins one morning that my friend saw it, and when he saw it, it sort of jolted him awake. One of the tall, lanky teenagers was wearing a black T-shirt with bold, white letters which said, "No One Gets Out Of Here Alive!"

At first, my friend thought it was a reference to the quality of the camp food, which left much to be desired, but then he realized he was making a profound comment about our human condition. No one knows more than ministers the truth of the statement, "No One Gets Out Of Here Alive." Our succession of funerals and burials at cemeteries remind us regularly and powerfully of our common mortality.

If that T-shirt was a solemn reminder, so was another experience common to most of us. You may remember it as I do, so very vividly. It was the experience of the first photographs of Mother Earth taken from the moon.

There we were, all five or six billion of us sharing this unique, magnificent, emerald blue spaceship in the solar system. All of us — white and black, red and yellow, rich and poor, educated and uneducated, male and female — all of us sharing the unique planet — unique perhaps in the universe. And more than ever before, we realized our common humanity and that we are all in this together.

This is the vision of our text written over 1,900 years ago — a vision of a common humanity, united on a common planet for peace, productivity, and hope. The writer of the text calls upon the church to be the model of a necessary future, because we are all in this together, and not one of us gets out of here without a stop at the cemetery.

I

In modeling a necessary future, the church needs to continue to do as Christ did — to break down the walls of hostility between people.

In Paul's day, the walls of hostility were very real between Jew and Gentile. In the eyes of many Jews in this time, there were two main divisions of humanity on Mother Earth — Jews and Gentiles, circumcised and uncircumcised, included and excluded, the chosen ones and the ones not chosen, insiders and outsiders.

Biblical scholar, William Barclay, says that many Jews of that time had contempt for Gentiles, believing God had created them to be fuel for the fires of hell. Orthodox Jews of the time often thanked God they were not created a woman or a Gentile. It was not lawful for a Jew to help a Gentile in childbirth because that would imply bringing another contemptible Gentile into the world. If a Jewish young person married a Gentile and converted, the Jewish family held a funeral service for their child as if he or she were dead.

It was only natural then, that this exclusivism should have been expressed in the Jewish temple in Jerusalem. Jewish historian, Josephus, says an inscription on the temple wall forbade any foreigner to go in under pain of death. Indeed, in 1871, archeologists found one of those stones with the inscription which read: "Let no one of any other nation come within the fence and barrier around the holy place. Whosoever will be taken doing so will himself be responsible for his death which will ensue."

But others were exclusive, too. Remember that there were Roman citizens and then all the others. The Greeks classified almost everyone but themselves as barbarians. The great philosopher, Plato, once said that the barbarians, the non-Greeks, are our enemies by nature, and in our time we have had iron curtains, bamboo curtains, Berlin walls, trade and tariff barriers, and barriers of race, caste, class, and religion.

But Christ came to put an end to these dividing walls and barriers of hostility and exclusivism. Rather than attempting to assert himself as a davidic messiah to build an exclusivistic, nationalistic kingdom based on heredity and narrow tradition, Jesus surrendered himself to build a universal kingdom where all are included, for he realized more than anyone, we are all in this together. And it is working. The church is universal and includes people from almost every nation, culture, class, race, and language group.

Nevertheless, Christians themselves often have continued the hostility. During the Middle Ages, the Christian treatment of Jews was often horrendous and despicable. In one of the Christian crusades to reclaim the holy land from the Infidels (by which they meant the Muslims), Christian crusaders slaughtered a whole village of Jews just because they felt like it.

The inquisition of the Roman Catholic church drove Jews and Muslims out of Spain where they had lived peaceably for centuries. Protestant and Roman Catholic hostilities of history are well known as are Protestant against Protestant intolerances.

In his book, *The Cross of Peace*, Sir Philip Gibbs says that "Modern progress has made the world a neighborhood: God has given us the task of making it a brotherhood and sisterhood."[1] Indeed he has, and we can begin by breaking down the walls of hostility between people, because we are all in this together.

II

In modeling a necessary future, we must not only work to break down the walls of hostility, we must work to build a new edifice of inclusiveness.

As we have noted, the ancient Jewish temple prohibited non-Jews, upon penalty of death, from entering the holy place surrounded by imposing stones. Non-Mormons are not allowed in the Mormon temple, and Protestant Christians technically are not allowed to receive the Roman Catholic Eucharist. Certain Protestant churches exclude other Protestants from their communion tables.

But the writer of Ephesians, like the writer of 1 Peter, envisions quite a different kind of holy temple. This temple is to be built not of stones, but of spirit-filled people who are themselves the living stones of an ever-expanding temple of God. Built on the prophets and apostles with Jesus Christ as the chief cornerstone, this temple is to be as expansive and inclusive as the very Spirit of God.

However, most of us wonder if God is as interested in people quite different from us as he is in us. Theologian Theodore Wedel said it was quite an experience for white, western Christians to see Fiji Island Christians with strange coiffures, black Pygmy Basutoland Christians, and other peoples so unlike our race or class, giving their heartfelt allegiance to the same Christ. I remember seeing a book titled, *God Is An Englishman*, and I loved the title, because it symbolized the way we tend to make God in our image.

I am reminded of a story told by Professor Fred Craddock, New Testament scholar and a professor of preaching. He was beginning a new semester and on the first day of class an unusual student entered. Not your typical seminary student, this older man had mustache and beard and ponytail. He wore black leather pants, a denim shirt, a black leather vest, a heavy chain necklace, and large metal bracelets. "To top it off," said Dr. Craddock, "the man was covered with tattoos."

Dr. Craddock confessed that he wondered if there must not be some mistake. This was a class for people preparing for the ministry. He wondered how this man could be a Christian, let alone a candidate for the ministry. And according to Dr. Craddock, he turned out to be one of the kindest, gentlest, most thoughtful and considerate men he had every known. He was reminded again of how inclusive Christ's holy temple of spiritual people can and should be.

So rather than putting up barriers of caste, class, race, and religion, we need to expand this living, holy temple of God to be tolerant and inclusive. This is not to say we must all become an amalgamated, conformist glob of saccharin sameness. Not that. God celebrates variety even more than we do.

It does mean, however, that we will practice tolerance and thoughtfulness. It does mean we will pray for diplomats and statesmen and peacemakers. It does mean we will work for peace, understanding, and harmony among the world religions. And as Christians, it means we will celebrate our love for Christ who calls us to break down the walls of hostility and build an inclusive spiritual temple of peace.

As the church, we are called to model this necessary future because, as we have seen from the moon, all five or six billion of us on Mother Earth are in this together.

---

1. Sir Philip Gibbs, *The Cross of Peace* (Garden City, New York: Doubleday, Doran & Company, 1935).

331

Sermons On The Second Readings

For Sundays
After Pentecost
(Middle Third)

Jesus Is The Recipe For Eternal Life

Richard Gribble, CSC

A Christian's daily walk with the Lord, that is living the great responsibility that comes with the privilege of bearing Jesus' name, requires much inspiration. We simply cannot walk our common vocation to holiness alone. As the expression states, "No man is an island, no man stands alone." While the famous Footprints in the Sand *poem clearly tells us that Jesus walks with us, we need the inspiration of human contacts as well. Ministry in the church provides me much inspiration, as I observe how good people struggle to find and live God's will in their lives. This book is appropriately dedicated to my dear friend, Sister Tania, whose daily close walk with the Lord always inspires me to follow Christ more closely and faithfully in a world with lights many times contrary to those of the Christian message.*

Preface

In the Roman Catholic liturgical tradition, the Pentecost season is referred to as "ordinary time," meaning this is a period when the church is not preparing for, or celebrating, the Incarnation or the Resurrection. However, we all know that there is nothing ordinary about the Word of God. As the Letter to the Hebrews tells us, "Indeed, the Word of God is living and active, sharper than any two-edged sword, piercing until it divides soul from spirit, joints from marrow; it is able to judge the thoughts and intentions of the heart" (4:12). Yes, the Word of God provides great comfort to those in pain, of mind, body, or spirit, and encouragement for those who are distressed, but it always provides challenges to those open to its powerful message. God's Word can flay us open like a sword, making us vulnerable, but it is only through such a process that we can ever move forward and make progress in the spiritual life. As athletes say, "No pain, no gain." Such it is with our relationship with God. We will never grow stronger and be better able to live the Christian life if we allow God's Word to pass in one ear and out the other.

The Second Readings during this liturgical season, found in the Revised Common Lectionary, come from Ephesians, James, and Hebrews. They provide many challenges as well as much comfort for our daily walk with the Lord. The Letter to the Ephesians, one of the three so-called pseudo-Pauline letters (along with Colossians and 2 Thessalonians), provides much comfort to its readers. While the authorship of this famous book of scripture is unclear (many scholars suggesting Paul is not the author), its message is very vivid and heartening. We can take comfort in the fact that while we have many responsibilities in our lives, we are not alone. We recall the words at the end of the famous poem, *Footprints in the Sand*: "During your times of trial and suffering, when

335

you see only one set of footprints in the sand it was then that I [Jesus] carried you." Similarly, Ephesians tells us that God will complement our honest efforts and bring them to fruition. We also learn that if we follow Jesus' lead, if we walk in his footsteps, then we will arrive home safely. Jesus will protect us with his word, faith, and presence. If we are wise and make the most of God's gifts, then most assuredly God's promise of eternal life will be ours.

The beauty and encouragement of Ephesians is complemented by the challenge of the Letter of James. Most probably written by the Apostle James, the leader of the Jerusalem church, the letter provides various manifestations on the general theme of being "doers of the word." Saint Paul says, "We walk by faith not by sight" (2 Corinthians 5:7). While we firmly believe this, James tells us that the true Christian, in response to God who first loved us, must live an active life. To talk the talk is insufficient; we must also walk the walk. How must we manifest a life as "doers of the word"? James gives several very concrete ways. First, he says we must daily live the Word of God; it must be applied to our daily lives, both the routine and mundane occurrences and those significant and highlighted events. We must learn to accept others, so we can become better, as individuals and community, when we believe and practice the expression, "strength through diversity." James teaches us to always be mindful of what we say; the power of the tongue is significant and must be used well and wisely. He concludes his message, telling his readers of the importance of prayer; it must become our way of life.

The Pentecost season concludes with a lesson from the Letter to the Hebrews. Clearly not Pauline in origin, the text nonetheless is very significant for Christians today, especially in challenging us to practice the priesthood of the faithful. In order to realize our efficacy as Christ's ministers, we must believe and practice the reality that Jesus is in solidarity with us. He is the source of our lives; we must stay close to him as he remains close to us. As Jesus is one with us, so must we seek to be one with our sisters and brothers.

The sermons in this volume reflect my own journey of faith and my belief that Jesus Christ has called all who bear his name to ply their efforts well and wisely in the construction of his kingdom in our world. Once we are confident of God's total and unrelenting love for us, we are called to be in solidarity with Christ and his people by being active participants in the Christian life. Christ's victories in the world are claimed not by those who watch on the sidelines, but rather by those who actively stand on the battlefield of life and choose to work for the common good by their ministry to those who have less. It is my hope and prayer that those who read these sermons will be inspired to more actively live their common Christian vocation to holiness and through such action help make the light of Christ shine more brightly in a world of confusion and contradiction. It is up to us; may we be worthy of our call and faithful to our baptism.

Richard Gribble, CSC

Let God Do The Rest

Once there was a boy who loved to look at the birds of the air, the flowers of the field, and the clear blue sky. These delighted him and he spent the majority of his time outside wandering about the countryside. One day he saw a crowd of people gathered and as he drew closer he saw that they were listening to a man. He was not sure what it was, but there was something magnetic about this man that drew the boy closer. He sat down on the grass and listened to what the man said. Never in his life had he heard someone speak so clearly from the heart.

From that time forward the boy kept an eye out for the man. Whenever he was in the area he hurried to listen to him speak. Over time the boy grew to love the man more and more. He truly envied the man's followers, his disciples. They traveled wherever he went. He could not wait to grow up so that he could follow the man as well. The boy received much from the man, especially the love and compassion present in his eyes and his heart-felt message, and he longed to be able to give the man something in return, but he had nothing to give.

One day the boy met the man's mother. She had come to give her son a message. The boy followed the woman to her home and begged her to tell him more about her son. She told him that shortly after her son was born three astrologers from the East had visited and presented him with gifts of gold, frankincense, and myrrh. She also spoke of one who gave her son a lamb. The boy recalled that he had heard that a woman in a local village had poured sweet smelling perfume over the man's feet and dried them with her hair. How he wished he had some great gift for the man.

Often the boy would go to the mother's home. He felt at home there as she spoke about her son to him. One day as he left her house to see if the man was in the area, she gave him a few loaves of bread she had just taken out of the oven. She thought he would need them for his journey home. As he went in search for the man he stopped by the local lake and caught a couple of fish. He then continued on his way with the loaves and two fish he had caught. Finally, he caught sight of the people who were listening to the man.

The man had much to say that day and the people listened and were fascinated. As it grew late the boy sensed that the people listening were hungry. He was happy that he had his bread and fish. He wanted to share with an old man to his side and a woman who was carrying her baby. What about all the others, he thought? There were so many of them and surely they did not anticipate being in such a deserted place where there was no place to buy food. It was a long way to the closest village. The boy felt badly, but he was only a youth; what could he do?

Then one of the man's disciples came to him saying that the man had asked for the boy's bread and fish. He was glad to give them, but felt badly for the tired old man and the woman with her child. How he wished he had more to give. Then he saw the man take the loaves and fish. He blessed them and gave thanks and then started to distribute them to all listening to him. He went through the crowd giving everyone some bread and fish. He came to the tired old man and then to the woman carrying her baby; there was enough for them. Finally, he stopped in front of the boy and gave him some bread and fish. The boy's heart stopped; never had he been so close to the man. He looked into the man's eyes and then realized that he did not need to give a lot. It really was quite simple. All he had to do was give the little bit he had and the man would do the rest.[1]

This story, patterned obviously after the synoptic accounts of Jesus' multiplication of the loaves and fish (Mark 8:1-10; Matthew 15:32-39), speaks of the Christian vocation to respond to the Lord.

Some of God's children have lots to give — material things, time, and spiritual advice — but others, like the boy, have what seems to be little or nothing to give. But we must realize, as the boy learned, whatever we have, if given fully and with proper attitude, is sufficient. God will supply the rest.

When one thinks about supplying something toward a goal, the concept of contract is applicable. We are very familiar with contracts for all of us participate in many varied types throughout our lives. We also know how contracts are supposed to work. Two parties agree to provide something, possibly services, money, time, material goods, toward a common goal. Most people have a contract associated with their home — a mortgage or lease agreement. We agree to pay a certain amount of money each month and in return the owner or loan broker agrees to supply a home which meets the standards agreed upon when the contract was signed. Many costly items, such as a car, necessitate a contract. Besides contracts with material things, the more important contracts of our lives are personal. When we agree to take a family member or friend to the doctor or assist someone in need we have made an important contract. We volunteer our time and some effort to assist others. While one party seems to be the giver and the other the receiver, both give and receive in hidden ways of friendship and love. A more fundamental human contract is marriage. Here the give and take is more obvious. Even students and teachers have contracts. If both sides work toward the common goal of education and enlightenment, all win; if either side fails to perform, the chain is broken and education is stunted.

Contracts are important, but often those that are most fundamental are the ones we think least about in our daily routine. People are very attentive to contracts for material things because failure to carry through results in harsh consequences. If we fail to pay our rent or the car payment we may be evicted or have the vehicle repossessed. Since the ramifications of our failure in such contracts is great, our attention to detail is greater. Unfortunately, however, our inattention seems greatest when, on the surface at least, there is nothing lost if we do not hold up our end of the contract. If we forget our arrangement to assist our neighbor, or fail to uphold our end of the marriage commitment we do not immediately see any consequences. Thus, we are at times are lulled into a state of complacency. We think we can "get away with" inattention or inaction. The results of our failures will one day return, however, and the results could be devastating.

One of the contracts that receives the "back-burner" treatment is our relationship with God. This contract is the same basic covenant that Yahweh initiated with Abraham and then more generally the Jews collectively as described in the Hebrew Scriptures. In essence the contract said that God would provide all that was needed if the people would be faithful and worship God and God alone. The failures of the Hebrews in their contract with God were numerous and profound, leading eventually to destruction of the northern kingdom of Israel and the infamous Babylonian exile in the southern kingdom of Judah. Like the Jews, we are many times unfaithful. Our half of the agreement is crystal clear. Jesus says we are to love God and love others as we do ourselves. The "Golden Rule" gives the basic format, the foundation for the contract, but in Matthew 25 we have some specifics of how we love God by loving one another. Our half of the contract requires us to feed the hungry, clothe the naked, and visit the sick and imprisoned. Rather than the proscriptions of the decalogue, Jesus presents a positive message of what is necessary to uphold our end of the contract.

God is not only eternally faithful to his end of the bargain, providing all that we need, but even promises divine gifts for those who hold fast to their end of the contract. The Pauline author reminds us, "If we have died with him, we will also live with him; if we endure, we will also reign with him; ... if we are faithless, he remains faithful — for he cannot deny himself" (2 Timothy 2:11b-12a, 13). The special reward that is God's promise is described by Saint Paul: "What no eye has seen, nor ear heard, nor the human heart conceived what God has prepared for those who love him" (1 Corinthians 2:9).

Saint Paul well understood the need to work toward a common goal and thus keep his contract with God. Jesus called Paul along the road to Damascus and commissioned him to be the apostle to the Gentiles. Paul gave what he had, possibly feeling inadequate

342

like the boy in the story, but trusting that God would do the rest. Paul did heroic things, traveling the Mediterranean world on three dangerous and arduous missionary journeys, but he realized that he was only the vehicle of God. He could only do so much, but he had total confidence that God would do the rest. Thus, in his travels he visited the great city of Ephesus, founded a fledgling Christian community, and instructed the people on giving what they had, and being faithful to their contract with God.

Today's Second Reading is a beautiful and powerful example of Paul's ability to instruct through prayer. The Pauline author tells the Ephesians through this prayer of their need for thanksgiving. He falls on his knees and prays that the Christian community will be strengthened through the power of the Spirit. Paul realizes that the people can only do so much; God will need to do the rest. He has total confidence that Christ also will bring strength to the community if the people are rooted in love. The apostle is suggesting that the people's relationship with God is based not on what they have but only on who they are and what they do. They must trust God to do the rest.

Paul next prays that the people will understand that the love of Christ surpasses all knowledge. He realizes that human nature often leads us to feel we need to control every situation and to provide what is necessary to complete tasks or remedy problematic situations. However, if we will allow God to do God's part, we will be filled with all the riches and understanding that the conditions warrant or require. If we do as the author of Proverbs suggests: "Trust in the Lord with all your heart, and do not rely on your own insight" (Proverbs 3:5), then we will have all that we need.

Paul summarizes his prayer with a doxology at the end. He reminds the Ephesians that God, working through us, will allow us "to accomplish abundantly far more than all we can ask or imagine." We must allow God to be God and do what only God can do. If we do our share, as much or as little as that might be or seem to be to us, God will fill in the gaps and complete the task.

Paul's prayer and his emphasis on a contract where we do our part but in faith allow God to do the Lord's part, is not easy. Two opposed generalities arise that become problematic in allowing God to handle things, to believe that God will do the rest. Some of us are like the boy in the story; we feel we have nothing to offer, that we are unworthy of God, but we should recall that the Prophet Isaiah (6:5a) considered himself unworthy. He cried out, "Woe is me! I am lost, for I am a man of unclean lips, and I live among a people of unclean lips." Yet, God demonstrated to the prophet his suitability for his mission by purging him of any sin. Recall as well, Peter's reaction to Jesus at the miraculous catch of fish: "Go away from me, Lord, for I am a sinful man" (Luke 5:1-11). But as with Isaiah, Jesus counters Peter's protest: "Do not be afraid; from now on you will be catching people." The story of the boy and the biblical examples clearly tell us that God is not concerned with the size or significance of our gifts, nor of our perception of personal worthiness; God is only interested in us doing our part and allowing God to do the rest.

The polar opposite of those who feel unworthy are people who want to do it all; they cannot wait for God to act because they may lose control. People in this category don't want to hedge their bets on a God they cannot see; the necessary trust in God does not exist. They want to control the situation; they cannot let God be God. Trust requires that one let go, but many find such an option threatening at best, and terrifying at worst. The story of the boy who met Jesus and Paul's prayer of thanksgiving to the Ephesians encourages us to let go and allow God to do what is necessary.

The boy thought he had nothing to offer, but he learned that all he needed to give was himself. Paul tells the Ephesians the same thing; they must place their trust in God and God will do the rest. Let us believe and practice the same!

---

1. Paraphrased from "The Boy Who Had Nothing to Give," in Jude Fischer, ed. *Be Always Little: Christian Fables for Young and Old* (Combermere, Ontario, Canada: Madonna House, 1996), pp. 91-93.

Proper 13
Pentecost 11
Ordinary Time 18
Ephesians 4:1-16

Finding Unity Through Christ

Nature is filled with examples of how the world functions better when things come together and act as one. Ancient philosophers understood this need for unity quite well. In their efforts to explain the world that they observed, they postulated, without the advantage of modern science, that all things were composed of four basic elements: earth, water, air, and fire. Everything that existed was a measured combination of these four elements and could exist in no other way. Earth was the "stuff" of the object observed. Water was added to the stuff to form it into various objects, be it a rock, tree, or human being; air was what filled the stuff. Fire was the glue that solidified the earth, air, and water combination. All things existed as a combination where four became one.

Ancient civilizations also discovered, I am sure quite by accident, the value of alloy metals. Probably around some evening fire two dissimilar metals were melted, mixed, and then when cooled formed a third metal which was stronger, longer lasting, and more durable than either of its constituent elements. Brass and bronze are good examples. Brass is a combination of copper and zinc; bronze is a fusion of copper and tin. The copper, zinc, and tin each contribute in important and unique ways to create the third metal. Brass and bronze can exist in only these ways.

A river system is another example of nature's desire for unity. The Mississippi River system is a good example. The Mississippi itself is formed in the northern regions of Minnesota from a combination of several tributaries. As it flows south it combines with additional rivers, two of which, the Ohio and Missouri, are mighty in their own rights. When the Mississippi flows into the Gulf of Mexico it is a unity of many rivers which act as one.

What is observed in nature is also found in human relationships. Why, one might ask, would fifty independent states choose to be one United States of America? The answer must be that these sovereign governments believe that they will be stronger, more serviceable, and better able to handle the normal ups and downs of life as a unity of one. Why do men and women come together in marriage? Again, the people believe they will be stronger and of better service to the world as a couple compared with individuals. Why do people who live in close proximity join together in neighborhood watch programs for protection and celebrate together in block parties? Surely the answer is that such unity makes for better ends for all.

The unity of the created world and human relationships is not accidental, but a very purposeful reality that presents an important message for Christians in their daily walk with the Lord. This same message of unity was preached by Saint Paul to the Christian community at Ephesus. We must listen to Paul and follow the natural movements of the created world and human relationships to find unity in our own lives, most especially in our relationships with our brothers and sisters.

The age-old adage, "united we stand, divided we fall," was certainly applied to the nascent Christian community after Jesus' return to the Father. The "New Way," or Judeo-Christian community, was forced to seek unity. During Jesus' life his disciples gathered together and followed in the Lord's footsteps, but after his ascension they came together out of fear and the hope that a united front would gain them strength. Through presenting a united front and a common message, including a common way of life, the fledgling Christian community gained strength. We must remember that the environment in which Christianity arose was quite hostile to the precepts and teaching of Jesus.

The pagan Roman civilization was at best tolerant and at worst openly aggressive against the Christian community. The early church tradition is filled with heroic stories of martyrs, like Ignatius of Antioch, Felicitas, and Perpetua. History tells us of infamous persecutions under Nero, Diocletian, and other Roman Emperors.

The Jewish community was often hostile as well. Jesus' claim to be the Messiah was rejected by many and his proclamation to be the Son of God was abhorrent for it threatened the monotheism which was so central to Jewish belief. The Acts of the Apostles (4:32-37) specifically says that the followers of Jesus banded together, holding all things in common. Christians, in imitation of Jesus, worked for the collective good; their very survival depended on their ability to be united.

Local Christian communities banded together in "house churches," meeting each Sunday morning and worshiping in secret, staying one step ahead of any authorities who might want to cease their operations. These small groups of Christians grew over time as a result of the strength that their unity provided. This vitality came not through numbers, but from common beliefs, goals, attitudes, and a standard way of life. People truly did their best to mirror the life and message of Christ in a world that rejected their message.

Saint Paul, having extensively traveled the Mediterranean world, knew better than most the hostile environment that the message of Jesus and his followers encountered. Paul, or as many scripture scholars suggest, one of Paul's close associates, wrote from prison to the Christian community at Ephesus. This was a pagan city where the worship of the goddess Artemis was widespread and significant. Many in the city made their living by selling souvenirs or attending to the other needs of the many pilgrims who came to Ephesus to worship Artemis. Having spent time in the city, Paul knew the environment and thus he calls in today's Second Reading for the people to live united by being faithful to the vocation to which they have been called. He suggests that this unity, this faithfulness to purpose, will be achieved through the Holy Spirit. The Spirit of God must be their bond and unity of peace. Paul did not believe that there were various types of Christians; the community needed to be united. Thus, he writes to the Ephesians and speaks of being "one Lord, one faith, one baptism, one God and Father of all" (4:5-6a). Paul is clearly trying to demonstrate that the Christian community must be one of heart, attitude, and way of life if it wants to survive in the hostile environment of pagan Ephesus.

While Paul is clear that a commonality in mind and heart is essential, there are several routes that individuals can follow to achieve this unified belief. There are various ways that the Spirit manifests himself as we practice different vocations depending on our talents and the opportunities that life sends our way. Some of us are apostles, others prophets, still others evangelists, pastors, or teachers. These varied ministries have, however, one unified purpose. Our solidarity is found in a common faith and knowledge of God. This common belief evolves and grows over time. We are called to grow from children into adults in our faith. We can do so by an openness to learning and a progressive attitude that says, "I do not have all the answers." We must in essence keep our eyes and attention fixed on Christ, who in the end must be both the source and the binding force of our unity as Christians. It is the unity we share through Christ that allows us to flourish in this world. Paul fully understood that this fledgling group of Christians would never survive in the hostile environment of the day if its members went their own ways. Thus, he shares with them the absolute need for a unified attitude, approach, and most importantly, faith.

The unity that Paul suggests for the Christian community at Ephesus has been the hallmark and tower of strength for countless groups and movements throughout human history. It is true, "united we stand, divided we fall." In American history we can look at just a few examples. How was it possible for a band of disorganized, ill-prepared, and fortified colonists to defeat the might of the British Empire in the American Revolution? We all recall from our history books that our forebears rallied around the common battle cry, "Taxation without representation is tyranny." I am sure as well, that Patrick Henry's immortal words, "Give me liberty or give me death," stirred many to unified action. The unity of purpose and attitude galvanized the rag-tag colonists into a force that shocked the world.

About one century later another group of Americans unified under the banner called the "Anti-Saloon League." Believing that drink was the cause of many social problems, League members banded together in a unified effort to change attitudes and practices in American culture. While the overall efficacy of this movement can certainly be judged in varied ways, historically, one cannot deny it was the League's united front that was the principle catalyst to the passage and ratification of the eighteenth (prohibition) amendment of the Constitution. More recently, it was the united movement of non-violent resistance, practiced principally by Martin Luther King, Jr., that was the rallying cry to the American Civil Rights Movement and the transformation in laws and attitudes of Americans. In each case it was the unity of people, their ideas, attitudes, and practices that brought success to their various efforts. Division and dissension would have been disastrous to the American colonists and would have frustrated the efforts of the Anti-Saloon League and the Civil Rights Movement.

People today unfortunately have a tendency to concentrate far too much on what is different or divides. While nationalism can create a great sense of unity, excessive nationalism or jingoism, can be highly problematic, for it creates major divisions. Nations divide on many lines — economics, political ideology, religion, and social structure. The tendency is to exalt one nation's beliefs or ways of operation to the detriment of others. Almost by definition, nations separate themselves by placing what they do and how they think above others. This type of thinking is highly destructive to the concept of a world community. We don't seem to see or recognize our need to view all people of the world as our sisters and brothers. In business we all know that competition is keen and central to the capitalism we practice. However, as with nationalism, excessive competitive spirit can lead to greed, unfair business practices, and unlawful methods of operation — all in an effort to get ahead of the other guy. The other company should not be the enemy, but a competitor that is seeking the same goal. In our personal relationships, too often we associate only with those who are the same economic, social, ethnic, or racial background. We see what is different and ignore the basic humanity we all share as creations of God.

Tragically, the area where we see division most is, as they say, in our own backyard — our practice of religion. All religious denominations protect their turfs, often using tactics, words, and methods that are completely inconsistent with the teachings that the faith proclaims as its creed. We seldom overtly seek what is common, but tend to concentrate on what divides. I am sure that Christ is somewhat disappointed with us in this area. Catholics and Protestants feud with each other and with their own members. Honest and sincere dialogue is one thing, but divisive words and actions are a whole other area. Christians and non-Christians divide over ideology and find it the source of world conflict. Jews and Muslims continue their seemingly perennial struggle in the holy land. Christians and Muslims often use religion as the pretext to promote the war on terror. It would be truly amazing to see what might happen if we worked together instead of acting in such distinctly separate ways. What might be achieved in the construction of God's kingdom in this world could be amazing!

The unity of God which Christians celebrate in the Trinity should be our goal. God is a community of love. We firmly believe that God is a unity of Father, Son, and Holy Spirit — Creator, Redeemer, and Sanctifier. It is this same unity that is found naturally in the created world, human relationships, and countless movements over history that have sought to effect change, growth, or revolution in our world. Saint Paul understood the need for unity and preached the same, but he was only following the lead of his Lord and Savior, Jesus of Nazareth, who expressed it best in a prayer: "That they may all be one. As you, Father, are in me and I am in you, may they also be in us, so the world may believe that you have sent me" (John 17:21). Let us, my friends, believe, profess, and act the same.

Jesus Is The Recipe For Eternal Life

Scientists tell us that if you take six molecules of carbon dioxide and combine it with twelve molecules of water, then add light, the result will be one molecule of glucose sugar, six molecules of oxygen, and six molecules of water. This process, known as photosynthesis, makes the world as we know it possible. Carbon dioxide, which is exhaled by all mammals, is converted into oxygen which allows us to breathe. Plants, which use this photosynthesis process, make our world possible. But, photosynthesis without light is not possible. The chemical reaction will not occur without light.

Light is an essential element in our lives. Light brings warmth to our earth and our feelings. We feel more comfortable in the light. Darkness is cold; it brings fear and danger. Light also gives us strength. We feel more confident and strengthened in will when we walk in the light. Light gives us direction as well. We can proceed forward when we walk in the light; we know which way to go. With the aid of the light we can see the path, the road of our daily journey as well as that of our lives.

Photosynthesis, a scientific phenomenon, and the light that makes it possible provides the created world with its formula for life. This process allows the world to function. Thus, it is in every possible way the recipe for life. Follow it and life becomes possible. While the world certainly needs a recipe to sustain its life, we equally need a formula to discover and attain the eternal life which is God's promise to all who believe. The scriptures, capped by our Second Reading from Paul's Letter to the Ephesians, provides the formula and path we need to follow.

God has demonstrated the path to eternal life throughout the period that theologians call salvation history. Like all recipes, God's formula and path require close attention on our part. If we follow the plan then we will find the goal, but if we take another route the result will be much less than we desire. God initiated the plan with Abraham, the first great Jewish patriarch and our father in the faith. In the book of Genesis we read how God spoke to Abraham. The Lord promised the patriarch progeny: "I will indeed bless you, and I will make your offspring as numerous as the stars of heaven and the sand that is on the seashore" (Genesis 22:17). The recipe, the path that Yahweh gave to Abraham, was rather generic. God asked that Abraham and his people place their faith in God and follow his commands with the promise that he, the Lord, would be with the people every step of the way. There was nothing to fear; there was only the need for trust. Generations later, when the Israelites found themselves in bondage in Egypt and they cried out to the Lord, the agreement was formalized and made more clear. The great stories of the Passover, exodus from Egypt, and giving of the Law are central to Jewish self-understanding. In an annual ritual from the time of Moses, Jews have expressed their commitment to God through Passover. God, in turn, left the people with a more specific path or recipe for being God's people. The Law, decalogue, or Ten Commandments, as it is variously called, provides a list of rules for following the Lord. As we know, some of these commandments are concerned with our relationship with God and others of our relationships with one another. Some of these rules are proscriptions of behavior and others are prescriptions for life. Through the decalogue, God made the path to eternal life much more specific.

The Hebrew Scriptures tell the long story of the up and down relationship between Yahweh and his people. God was ever faithful to the covenant and gave the people all that was necessary to find and follow the path toward life, but often the people, for various reasons, chose other paths. Prophets were sent before, during, and after the infamous Babylonian exile to point out the errors of the people, especially religious leaders, and to direct them along the right path. Still the people failed to heed the unmistakable warning of God. God sent the Prophet Jeremiah (31:31, 33b) to renew the covenant and provide another important part of the recipe to eternal life. This renewal was to be written on the hearts of the people. "The days are surely coming, says the Lord, when I will make a new covenant with the house of Israel and the house of Judah.... I will put my law within them, and I will write it on their hearts; and I will be their God, and they shall be my people."

The path to eternal life was made more clear and specific with the ministry and message of Jesus. Christ spoke in generic terms about reconciliation, loving God and neighbor, demonstrating an attitude of peace, and the need for prayer, but he was also very specific in many areas of what the recipe of eternal life required. Jesus often, and in varied ways, spoke of the need for personal conversion and daily renewal. In his conversation with the Pharisee Nicodemus, who came to Jesus at night, we have the essence of the Lord's message. Jesus told him, "You must be born anew" (John 3:7b). Nicodemus did not understand the Lord's words, thinking only of a physical rebirth, not a spiritual one. Some people have seen this call as a one-time conversion to the understanding that Jesus is our Lord and Savior, but many others, such as the scripture scholar, Marcus Borg, see Jesus' words as a call to daily conversion. We must answer the call to follow the recipe that Jesus lays out. In order to do this, however, we must better understand what that recipe is and how to follow it.

Jesus describes the path, the basic recipe, by addressing the idea of renewal in Christ through a greater concentration on the things of God and God's people and less on our own needs and desires. In John's Gospel, Jesus says, "Unless the grain of wheat falls to the ground and dies, it remains just a grain of wheat, but if it dies it produces much fruit." In the synoptics the Lord presents the same message in varied ways. Jesus told his disciples, "Whoever wants to be first must be the last of all and servant of all" (Mark 9:35). In another context, Jesus put it this way, "If any want to become my followers, let them deny themselves and take up their cross and follow me. For those who want to save their life will lose it, and those who lose their life for my sake will find it" (Matthew 18:24-25).

In essence Jesus is saying that the recipe for eternal life is not about me only, but rather our ability to give of ourselves for others. This message is dramatically presented in Matthew's famous vision of the final judgment in chapter 25. Interestingly, here Jesus tells his disciples, and all of us as well, that it is not right belief that gains us the eternal life we seek, but rather how we treat our sisters and brothers. Clearly the recipe has now focused on right action. The Christian life is about our relationships with one another.

Saint Paul, the great evangelist and teacher, realized that Jesus' message for the recipe for eternal life needed to be amplified. Last week he spoke of the unified community that we must seek; now we must see how that community, individually and collectively, attains salvation. Paul begins, in a general way like Jesus, speaking of the need to be renewed in Christ. He wrote, "So if anyone is in Christ, there is a new creation: everything old has passed away; see everything has become new!" (2 Corinthians 5:17). Paul was renewed in a very dramatic way, but certainly this was only the beginning of a process of daily conversion that was played out in his lived experience.

Thus, Paul presents to the Christian community at Ephesus a series of very specific ideas that form for him the recipe for right treatment of others and thus the path to eternal life. First, Paul speaks of putting away falsehood and speaking the truth. If we are to treat others with dignity we cannot deal in untruth. As Jesus himself said, "You will know the truth, and the truth will make you free" (John 8:32). Paul then speaks of the need to rid ourselves of anger, bitterness, and wrath. We must not allow the sun to set on our wrath. In other words, we must let go of the things that keep us apart from one another. We are to live peaceably. The next ingredient in Paul's recipe is the need for honest work. Paul was a tentmaker and thus a laborer who knew and probably experienced the human tendency to work for ourselves alone and thus to short-circuit things and possibly use an unethical practice or two. Thus, he tells the Ephesians to labor with their own hands for the betterment of all. The apostle places charity in his recipe for eternal life. He calls his readers to give to those in need. Our charity to others is not only in material possessions but in time and attitude as well. Charity requires that we realize that all is gift and, therefore, is not ultimately ours. All belongs to God and, thus, all must be shared with God's children. Saint Paul's recipe continues by an exhortation to right and proper speech. Again, he realized that humans often grow angry at others. Thus, he tells the people that they must say only things that build up and allow the people to be filled with the grace of God. Speech that tears others down, slander of any kind, must be eliminated from our daily lives. He encourages the people to not grieve the Holy Spirit; do not try the patience of God as the Jews had done so frequently in the past. Paul closes by encouraging the Ephesians to be kind to one another and forgiving, as Christ has forgiven them. Paul thus presents to the Christian community at Ephesus a long list of ingredients, but in essence he is telling the people that the formula for eternal life is centered in how we treat one another.

We are all familiar with recipes of various things we enjoy. Experience in the kitchen tells us that if we follow the directions to the letter, add the right ingredients, follow the proper procedure, and bake things at the proper temperature and amount of time, the final result will be what we hope and expect. In similar ways, if we follow the plan, procedure, or recipe for our daily work things will come out as we hope. Whether we are filing reports, preparing presentations, studying for an examination in school, or simply driving home after a hard day at the office, there are generally accepted recipes for success. We all know them, specific as they may be for individuals but common as they are for many or most. We know as well that if we choose not to follow the recipe, the end will not be what we want or intend. The choice is ours!

The challenge to fulfill the recipe for eternal life is twofold. First, we must be willing to follow the path marked out by Christ. Too often, however, we think that we know the path better than Jesus. We place greater trust in our own ability, knowledge, confidence. We value our self-autonomy over following a plan that we did not create. We have a "do it our own way" attitude. We sometimes feel somewhat self-righteous and think that we are better than others. We can, therefore, follow our own plan. Yet, when we think like this, God, sometimes gently and other times more forcefully, reminds us of our need for God. A simple story demonstrates how God can correct such an attitude of self-righteousness. There was a woman who had a reputation for being a very holy person. She came to church every Sunday. In fact, she came to church every day. In fact, she often came to church more than once per day. A good friend asked her, "How many times do you come to church in a year — over 400?" The question intrigued the women, so she decided to start keeping count. She bought a large box with a lid in which she cut a whole and put a lock on it. She hid the key in a safe place that only she knew. Each time she returned from church she placed a stone in the box. She never failed upon returning home from church to place a stone in the box.

As the year drew on, the woman wondered how many stones were in the box. She was certain that the box was very heavy so decided that she needed a strong man in the village to help her lift it outside. When the man arrived to help she said, "Be careful, it is very heavy!" The man lifted the box effortlessly. "This box is very light," he proclaimed. "You don't need me to help you lift it." The woman went to her secret hiding place to obtain the key. She opened the box and when she peered in she was speechless. The box was almost empty; there were only five small pebbles inside.

It took a couple of days for her to recover from the shock of the almost empty box, but when she did, she went to the local pastor and told him the whole story. With kind words he told her, "Your box tells us that when you came to church, God was not central in your mind and your neighbors were not central in your prayers. It is clear that most of the time you were thinking how pious and holy you are and how everyone ought to know how devoted you are to the church. The pebbles are a sign that only five times have you entered church with a heart turned to God." True worship is not the number of times we worship, but our attitude when we worship. Yes, God will show us the correct path, even if we are humiliated in the process.

The other great challenge in following the recipe of eternal life is to help others follow this path. As the light is essential to photosynthesis, so must we provide the light to others to light their path to Christ. This way is certainly the most difficult, but Jesus, understanding the challenge nonetheless, told us directly what was necessary: "Enter through the narrow gate; for the gate is wide and the road is easy that leads to destruction, and there are many who take it. For the gate is narrow and the road is hard that leads to life, and there are few who find it" (Matthew 7:13-14). The basic call of Christianity tells us that we do not live alone; we are a community. Thus, we have a responsibility to assist our brothers and sisters in their efforts to find and live the recipe of eternal life. We might not think it is our job; we may be too preoccupied with ourselves and our immediate family, but Jesus' message of service to our brothers and sisters is crystal clear.

While there are many paths in life, and at times we might feel we are in a maze, there is one and only one path that leads to eternal life. Throughout salvation history we have been shown the path. Paul, taking his lead from Jesus, knew the tradition. He experienced conversion on the road to Damascus and knew with complete certainty that Jesus had the recipe for eternal life. We know from science that the created world can only exist and function through the process of photosynthesis. It provides our world its basic sustenance and gives us life, but Jesus provides the more important recipe for life eternal. Let us, therefore, listen to Saint Paul (1 Corinthians 2:9), follow his lead, and find the gift which he has described so well: "What no eye has seen, nor ear heard, not the human heart conceived, what God has prepared for those who love him."

357

Make The Most Of God's Gifts

John Harding had it all; his credentials were impeccable. He had a wonderful family. His wife, Sally, was one of those people everyone enjoys meeting. His eight-year-old son, Rick, was a good student, enjoyed athletics, and obeyed his parents. John himself had moved up the corporate ladder. After graduating from Arizona State University, where he played baseball well enough to be offered a professional contract, he moved to California's "Silicon Valley" and signed on with one of the many software companies with headquarters in the region. Through his brains, diligence, and much hard work he rapidly moved into management, beginning at the bottom and moving up. Still in his thirties, national publications such as *Forbes*, *U.S.A. Today*, and *The Wall Street Journal* commented favorably on his managerial style. John Harding seemed to have the perfect resume for life: academic achievement, awards, and many positions of importance. Yet, he sometimes wondered if he used his gifts wisely.

With such a record it was not a big surprise when Millennium, the third largest software manufacturer in the world, asked Harding to be its chief executive officer. John jumped at the offer. Not only was it a great position, but it would allow him to return to his native New England. He settled in his home town of Boland, New Hampshire, only twenty miles or so from Concord, the world headquarters for Millennium.

Everything seemed to be going well for John. The town welcomed a favorite son; the company liked their new boss. Then in the twinkling of an eye everything changed for John Harding. Sally and Rick were riding in the family car. A drunk driver crossed the centerline and an instant later they were both gone. John Harding had the all the gifts for success, but when tragedy struck, he did not know how to use them. He was a man who placed all his trust in his own ability; he never had to rely on others. Now, however, in grief and shock, he crawled into a shell of mourning and refused to come out.

After a couple of months, an old friend, Bill West, came to John to see if he could pull him from his state of grief. He knew that John liked baseball; maybe he would consider being the manager of one of Boland's four summer little league teams. Harding tried to run away, but Bill West was persistent and so John agreed. His team was the Angels.

It was at this time that John Harding met little Timmy Noble. Timmy, a member of the Angels, was eight years old and a towhead just like his son Rick. Unlike his son, however, Timmy was not a good player; he did not have the gifts for baseball. He did not possess the keen eye to be a good hitter and he did not have the strong arm needed to be a good fielder. But Timmy Noble had some very important qualities, nonetheless. He had courage and a big heart — how can one measure such qualities? He had determination and, most especially, Timmy Noble had faith in God. He didn't worry about what he couldn't do; he was grateful for what he had. He had decided a long time ago to place his trust in God.

The Angels did well that year; in fact they won the league championship. Timmy Noble was not one of the stars; he just was not gifted as a baseball player. But there was something wrong, something radically wrong. Timmy Noble was very sick. He never told anyone; he never complained. He came to every practice and played in each game, even though he had to ride his bike five miles each way to the field. When the season was over and it was revealed that Timmy Noble had terminal cancer, John Harding knew the reason that God had led him to manage the Angels. John had the perfect gifts for personal success, but Timmy Noble used his gifts for the benefit of others.[1]

Timmy Noble was not blessed with natural talent as a baseball player, but he had great gifts nonetheless and used them to their maximum. His seemingly limited gifts were actually abundant for he used them to convert John Harding from his personal misery and sadness into a man who was able to care for others. This is precisely what Saint Paul tells the Ephesians in today's Second Reading from scripture.

The religious world of Saint Paul was characterized by a minority status. The vast majority of the people with whom Paul had contact were pagans; monotheism as practiced by the Jews was a unique concept in religion and was not popular. When Paul was converted on the road to Damascus his religious purview became even more narrow as he became part of the Judeo-Christian community, a small sect that found itself alienated not only from the polytheism of the pagans but increasingly also from the Jewish community in which he was firmly rooted as a Pharisee. Paul's mission to the Gentiles thus had a certain sense of urgency. Not only was he surrounded by those who opposed his views, but additionally and probably more fundamentally Paul firmly believed that Christ's promised return to claim the world, the Parousia, was imminent. This belief was certainly a major factor in Paul's teaching on marriage and vocation. Convinced that Jesus would soon return, Paul thought it wise to suggest to the Corinthians: "In whatever condition you were called, brothers and sisters, there remain with God" (1 Corinthians 7:24).

Paul also dealt with this issue with the Thessalonians. Here, the question was whether those who died before the Lord's return would inherit the promise of eternal life. Paul answered, "For this we declare to you by the word of the Lord, that we who are alive, who are left until the coming of the Lord will by no means precede those who have died" (1 Thessalonians 4:15). Thus, for Paul procrastination in the Christian life was not an option. Those who chose the "new way" needed to get going and waste no time. They were to be active about the business of the Lord. Paul realized that Jesus came to inaugurate the kingdom of God, but it would be the task of his followers to do their share to complete the work and make God's reign a reality.

Thus, as we heard this morning, Paul writes to the Ephesians with a message of urgency in the right and proper use of the gifts we have been given. First, Paul tells the people to live as wise people and make the most of every day, for the days are evil. This was certainly good advice, but in the environment of the pagan city of Ephesus and with the understanding that the days were short, such a warning was essential. Paul was telling the people that Christians had a special vocation to fully and rightly use each and every day. Each day brought many opportunities to give praise and glory to God, occasions to continue the construction of God's kingdom in this world. The apostle understood human nature well and the tendency we have to procrastinate, to let things go, the attitude that we will always have tomorrow. Paul was most probably aware of Jesus' teaching on the coming kingdom (Luke 17:20-37) and the need for vigilance. Jesus was very clear, "Beware, keep alert, for you do not know when the time will come" (Mark 13:33). Paul himself warned the Thessalonians: "For you yourselves know very well that the day of the Lord will come like a thief in the night. When they say, 'There is peace and security,' then sudden destruction will come upon them, as labor pains come upon a pregnant woman, and there will be no escape!" (1 Thessalonians 5:2-3). Time was of the essence; it should not be wasted.

Next, Paul tells the people not to be foolish, suggesting that they seek God's will. Again, Paul understood that people often wish to "go it alone" and not be tuned into God. He tells the Ephesians they must do their best to know God's will in their lives. The apostle goes on to say this can best be accomplished by not wasting time with foolish things, such as with excessive drinking, but to be filled with the Holy Spirit. He suggests using time to praise God and most especially to thank the Lord for all he has done. Paul understood that prayers of contrition and petition were important, but also prayers of praise and thanksgiving were necessary for all of the Lord's many and manifest blessings.

Paul's teaching tells us there is a need to strike a balance in our lives in using our time and gifts wisely. Two polar extremes exist in our world that make this balance hard to achieve. One pole is associated with those the world labels "workaholics." The popularity of this expression is certainly associated with the old adage, "All work and no play makes a dull Jane or John." This statement forces us to consider the need to balance the demands of contemporary life with some personal time, spent alone, with God, or in recreation with family and friends.

The other end of the spectrum is less addressed and thus, as Saint Paul suggests, some significant reflection upon the human tendencies toward procrastination and laziness is needed. One might label the procrastinator's creed as: "Leave until tomorrow what can be done today." As excessive work, the "workaholic" mentality can lead the wrong way, so too can an attitude of continually letting things go. We need to strike a balance, a lesson that John Harding only learned "through the back door."

There are several ways we can challenge ourselves and others to address the important questions Paul raises in today's lesson. He suggests the need for diligence concerning the things we do. Last week we heard Paul's recipe for eternal life; now we must sincerely and forcefully do what is necessary to put all these ingredients together; it will not happen without a high level of effort on our part. All the ingredients for the pie may be present, but until the baker diligently applies her skills there will be no result; no one will reap the benefits of the gifts, talents, and opportunities given by God.

There are many reasons why we are less diligent than possibly we should be and few, I suppose, have much to do with genuine laziness. We may feel inadequate to the task, perceiving that our God-given skills are not sufficient to successfully complete the job. There are occasions as well when the time we have, considering our ever-increasing list of responsibilities, or lack of opportunity to engage a particular task, is insufficient. As important as a task may be and as much as we might want to help, we cannot respond to all possibilities. All people need "down time"; we must choose among the myriad of tasks and opportunities that come our way.

We must admit, however, that inside each of us lies a sense of complacency. We should listen to the Prophet Amos concerning such laziness: "Alas for those who lie on beds of ivory, and lounge on their couches, and eat lambs from the flock, and calves from the stall; who sing idle songs to the sound of the harp, and like David improvise on instruments of music; who drink wine from bowls, and anoint themselves with the finest oils, but are not grieved over the ruin of Joseph! Therefore they shall now be the first to go into exile, and the revelry of the loungers shall pass away" (Amos 6:4-7). We all have a tendency to concentrate first on our own needs and then secondarily on others. But Jesus addresses this question as well: "For everyone to whom much has been given, much will be required; and from the one to whom much has been entrusted, even more will be demanded" (Luke 12:48b). We have all been given by God many wonderful gifts and talents. We are to use them well and wisely to make the most of what God has given us. Paul certainly had heard of Jesus' parable of the talents (Matthew 25:14-30) and realized his need not to hide but use fully what he had been given. He could, therefore, proudly claim as his ministry came to and end: "I have fought the good fight, I have finished the race, I have kept the faith. From now on there is reserved for me the crown of righteousness, which the Lord, the righteous judge, will give me on that day, and not only to me but also to all who have longed for his appearing" (2 Timothy 4:7-8).

Timmy Noble also fought the good fight, using the gifts he was given, limited as they were. Yet, his efforts transformed one with greater talent and opportunity. He, like Paul, deserved a merited crown, and I am sure he found the same. If we have the courage to act and to use our gifts well and wisely, then the merited crown of God's eternal life will be ours as well. Let us, therefore, be pro-active, work hard, and see through our efforts a certain wisdom that only God can bring. Can we say and believe, "The difficult I'll do today and the impossible tomorrow"? Only you can answer!

---

1. Summary of: Og Mandino, *The Twelfth Angel* (New York: Fawcett Crest, 1993).

Proper 16
Pentecost 14
Ordinary Time 21
Ephesians 6:10-20

God Our Protector And Shield

James Gillis, a priest and writer in the mid-twentieth century, became well known as a commentator on American life. He saw himself as a champion for the cause of moral righteousness and absolutism against the forces of darkness that manifested themselves in various ways. This "war" continued throughout his life with battles waged on numerous fronts, all prosecuted to protect the American Christian way of life that was instilled in him from childhood. Gillis believed that truth should enwrap all decisions and be the basis for all policies; it was the belt that bound the world to God. Justice and freedom for the individual, who was constantly in jeopardy of absorption by organizations, was the foundation from which he built his argument against statism. Zeal was apparent in every aspect of his life; he attacked all tasks with a degree of fervor that bordered on obsession. His activity, that at times in the 1930s found him speaking on two weekly radio programs, writing editorials and columns, and traveling the lecture circuit makes an industrious worker today appear as a moderate activist.

James Gillis' faith was manifest in his fear of God; it was his shield and protector. His views were at some points out of touch with time and reason, as in his inability to grasp that World Wars I and II had changed America's international role and his refusal to recognize the outrageous tactics of Joseph McCarthy's anti-Communist crusade. Additionally, Gillis possessed a rigid attitude of absolutism, rejected relativism, and outwardly offered little compassion, peace, or forgiveness to opponents. Yet, his uncompromising method demonstrated that his ideas and opinions were held as convictions of faith; he stood his ground and never backed down. Gillis believed with complete sincerity that not only were his opinions correct, but that failure to reform along his recommended line would be disastrous and possibly fatal for the nation. His belief in America's democratic principles that originated with the founding fathers never wavered. With the fear of God as his shield Gillis fended off the forces of darkness, as he perceived them, which imperiled America, while he attacked perceived wrongdoing or faulty ideas, using the pen and fiery oratory as his swords.

Gillis' contribution to American society, therefore, must be found in his courageous stand against any person, ideology, or program which jeopardized his sense of the integrity or future of the United States and its Christian principles of democracy. His vision was not complex or ambiguous; in a polemical manner he voiced clear arguments and proposed a return to God as the solution to society's ills. James Gillis' place in American history will be maintained from his extant record, but it is his strength of belief and unqualified devotion to purpose which will continue to serve as an example of faithfulness in ministry for future generations.

James Gillis wrapped himself in the flag he respected and cherished and the banner of God's righteousness which he loved. While many men and women of great faith could serve as illustrations, Gillis' life presents the words of Saint Paul as a lived experience. He truly was a man who, while flying the stars and stripes, saw God as his protector and shield.

The concept of God serving as a protector and shield for his people is what scholars call salvation history, as related in the scriptures. The story of the Exodus serves as one illustrative example. When the people cried out to God from their place of bondage, the Lord sent Moses to be the great deliverer. God wrought the plagues upon the Hebrews, led the people through the Red Sea and provided a cloud by day and a pillar of fire by night to lead the people to the promised land. The former prophets or historical books of the Bible are filled with stories of how God took the side of Israel against their many enemies, especially the Philistines, with whom Israel constantly seemed at war. Even after the darkest moment of

Israel's history and its destruction by the Assyrians, God fought on the side of Judah in the south. Sennacherib, King of Assyria, after conquering Israel made ready for the conquest of Judah, but Hezekiah, King of Judah, cried out to God who sent his angel striking down the whole of the Assyrian army and forcing their retreat (2 Kings 19:9-36). God was the protector and shield for the Hebrews.

God not only provided victory in battle, but was the primary provider of life and sustenance as well. The powerful image presented by Isaiah demonstrates God as the protector-provider: "On this mountain the Lord of hosts will make for all peoples a feast of rich food, a feast of well-aged wines, of rich food filled with marrow, of well-aged wines, strained clear" (Isaiah 25:6). The psalmist provides some of the most powerful images of how God is the protector and shield of his people: "You are indeed my rock and my fortress; for your name's sake lead me and guide me, take me out of the net that is hidden for me, for you are my refuge" (Psalm 18:3-4). In Psalm 62:5-8 we hear: "For God alone my soul waits in silence, for my hope is from him. He alone is my rock, and my salvation, my fortress; I shall not be shaken. On God rests my deliverance and my honor; my mighty rock, my refuge is in God. Trust in him at all times, O people; pour our your hearts before him; God is a refuge for us."

As a Pharisee, Paul had read and studied the Torah and through his life experience he came to realize in the end that human answers to the situations of life were bankrupt. He understood what the author of the book of Proverbs stated: "Trust in the Lord with all your heart, and do not rely on your own insight" (Proverbs 3:5). Paul realized that while the world was filled with many possibilities and great goodness, it was also infected with evil, the multiple manifestations of the presence of Satan. Therefore, it was necessary to battle against the forces of evil in the world.

Thus, as we just heard proclaimed, Paul tells the Ephesians to put on the armor of God to protect themselves against the wiles of the devil. The battle was not against the forces of the world *per se* but against the spiritual hosts of darkness that manifest their presence in humans. The Ephesians are not fighting against flesh and blood, but a much stronger enemy. Thus, Paul again extolls the people to use the whole armor of God; the people are to protect themselves fully and completely.

Paul proceeds to break down the various pieces of God's armor and how they must be used to protect the people against the wiles of evil and darkness. First, Paul tells them to gird their loins with the truth. He must have been told what Jesus had said to his disciples: "If you continue in my word, you are truly my disciples; and you will know the truth, and the truth will make you free" (John 8:31b-32). Anything but the truth is a masquerade, but God sees through the disguise. God's truth will protect us. Next, Paul says to put on the breast plate of righteousness. The apostle believed that justice must govern our relations with each other. Saint Matthew's depiction of the final judgment (ch. 25) clearly demonstrates it is what we do or do not do for others, rather than our particular belief, that brings us to eternal life. Paul then tells the people they must protect their feet with the gospel of peace. Jesus preached a message of love and peace; anger and violence solve nothing. Next, the shield of faith is provided to ward off the slings and arrows that the enemy may hurl. But what is faith? The best answer is in the scriptures: "Now faith is assurance of things hoped for, the conviction of things not seen" (Hebrews 11:1). Paul challenges the people to protect themselves with the helmet of salvation, that is the realization that there is more that awaits those who believe. As he wrote to the Corinthians: "What no eye has seen, nor ear heard, nor the human heart conceived what God has prepared for those who love him" (1 Corinthians 2:9). Lastly, Paul suggests that the people arm themselves with the sword of God's word. Scripture must be the basis for our life, the testament we preach in word and deed. Again, Paul knew of the efficacy of God's word: "Indeed, the word of God is living and active, sharper than any two-edged sword, piercing until it divides soul from spirit, joints from marrow; it is able to judge the thoughts and intentions of the heart" (Hebrews 4:12). Paul concludes his exhortation to the Ephesians with some important additional challenges. The people are to pray at all times and to keep alert with all perseverance. He asks the people to pray for his ministry so that he may continue to boldly proclaim the mysteries of the Gospel.

Paul's exhortation to the Christian community at Ephesus, as seen in the life of James Gillis, must be a source of hope and a guide for life in an often alien and hostile world. The twenty-first century is obviously more advanced technologically, more diverse, and certainly different in many ways from the world that Saint Paul experienced, yet in some important ways it is still the same. The Christian community lives in a foreign world. Even though the United States is a so-called Christian nation and many of the precepts upon which the country was founded are found in the Bible, we cannot be ignorant nor blind to the reality that our society, like that of the first century Mediterranean world, is filled with many manifestations of darkness. Thus, we are daily challenged to stand tall against the various revelations of evil that come our way.

Therefore, as Paul suggests and as James Gillis lived, we must put on the armor of God, in all its various manifestations. God must become our protector and shield. We must gird our loins and speak and live the truth. This means much more than being forthright in what we say. Certainly we must be truthful in our dealing with others, our relationships, and business responsibilities. More importantly it means being true to ourselves, accepting who we are and not pretending to be someone we are not. People must see in us what they get; there should be no need to present a false front. Who we are, with our strengths, weaknesses, and incompleteness is precisely how God made us. We must accept the truth of who we are and rejoice in what God made in us.

We must also live righteously, using it as our breast plate. Being compassionate and just in how we conduct our lives is extremely important, especially in a society that practices discrimination and fuels prejudice on all levels. We are called to live a life of inclusivity, an ecumenical existence, seeking the good in all and rejecting any and all ideas and propositions that seek to isolate individuals. We must be just in business. Employers and employees must work together in mutual respect toward the common goals of economic success and the construction of a better society that will benefit not only the privileged but all citizens. If we conduct our lives as peacemakers and lovers of serenity we will live righteous lives. As the lyrics of a popular Christian hymn state, "Peace is flowing like a river, flowing out of you and me." In a world rampant with violence, hatred, and discontent, we need to be peacemakers in attitude, word, and action.

Faith must be the shield that wards off the blows and insults of our world. As the Letter to the Hebrew suggests, our faith must provide us with assurance of things hoped for and unseen. Thus, our faith in God whom we cannot see must be manifest in God's people who we see all around us. It must be found in a certain self-confidence that allows us to use well and wisely the many gifts and talents given us by God. It is found in an optimistic attitude toward life, encouraging others to believe that with God all things are possible.

The sword of God's Word must be the vehicle used to fight our battles. The gospel must be our constitution, the written and lived word by which we bring hope and strength to a world that badly needs our assistance. Guided by God's Word we are daily challenged to bring the message of Christ to our world. Since, as Saint Teresa of Avila once wrote, "We are the hands and feet of God," we have a mandate as baptized Christians to do what we can to finish the work Jesus inaugurated during his public ministry. We cannot do it alone and the work will most probably not be completed when God calls us home, but our membership in the Christian community mandates our need to go to the fields and harvest the crop of God's love. Prayer must be the source of our strength, assisting us to boldly proclaim the message of Christ to our broken world.

Many women and men of great faith have provided examples of the words of Saint Paul. Some have been recognized as saints; others, like Father James Gillis, were notable in their time. Still others are the simple and ordinary men and women who cross our paths in life every day. Paul understood human nature and the life of the spirit through faith. Thus, if we wish to follow the Lord and grow in his love, we must heed Paul's advice and clothe ourselves with the armor of God, that is with truth, righteousness, and justice, peace, faith, salvation, and the Word of God. This will allow us to break through the darkness, be bathed in the light and live the resurrected life — God's promise to all who believe.

Living The Word Of God

Mohandas Gandhi was born in Porbandar in the present state of Gujarat, India, on October 2, 1869. After completing his initial schooling he went to England where he earned a law degree from University College in London in 1891. He then returned to his native land and established a law practice in Bombay, but his lack of success led him to accept an invitation to go to South Africa to work for political rights for Indian immigrants in that land. He was appalled to discover the widespread denial of human rights and to realize that he was considered a member of an inferior race. He felt compelled to respond to this injustice. Thus, he remained in South Africa twenty years and was imprisoned several times for his views and verbal protests. Influenced by the Russian novelist, Leo Tolstoy, and the American essayist, Henry David Thoreau, he developed a system of nonviolent resistance, called *satygraha*, that became his hallmark.

He returned to India and immediately was drawn into the ongoing struggle for home rule against the imperialist policy of England which ruled the land. When the British failed to make amends after their massacre of scores of Indians at Amritsar in 1920, he proclaimed an organized campaign of non-cooperation against the ruling government. Indians in public office resigned, children were withdrawn from schools, and thousands of citizens blocked streets in a protest heard round the world. He spoke little, but acted to secure justice for his people.

As the 1930s dawned, Gandhi continued to lead the campaign for freedom and proclaimed a new program of civil disobedience.

He was arrested several times but only answered by initiating hunger strikes and championing the ascetic life. He never compromised his values of nonviolence, but rather, used his method successfully attracting world attention in the process. By 1944, the pressure he and his followers exerted was so great that Britain was ready to capitulate and grant independence. In 1947, after the end of World War II and following the division of the country into two, India for the Hindus and Pakistan for those practiced Islam, independence was granted. Riots, however, continued to engulf the country and, thus, as was his custom Gandhi began a fast asking for peace. On January 30, 1948, twelve days after his fast ceased, Mohandas Gandhi, known as Mahatma or "Great Soul" to his people, was assassinated as he walked to evening prayer. The world mourned the loss of one of its great men, one who acted on his beliefs to secure justice for all.

Mahatma Gandhi was a Hindu, but nonetheless he read the Christian scriptures and was highly influenced by them. He realized that it was necessary to put into action and to live the precepts of the scriptures. This he did well in leading a nation to sovereignty and a people to freedom. Gandhi brought hope to our world. He became the source of inspiration to many, including Martin Luther King, Jr., as an example of how to live the Word of God. Both men took Jesus' message of nonviolence and applied it to the situation of their lives. Rejecting violence and sordid behavior they became doers of the word. Today, as we begin to read the Letter of James, the apostle gives us the same message.

The Letter of James provides an important message of an active Christianity that is necessary for our contemporary world. It seems that the author of this letter was an official of the early church, but it is not certain it was James, "the brother of the Lord," although many scholars believe it was. The tract is more a sermon or written instruction as opposed to a letter. The one distinctive characteristic or theme that binds together the many short exhortations on faith is not theoretical or abstract. On the contrary, James calls for implementation in every aspect of one's life the message Jesus proclaimed. The letter serves to warn against the tendency toward an abstract and unfruitful practice of Christianity that threatened the local churches. James most likely was familiar with Jesus' words as recorded by Saint Matthew on the need to practice a religion of deeds not words: "Everyone then who hears these words of mine and acts on them will be like a wise man who built his house on rock. The rain fell, the floods came, and the winds blew and beat on that house, but it did not fall because it was built on rock. And everyone who hears these words of mine and does not act on them will be like a foolish man who built his house on sand. The rains fell, and the floods came, and the winds came and beat against that house, and it fell — and great was its fall!" (Matthew 7:24-27).

The central message in this passage from James, namely that we must "be doers of the word," requires important preparations that the apostle outlines for his readers. In order to build the kingdom we must first realize that all are born for a purpose. James says that God gave us birth so we could be first fruits of his creation. In other words, God brought us into this world to be active; we are not here to sit around and allow others to be livers of the word while we observe from the sidelines. Armed with such knowledge we must stand away from the tendencies to laziness, complacency, or procrastination that exist in each one of us. Christianity is not for observers; it is best lived in a pro-active way.

James then provides more important advice on one's preparation to be good doers of the word. He says we cannot be active doers if we are always speaking. Thus he says, "be quick to listen, slow to speak, slow to anger," for none of these produce God's righteous. A Catholic nun once told me many years ago, "God gave us two ears and one mouth, so we should listen twice as much as we speak." James, I am sure, would say the same thing. Next, he suggests that we remove all sordidness and wickedness. These things impede our progress because they cause us to concentrate too much on our own needs and not those of others. We are to welcome the active message of the Gospel, which has the power to save.

With our preparations complete James says we are now ready to be a doer of the word, to live the Gospel message. People who simply listen and do not act, deceive only themselves; but they are not fooling God. James provides an image of how we deceive ourselves by self-observation in a mirror. When we look into the mirror we see all the imperfections, blemishes, and problems. If the user forgets what is seen in the mirror the situation cannot be corrected; things will remain in disarray. James is telling us that we must live the Word of God, as did Mahatma Gandhi, not only in what we say, but more especially in what we do. The apostle continues by saying that we cannot be true practitioners of the faith we profess if we cannot bridle our tongues. James would say, think before your speak. Furthermore, we are not simply to talk about what we will do, but to care for orphans and widows in their distress. Again, James must have remembered or been told about Jesus' words, "Truly I tell you, just as you did it for one of the least of these who are members of my family, you did it for me" (Matthew 25:40b). Any other approach is self-deception making our religion worthless.

Actualizing the precepts, ideals, and beliefs of any ideology, religion, or creed is difficult; it presents a significant challenge. The United States of America's foundational document, the Declaration of Independence, states that all people have the rights of "life, liberty, and the pursuit of happiness." Yet, we know from our study of history the many struggles our nation has endured, continuing today, to make this ideal a reality. The horrors of slavery and racial injustice that Abraham Lincoln's "Emancipation Proclamation" sought to end required the additional support of constitutional amendments and the work of many people, like one of Gandhi's disciples, Martin Luther King, Jr. However, the ideals expressed by Thomas Jefferson still are not fulfilled, not only for African-Americans, but many others who find themselves, often through circumstance alone, on the margins of American society, suffering social injustice in the midst of the wealthiest and most powerful nation in the history of the world. Immigrants suffer much injustice simply because they speak differently or practice different customs. Women fought long and hard for their right to vote and for greater equality in the workplace. As we all know, however, despite the positive strides, women are generally paid less for equal work performance, simply because they are female. We must admit that America does not live the ideal that the Declaration of Independence proposed.

In our lives of faith we strive for the ideal, but again we fall short. Jesus' message is clear but very challenging and, therefore, often not fully actualized. The British essayist, G. K. Chesterton, got it right back in 1910 when he wrote in *What's Wrong with the World?*: "The Christian ideal has not been tried and found wanting. It has been found difficult and left untried." We know the scriptures; we are aware of what is necessary, right, and wrong. We, too, often talk the talk but cannot adequately walk the walk. We say all the right things, but too often we cannot put into practice what we know is right and proper. Our failures make us hollow shells that need to be filled.

The hollowness that sometimes is the reality of our lives must be filled with lives of faith that not only speak but live God's Word. Sometimes things get in the way of our goal. Pride, laziness, preoccupation with other things, and feelings of inadequacy can all get in the way of our ability to live the Word of God. Thus, we must remove all obstacles so that we can hear the word clearly and then actualize what we hear.

Mahatma Gandhi came to his vocation in life rather suddenly and unexpectedly by observing injustice in South Africa. Seeing injustice first hand, he chose to act. He had the ability to listen and speak softly. He was able to keep his attention fixed on his mission and his call to action. Never a Christian, Gandhi nonetheless exemplified Jesus' call to action, as expressed by Saint James. Without knowing it, the fabled Indian freedom fighter took the advice of today's scripture and prepared himself properly to actualize the Christian message. Let us remove all obstacles that prevent us from hearing God's Word. Let us respond generously as doers of the word so that one day we will hear Jesus say to us, "Come, you that are blessed by my Father, inherit the kingdom prepared for you from the foundation of the world" (Matthew 25:34b).

Strength Through Diversity

A wealthy businessman decided to take a walk and eat his lunch at the same time. He strolled through a park and purchased a hot dog and a soft drink. As he walked, enjoying the view, two different street people approached him one by one. Each asked, "Can you help me, I am hungry?" Each time the businessman looked straight ahead and kept walking. After finishing his lunch he began to walk back to his office. He stopped and bought a chocolate eclair for dessert. As he was about to take the first bite, he was forced to jump out of the way as a young boy raced down the sidewalk on his skateboard. The eclair went flying and landed on the ground. The man picked it up and tried to clean it off, but it was no use. It was now a dirty eclair. Before discarding it, however, he had an idea. He strolled over to one of the beggars who had approached him and handing the man the eclair said, "Here you are my good man. This is something for your hunger." The businessman walked away smiling and returned to his office.

That night the man had a dream. He was sitting in a large and crowded cafe. Waitresses were scurrying about bringing customers delicious cakes and tortes. All the waitresses ignored the businessman, even though he was waving his hands at them continually. Finally he caught the eye of a young woman and asked for something to eat. She returned a few minutes later with a dirty piece of pastry. The man was outraged. "You can't treat me this way. I have a right to be served like all the others. I expect good service and food for my money." "You don't seem to understand," the waitress responded kindly. "You can't buy anything here. We don't accept money. You have just arrived in heaven and all you can order here is what you sent ahead while on earth. I just checked the records and the only thing we have for you is this dirty eclair."

The businessman obviously thought quite highly of himself and the finery that his life and talent had given him, but he could seemingly care less for the needs of others. He learned, "through the back door," that the second half of the Golden Rule, "to love our neighbor as ourself" is a necessity of life. Today, Saint James, following the lead and message of Jesus, tells us that we must never think that we are above or better than others; we are all sisters and brothers, members of the same Christian, even world family. All people deserve our respect. The Christian virtue of welcoming others allows us to welcome Christ. We have no option; this task is part and parcel of our Christian vocation.

Even a cursory reading of the New Testament demonstrates clearly that Jesus welcomed all people. No one was ever rejected; all were given a chance. Jesus freely associated with those people whom society shunned. Lepers, due not only to the contagious nature of their physical condition, but also their uncleanliness according to the Hebrew Law, were rejected by all, but not by Jesus. Saint Mark reports: "A leper came to him begging him and kneeling he said to him, 'If you choose, you can make me clean.' Moved with pity, Jesus stretched out his hand and touched him, and said to him, 'I do choose. Be made clean!' Immediately the leprosy left him, and he was made clean" (Mark 1:40-42).

We all recall the popular story (Luke 17:11-19) of the ten lepers who came to Jesus and were cured, yet only one, a Samaritan, returned to give thanks. Jesus also welcomed foreigners, even those who were despised by Hebrew society. Recall how amazed were both the Samaritan woman and Jesus' disciples when he entered into a long and significant conversation with her at Jacob's well (John 4:1-42). Jesus took the time necessary to welcome the sick and infirmed. Saint Luke reports, "As the sun was setting, all those who had any who were sick with various kinds of diseases brought them to him; and he laid his hands on each of them and cured them" (Luke 4:40). Christ also reached out to those rejected by society. He called a tax collector, Matthew, to be a member of his inner circle. While scholars are not certain, tradition suggests that Jesus' friend Mary Magdalene, the first person to see him after the resurrection, was a former prostitute. Jesus summarized his preferential outreach to the marginalized of Hebrew society: "Those who are well have no need of a physician, but those who are sick. Go and learn what this means, 'I desire mercy not sacrifice.' For I have come to call not the righteous but sinners" (Luke 9:12b-13).

Jesus' message of love and peace was announced to a wide spectrum of people and it was delivered to create a unified society of mutual trust and love. In treating all with respect and rejecting none, Jesus demonstrated that unity and inclusivity were to be sought and division and exclusivity were to be avoided. The Lord put it this way, analogizing the unity of peoples to that of God: "I ask ... that all may be one. As you, Father, are in me, and I am in you, may they also be in us, so that the world may believe that you sent me" (John 17:20-21).

Saint James, in direct and challenging words, takes the message of Jesus and applies it to his audience, "the twelve tribes in the dispersion." Apparently partiality and favoritism have been practiced for James immediately equates such behavior with a lack of belief in Jesus. Thus, consistent with his basic message of an action-oriented Christianity, namely to be doers of the word and not merely listeners, James attacks the problem through example. This illustration is one to which we can all can relate, now as well as the apostolic period. Yes, this very scene is happening in our churches today. We often make distinctions, creating separations and divisions based merely on what we observe or the previous opinions we have formed. We do this both with people we know and those we know not. We make decisions and classify some people and groups as acceptable while rejecting others. An ecumenical, inclusive spirit too often loses out to an exclusivist mentality and approach.

James tells us, however, that Jesus has preferentially chosen the poor and those on the margins of society. He writes, "Listen my brothers and sisters. Has not God chosen the poor in the world to be rich in faith and to be heirs of the kingdom that he has promised to those who love him?" (James 2:5). He says to distinguish between people, choosing some and rejecting others, dishonors the

379

poor, the very ones to whom Jesus ministered in a preferential way. He goes on to say that partiality is sinful and, thus, must be avoided. He summarizes his teaching by returning to his basic premise of the need to live an active Christian life. We must not only respect all, but act on their behalf. Our actions toward the poor can truly make a difference. This reality is clearly demonstrated through a little story.

One day a businessman was rushing to a meeting. As he hurried along the sidewalk he passed a homeless man sitting on a bench with a pot of somewhat wilted flowers and a hat ready for donations. Feeling sorry for the man, he reached into his pocket and threw in about a dollar of change, but he took no flower. He continued down the sidewalk but was forced to stop at a traffic light. As he waited he thought, "That man was selling flowers and I did not take my purchase. I must return and take a flower." Although he might be late for his meeting, the man turned about and found the homeless flower salesman. "I apologize, my good man," said the businessman. "Your flowers are fairly priced and you have a good business. Please excuse my earlier lack of concern for your livelihood." The businessman then chose a flower and hurried off to his meeting.

One month later the same businessman was eating lunch with some clients in one of the city's finest restaurants. Unexpectedly one of the waiters came to him and said, "Sir, I am sure you do not remember me, but I will never forget you. One month ago you spoke to me as I sold flowers on the street. You restored my self-dignity and encouraged me to get my life in order. It is because of your faith in me that I have this job today."

When we welcome others and show them respect, we welcome Christ and honor him. Spanish-speaking peoples have an expression that illustrates this point: *Mi casa es tu casa.* Literally translated it means, "My house is your house," but these words do not adequately convey the significance of this greeting. It is not only an expression of welcome; the words express the reality that for the time guests are entertained in the house, they are members of the family and are treated as such. This is true regardless of who the guests are, their backgrounds, or past histories. All that matters is that they are under the roof of the house and, thus, very special. No one is left on the outside; all are welcomed as if they were Christ. We should not look upon others as strangers, foreigners or create any other categories. All that is necessary is to realize that they are God's children. To honor them is to honor Christ. We can have no greater privilege.

The preferential option for the poor and marginalized in society, seeing strength through diversity, has been a hallmark of many Christians in the twentieth century. Walter Rauschenbusch, a Baptist minister who worked in New York's "Hell's Kitchen" district at the outset of the twentieth century heard the cry of his people for justice and peace. He saw poverty firsthand and rallied to the support of his people. His response was more intellectual as he became a leading proponent of the Social Gospel Movement through such famous books as *Christianity and the Social Crisis* and *A Theology of the Social Gospel*. One generation later, the Catholic radical, Dorothy Day, heard the cry of the poor and responded through the initiation of the Catholic Worker Movement, which featured houses of hospitality to shelter and feed the homeless, and its penny newspaper, *The Catholic Worker*, which even today stridently promotes the rights of the poor. Dorothy Day's outreach to the marginalized of society was patterned after scripture. In the Letter to the Hebrews we read, "Do not neglect to show hospitality to strangers, for by doing that some have entertained angels without knowing it" (Hebrews 13:2).

It is sad but true that many times we, as individuals and a society, live life in a manner completely contradictory to the message of Saint James. We separate and discriminate on many levels and various criteria. We separate people on the basis of intelligence, appearance, and personal habits. Only those who are sufficiently bright, beautiful or handsome, and sophisticated are acceptable; others are given the proverbial dirty eclair. We make distinctions based on political and religious views and ideologies. Again, some are acceptable and others are not. We categorize and separate ourselves based on physical and mental condition, ethnic and racial origins, and even cultural views.

Our tendency to be exclusive occurs not only in our relationships with those who are different; it also happens with those who, at least on the surface, are in "our own group." Believe it or not much of our attitude can be explained by observation of how dogs treat each other. One day a woman observed an interesting occurrence. She began her story: "There was a terrible racket outside my home and I went to the window to see what was happening. I saw a large dog standing outside the front yard fence and my dog was barking wildly at it. Have you ever noticed how the dog on the inside usually barks wildly if another dog passes by outside, yet, the dog on the outside does not bark at all? I guess that is the way it is with dogs."

The woman continued saying, "I knew that the dog outside belonged to a neighbor, so I went outside and opened the gate. Almost instantly the barking stopped. There was some sniffing as they wanted to make sure of each other, but then the two dogs proceeded to ignore each other. I guess that is the way is it with dogs."

She then continued in a reflective mode, "It seems that the way the dogs act is the way church members act as well. The ones outside never bark, but the ones inside often bark angrily at those not on the inside with them. However, after they come inside and we are familiar with them, we come to completely ignore them, unless they happen to be in our social crowd." She thought, "It would be nice if we changed the rules and stopped acting like dogs. Wouldn't it be better if we extended our hands and were friendly to those on the outside? Wouldn't it be so much better if we did not ignore each other, except for the occasional sniff or handshake at church or greeting during a holiday?

"Just think how many broken hearts would be mended, how many tears dried if we cared enough to notice and to share a bit of genuine love. It's too bad that more love can be generated by a puppy wagging its tail to cheer one up than what we do. But I guess that's the way it is with dogs! What about us?"

James provides us with a significant challenge — to actualize the second half of the Golden Rule. We are called to live an active faith by seeking to accept all. Moreover, we are told to have a preferential option for the poor and those who need our attention the most — those, in other words, who need a doctor. Let us learn this lesson well. May we give others the best we have and not a leftover dirty eclair. If we can our reward in heaven will be great.

Proper 19
Pentecost 17
Ordinary Time 24
James 3:1-12

Engage Mind Before
Putting Mouth In Gear

When we were children our parents often quoted us the expression, "Sticks and stones can break my bones, but words can never hurt me." Generally this was a welcome comment that brought significant comfort, especially after the callous and thoughtless words of one of our friends or classmates hurt us. As children this expression works well and alleviates many problems, but as we mature we begin to see that this catchy phrase really does not help, for it simply does not apply. The reality is that words can be very hurtful and damaging. They might not hurt us physically as a blow to the body, but they can be even more destructive for their damage does not generally heal as rapidly and as well as wounds we can readily see. The power of words is real and, thus, their use must be recognized and guarded appropriately.

There are numerous examples in history of how words have been effectively utilized to aid, encourage, and inspire, both individuals and groups. On November 19, 1863, when President Abraham Lincoln spoke at the dedication of the Gettysburg National Cemetery, he finished his remarks with words that have echoed and been memorized by school-age children since that time: "That government of the people, by the people, and for the people shall not perish from the earth." Lincoln's words have been the source of inspiration not only for Americans, but all people who seek freedom. Some seventy years later, another president, Franklin D. Roosevelt, uplifted the American people in the midst of the Great Depression by stating, "There is nothing to fear but fear itself." He went on to articulate his four freedoms: freedom of speech and worship, and freedom from want and fear. He called upon Americans to unite for the common cause and good of all.

In the 1960s, Americans continued to be inspired and motivated by the words of great leaders. John F. Kennedy in his inaugural address on January 20, 1961 challenged Americans: "Ask not what your country can do for you, ask what you can do for your country." Volunteerism in programs such as the Peace Corps and many other civil and religious groups, seeking to aid those less fortunate, sprang up and gave people reason for hope. Dr. Martin Luther King, Jr., in probably his most famous speech told those assembled during the "March on Washington": "I have a dream that my four children will one day live in a nation where they will not be judged by the color of their skin, but by the content of their character." King dreamed of a colorless society where people would live in an ecumenical spirit of harmony with one another. His words gave inspiration to those associated with the American Civil Rights Movement.

The positive and uplifting use of words has been equaled, unfortunately, with many examples of the destructive use of rhetoric and language. The Ku Klux Klan preached hatred, racism, and religious intolerance against all who were not white, Anglo-Saxon, and Protestant during its heyday in the 1920s. Adolf Hitler proclaimed death to Jews, leading to the great genocide of the Holocaust. Our contemporary scene continues to experience hate-filled speech between Muslims, Jews, and Christians and even nasty and often "below the belt" verbal jabs in political campaigns. Playing by the rules of decorum no longer seems applicable. In order to get ahead the rule is not to promote your own initiatives but to downplay what others are suggesting.

Unquestionably, words have been used to inspire, rally, and produce the very best in human society, but they have equally been used to tear down and destroy, bringing great harm to individuals and groups. We need to learn how to use words wisely and constructively to build up and enhance our society. Saint James warns us today of the care that is needed in our use of words.

James provides much food for thought in his epistle this day. He begins his lesson by speaking of the significant and great responsibility of being a good teacher. He suggests that not many should be teachers, but this in only in a formal sense, for all of us are teachers in significant ways in the varied aspects of our lives. Parents, as we know, are the primary teachers of their children in every aspect of their lives. From learning to tie your shoes, to riding a bike, to how to conduct yourself in public, to the important lessons of our faith, parents are the frontline soldiers as our teachers. As teachers, as humans, we will make mistakes; this we know for certain, but it must be a great consolation to hear James say it. Thus, while we know, all too well at times, of our own failures and inadequacies, we must realize that God understands. After all, God made us incomplete and imperfect. All God asks of us is our best effort. Still, James reminds us that God has called us to a higher standard, a Christian life. Our road will encounter some detours, potholes, and roadblocks, but then God never promised us a smooth path to eternal life. In fact, Jesus is very clear in the Gospel: "If any want to become my followers, let them deny themselves and take up their cross and follow me. For those who want to save their life will lose it and those who lose their life for my sake will find it" (Matthew 16:24b-25).

James then gets into the heart of his message on the importance of the tongue to the body. Using the power and grandeur of a horse and a ship as examples, James demonstrates how the tongue can control the whole body. As a bit guides a powerful horse and a small rudder directs a large ship, so the tongue, seemingly so insignificant, directs a human by the words one uses. The apostle uses a reference from the book of Genesis to show how, through God's plan, all of creation is subject to humans. We have the ability to subdue all things; the created world has been made subject to humanity. All is subject to us, that is, except the tongue. He calls it "a restless evil, full of deadly poison." While, as we have seen, words can be used effectively to praise and uplift, so too they can be used to tear down and injure.

James tells us that with the same tongue we praise God and curse God's people. We know all too well the reality of this statement. We gather together this day in praise and worship of God. We use many words, all of which in some way are articulated to bring something positive to God's people. Yet, if we are not careful, before the day has ended, we will use the same tongue with which we utter praise to be the vehicle that speaks ill of others, especially behind their backs, where it is easy, convenient, and "safe." Unfortunately, this is a common failure in which we all participate. The apostle suggests, however, that this reality need not occur. He provides examples from nature that show that the tongue need not participate in both good and evil. He says a spring does not yield both fresh and brackish water nor does a fig tree yield olives nor a grapevine figs.

The challenge of Saint James is highly significant. The laws of nature govern the reality that apple trees do not yield grapes nor do seeds for squash yield carrots, but the tongue is under our control; it is not governed by the laws of nature. Personal choice, one of the two ideas (along with the ability to think) that separates humankind from the rest of God's creation, is operative with the tongue. We must choose to use the tongue to build up, praise, and challenge, rather than ridicule or condemn. Thus, the choice is ours. The choice is always ours!

The words of James, I am certain, must have been the inspiration apparent in a teacher who, the first day of class placed in huge block letters above the blackboard (so it would not be erased): "Engage mind before putting mouth in gear." In other words, we must think before we speak. These words of wisdom should be heeded by all. All of us have a tendency to be impulsive. We use words to get our way and to get it now, not in a few days or even a few minutes. When things don't happen as we think or the schedule we have set, we lash out, often at others who have absolutely nothing to do with things for which we give them responsibility. We all have a tendency as well to react, often harshly, especially when someone speaks ill of us or is less than positive. All of us at times are defensive. It is natural for us to "circle the wagons" and create a defensive shield around ourselves when be believe we are being attacked. Even when we know in our hearts that what the other person is saying may be true, we do not want to admit it. We defend ourselves, often with significant barbs for the person who we perceive is attacking our person. We simply cannot allow what others say to go without our response.

Words are easy to use — as the expression says, "talk is cheap." Yet, in the end, words can be very expensive. They can cost us dearly if not properly used. When loose and thoughtless words, often expressed without engaging our minds, reach unintended ears, we pay a heavy price. We may only receive a lecture or a reprimand for our casual use of speech. We could, however, lose a friendship or our job. Thus, we must always be mindful that while words are free, their use must be tightly controlled.

Jesus provided the best examples of how to properly use our tongues. The Lord used his tongue wisely to instruct. The Gospels are filled with examples of how Jesus taught his disciples and even those who were allied against him, the Scribes and Pharisees, what was necessary to gain the eternal life of God. Jesus spoke directly in the "Sermon on the Mount" (Matthew 5-7), and metaphorically through the use of parables, stories which are timeless for all peoples. Jesus used words to praise. The Lord praised the widow who contributed to the collection only a few pennies, but it was all she had for her livelihood (Mark 12:43-44). He congratulated Mary of Bethany for her wisdom in choosing to sit at his feet and listen to his words (Luke 10:41-42). Jesus used words to console the widow of Nain (Luke 7:11-17) and to bring hope to the centurion whose servant was sick (Mark 8:5-13; Luke 7:1-10) and to the blind man at Jericho (Luke 18:35-43). Jesus used words to forgive the penitent thief, "Truly I tell you, today you will be with me in paradise" (Luke 23:43), and the woman caught in the act of adultery: "Neither do I condemn you. Go your way, and from now on do not sin again" (John 8:11b). Christ also used words when appropriate to challenge. He said to his parents after their three-day search resulted in his discovery in the temple, "Why were you searching for me? Did you not know that I must be in my Father's house?" (Luke 2:49). His parable of the Good Samaritan (Luke 10:25-37) challenged Jewish officials on who they considered their neighbor. He used strong language, even to the point of losing a part of our body (Matthew 5:29-30; Mark 9:43-48), to suggest that nothing must interfere with our relationship with God. Jesus even used rather harsh words to speak of the future and the division his reign would bring (Matthew 10:34-39; Luke 12:49-53).

Jesus did not always use words to praise, but they were always directed in positive ways, to right the ships of others, spiritually and socially, and guide them toward more calm waters. The Lord used words to assist people toward the one and only goal that has ultimate meaning — our eternal life with God.

In our lives we want to change the world and change others, but we need to control ourselves first. The Indian Jesuit and spiritual writer, Anthony de Mello, tells of a Sufi Bayazid who once commented about himself: I was a revolutionary when I was young and my single prayer to God was, "Lord, give me the energy to change the world." As I approached middle-age and realized that half my life was gone without my changing a single soul, I changed my prayer to, "Lord give me the grace to change all those with whom I come in contact. If I can change my family and friends I will be satisfied." Now that I am an old man and my days are numbered, my one prayer is, "Lord, give me the grace to change myself." If I had prayed for this at the outset, I should not have wasted my life.

Words truly are an important element in our lives. We speak casually; we speak seriously. We joke with others and we bring challenges. Yet, in all that we say there is a need to think seriously about what we say before we say it. Too often we hear people say, "Oh, I wish I had not said that," or "I should have said something." In short, we need to think about what we say. We must follow the lead of Jesus and use words in ways that instruct, praise, forgive, and when necessary, challenge and admonish. Let us do our best to tame our tongues. Let us make sure to engage mind before putting mouth in gear!

God's Wisdom Or The World?

Once upon a time there was an old man who lived on the outskirts of town. He had lived there so long that no one knew who he was or where he had come from. Some thought that he had been a very powerful king, but that was many years ago. Others suggested that he was once famous, rich, and generous, but he had lost everything. Still others said that he was once very wise and influential. There were even some who said he was holy. The children in the town, however, thought he was an old and stupid man and they made his life miserable. They threw stones at his windows, left dead animals on his front porch, destroyed his garden, and yelled nasty words at him at every opportunity.

Then one day, one of the older boys came up with an idea to prove once and for all that those who thought he was a former king, or rich, famous, and generous, or wise and influential, and most especially those who considered him holy were all wrong. No, he truly was just a stupid old man. The boy knew how to catch a bird in a snare. He told his friends that he would catch the bird and together they would go to the old man's home and knock on the door. When the man would answer the boy would ask, "Old man, do you know what I have hidden behind my back?" Now he might guess that it is a bird, but with the second question I will get him. I will ask him if the bird is alive or dead. If he says dead, I will allow the bird to go free, but if he says the bird is alive, I will crush it to death with my hands. Either way he will prove he is only a stupid old man.

The children thought it was a great plan. Thus, the older boy caught the bird and together they went off to the old man's house and rudely knocked on the door. The man opened the door and seeing the large gathering of children realized something was up. The boy spoke quickly, "Old man, do you know what I have hidden behind my back?" The old man looked at the children one by one and out of the corner of his eye he saw a white feather fall to the ground. He answered, "Yes, I do. It's a white bird."

The children's eyes grew large. How could he know it was a white bird? Maybe the people in town were right all along. The older boy was not to be deterred from his goal and quickly asked the second question. "Well that was a good guess, but is the bird alive or dead?" Again, the old man looked with sad eyes at each of the children. Finally his eyes met those of the boy. He answered, "That depends on you; the answer is in your hands."[1]

Certainly the old man was filled with wisdom and knowledge. Not only could he "outfox" the children, especially the boy, at their own game, but he was wise enough to be able to teach them an important lesson at the same time. We have the choice to do good or evil. We have the chance to choose the wisdom of God or that of the world. Which will you choose?

The Hebrew Scriptures provide many examples of how the Lord laid before the human race distinct options that require humans to choose between God and the world. The Genesis account of creation related how God gave Adam and Eve all that they could possibly need or want, yet, they were not satisfied. Satan tempted them by claiming they could be like God, but in reality they were being asked to choose the world over God. They took the bait; they chose unwisely, seeking ambition over what they had been given. The end result was the disorder and wickedness in the world, what many contemporary theologians call the "original sin" as it is the common lot of all; none can escape from this reality. Later in the Pentateuch, God, in a conversation with Moses, places another fundamental choice before the great deliverer. We read in Deuteronomy: "I have set before you life and death, blessings and curses. Choose life so that you and your descendants may live, loving the Lord your God, obeying him, and holding fast to him; for that means life to you and length of days, so that you may live in the land that the Lord swore to give to your ancestors, to Abraham, Isaac, and to Jacob" (Deuteronomy 30:19b-20). God is telling Moses that the choice for God is a choice for life; to choose the world is a formula for death. This fundamental choice is placed before the rulers of Israel and Judah numerous times by the many prophets sent by God. In short the message of the prophets is a basic choice. Isaiah, Jeremiah, Amos, Hosea, and all the others placed before the ruling elite the choice to follow God or the way of the world, manifest by false gods, such as Baal, or even more common, the false avenues of power, wealth, and prestige.

God did not simply place choices before the Hebrews, but showed the people how to make the wise and proper decision. When Jesse parades before Samuel his sons to see which one has been chosen by God to replace Saul, he does not even consider the youngest, David, because he is a youth and ruddy in complexion. In other words he does not "look the part." God, however, corrects this attitude saying to Samuel, "Do not look on his appearance or on the height of his stature, because I have rejected him; for the Lord does not see as mortals see; they look on the outward appearance, but the Lord looks on the heart" (1 Samuel 16:7). God is telling Samuel and Jesse that they must not look at what the world considers important when selecting a king, but what God deems valuable. As always the choice is clear — the world or God.

Jesus, in his ministry, also provided many examples of the need to choose God over the world. We recall the story of the Pharisee and the tax collector. The former thought himself important because of his perceived righteousness, while the latter only beat his breast and admitted his sinfulness. Jesus is clear, "I tell you this man [the tax collector] went down to his home justified rather than the other; for all who exalt themselves will be humbled, but all who humble themselves will be exalted" (Luke 18:14). Humility comes from God; arrogance comes from the world. The parable of the man with a super abundance of wealth (Luke 12:13-21) is another example of making the choice between God and the world. All the man seems to be concerned about is where to store his great wealth; he seems totally oblivious to the source of his prosperity.

Thus, his life will be taken. Jesus concludes, "So it is with those who store up treasure for themselves but are not rich toward God."

In the story of the rich man, traditionally known as Dives, and the beggar Lazarus (Luke 16:19-31) we recall how Dives seemed unconcerned about the beggar until it was too late. He made his choice and so, too, will his family have the opportunity to choose, God or the world. All the synoptic evangelists (Matthew 19:16-30; Mark 10:17-31; Luke 18:18-30) report the story of Jesus' encounter with the rich young man who was challenged to divest himself of his wealth. Again, in essence it is a choice between God and the world. Jesus provides a great challenge to those who are attached to the world: "Truly I tell you, it will be hard for a rich person to enter the kingdom of heaven. Again I tell you, it is easier for a camel to pass through the eye of a needle than for someone who is rich to enter the kingdom of God." Jesus continued, "For mortals it is impossible, but for God all things are possible" (Matthew 19:23b-24, 26b). Clearly Jesus is telling his disciples that they must choose God and not the world.

Lastly, Jesus himself was given the challenge of choosing the world or God. After his baptism, he chose to go to the desert to prepare himself for his public ministry (Matthew 4:1-11; Mark 1:12-15; Luke 4:1-13). There Satan tempted him with the three great challenges that have always faced humanity: power, wealth, and prestige. In each case Jesus rejected the world, saying that the things of God were more important. We must choose the same.

James, as one of the select disciples of Jesus, took seriously his Master's challenge and passed it on to his readers, including you and me. He begins this passage by basically asking the people how they understand wisdom and understanding. In a rhetorical manner he answers his own question by suggesting there are two possible responses. One form of wisdom is characterized by envy, selfish ambition in one's heart, boastfulness, and lack of sincerity. This is earthly, unspiritual, and devilish; it is an understanding of life that creates disorder and wickedness of all kinds. James, as a contemporary of Jesus, wrote from personal experience of what such an earthy attitude had done in Christ's ministry.

There is, however, a second form of wisdom, the pattern of life that comes from God. This is what James wishes to emphasize. He provides some powerful words to describe the wisdom of God. First, he says it is pure, peaceable, and gentle. God's wisdom is not tainted by the world, but rather seeks the good for all. Next, he suggests that God's wisdom is willing to yield and is full of mercy. God's wisdom, in other words, watches over the individual. Where the world's wisdom often unceremoniously "runs a person over," God's wisdom yields and gives people freedom. And, when one makes a mistake, God forgives, where the world is often very unforgiving and intolerant. James says God's wisdom is without a trace of partiality or hypocrisy. In other words, God is inclusive, not exclusive like the world. In the world, social Darwinism continues suggesting that the powerful, rich, and beautiful should dominate others. God's wisdom does not differentiate; all are God's children. Finally, the apostle says that those who demonstrate the wisdom of God will manifest peace and yield a harvest of righteousness.

James next addresses what happens when we make friendships with the world. Conflicts and disputes are the general problem. If we make alliances with the world, the tendency is great to covet and when we cannot obtain what we wish, we even use force and violence to achieve our perceived needs. We engage in disputes with others. We seldom if ever ask God for what we need, only what we want. And, if we do ask for our needs, we ask wrongly. Possibly James recalled Jesus' promise that all our needs would be met: "Ask, and it will be given you; search, and you will find; knock and the door will be opened for you. For everyone who asks receives, and everyone who searches finds, and for anyone who knocks, the door will be opened" (Luke 11:9-10). Thus, it is clear that God will meet all of our needs. We may not receive it when we planned or in the manner we thought. We must also remember that our needs and desires are not always the same. God will, however, meet all of our needs.

James does provide the proper means to choose God over the world. First, we must submit to God. Submission does not violate our free will; we should choose to make God and God's wisdom the pattern of our lives. Next we are told to resist evil and Satan will flee and to draw close to God and God will draw close to us. We must, therefore, seek the wisdom that God can provide and then all other things will fall in place.

James' message that contrasts two forms of wisdom is an excellent example of the dilemma we have in exercising one of the greatest gifts given us by God, namely the opportunity to choose. Animals have no choice; even the most intelligent of God's creation operates on instinct. They are programmed to do whatever they do. However, humans are given free will. God does not demand compliance; we are never placed into handcuffs or a straightjacket so as to force our actions.

Free will, that quality along with the ability to think, which separates us from the rest of God's creation, always must be used judiciously and wisely. Thus we might ask, why does the world suffer? Why do pain, problems, and suffering exist in such abundance? We all believe that God is all-good, all-love, full of compassion, and all-powerful. This is how we define God. Thus, the question bears repeating, why does our world suffer? Why do wars exist and people die in innocence? Why do people in positions of public trust commit acts that cause others not only to lose faith in the individual, but in the system as well? Why do people fight one another and the only question between them is the color of their skin, their political preference, or religious belief?

The basic answer to these challenging questions is personal choice, our free will to choose the wisdom of the world or that of God at any time in any way. Soren Kierkegaard, the famous nineteenth-century existentialist philosopher and theologian, once wrote, "Faith is a matter of choice, our personal decision in finding God." This personal decision, our free will, is why the world suffers. It is free will that allows the drunk to drive and kill others. It is free will that allows people in public service to break the law and thus lower the integrity of the system. It is free will that places certain members and groups in society on the fringe and does not allow them to participate. Free will moves us closer to or further from God. As Kierkegaard wrote, it is our decision; faith is our choice. As God said it to Abraham, "I place before you death and life; thus choose life."

Too often we willingly choose the world and, thus, death, but if we wish we can choose the wisdom of God and life. Yes, we must use our gift of free will wisely, to always choose God's wisdom over that of the world. Often we hesitate; we are unsure how far we can go or how much we are willing to risk. Thus we balk and miss opportunities.

A little story illustrates how our tendency to hesitate can lead to loss. Three wise men were encouraged to experience what others called the cave of wisdom and life. They made careful preparations for what would be a challenging and arduous journey. When they reached the cave, they noted a guard at the entrance. They were not permitted to enter the cave until they had spoken with the guard. He had only one question for them, but he insisted that they answer only after talking it over amongst them. He assured them they would have a good guide to lead them through the various regions of the cave. His question was simple, "How far into the cave of wisdom and life do you wish to go?" The three travelers discussed the question and then returned to the guard. They said, "We do not want to enter very far. We only want to venture far enough to say we have been there." The response of the guard manifested none of the disappointment that he felt as he summoned a guide to lead them into the cave. Then he watched as they set out to make the return trip back to their own land.

The children in the story were wrong; the old man was not a nasty and dumb person. On the contrary, he was a man of great wisdom and prudence who, at the same time, was a great teacher. Let us consider the options that stand before us. Let us have the courage to go forward, confident of God's presence with us. May we always choose wisely the wisdom of God. If we can our reward in heaven will be great.

---

1. Paraphrased from "The Answer's in Your Hands," in William J. Bausch, *A World of Stories for Preachers and Teachers* (Mystic, Connecticut: Twenty-Third Publications, 1999), pp. 219-220.

Prayer: A Way Of Life

Once there was a monastery in the woods that had fallen upon hard times. In the past it had been a thriving community that was well known and respected throughout the region, but over the last generation the monks had died one by one and there were no new vocations to replace them. Besides this, the monks did not seem to be as friendly to each other. Something just wasn't right. The Father Abbot was quite concerned about the future of his monastery, now consisting of himself and three brothers and, thus, he sought counsel from the local rabbi who was known to be a great sage. The abbot went to the rabbi and asked him if he had any advice on what to do to save his monastery. The rabbi felt at a loss and said that he, too, worried about his own congregation; people were too busy and simply were not coming to the synagogue any longer. The two commiserated together and read the Torah. As the abbot was getting ready to return home the rabbi looked at him and said, "One in your home is the Messiah." The abbot walked home puzzled as to what the rabbi's words meant.

When he arrived at the monastery the monks asked the abbot what he had learned. He responded that the rabbi had given him no concrete advice, but he had said in cryptic language, "One in your home is the Messiah." Over the next days and weeks the monks pondered what this might mean. Was it possible that one of them was the Messiah? If that was the case then most certainly it was Father Abbot. He had been the leader for more than a generation. On the other hand it might be Brother Thomas, for he is a holy man and full of light. Certainly it could not be Brother Eldred. He is old, crotchety, and often mean-spirited, but he always seems to be right, no matter what the situation or question. The rabbi could not have meant Brother Phillip. He is very passive — a real nobody, but one has to admit that he is always there when someone needs assistance.

As they continued to contemplate this question, the old monks began to treat each other with great respect, on the off chance that the one with whom they were dealing really was the Messiah. They again began to live the gospel message. The monastery was a much more prayerful place once again.

Because the monastery was located in a beautiful portion of the forest it was common during the spring, summer, and fall months for families to come and have picnics on the grounds. During this period people who came seemed to sense the new spirit of respect and love that was present at the monastery. The people returned often and one day a young man came to the Father Abbot and asked if he could join the community. Soon others inquired and joined and, thus, after several years the vibrant community at the monastery was again restored because the wisdom of the rabbi had transformed hearts. The monks had once again started to live their lives according to the Golden Rule.

The monks in the monastery learned, "through the back door," of the need to treat their brothers with respect. They were converted to an understanding that prayer must be a way of life. Prayer is vocal, but it must also be action. It must be the way we live our daily lives. Saint James, as he concludes his epistle, a letter based on action, that is being doers of the word, makes this point abundantly clear.

Prayer, one's daily communication with God, is a staple of all organized religion and a central tenet to the Judeo-Christian tradition of which we are all members. In the Hebrew Scriptures there are numerous examples of various kinds of prayer that are used to invoke God to act. In Numbers 21:7 the Israelites ask Moses to save them, "Pray to the Lord to take the serpents from us." More positively, Ezra calls the Hebrews to "pray for the life of the king and his children" (Ezra 6:10). Jeremiah wrote to the Jews in exile telling them, "Pray to the Lord on its [the city of Babylon's] behalf" (Jeremiah 29:7). King Zedekiah asked Jeremiah, "Please pray for us to the Lord our God" (Jeremiah 29:7). The book of Psalms is filled with prayers of praise to God. The psalmist writes, "You who fear the Lord, praise him! All you offspring of Jacob, glorify him" (Psalm 22:23). Psalm 148, familiar to many, begins: "Praise the Lord! Praise the Lord from the heavens; praise him in the heights! Praise him, all his angels; praise him all his host! Praise him, sun and moon; praise him, all you shining stars! Praise him, you highest heavens, and you waters above the heavens! Let them praise the name of the Lord."

The New Testament is equally filled with references to the importance of prayer. It is clear that Jesus was a man of great prayer; it was the center of his life. Many times Jesus went off by himself to an isolated spot to pray to the Father (Matthew 14:23; Mark 6:46; Luke 6:12), sometimes spending the whole evening in prayer. Jesus encouraged his friends to pray. He took Peter, James, and John up on a mountain to pray and there he was transfigured before them (Luke 9:28-36). After the Last Supper, Jesus went to the Garden of Gethsemane to pray and he told these same three apostles to pray as well (Mark 14:32-42). When Jesus' hour had come he prayed for those who would be left behind; he never forgot his friends (John 17:1-26).

Besides being a man of prayer, Jesus also instructed his followers on how to pray. He taught his disciples that prayer was a private matter; it was not to be used to make others think you are important. In the Sermon on the Mount, Jesus said, "Whenever you pray, do not be like the hypocrites; for they love to stand and pray in the synagogues and at the street corners, so that they may be seen by others ... Whenever you pray, go to your room and shut the door and pray to your Father in secret" (Matthew 6:5-6). Jesus then went on to tell his friends the multiplication of words was not important, rather a more simple approach is best. Then he taught them the Lord's Prayer, which for many, if not all of us, was the first prayer we ever learned.

Jesus' disciples took his instructions on prayer and through their evangelistic zeal spread the practice to all lands and people.

While it was clear from Jesus' practice, Saint Paul, the apostle to the Gentiles, made explicit a fundamental tenet of prayer: "Pray in the Spirit at all times in every prayer and supplication. To that end keep alert and always persevere in supplication for all the saints" (Ephesians 6:18). In his Letter to the Colossians he put it this way, "Devote yourselves to prayer, keeping alert in it with thanksgiving" (Colossians 4:3). Paul in essence was telling his fledgling Christian communities that they must make prayer a way of life. Today Saint James makes this same important point.

Since James' message in his epistle has been centered about action, it is totally appropriate that he closes his letter with an exhortation to make prayer, in word and action, a way of life. James begins by speaking of the more traditional forms of vocal and mental prayer. He asks those who suffer and those who exalt to pray. One must pray in petition to God and, as James says, such prayer will save the sick person. Next, the apostle says the cheerful should give praise and thanksgiving to God. We should never forget the source of our sustenance. James then moves to a more active understanding of prayer. He first says that we should pray for one another. We can verbalize and more mentally pray for our family and friends, but we can also act on their behalf. If prayer is communicating with God, there can be no better way than to demonstrate by action what one wishes or hopes for another. James uses the example of Elijah to demonstrate the power and effectiveness of prayer, in word and action. Clearly, James wants his readers to know and practice the idea that prayer is essential; it must become an integral part of our everyday lives. We must broaden our often-narrow understanding of prayer to include an active response.

When people think of prayer, generally, as we have said, they are referring to verbal or mental communication with God. Certainly this is the most common idea. We converse with God in five general ways: petition, intercession, praise, thanksgiving, and confession. Christians call upon God in prayers of petition and intercession when they need something. We may pray for something in our personal lives, the life of a family member or friend, or more broadly for a group of people, a nation, or even the world. We call upon God to intercede; we say with the psalmist: "God is our refuge and strength, a very present help in trouble" (Psalm 46:1). People must praise God daily. We should wish to praise the one who has provided everything, who is the source of the goodness and peace we seek and generally enjoy, and the one who challenges us to move forward and continue walking the Christian road toward holiness. When we gather in our churches on Sunday morning we pray in praise as a community. Many Christians find great fellowship through charismatic prayer of praise in the Spirit.

We must pray to God in thanksgiving. As a nation, we annually set aside the last Thursday in November to give thanks for the many blessings we share. However, our daily prayer must be one of thanksgiving. Jesus was very disheartened when, after curing the ten lepers only one, a Samaritan, returned to give thanks: "Were not ten made clean? But the other nine, where are they? Was none of them found to return and give praise to God except this foreigner?" (Luke 17:17-18). Our daily prayer must be one of thanksgiving. We seldom think to thank God for our lives, the beauty of the day and creation, and even the challenges that come our way.

Lastly, we must also pray for the forgiveness of sins. Jesus specifically calls for this in the Lord's Prayer and so does James today. We are all sinners and thus in need of God's healing touch. We should never be too proud to admit that we are wrong and have failed. We must not forget how Jesus exalted the publican who could not raise his eyes to God, but had the courage to beat his breast and say, "God, be merciful to me, a sinner!" (Luke 18:13c).

While we generally think of prayer as a mental or verbal exercise, such a view is far too narrow. We must see our lives as a prayer. If prayer is communication with God, all that we do and say, even think, is a prayer. Thus, our lives of action must echo the fivefold process of mental and verbal prayer. If we petition God to act, for ourselves or others, are we willing to act as well? We cannot passively stand still as the world races by. That is precisely the problem that was at the monastery; no one was willing to take responsibility; nobody acted. If we want God to act for us, we must be willing to act, to do our share, to lift our portion of the load. God will always do God's part, but too often we expect God to do it alone. The Lord has given each one of us many talents and opportunities to act. We should not disappoint him.

Sometimes we call upon God to intercede, to act for justice and righteousness for others. We pray for God to intercede, but what are we willing to do; what intercession can we make? Can we march for justice and human rights? Can we stand in solidarity with the poor and marginalized peoples in our world? Can we lobby our elected officials to act for others? Can we work to change things and make our world a better place? We might not be able to effect systemic change, but a powerful call to action challenges us, "Think globally, but act locally."

If we truly wish to praise God, how do we show it; how is it manifest? If we wish to praise God should we not be more actively involved in our church, the Christian community that binds us together as a family, namely the people of God? Are we willing to challenge others in their Christian duty to praise God? Do we praise God by standing up for what we know is right, that is what God says and not the world?

We must thank God with actions as well. It is very easy to say, "Thank you," but much harder to go out of our way in some gesture of thanksgiving. When God acts as we hope, we often give thanks and praise in return. But does our thanksgiving end with a word and a nod of the head? What can we actively do to demonstrate our thanks? Writing a thank-you note to God is a start, but we can do better. We must actively work on God's behalf in our world. Do we consider giving thanks to God when the response we receive from our prayer of petition or intercession is not what we expect or does not come in the timely manner we want or even demand? Do we only give thanks for "positive" results? Is it possible to give thanks to God under these unexpected circumstances, confident that God's answer may be the proper one after all?

The ease of saying, "Thank you," is also found in the curt expression, "I am sorry." Although it may take some courage to express sorrow and admit guilt, can't we do more? What can we do to demonstrate contrition to others for the ways we have hurt them? If we have wronged another, can we make amends? If we have failed someone by omission can we work harder to assist their needs

404

in the future? Can we show God that we have turned over a new leaf, a new chapter in our lives? Realizing that we have done wrong, can we demonstrate clearly and forcefully a better way to live? The monks in the monastery learned through the wisdom of the rabbi that their lives needed to mirror the one whom they worshiped; they had to become like the Messiah. Jesus' whole life, every word and action, was a prayer. Saint James today presents us with the message to make our lives a prayer. The apostle's missive is consistent with the whole of his epistle, the need to be doers of the word and not simply listen. We are challenged to transform every action of our lives into a prayer, communicating to God our desire to be his disciples. Let us, therefore, resolve today to be doers, active participants in God's life. The game of life is not won by sitting on the sidelines; we must actively participate. Let us do so by living our lives as a prayer that will help build the kingdom of God today and each day of our lives.

In Solidarity With Jesus

"Rags, rags! Give me your tired, dirty, and old rag and I will give you a new, clean, and fresh one. Rags, rags." That was the cry to which I awoke one bright sunny Friday morning. I sprang from my bed and peered out my second-story apartment window. There he was, the ragman of our town. He was 6'4" if he was an inch, youthful in appearance and strong of build. I had heard so much about him but never actually seen him. I threw on some clothes, bounded down the stairs and out the front door of my apartment building. I thought, this is my opportunity to see where he goes and what he does. I decided to watch at a distance.

The ragman pushed his basketful of rags ahead of him. He continued his cry, "Rags, rags. Give me your old, tired, and dirty rag and I will give a fresh, clean, and new one. Rags, rags." As the ragman pushed his basket of rags he came across a young woman who sat on the front porch to her home. Even from a distance, I could see that she held a handkerchief to her face which was swollen and her eyes were red. She had been crying. "Please," said the ragman to the young woman, "give me your old and soiled handkerchief and I will give you a clean and fresh one." The woman looked at the ragman with a puzzled stare, yet she agreed to his request. The ragman pulled out a clean and fresh linen handkerchief. When the woman put the cloth to her face, something wonderful happened. Her face was no longer swollen; her eyes were no longer red. She appeared happy and gay. But when the ragman put the woman's handkerchief to his face, he began to cry, his eyes turned red and his face began to swell. My amazement at what I was witnessing knew no bounds. And the ragman continued on.

He pushed his basket of rags ahead of him as he walked through the city streets. He came to the main square and there on a park bench he encountered another woman. She was older and her clothes were dirty and torn. Around her head was a bandage from which blood oozed from a fresh wound. The ragman said to her, "Please give that old and dirty bandage and I will give you a new and clean one." The woman looked at the ragman somewhat with disdain. Yet, there was something in what he said or how he said it that attracted her. She took the bandage from her head and replaced it with the fresh one given her. As she placed the bandage on her head, the blood flow stopped. No longer was her face tortured with pain. When the ragman placed the old bandage on his head, he began to bleed in the same place the woman had been injured. His face took on the look of one in pain. I continued to wonder at what I saw. And the ragman continued on.

Bleeding and crying, the ragman continued to push his basket of rags. He came upon the local town drunk who was sleeping off his night of frivolity between two buildings in the center of town. The ragman approached, quietly so as to not disturb the man. He pulled the old blanket from the man and covered him with a new and clean one. He also left a set of new clothes. As the ragman wrapped the old blanket around him, he began to stagger and stumble as if he was the one who had been drinking. And the ragman continued on.

The ragman continued to push his cart, stumbling as he went, leaving a trail of blood and tears. He came to the edge of town. There he encountered someone with whom I was not familiar. He must have been a new person in town. He was an older man with a tattered old jacket. He had only one arm. "Give me that old coat," said the ragman, "and I will give you a new and clean one." The man readily agreed, after all he was to get a new coat out of the deal. As the old man put on the new jacket not one but two arms came through, arms that were strong and youthful. But when the ragman put on the coat of the old man, only one arm came through.

As I watched I could not believe what I saw. And the ragman continued on.

The ragman, bleeding, crying, stumbling, and now with only one arm, continued to push his basketful of rags. At the outskirts of town he found the local dump. With his remaining strength he pushed his basket through the gate and up the hill. There in the middle of the garbage dump he lay down to sleep and as he slept he died. From a distance, I found safe haven in the front seat of an old abandoned vehicle in the dump. I began to cry, so powerful were the events that I had witnessed. My tears put me to sleep — a deep and restful slumber. Friday was lost and Saturday passed without my knowing it. But the next day, Sunday morning, I awoke to the most brilliant light. There before me stood the ragman. He had a small scar on his head, but both his arms were restored. He was dressed in the most glorious white clothes I had ever seen. Yes, he was the ragman of our town; he was the Christ.

Walter Wangerin, Jr.'s powerful tale of the ragman[1] demonstrates how one took on the cares and concerns of those he encountered; he took on their pain. In every way he became one with the people. His ability to be in solidarity with others brought him several trials, but in the end he received the exaltation that is the reward for those who love God. Today's reading from the Letter to the Hebrews tells us that Jesus found perfection, through suffering and becoming one like us in all things but sin. God becomes one with us; we must, in turn, have the courage to become one with Christ by being one with each other. Our solidarity with Christ is our solidarity with our brothers and sisters who bear his name.

Salvation history relates how Jesus came to be in solidarity with us. This story begins in the Hebrew Scriptures with the prophecy of the coming of the Messiah. The scriptures present two contrasting images of the Messiah, one that speaks of a great warrior and a second which describes a peaceful and obedient servant. The prophet Jeremiah provides an excellent description of the first image: "The days are surely coming says the Lord, when I will raise up for David a righteous branch, and he shall reign as king and deal wisely, and shall execute justice and righteousness in the land. In his days Judah will be saved and Israel will live in safety. And this is the name by which he will be called: 'The Lord is our righteousness'" (Jeremiah 23:5-6). The prophet thus describes one who will be a great champion for Israel, conquering its enemies, restoring the davidic kingship, and bringing greatness once again to the nation. This was clearly the dominant image among the Jews at the time of Jesus.

There was, however, a contrasting portrait, that of a peaceful servant, which Isaiah often references. We read, "For a child is born for us, a son given to us; authority rests upon his shoulders; and he is named Wonderful Counselor, Mighty God, Everlasting Father, Prince of Peace. His authority shall grow continually and there shall be endless peace for the throne of David and his kingdom" (Isaiah 9:6-7a). More importantly, Isaiah also speaks of a "suffering servant": "He was despised and rejected by others; a man of suffering and acquainted with infirmity; and as one from whom others hide their faces he was despised, and we held him of no account" (Isaiah 53:3). Thus, when Jesus began his public ministry, exhibiting this latter image, he and his message were not accepted by the Jews.

Jesus came, not as a warrior or great king in an earthly sense, but rather as a servant. He made this abundantly clear to his followers: "The Son of Man came not to be served but to serve, and to give his life [as] a ransom for many" (Matthew 20:28). How did Jesus manifest his desire to serve, to be in solidarity with us? First and foremost, he chose to become human and, thus, experience our daily life in every aspect, save sin. Next, Jesus associated freely with all people, but in a preferential way with those whom society had placed on the margins — foreigners, the poor, the diseased, tax collectors, sinners, and women. No one was excluded in Jesus' mind. Third, Jesus constantly spoke of and lived a life of personal humility that was centered on the needs of the common good of all. We recall how Jesus instructed his disciples to always sit at the lowest place of honor at the table so one might later ask them to come higher, concluding, "For all who exalt themselves will be humbled, and those who humble themselves will be exalted" (Luke 14:11). Lastly, Jesus was in solidarity with his people by accepting his fate and not running from it. As he says, legions of angels

(Matthew 26:53) would have come to his rescue, but he chose the route of suffering and death so his human experience would be complete. Saint Paul has summarized Jesus' solidarity with us in his famous Christological hymn in Philippians: "Though he was in the form of God, [Jesus] did not regard equality with God as something to be exploited, but emptied himself taking the form of a slave, being born in human likeness. And being found in human form, he humbled himself and became obedient to the point of death — even death on a cross" (Philippians 2:6-8).

The Letter to the Hebrews, which we begin to read today has an interesting history. Originally ascribed to Paul, biblical scholars today tell us that due to significant differences in language, style, theme, and theology the letter was not from Paul's hand, but rather another Jewish Christian of Hellenistic background. Scholars also tell us that the letter was most probably addressed to Jewish Christians to assist those who wavered in their belief that Jesus was the promised Messiah of the Torah.

The author, therefore, at the outset sets forth his argument about the connection of the Messiah to God and God's people. We learn that God speaks to us through the Son, who has been appointed heir to all things. The Son, Jesus, is the reflection of the Father's glory and the exact imprint of God's being. Jesus is God and sits with the Father in majesty on high. Next, we learn of the dignity of the human race. Although humans are lower than the angels, they are crowned with glory and honor. We are reminded, as Genesis tells us, that all of creation is subject to humans. The human race is the crown jewel of God's creation. With these two premises set, the author then makes the connection that Jesus, although God, was, for a period of time, made lower than the angels and crowned with glory and honor. That is, Jesus took on the human condition, choosing to suffer, like the ragman in Walter Wangerin's story. Jesus tasted death for all of us. It was through his suffering and death that Jesus was perfected. Then we hear the most important verse, "Jesus is not ashamed to call them [us] brothers and sisters, saying 'I will proclaim your name to my brothers and sisters, in the midst of the congregation I will praise you.' " Yes, Jesus is one with us; we are in solidarity.

Jesus, the Son of God came among us as a human, walking on our earth, living our life, and calling us his sisters and brothers. God's oneness with us challenges us to be one, that is, in solidarity with one another. Like Jesus, we must be in solidarity with the marginalized peoples in our society; we must follow the pattern of life that the Lord laid out for us. We must reach out our hand to the lowly and poor, the *anawim*, those who count for little or nothing in our world. It is our responsibility as Christians to lend our efforts and place ourselves at the service of the sick and aged, the sinner, those who are imprisoned. In short, we must carry out the exhortation of Jesus, as described by Saint Matthew in his famous scene of the Second Coming of the Lord (25: 31-46). We must feed the hungry, clothe the naked, and visit the sick and imprisoned for as Jesus says, "Truly I tell you, just as you did it to one of the least of these who are members of my family, you did it to me." We must be willing to spend our lives in the service of others, to grow rich, not in the eyes of the world, but the eyes of God (Luke 12:21). Jesus told his disciples, "If any want to become my followers, let them deny themselves and take up their cross and follow me. For those who want to save their life will lose it, and those who lose their life for may sake, and for the gospel, will save it. For what will it profit them to gain the whole world and forfeit their life?" (Mark 8:34b-36).

We are called to take on the pain and suffering of the world and transform it into something that is life-giving. We cannot take on the burden of all, but we must be open to sharing the pain of others so as to be in solidarity with them. Jesus shows us the way, "Come to me, all you that are weary and are carrying heavy burdens, and I will give you rest. Take my yoke upon you, and learn from me; for I am gentle and humble in heart, and you will find rest for your souls. For my yoke is easy and my burden is light" (Matthew 11:28-30). We must allow others to use us as a vehicle, a conduit to God. We must be in solidarity, even for a time if necessary to lower ourselves to be in solidarity. We would only be following the lead of Jesus.

The ragman was the Christ, taking on the pain and suffering of others and truly being in solidarity with them. The author of the

Letter to the Hebrews, in a similar way, tells us that Jesus, while the reflection of the Father, calls us his sisters and brothers. He chose to be one with us. We, in turn, need to be one with each other. Let us, therefore, break down barriers that separate us from others and actively seek to be sisters and brothers to all. It is Jesus we seek to emulate. It is his kingdom we wish to build, today and each day of our lives.

---

1. "Ragman" paraphrased from Walter Wangerin, Jr., *Ragman and Other Cries of Faith* (San Francisco: Harper and Row, 1984), pp. 3-6.

Sermons On The Second Readings

For Sundays
After Pentecost
(Last Third)

Travel Tips For Fellow Pilgrims:
Lessons Learned Along The Way

Lee Ann Dunlap

To Nancy and Suzie,

"Mis amigas" and fellow pilgrims on the journey,
who convinced me I could do this.
Many thanks for evoking the laughter,
listening to the heartaches,
and gently providing your wise "travel tips" along the way.

Introduction

From the *Iliad* and *Odyssey* to the *Tales of Tom Sawyer and Huckleberry Finn*, humans have oft been entertained and taught by the stories of people on a journey. Whether the quest be for the golden fleece, the city of Oz, or the Twin Towers, the real story is about lessons learned and relationships forged along the way. The literature of many cultures throughout human history is rich with travel tales of adventurers and pilgrims. The Bible is no exception. It is no coincidence that the theme of the journey has become a biblical symbol for life — both individual and communal.

From the call of Abraham to the travels of the apostles, God has called individuals away from the safe and settled and into the unknown. Both the Hebrews of the Exodus and the church of the early Christian era were people on the move — sometimes by choice and often by the decree of malevolent forces. Yet behind, in, and through those travels the power and truths of God were made known for all time and all people.

The book of Hebrews takes up this metaphor of the journey, using the experiences of the wandering tribes of Israel and their quest for a proper relationship with God as a parable for life in the church of the first century. Like so many "guidebooks" written for modern travelers, this book offers the best wisdom and guidance to help fellow pilgrims arrive safely at the heavenly destination, while gaining the full richness and beauty to be savored "on the way."

I make no claims to be an expert Bible scholar, nor to possess exceptional eloquence from the pulpit. This volume is an offering of "travel tips" from one pilgrim to another, based on the best guidebook of them all, the Holy Scriptures. I am indebted to the real scholars on whose work I have relied, and whose insights I have sought to translate into the everyday journeys of those "fellow pilgrims" to whom these sermons are proclaimed. I am especially

417

grateful for Robert Jewett's *Letter to Pilgrims* commentary on Hebrews, and to a little book called *God's Tent, the Tabernacle for Today*, by Aldworth Cowan. They contributed much to the overall theme of this book.

In no way do I expect these chapters to be the only valid insights into these scriptures, or the only way to proclaim them; nor do I believe they are necessarily the best. I offer them only as a springboard for the preacher or teacher's own imagination, in the hopes that these words might inspire fresh consideration of the texts and a more enthusiastic proclamation of the truths they teach.

Like A Child

Angela was still a pre-schooler the Christmas Grandpa Harvey got her the red Radio Flyer wagon, and by summer it had become a popular item in the family's backyard. When her younger sister learned to toddle along sometime later they made a game of pulling each other, often with the help of Mom or Dad.

As is known to happen with siblings, one afternoon the cooperative play turned competitive, then became a heated argument. And so it was that Angela informed her little sister in a physical way that this was indeed *her* little red wagon, and hers alone. Before their parents could intervene the whole matter was succinctly solved. "Don't cry. It's okay," Angela declared to her sobbing sister with absolute confidence. "I'll just tell Grandpa, and he'll buy you a wagon, too."

Now little red wagons are *not* a dime a dozen, and Grandpa Harvey was not known to be a doting grandparent, nor was it his habit to lavish toys willy-nilly — even upon his grandchildren. In all her four years of living, Angela had never once asked him for anything more than to sit on his lap, but when the story made its rounds amidst the family grapevine her words of trust found their mark. And as if on cue, her prophecy was fulfilled and a second little red wagon found its way into the backyard, courtesy of Grandpa Harvey. For Grandpa, it was a matter of honor.

It would seem that a child's unqualified trust has the power of nearly supernatural proportion at times, melting the resolve of even the most rigid adults. That power is matched by some children's unlimited capacity to ask for anything from anyone, at anytime —

strangers included. Ask any adult with a freezer full of Girl Scout cookies or twenty chocolate candy bars from the fourth grade class fundraiser.

Take for instance eight-year-old Travis and his cousin Lisa, who knocked on an elderly neighbor's door one afternoon with a handful of dried wildflowers and an intriguing business proposal:

"Um, you don't want to buy some weeds, do you?"

"Well, how much do you want for them?"

"Oh, a penny."

And he got it! He got a *nickel* in fact. Of course he got it — and more. What adult could resist?

Absolute dependence and absolute trust, combined with a penchant for shameless petitioning — that pretty much describes the spirit of early childhood. Then, somewhere along the way, things change. Sometimes we get rebuked and scolded; some of us get neglected or abused — and we stop trusting. Sometimes we are made to feel ashamed of our need, and we stop asking. We learn, "I can do that *myself*," and we are *expected* to do just that, and we stop depending.

Somewhere along the line we stop asking and we start demanding. We stop believing in others' generosity, and we start fending for ourselves. We stop trusting and we start manipulating; we stop begging and we start earning. It's called growing up and, for the most part, growing up is a good thing — but sad in a way, too.

Odd, isn't it, that our healthy physical and emotional growth toward maturity involves moving from infantile dependence to adult autonomy; but our spiritual maturation requires movement in the *opposite* direction? Those to whom we would point as saintly, or "perfected in faith," display as the hallmark of their lives a total trust in God's benign providence, a recognition of their own absolute dependence upon that providence, and the intimacy to "take it to the Lord in prayer." Growing up spiritually means that we live before God in the same condition that we entered the human realm — exposed, helpless, and crying out for what we need. Getting to that place is the journey of a lifetime.

But too many times, when it comes to our prayer lives, we just don't get it. Few of us hesitate to pray for the needs of others, particularly our friends and family. We are even able on occasion to petition for our own physical needs, but if we tell the truth about ourselves, most of us would admit that the journey to a place of childlike honesty and innocence, of intimacy and vulnerability before the face of God, is a journey we humans tend to avoid rather than embrace. Like the Hebrew children traveling to Canaan's promised land, we seek out the shortcuts and safe havens of false gods and false security, only to end up wandering the wastelands. Sadly enough, many of us, like them, perish in those wastelands. Dealing with a zealous God face-to-face is a frightening thing, and many choose alternate routes.

One of those all-too-perilous detours on this journey we might call "the head trip." It is a path chosen by clergy and laity alike, and can be recognized at denominational conferences, in local church Bible studies, as well as the local coffee shop. The first step on this path begins when we shift our focus toward conversing (and often arguing) with others regarding the finer theological propositions *about* God rather than engaging in intimate conversations *with* God.

The preacher who penned the Epistle to the Hebrews saw his own congregation wandering this treacherous path as they entered their popular culture's dialogue regarding the nature and activity of angels and other heavenly beings. Many converts from a pagan background practiced a kind of angel reverence as a way of hedging their bets against the chaotic forces that seemed so threatening. These heavenly creatures have their role, the preacher acknowledged, but that role is secondary to the glory of the crucified Christ. It is Christ and Christ alone who has the power to intercede on our behalf. No other intermediary is necessary or effective.

Make no mistake, theological reflection and dialogue are a necessary part of spiritual growth, but books and seminars and exegetical debates are no substitute for personal prayer and corporate worship. Separated from a healthy devotional life these "head trip" activities leave us as hungry and thirsty as those wandering Hebrews. Before we begin spouting our ideas and doctrines *about* God we must first engage in conversation *with* God. Only then will we have any proclamation worth hearing.

Another dangerous detour that tempts us on the spiritual journey could be called "the business trip" (or rather the "*busy-ness* trip"). We might recognize this path by its hectic pace and flurry of activity, often centering on church or community work under the banner of Christian service. Caught up in the busyness of *doing for* Christ we neglect *being with* Christ.

The congregation to which Hebrews was written was wrestling with their Jewish heritage and some persistent voices from within their group that demanded adherence to the Mosaic traditions and Law in addition to the Christian confession. Faith in Jesus is well and good, they declared, but those "good works" insured extra protection from the perils of the journey.

No one wishes to discourage Christian service. Most certainly, service projects, social justice campaigns, charitable fund-raisers, and church committee meetings all have their necessary place in Christian community. But when they become a diversion from the more rugged path of intimate prayer time our trek toward spiritual maturity takes a dangerous turn indeed. For the spiritually mature, service to others flows *from* our devotional life, and makes a poor substitute *for* it.

What is it about the steep path of prayer that scares us so? — so much so that we seek out the easier routes? Like those Hebrews gazing upon the fire and smoke of Mount Sinai we recognize that penetrating the presence of the living God is cause for awe and wonder, and more than a little fear. Placing one's self in the presence of such a God does indeed make one vulnerable and powerless. The word used in the text from Hebrews carries several nuances:

- "laid bare" and vulnerable — as in the jugular vein of an animal about to be slaughtered
- laid out like a patient on the operating table before the surgeon — that's Eugene Peterson's image
- "all are naked" before God — that's the NRSV translation

None of these images are particularly comfortable. Adults have hang-ups about nakedness and vulnerability — particularly in the presence of someone with power over us, but for little children this is not so. If you've ever chased a naked two-year-old around the room (or the front yard!) with a diaper in hand, you know it's the truth. Little children have no concern about who sees their private parts, and a few downright enjoy the exhibition!

But before long, we learn to cover up — not just our bodies, but also our emotions, and our hopes and dreams — and, more than that, our flaws and failures and misdeeds. Like Adam in the Garden of Eden, we weave garments to hide our shame. We hide our guilt beneath garments of rationalization and blame; we cover our fear and pain with the mantle of addiction. We conceal our true neediness with an attitude of indifference, and we avoid true intimacy with God and others under the disguise of self-righteousness.

But, as the scripture insists, it is a futile endeavor. The Word of God is sharper than any two-edged sword. Eugene Peterson's paraphrase reads "a surgeon's scalpel." It cuts through the surface of skin, muscle, and bone into the depths of our soul. Jesus, the Living Word, penetrates our defenses and cuts to our core. No body-armor can stop him. No head trip can deflect him, and no busyness of life can obscure his gaze.

What we tend to forget, however, is that the knife which penetrates our soul is the Word-Made-Flesh — sharing our humanity and interceding on our behalf. In the hand of the Great Physician, the scalpel becomes an instrument of healing. From the heart of God, the word of judgment we so often fear, becomes the word of forgiveness and restoration.

"For we do not have a great high priest who is unable to sympathize with our weakness, but we have one who has been tempted in every way, just as we are — yet was without sin." The beauty of a two-edged sword is that it cuts both ways. The one who is able to see into the depths of our soul is also our high priest who has penetrated the mysteries of heaven and gained access to the very heart of God.

In Old Testament tradition, the function of the high priest is to "draw near" (that's the meaning of the word in Hebrew). He functions as an intermediary, drawing the people into the presence of God, and bringing God into contact with the people. In Christian understanding, it is Jesus who embodies this work most completely. In his humanity, Jesus, the Son of God, made himself totally vulnerable and obedient and dependent — living his life in a state of complete reliance upon God. Because of that reliance, this great high priest goes before heaven's throne to petition the Almighty without shame or embarrassment of his need or desires. "Don't worry, it's okay," he assures us. "I'll just tell the Father, and he'll provide exactly what you need."

"Let us then approach the throne of grace with confidence, so that we may receive mercy and find grace to help us in our time of need." Let's stop trying to manipulate God's favor and instead trust in God's generosity. Let's stop laboring to acquire for ourselves what God has promised to provide in due time. "Let us hold firmly to the faith we profess." Let us pray with the confidence of children.

Power And Compassion

Many of you may remember from your grade school days a novel by Mark Twain titled, *The Prince and the Pauper.* It has been adapted in various forms of Disney productions and even a few cartoon tales. The Twain story begins with two boys with identical features — one a spoiled royal heir, and the other a street urchin surviving on his wits. By chance they meet. The pauper is enamored with the fineries of the palace, while the prince envies the pauper's freedom to come and go as he chooses.

Eventually, they agree to change clothes and identities, and each then endures a series of misadventures as they seek to survive the other's life. In the process, the pampered prince discovers the hard realities of being subject to another's merciless power, and the pauper learns that having royal authority also carries with it the responsibility for the welfare of others. When the king dies unexpectedly, the prince comes to the throne much wiser and kinder for his adventure.

Power and compassion — a divine combination, and also a difficult balance for any leader to keep. The best of our leaders are those with the clout to get things done but who are devoted to using that power for the enhancement of those over whom they have authority.

Power wielded without compassion is cruel and corrupt, while sympathy without competency is ineffective and futile. Anyone facing criminal prosecution or a costly civil suit wants a lawyer not only with the highest skill level, but also with a passion to fight ferociously for the client. Likewise, when we need a heart transplant to survive, a well-meaning friend with a penknife and no medical training won't do us much good; and neither will a cardiac surgeon who chooses to vacation in Maui in our hour of need. What we most need is a physician with skill *and* a deep commitment to the patient.

Those of us with sin-sick souls require that similar combination of sensitivity and compassion, balanced by the power to effectively heal and forgive. We need to know, in the words of the children's table grace, "God is *great* **and** God is *good*." Goodness without power is ineffective, and power without goodness is demonic.

The quest of the human spiritual journey is to connect with a higher power that can deliver us from our human predicament and engage that power to come to our aid. In the history of that human journey, it is the role of the priest to help us make that connection. One could argue that, historically, the so-called "oldest profession" is that of the priest, or "holy man." In religious cultures all around the world it is the sacred duty of the priest to represent the divine mystery to mortal men and women — and to intercede with the deity on the worshiper's behalf.

In the Old Testament, the very meaning of the word for priest means "to stand between." For the most part, the task was accomplished with cultic ritual. The role of the priest was to receive the offerings of penitence or thanksgiving from the worshiper and to in turn offer those gifts as an intercession on the worshiper's behalf. In Genesis, Melchizedek, the King of Salem (meaning "righteousness" and "peace") received the tithe from Abraham following a successful military campaign, and in turn pronounced God's blessing upon the patriarch. In later history, it was Aaron and his descendents who were chosen to make those offerings and intercessions — first in the traveling tabernacle, and later in the Jerusalem temple(s). In one particular ritual, on the Day of Atonement, the high priest would enter the holy of holies in the central part of the Jerusalem temple. There in the place where God had promised to dwell, he would offer sacrifices for the sins of himself, his family, and the whole nation in hopes of assuring God's continued presence with the nation.

But by the time Jesus came to Jerusalem, the office of high priest was *not* what the scriptures intended. Rather than a lifetime position for a man chosen by God, the high priest office had become a political reward granted by Rome for loyalty given, services rendered, or price paid. It was a ceremonial function, emptied of spiritual power, and by the time our preacher wrote the book of Hebrews, there was no longer a temple in which to offer sacrifices; and thus no functional need for a priesthood.

Some folks in our own day and time seem to insist this is still the case. For the enlightened, scientific mindset of our generation, prayers of penance and thanksgiving to the deity are irrelevant superstition from a bygone day. We like to think we control our own destiny and that we have progressed far beyond ritual and homage to deal with life's uncertainties.

In our modern world we do still have similar intermediaries to ensure our safety from the perils of daily living. We have sought to forge our own path into the mysteries of the universe. Rather than relying upon priests, we turn to science and technology, medicine, economics, and politics to solve our daily woes and save us from the terrors of our enemies. But even these require human faces to interpret to us their mysteries, and to guide us to the proper rituals for successful results — a kind of modern "priest" if you will. To plumb these mysterious forces we will offer any number of sacrifices: we will pore over self-help books, consult our financial gurus, and call our psychic hotlines; we hire our attorneys, and tune-in to Dr. Phil in our efforts to fix the troubles and predicaments in which we find ourselves.

But if the truth be told, even with our knowledge and technology, and all the material resources at our disposal, most of us feel helpless in the face of chaotic forces beyond our control. We blanket our fears behind a guise called "homeland security," all the while knowing we are never truly safe. We pad our pension plans, not wanting to admit that one catastrophic illness or injury could wipe out our life savings. Factories get bought out and jobs get moved to another country. Months of drought or a siege of rainfall can wipe out a season's crop. A phone call from the police in the middle of the night — our child in jail, or worse — and our lives are changed forever. A stroke or heart attack, and our youthful strength and vitality vanish like a vapor.

How do we cope? To whom can we turn? Our friends may be sympathetic, but what can they do? The government could redress grievances, but what does it care? We need a friend. We need a Savior. We need a merciful someone with power and might.

Most firefighters and rescue workers know that effectiveness at their job requires the proper equipment and skills training, as well as character, and the courage to face danger for the sake of those in peril. When your car has stalled out in the midst of a flash flood, having rescuers shout encouragements from the flood banks is of little comfort. Likewise, having courageous people dive in without the equipment or the stamina and skills to endure the current, leads only to disaster for everyone. We need someone with enough courage and compassion to brave the winds and currents, but also with the lifeline to secure us and guide us to safety.

To be effective in the rescue of the human soul requires an unbreakable connection with the saving power of God as well as a willingness to enter the torrents of sin and death to deliver that saving power to those in peril. We need a rescuer who is both great and good.

The problem with our modern "priests," however, is that they are all mired in the same human predicaments as we. Many have worldly power and influence, but lack true goodness, and others offer grandiose solutions that are irrelevant to our particular situation. And for all of them, even their best efforts produce only limited success. Knowledge is incomplete, and power is relative. Their guidance may help us avoid a few calamities and cushion a few of life's bumps; but in the end they cannot restore our innocence, transform our fallen nature, mend a broken relationship, or walk with us beyond the grave.

But we know the one who can. His name is Jesus. Like Melchizedek before him, he is the king of righteousness and peace. Just as Melchizedek offered a blessing from Almighty God before and beyond the Levite priesthood of the Jewish tradition, so also does this Jesus intercede with God on our behalf, standing on his own eternal authority.

As the floodwaters of human inhumanity thrash and churn around us, and threaten to sweep us away — we reach out to Jesus, our lifeline to God's saving power. Jesus, who is both willing and able to wade into the torrents on our behalf, and able to reach us where we are, and wrap us securely in the strength of his loving arms — arms that once were stretched wide for us upon the cross of Calvary.

In the words of the Apostle Paul, Jesus, God's royal Son "did not count equality with God as something to be grabbed, but made himself nothing ... He humbled himself, and became obedient to death, even death on a cross" (Philippians 2:6, 8). The prince — for the sake of his royal subjects, became a pauper.

The preacher of Hebrews asserts that both power and compassion are the qualities required for the priestly role of uniting a holy God with a sin-soaked, struggling humanity. In his journey to Calvary, we easily recognize Jesus' compassion for us. We recognize in his suffering and agony our own sorrow and grief and loss. Many of the pagan mindset in the preacher's community, as well as in our own, insisted that a suffering Savior is no Savior at all. They declared that the path to salvation lay in escaping human suffering by moving beyond it, or desensitizing ourselves to it. Some deny its reality altogether. The gnostics of the preacher's community insisted that Jesus the Christ only appeared to be human, and thus was not tainted by the carnal existence.

Not so, declares the preacher, and generations of Christians after him. The Jesus of history was, and remains fully human, and that humanity does not diminish his divinity but only serves to enhance it. He "learned compassion through what he suffered." Compassion is at the center of the divine Spirit. Jesus is able to deliver us from the torrents of human sin and suffering precisely because he has entered them with both feet. Because he lived and died in complete obedience to God, he is able to ford those powerful currents and to offer forgiveness with the very authority of God.

Just as Jesus embraced his own human vulnerability and mortal limitations, so are we likewise called. In the presence of our God, who is both great and good we are challenged to pray without fear or embarrassment. Praying for our real human needs, and those of others means we recognize our weakness — our inability to attain for ourselves what is ultimately God's to give. In the process we place ourselves at the mercy of this God, who may or may not respond exactly as we desire. Prayer makes us vulnerable, but it also draws us into closer relationship with God, and in that prayer life we gain strength beyond our human comprehension. Trusting both in Christ's greatness and goodness, we come before the royal throne of heaven as the poor and helpless pauper, and in turn we gain all the power and favor of the Prince of Peace.

The Unshakable Foundation

On Top Sail Island, North Carolina, stands the ruins of a dream in a shell of a house. Before the hurricane, both the house and owner had proudly stood on the oceanfront daring the challenges of wind and wave. Six years before, John (not his real name) had left his wife of eleven years in search of something he could not define — something that would make his life complete and happy. He wanted adventure and fun; he wanted big-boy-toys. He wanted a beautiful home and a beautiful wife, and he was willing to live beyond his means to get it. He wanted his youth and strength and female attention, so he worked out at the gym, had his teeth professionally polished, and he ran daily in the best running shoes available. He married the woman who peaked his fancy and together they financed their $300,000 dream home on the ocean, with payments neither of them could afford.

And then came Hurricane Andrew. The house was ripped apart, and many of the big toys were ruined. The bills came due, and within five years the marriage crumbled along with the dream. The bank reclaimed the property, and the last of the big toys were sold at a yard sale in Ohio.

Today John is forty years old, "But I look like I'm 25," he brags to his sister. He has determined to change his lot in life through a self-guided course of self-help books. He rarely sees his children (from the first marriage) or visits his family; but he is once again living beyond his means with a younger woman and destined for another marriage. The house on the beach is the property of yet another couple searching for their dream.

John's story plays like a modern tragic romance — two people seeking to find their dream in each other and in the things they yearn to acquire, and losing it all in the contest with fate. Flannery O'Connell could hardly write it better. But John's story is true-life — perhaps not unfamiliar to you or someone you know. The house and the man are real, and they stand as a reminder to those of us who would build our lives and dreams on the shifting sands of what we can possess, or what we can make of ourselves.

John's story is not unique, nor is it new. Trade the hurricane winds of North Carolina for the sand storms of the Middle Eastern desert and you might well be telling the story of the ancient Hebrews. Exchange the mortgage payment for empirical taxes and we might easily be speaking of the early Christian converts. Whether the plague be the devouring locust consuming the year's grain harvest, or a catastrophic illness consuming our life's savings — our fear and dread is the same, as is our overwhelming desire to fend it off.

In their age or in ours, life's journey is fraught with perils that threaten to wipe us out — physically, emotionally, and spiritually, and above all else we want to survive and thrive. Almost from the beginning of our human quest we have sought the help of the divine to ensure that survival. Nearly every human culture offers tribute and prayers to the deities with hopes of gaining aid and favor of the forces that lie beyond our control. Some of us, like John, seek to hedge ourselves from life's uncertainties with a wall of material possessions. We brace ourselves against disease and death with a facade of youth and strength. Others embrace a shield of religious ritual and moral codes as the path to health, wealth, and eternal bliss.

But whether we seek salvation and safety through moral conduct, by ritual observance, by appeasing the local ruling powers, or by trusting in our own inner strength and wits, the result is always the same — disaster. Human strength eventually declines, human social structures fail, and human philosophies offer us no sympathy or forgiveness in desperate times. Eventually the waves of chaos get mightier than our ability to withstand, and the sands upon which we have built our dreams crumble and wash away.

432

What, or who, can protect us from the perils that threaten at every turn? That is the very question the early Christians faced in the community to which Hebrews is addressed. Like the Hebrew community of earlier times, the faith trek had become rugged, and many were weary and tempted to quit. Harassed and sometimes persecuted they saw the world as "stacked against them." They needed to know with certainty that God's favor was with them. Like so many of us, they wanted relief. They wanted control. Find a way to appease and manipulate those cosmic forces and they would find their home on "Easy Street."

The society of their day offered two appealing possibilities: the moral rectitude and sacrificial observances of the Mosaic Law advocated in their Jewish tradition, and the repetitive rites and rituals practiced in the pagan cults of their neighbors.

The sacrificial system practiced by the Hebrew community in the tabernacle at Sinai, and later at the Jerusalem temple was, at its best, a way of giving the sojourners access to their mysterious God amidst the journey. But as the scriptures warn, encountering this God directly must be approached with awe, reverence, and a great deal of fear and trembling. With full recognition that a holy and righteous God could not travel long or far with sinful, rebellious humans without somebody getting killed (as in the fiery serpents of Numbers 21), the tabernacle was a kind of "mobile home" by which this holy God could travel with the chosen people, instead of merely awaiting them in the promised land or on the heights of Mount Sinai.

The rituals of sacrificial offerings conducted by the appointed priests in this tabernacle, and later in the Jerusalem temple, became a means by which the people could acknowledge the great distance between themselves and this holy God, and yet it also provided the means by which their sins could be covered and that distance overcome. The priests played a pivotal role in bridging that chasm. Primarily, this was accomplished through the performance of ritual sacrifices, it was initially their responsibility to represent the people before God through the rituals proscribed in the law. Only they had the God-given authority to approach God with offerings. Only they were given permission to enact the sacred ceremonies and pronounce God's forgiveness and favor on the people. No others dared approach.

In addition to representing the people before God, the priest was also charged with interpreting God to the people through the periodic public reading of the law to the assembled people. Early on, it was the priest who was called upon to seek out God's guidance when crucial decisions had to be made. (Later, of course, the prophets assumed this function.) All these responsibilities of mediating human concerns with the divine presence were most completely embodied in the office of the high priest. His clothing and sacred equipment were distinct from the others. Appointed for life, he alone had authority to enter the holy of holies once each year, offering animal sacrifices to atone for the sins of the nation.

To our modern "enlightened" minds, rituals of grain offerings and animal sacrifices are dismissed as archaic and superstitious. Yet, if we tell the truth about ourselves, we have our own ways of seeking to alleviate our sufferings and control our own destinies and gain access to the mysteries of the universe. Organized religion is unnecessary we are told, even detrimental. The path to a "heaven" of inner peace and enlightenment is within our own power. Being a "morally good" person is good enough, we are told. Education is the path to salvation, so we seek out the hidden knowledge to success and happiness through a library of self-help books or flashy seminars in posh resorts. We buy lottery tickets with hopes of striking it rich. We consult the so-called experts. We buy videos and listen to audiocassettes from nearly any charismatic person who will promise to make us wealthier, sexier, or more popular at work. We sacrifice our family ties on behalf of the job and labor long hours to please the company, so that we can have health and pension benefits once we've worked ourselves sick and tired. All of this is in hopes of attaining a place and time on Easy Street when we need no longer labor, or suffer, or struggle with our human relationships or mortal circumstances.

Eventually, we discover it is all in vain. The people in whom we have trusted succumb to the same mortal limitations that threaten us. The material possessions we have obtained crumble away. Old age eats away at our youth and strength, and our financial investments drain away through taxes, inflation, and catastrophic illness. In the end, there is no Easy Street. There is nothing and no one to sustain us in a lasting way — except God.

And that is the very point the preacher of Hebrews is hammering home: It is Christ, and Christ alone who can deliver us from sin and death. Christ's priesthood is superior to both the Jerusalem temple cult and the local pagan philosophies. His power to save is superior because it is the promised plan of God to save us, and not our human attempt to save ourselves. Christ's priesthood — his authority to bring us into God's presence — is built not on the shifting sands of human effort, but rather on the unshakable foundation of God's own oath, "You (Christ) are a priest forever after the order of Melchizedek" (Hebrews 7:19). Human agents will fail, and philosophical truths have no personal commitment, but Jesus Christ can save forever. Unlike the mortal humans in whom we place our trust, Christ will never be diminished by mortal frailties and limitations. Unlike the eternal truths and philosophies of the pagan culture, Christ's love for us is relational — "a very present help in times of trouble."

In the end, the goal of our striving here on earth is not to finance and build our dream home on Easy Street; it is far better to build Easy Street as we go with the daily help and guidance of our risen Lord. Rather than striving to reach a place and time when life is perfect, let's strive to perfect the place and time where we find ourselves by letting Christ perfect us daily in holy love. By accepting our human limitations and giving up all pretense of having control of our destiny, we receive the perfection that cannot be earned or finagled. Our home on Easy Street is already ours as a gift! The payment was made on Calvary, our title is clear and the deed is signed in the blood of Christ. All that is left for us is to enter in.

Where Is Love?

Several years ago, a fellow named Lionel Bart wrote a hit song, "Where Is Love," for the Broadway musical *Oliver*. Based on the Charles Dickens classic, *Oliver Twist*, the musical tells the story of an orphaned child struggling to survive the cruelties of the streets of England amidst the Industrial Age. No one seems to care, except those trying to use him for profit. "Where is he, whom I close my eyes to see?" Oliver sings. "Will I ever know the sweet 'Hello,' that's meant for only me? Where is love?"

Few of us have ever faced the hardships of life as a street orphan, but we need not look far to see that the cruelties of Dickens' world still exist in our own. The young and the very old, the ill and the poor are still exploited and abused, forced to scrounge for daily sustenance. Orphaned or not, nearly all of us can identify with the spirit of Oliver's song — yearning for love and acceptance, yearning to belong to one someone, and to community — thirsting for God "as the deer pants for the water" (to use the psalmist's words).

We have, in fact, been created with the capacity for just such a thirst. As an infant instinctively knows to suckle its mother for life-giving milk, so, also, do human beings yearn to be near to the heart of another, and ultimately to be "near to the heart of God" (to quote another songwriter). Yet, as we look around us, and look within ourselves, we recognize that so many of us are still thirsting, and perhaps in our more desperate moments we ourselves have uttered the plea (although not so melodiously), "Where is love?"

What is it that stands between us and the Creator's life-giving love that our spirits so desperately need?

For Oliver Twist and so many like him, the barrier is human ignorance and cruelty, along with the physical hardships of life that so often lie outside an individual's control. Little souls, and little souls in adult bodies, are told first by their families and then by the world that they are unwanted and unlovable, that they are ugly or stupid or bad. In turn they begin to act that way. They are told that they are inferior human beings because of the color of their skin, or their gender, or the gender of the people they choose to love. Instead of a "sweet hello" they anticipate only condemnation from the church, and from God.

For others, that barrier to God stands *inside* us rather than beyond us — pride, arrogance, and the guilt of our own rebellious deeds. Although religious in outer form and ritual, we dare not approach God in honest prayer, because coming near to the heart of God means we are forced to recognize our own ungodliness — our human weakness and fallibility. In our culture admitting our flaws and misdeeds makes for disaster at the hands of our competitors and political enemies.

So where is love, and how do we secure it for ourselves? Perhaps the church community first addressed by the preacher of Hebrews felt a bit like the orphaned Oliver Twist. They had earlier stood their ground amidst persecution and had faithfully supported fellow Christians who lost property and personal freedom. But they were growing weary, and the stakes were getting higher, and many were questioning whether the struggle was worth their continued efforts with no apparent end in sight. They were seeking a place of rest from the debating, the theological wrestling, and economic and physical suffering. And close at hand were those well-meaning teachers and philosophers offering easy answers and easy solutions.

Biblical scholars and historians have suggested that this easier alternate route to Easy Street was a kind of amalgamated heresy based on the pagan, gnostic (knowledge-based), and popular Jewish beliefs of their time and place. It might best be described as a kind of universalist "whatever works" religion like some of the New Age stuff floating around in today's religious neighborhood.

As best these scholars can conjecture, this ancient New Age religion suggested that the path to the realm of God could be cleared of obstacles if one only possessed and practiced the secret knowledge and rituals that could appease those opposing cosmic forces that were causing the havoc.

The Old Testament story of the wandering Hebrews recalls how the earlier generation of pilgrims had struggled with this same quest to find a place "near to the heart of God." In the midst of their travels, the path to God's presence was laid out legally in the holiness code, as well as architecturally and symbolically in the tabernacle (and later the Jerusalem temple). Although the exact details and specifications have been lost in antiquity, enough remains in the Old Testament for a good artistic rendering.

In the days when Moses and the Hebrews traveled the desert the tabernacle served as a kind of divine "mobile home" in which the holy and transcendent God could travel with the chosen people, a "visual parable" to use Eugene Peterson's phrase, showing that "people just can't walk in on God." (That's his paraphrase of Hebrews 9:8, which the NRSV translates, "The way into the sanctuary was not yet opened.")

For a typical Israelite of Moses' generation to find God, he had only to enter the tabernacle, that architectural expression of the path to the divine presence. Any Hebrew feeling a need to reconnect with God would approach the tabernacle through its singular opening. No class separation here, all came to God through the same door. Immediately inside that opening the worshiper encountered the large altar where the animals were sacrificed to atone for sin. One could not gain access to the holy one of Israel without first confronting the reality of one's own sin and failures. Only after that could the other offerings be proffered or advice sought.

Physically, that was as close to God as the average Israelite dared to go. Beyond that — the holy area — was entirely the domain of the priests — the intermediaries sanctioned by God and ritually cleansed for service in God's house, kind of like divine butlers, if you will. It was in that holy area that the priests engaged in an array of religious ceremony — rites and rituals laid down to properly acknowledge God's "otherness." Among other things, this partitioned area contained the lampstand and a table with special bread to symbolize God's past favor and continuing presence with the people.

But even the designated priests went only so far. At the very center of the sanctuary was the holy of holies — and central to that was the Ark of the Covenant with the tablets of the Ten Commandments given to Moses by God on Mount Sinai. At the center of that — the cherub-guarded mercy seat, where God promised Moses would find divine audience. Only once each year was this inner sanctum to be entered, and then only by the high priest. He entered twice on that day — first with a young bull to be sacrificed for the sins of the high priest and his family, and then again with a ram to be offered for the sins of the entire nation. If the high priest returned from the divine presence alive, the people saw evidence their sins were forgiven and God's favor was assured for yet another year.

All of this seems strange and archaic to our modern intellects. At best, it was a physical and symbolic representation of the spiritual quest, a tangible path to an encounter with divine mystery with appreciation for some deep spiritual truths about guilt and innocence and the need for reconciliation, not only with God but also with each other. To express it in our own liturgical tradition, "an outward and visible sign on an inward and spiritual grace."

But as the preacher of Hebrews points out, this path through the tabernacle is temporary at best. The fact that the activity is continual and the barriers remained indicates that nothing was ultimately resolved, particularly any lasting restoration of the human soul. People continued to fail and continued their need for reconciliation.

Later in Jewish history, a conquering Roman general would ride his horse into the inner sanctum of the holy of holies — to announce that he found nothing. No god resided there. Just as centuries later a Russian cosmonaut would walk in outer space and triumphantly declare that he had been to the heavens and no god resided there, either. Did that come as any surprise to believers?

Where and how do moderns strive to find God, who is known to be aloof and mysterious? How do *we* seek to resolve the brokenness

440

and alienation of our inner selves and to confront the breaches of our human relationships? Our suggested paths to healing often lie with doctors and psychologists. Some of our solutions are legal — both civil and criminal; some are technological, and some military. But are these any more effective or permanent than the path to the holy of holies through the tabernacle? We build bigger jails, but the violence continues, develop more sophisticated weapons and broker more peace treaties, but one war erupts even before another is concluded. We develop a cure for one dreaded disease only to hear news of a new one. Are the paths we have forged toward peace and wholeness any more effective than the one leading through the temple?

Back to Oliver's question, "Where is he, whom I close my eyes to see? Will I ever know the sweet 'Hello' that's meant for only me?" The preacher insists that the path to God does not ultimately lie in any physical route, nor in any secret knowledge available on the worldwideweb. It does not lie in slaying one's enemies in the name of God, nor in denouncing others as eternally damned in order to solidify one's own creed. To find love, to encounter God, and receive assurance of divine forgiveness one must confront Jesus. It is Jesus Christ, and Christ alone, who is the Way, the Truth, and the Life.

Through his total submission to the human condition, with all its accompanying limitations and sufferings, Jesus offered to God the only sacrifice of lasting impact. Rather than offering the innocent blood of another in place of himself in atonement for sin (as in the Hebrew ritual), he chose to offer himself, his own innocent blood, in place of the guilty humanity. In his death upon the cross and in his Easter resurrection the preacher assures us that Jesus ascended beyond the physical realm and entered the real holy of holies — the very presence of Almighty God.

On our spiritual journey, our quest to connect with what is truly real and ultimately meaningful, how do we seek the path that leads to the heart of God? The path to God has been cleared for us, not by rituals or incantations, and not by our continual efforts to impress God with our sacrifices and gifts and good behavior. Sacrificial offerings won't get us there, even in our official church envelopes.

Succeeding at all our life's grand ambitions won't either. Neither will intense psychotherapy or a degree in theology. Continual religious activity and successful church growth statistics won't pave the way, either, and neither will your preacher. He or she is only a fellow pilgrim. None of this will pave the way to God, because through Christ, God has already paved the way for us, and so we do not despair:

> *There is a place of quiet rest, near to the heart of God.*
> *A place where sin cannot molest, near to the heart of God.*
> *O Jesus, blest Redeemer, sent from the heart of God —*
> *Hold us, who wait before thee, near to the heart of God.*
> — Cleland B. McAfee, 1903
> "Near To The Heart Of God"

Dots On A Screen

Several years have now passed since the television series *Survivor* first debuted to become a summer ratings sensation. The concept was simple: place a group of individuals with diverse backgrounds, skills, and personalities into close proximity with a common purpose, namely survival on a deserted island, and let the audience watch as their relationships develop, or fall apart.

This, of course, is not to be confused with a much earlier comedy series based on the "seven stranded castaways" of *Gilligan's Island*. The *Survivor* contestants were to live similarly, with "no lights, no phone, no motorcars — not a single luxury," but unlike the Sherwood Schwartz series, the basic theme is competition, and someone gets booted off the island each week.

Like a hybrid version of the old daytime drama mixed with the competition of professional wrestling, what we now term "Reality TV" was born. Other shows have since emerged with exotic locations or other variations to the theme. Some have a more romantic angle, placing couples in separate exotic island resorts to test their fidelity. Music channels like MTV and Nashville Network feature a variation which is more like *Star Search*. Some have a more profiteering angle. (Who *really* would want to work for Donald Trump, anyway?) Some are just plain silly (as if the above mentioned are *not*).

Yet, with each fall's schedule come new variations to the plot. The appeal of such shows is measurable, if not comprehensible. People are tuning in in amazing numbers. But no matter what the location or personalities involved, reality television is in reality an oxymoron — a pairing of mutually exclusive ideas — like "jumbo shrimp" or "dry hydrant" or "government intelligence."

Television, by its very nature, is not reality. Although some household pets may bark or paw at their television counterparts, young children and even most animals learn quickly that television is really just shades of light or dark on a flat screen. The real people or objects are, in fact, unseen and in another place, usually far away. While the television screen can project meaningful images of an invisible reality, it is not the reality itself, and while the dramas and events portrayed upon the television or cinema screen can often be an important glimpse into an unseen reality, they are not to be confused with real life. Not all adult humans seem to grasp this fact and often confuse the actors with the characters those actors portray.

For some folks in isolated areas, the television screen can provide a glimpse into the larger reality that lay beyond view. Images of the wonders of nature and architecture, and nowadays history-in-the-making, can be transmitted into homes and public gathering places half a world away. Still, it is always fascinating to see the recognition and even awe on a person's face when they first spy the real thing. Comments like, "He (or she) looks much different in real life," are often heard, often in a disappointed tone. Or, on the other hand, one can see pictures of Mount Rushmore on postcards, in travel books, or on the picture screen, but only with an up-close, in-person visit can one fully grasp its beauty and grandeur. That fact is usually audible as folks gasp in wonder at their first view. Compared to that firsthand vision, everything else is just dots on a screen.

Our biblical ancestors traveling the desert obviously had no concept of television, yet in some sense the ancient tabernacle (and the later Jerusalem temple) and the accompanying rituals functioned as a kind of television screen that offered worshipers a glimpse into an unseen heavenly reality. Some Greek and Jewish philosophers of the first-century period conceived of the earthly realm as a kind of parallel universe to that of the heavenly existence, and as such, the Jerusalem temple was viewed as having a spiritual equivalent in the heavenly realm. In the human quest to encounter God, the temple and its rituals served as a kind of television screen that projected an image of the heavenly reality, invisible and far away. Every detail of architecture and ritual pointed to a cosmic truth in the human relationship with God: "dots on a screen" so to speak, or in the words of the Hebrews text, "a copy of the heavenly reality." The annual observance of the Day of Atonement represented the holiest of cosmic dramas to be played out before the audience of worshipers.

At the appointed day each year the high priest would enter the holy of holies at the very center of the temple, and there he would ritually sacrifice two animals, the first in recognition of his own sins, and the second for those of the nation. If he emerged alive, the people rejoiced in Yahweh's forgiveness and continued presence and favor. Scripture does not say if any high priest ever actually died during the ceremony, only that a cord was attached to retrieve his corpse should God's wrath go unappeased.

The yearly ritual bears some resemblance to the dramatic re-enactments of the cosmic myths performed in the temples of the pagan gods of Israel's Canaanite, Egyptian, and Greek neighbors. Acknowledge the breach between God's holiness and rebellious humanity, offer the appropriate sacrifices and receive divine favor for another year. Dots on a screen, so to speak: visual representations of a bigger, richer reality that is far away and out of sight. Nevertheless, such dramas played a vital role in the shaping of the people's minds and spirits. Like the plays, television, and motion pictures of our own day, people's lives were touched and "cleansed." The Greeks called it *catharsis*, a kind of emotional purification. The audience of worshipers could be drawn closer to God as they watched and participated.

And yet, like the veil in the temple, the barrier between divine and human reality remained. For all its powerful imagery the experience remained "dots on a screen" — a faint copy of the heavenly reality.

Then along came Jesus. The preacher of Hebrews insists that, unlike the pagan myths or the Jewish ritual, Jesus is no actor playing a role, he is the real thing: More than a screen image of God, he is God incarnate — love in human skin. His trust in God was

445

uncompromising, his obedience unwavering; his love for us is undeniable. His bloodshed was real and human — not that of a lamb or bull or goat.

The community of Christians to which Hebrews was first addressed was surrounded by pagan cults and idol worship — "dots on a screen" that had enamored the congregation and diverted their attention from the real life-giving power necessary for their continued faith journey. The preacher adamantly insists that Jesus' death upon the cross was the real and final salvation event — not a mystical ceremony but the reality itself. And, unlike our modern television dramas, there are no repeats! One historical sacrifice offered by Jesus — once for all — the real live event. No other performances are necessary. All others are merely "dots on a screen."

Jesus' ultimate sacrifice went far beyond eating slimy worms and bugs. The test of his fidelity had no connection with scantily clad bathing beauties or office politics. They put nails in his hands and a crown of thorns on his head and a spear in his side. The prize to be won surpassed all human treasure. He confronted human sin and depravity, and it cost him his life in exchange for ours.

Through his absolute obedience and pure love and faith, Jesus entered the heavenly holy of holies and accomplished the atonement to which all previous sacrifices merely pointed. The final sacrifice is accomplished — our sins are forgiven and our high priest is now in God's presence offering prayers and intercessions on our behalf.

Like that high priest of the Jewish temple, we await his promised return, a survivor of death itself. Like the crowd of Hebrew worshipers outside the holy of holies, we await the moment when our high priest Jesus shall reappear and we shall sing and shout for joy with his pronouncement of God's eternal love and continuing presence.

In the meantime, we are called to "get real" in our own faith journey. Our response to the "reality television fad": "Get a real life!" Rather than peering in as others exorcise their fears and passions in a half-scripted "reality show" why not confront the very real dangers presently threatening our real world? Real life-and-death dramas unfold all around us each day:

- Little children need to be loved and cherished.
- Our elderly in nursing homes need to be visited.
- Teenagers are struggling with the meaning and purpose of their lives, and are considering ending them.
- People are tortured by guilt and shame and desperately need redemption.
- Unchurched family, neighbors, and strangers need to hear the gospel.

Rather than escaping to watch other people's melodramas on soap operas and so-called "Reality TV," we are called to invest our time and our passion in the people who are right in front of us each day.

- Would you like to be part of a diverse group of people with various skills and talents challenged to work together toward a common destination with an "eye on the prize"? Join the church!
- Do you want adventure in exotic places with danger, physical challenges, and an unscripted outcome? Become a missionary!
- Are you willing to lay personal relationships on the line for the sake of authentic love and true intimacy? Share your faith story!
- Are you ready to risk it all in the realm of high finances? Learn to tithe!
- Do you want to show off your hidden talents for all to see? Use them in Christian service!
- Do you want to experience life-altering drama? Volunteer at a crisis-counseling center!

Let us not be distracted by dots on the screen, caught up in mere images and reflections of life. Let us instead focus on the real thing — our daily journey of communion with God and each other

— real relationships, real struggles, and an honest-to-God prayer life. Together, let us turn our attention toward Christ and aspire to living reality in accordance with God's script(ure). As we trek toward the heavenly realm let us strive to be more than survivors, let us seek to be true children of God.

Practicing God's Presence

In the early years of the sixteenth century, a young adventurer named Nicolas Herman left his parents' home near Lorraine, France, to join the French army. Wounded in war, he returned home to recuperate and thus began a process of soul searching that led to Christian commitment.

His quest for closeness to God first led him to life as a hermit. He found that unfulfilling, so he eventually joined a Carmelite monastery where he was assigned to menial duties in the kitchen. Kneading bread might truly seem an unholy task to an ex-soldier, but Nicolas soon found his home in the labor of the kitchen.

In later years, this "Kitchen Saint," as Brother Lawrence was called, would write about how his soul discovered intimacy with God by prayerfully inviting God into each and every assigned task, every conversation, and every relationship. He once wrote that he felt nearer to God in the sanctuary of the kitchen than in the liturgy of the chapel. The experience changed his life and those around him. It was said of him, "He pretended nothing, was compliant with everyone and tended to treat his brothers and friends amicably without being pretentious." His written reflection, titled *The Practice of the Presence of God* is today considered a spiritual classic. It continues to change lives.[1]

For the most part, the goal of the human religious quest is a direct encounter with divine being. Various religious traditions have different names for it — paradise, heaven, nirvana, but the images are similar — a place of peace and rest, of enlightenment and bliss. Getting there is the journey of a lifetime. For some, it is the reward

for a life of obedience, for others a state of conscious connected-
ness. For most it is a "someday" kind of place, with occasional
glimpses here and there along the way. For Brother Lawrence, it
was an everyday discipline, breathing divine reality into every loaf
of bread and every dish he washed.

What would it be like to know the joys of paradise here and
now — not as a reward for services rendered, but as the serendipi-
tous gift of a generous God? What would it be like to "practice the
presence of God" on earth as it is in heaven?

We usually find it easy to encounter God in the grandeur of
majestic mountains, in the vastness of ocean waves or the splendor
of a clear night sky. But far fewer of us experience intimacy with
God in grimy urban streets, in a heated debate of a church board or
town meeting, or through changing a baby's stinky diaper. We might
send our children to parochial school to learn about God, but hardly
ever would we inspire spiritual growth by engaging in so-called
"menial" tasks like scrubbing toilets, changing linens, and empty-
ing bedpans. Where is God in that?

The community of believers who first heard the Epistle to the
Hebrews was a people struggling to survive hard times and social
persecutions. Many had lost their property and lived with the threat
of losing even more — their family relationships or even their lives.
Some were giving up, and others were wondering if the outcome
was worth the struggle. Through the lens of their culture's wisdom
hard times meant either they were doing it wrong or else the opposing evil forces were more powerful than the friendlier ones.
Some sought the easier path of a private faith — believing in their
heads and hearts but keeping their commitments secret.

If these believers were to survive the trials and grow in faith,
they needed a hope on which to lean. The preacher sought to give
that hope using the story of another group of struggling pilgrims
— the Hebrews on their journey to the promised land.

Remember that tabernacle — the physical signpost of God's
continuing presence as the Hebrews traveled to Canaan? God did
not send Moses a roadmap and say, "See you when you get there!"
God chose to journey with them all the way. But remember the
story. Even in the tabernacle and the temple there was separation

450

— that veil which separated a holy God from mortal humans — a reminder of human sin and human mortality which kept them from the fullness of God's presence. The cultic sacrifices of the temple symbolized that breach.

But, we have good news, the preacher says. In Christ, God is not waiting beyond us and God is no longer separated from us. In Christ, we have access to heaven here and now. In Christ, the ultimate sacrifice has been offered and the breach has been bridged. In the earthly temple there were no chairs — the priestly work of offering sacrifices was continual, yet in Hebrews, Christ, the great high priest, is presented in a sitting posture.

The sacrifice is finished and the priestly work is accomplished, so now Christ sits as a king. He is truly a priest-king after the order of Melchizedek, the King of Salem. A new deal has been accomplished as promised by the prophet Jeremiah. Forgiveness has been granted; no more peace offerings are needed. The intimacy with God once known in Eden's garden is now possible for all of us.

Do we get it?

Too often in the minds and lives of church folk, salvation is a human achievement. "I got saved" (back when) we say. Too often salvation, or heaven, becomes a consequence of right belief and doctrine or a reward for good conduct. That's really not too different from the preacher's community and their mindset — right knowledge and proper ceremonial observance and timely sacrifices as the stepping-stones to eternal bliss.

"Don't you get it?" the preacher asks. Jesus has already opened the door. He cleared the path to heaven's bliss through his own life's blood. Anything more is unnecessary and in fact denies his victory.

Therefore, my friends, we have confidence to enter the sanctuary by the blood of Jesus. We need no longer concern ourselves with manipulating God's favor with right doctrine or right sacrifices or even right behavior. God's favor is already ours through Jesus Christ! We don't have to clean up our act to encounter God; we have been cleansed by Jesus. All the barriers that have kept us from God in the past: the emotional garbage others have laid on us and the sin garbage we have created ourselves. All of it has been swept away by Christ's life and death and resurrection!

So if we no longer are required to invest our lives in acquiring our own salvation, what is left for us to do? **Worship!**

What's left for us to do? Abide in God's presence. Make passionate love with God in each and every daily task, and passionately love and encourage each and every person who crosses our path along the way.

What would your life be like if you, like Brother Lawrence, "practiced the presence of God"?

- How might your day be different if you were to invite God into each task of your workday and each relationship in your job? Would you use the time differently?
- What if you were to invite Christ to sit with you behind the steering wheel each time you enter the highway? Would your driving habits change?
- What if you invited Christ to go with you to the grocery store or the mall? Would your purchases be different?
- What if you "practiced God's presence" in your leisure time? Would you volunteer more time and talents to help others?
- What if you asked Christ to help you balance your checkbook? (That's the *only* way some of us get it done!) Would your spending habits change?
- What if you "practiced God's presence" at your child's ball game? Would your attitude toward the umpire change?
- What if we truly practiced God's presence at our church committee meetings and denominational gatherings? Would our decisions be different?
- What if you breathed Christ into every word you spoke? Would your language change? (Particularly at church meetings and your child's ball game!)
- What if you went to church fully expecting to experience the movings of God's Spirit? How often would you attend?

Practicing the presence of God means that when times get tough and the journey gets rugged we do not avoid community nor break

452

away from others, and we don't walk away from the church; we *seek* it out, we *talk* it out, and we *work* it out. When times get tough and the chaos caves in around us we do not run from God but look for God's hand at work. We do not abandon each other but we come together — to worship. We sing, we pray, we praise, and we intercede on behalf of each other.

What would our daily lives be like if we, like Brother Lawrence, "practiced the presence of God" in the here and now? If we sought daily to do God's will "on earth as in heaven"? Well, it would be heaven on earth, would it not?

In the communion liturgy of the church we recognize Christ in the breaking of the bread as being present in our midst as he promised. But we also anticipate a fuller, richer divine presence that will be ours when we gather around the table of the heavenly banquet that is to come. In the words of a Charles Wesley hymn, we "anticipate that joy below and own that joy of heaven." The messianic banquet is eaten with each Eucharist. In fact, it is tasted each time we dine in Christian fellowship.

So it is also when the community gathers for worship. As we traipse the terrain on the human journey we are invited to rest periodically on the way to experience a foretaste of the heaven to which we are headed. One day all the saints shall be gathered in the realms of heaven to sing praises and shout victory chants to the Lamb of God. But we need not wait to experience the joy of the party, we can gather with our fellow pilgrims to sing praises and lead the cheers of victory even before the journey is complete. Our communal worship anticipates the future home and makes it real, here and now, as we "anticipate the joy below and own that joy of heaven."

---

1. Biographical details on Brother Lawrence are from the section by Elmer H. Douglas, in Lawrence's book, *The Kitchen Saint and the Heritage of Islam* (Eugene, Oregon: Pickwick Publications, 1989), p. 7.

Looking In All The Wrong Places

Author's Note: a fun way to animate this sermon might be to play sections of the several hit songs mentioned. In my case, the music program director at the local "Golden Oldies" station was immensely helpful.

The song has long been relegated to the "Golden Oldies" category, but occasionally it can be heard on the airwaves. Long before one-name singers like Cher, Blondie, or Madonna made their mark in pop music, a little-known and even less-remembered singer named "Charlene" topped the charts. The song was addressed within the lyrics to the "frustrated mother" and "unappreciated wife" from the perspective of a woman who has been everywhere and "seen a thousand things a woman ain't s'posed to see." Yet for all her adventures and exciting travel she feels unfulfilled, even a bit envious of those with a man to fight with, and sleep with every night. She grieves for the children she will not bear and reflects, "I've been to Paradise, but I've never been to me."

The song was released amidst the turmoil of the women's liberation movement and the aftermath sexual revolution of the 1970s; and even then not everyone agreed with its sentiment (or even understood it). It stood as a kind of counterbalance to Helen Reddy's earlier smash hit, "I Am Woman." Taken together, both songs musically depict the struggle of the gender throughout the last century to find the female place in the world.

For centuries, women have been told by their cultural and religious leaders that the way to fulfillment was through homemaking

455

and motherhood — a kind of "Stand By Your Man" mentality (to quote another female music artist of the era). But World War II and its production demands brought economic independence to thousands of women who entered the workforce. And after that "the Pill" brought reproductive choices to millions more. Yet with those choices also came consequences. To succeed in the work place challenged the relationships of home and family. Even today, most women struggle to find the balance. Some balance their Daytimers in one hand and their children's soccer schedules in the other, all in an effort to "have it all" — only to lose their sense of self in the process. "Finding me" has become as an intense a spiritual quest to the present generation as "finding God" has been to previous ones.

Not that men have it any easier. At the same time Helen Reddy was singing "I am woman hear me roar," the guys were watching *Easy Rider*, lip-synching "Born To Be Wild," and saving their money to buy a chopper. After trying to fulfill the demands of duty to family and community and nation instilled by culture and tradition, many males also experienced a loss of self. In the 1960s many did their civic duty in a place called Vietnam only to come home physically mangled and spiritually disillusioned. Even today, a man in his quest for self might abandon family and career for a flirtation with a younger woman, a fast car, and social independence. And, while only a minority of men and women actually take such drastic measures, many agonize in silence through a dull and seemingly pointless cycle of eating, sleeping, and working.

The tragedy in all of this is that, even today, we humans expend so much of our time and energy looking in all the wrong places in our search for meaning and connection. The idols of household and duty to which we were taught to bow offer precious little comfort or inspiration, and ultimately no wholeness.

None of these are evil in themselves except when they become our top priority. In fact, all have great value. Family is vitally important and enriching; but no other person can fulfill one's needs completely (even the one with whom we are madly in love, or the one to whom we gave birth). Community is essential, but likewise, it can't be counted on to meet our greatest needs. Then on the other

456

side of the spectrum we find those who sacrifice both family and community for the sake of the quest — for fun, for freedom, for adventure or excitement, or for the profit margin. But these also fall flat in the end.

So, do we stay in the proper place dictated to us by social conventions and traditions, or do we break all the rules and do it "My Way"? That's another "Golden Oldie" we used to play until the record broke.

In the end, the goal of the modern spiritual longing is not all that different from that of our ancient ancestors — to be free, but connected, to experience the adventures of the world beyond the everyday *and* still have the comfort of human love and friendship. The goal is to escape the dirty diapers, but keep the cuddly kisses; to find both intimacy and transcendence, relationship without vulnerability. And if we are *really* good we'll put these experiences to music so others can sing along!

It's a tall order.

The Christians in Rome to which the Apostle Paul wrote were part of an urbanized culture similar to our own. The gathered community had believers from various pagan and Jewish backgrounds. Voices from the synagogue insisted that the path to wholeness lay in strict adherence to the rules (of the Jewish faith, that is). Belief in Jesus was tolerated at the time for the most part, yet they insisted that salvation lay in observing the Law. But many Gentiles saw little value in circumcision or dietary demands of the Old Testament. To the Greek way of thinking, what happened to the body had little to do with the state of the soul (which departed at death). For the hedonists sensual pleasure was the ticket, "If it feels good — do it!" And in Rome's civil religion fulfillment lay in good citizenship.

All of these approaches have their appeal. Some valued freedom and others connection. Some emphasized the earthly realm and others the heavenly. Some focused on paradise, and others on self-knowledge and pleasure.

Sadly enough, they all leave Christ and his love on the periphery, as do we at times. As both a Pharisee and a Roman citizen, Paul knew both sides of the religious quest. He had seen the moral decay of pagan idolatry and self-indulgence, and he had witnessed the self-righteous legalism of his Jewish colleagues. His zealousness for his Jewish traditions had once led him to participate in the murder of the believer Stephen. And in his own ministry he had witnessed Gentile converts exhibiting the fruits of the Holy Spirit without the trappings of Jewish covenant.

We can follow the rules and do our religious duty to the utmost, and never experience divine love. We can amass fortunes, achieve world renown, and view all the wonders of the world and still be empty inside. In the end, there is nothing we can do to get God's attention and earn God's favor, because it has already been given us through Christ.

In the end, Paul insists, it is neither obedience to the Law nor defiant self-determination that gains us access to God's divine favor. In the end, it is only Christ who opens the door and only by faith do we gain entrance. Neither Jew nor Gentile can lay claim to God's favor, because all have broken faith and sinned. Both Jew and Gentile can lay claim because Christ died for all.

It is a wondrous truth; but we forget from time to time, and because we find it hard to believe that our holy Creator could love us so much, we tend to look for insurance. We'll trust in Christ and obey the rules. We'll ask God to "give us this day our daily bread," but stock up our cupboards just in case. We'll pray for deliverance from our enemies, but stockpile our weapons to be sure. We'll confess Christ as Lord, but take charge of our own lives when it suits our purposes.

The church forgets this truth from time to time, as well. For a while, a few centuries ago, the Roman Catholic church was the only religious establishment in town, in western Europe at least. And, for a while, its priests and bishops and popes mistakenly believed they had a monopoly on divine grace. They sought to meter it out to those who professed their doctrine, obeyed their rules, and paid their apportionments (oops! make that *indulgences*). And when a priest named Martin Luther begged to disagree, they threatened to kick him out, or do even worse. They said if he valued his eternal soul, he'd best do his priestly duty and not question orders.

Now Martin Luther had read Paul's letter to the church at Rome, and he figured that if grace is God's prerogative and Jesus' gift to those who trust in him, then nobody but Christ could take that grace away from him, or any other believer for that matter. If Jesus' death on the cross atoned for his sins then nobody had the power to renege on the promise made in scripture: "we are justified by faith." He figured his eternal soul was in God's hands and none others'. So he nailed his protests to the door of the church and changed the course of Christian history.

Not that the *protest-ants* who agreed with him have lived happily ever after, mind you. We still struggle with many of the same issues. We hear many of those same voices from our world that Paul and Luther addressed in theirs. Right doctrine and correct behavior are still held up as the path to salvation. Giving homage to earthly forces, or learning to manipulate them, is still proclaimed as the ticket to ultimate success and fulfillment.

Martin Luther, like the Apostle Paul, knew that real salvation — real connection with our divine Creator — is made possible only through Christ's love for us. Other reformers like Wycliff, Calvin, and the Wesley brothers understood it, too. Deep down, the whole church does, but we profess this grace in different ways and with differing emphases.

In Christ, our spiritual quest is complete, our longings are fulfilled by:

- trusting in his mercy we are freed from our guilt.
- submitting to his dominion we are emancipated from bondage to legalism and delivered from slavery to selfishness and empty pleasures.
- being filled with his Spirit we are given liberty to love others in creative and inspired ways without regard to their return of affection. We are freed to connect joyfully with others without fear of their demands.
- being perfected in his love. Through this perfected love we are able to know ourselves through the eyes and heart of our Creator, and we are challenged to grow and achieve beyond anything we thought possible. In serving Christ we find our

true selves, and achieve our true calling. We are given a purpose beyond ourselves and find our true life beyond our mortal existence.

It is not by our own efforts, our own striving, our own brilliance, that we find our place in the cosmos, or find purpose and power in our place on earth. By trusting in Christ and yielding only to his command, we find both ourselves and our home in paradise.

Our Ultimate Destination

On U.S. Route 40 just west of New Concord, Ohio, stands an S-shaped bridge spanning a creek on the old National Road. Standing uphill from that bridge a traveler can simultaneously observe five historic transportation links that helped to build a nation:

- The original trail blazed by Ebenezer Zane, also known as "Zane's Trace."
- The brick roadbed of the old "National Road" that followed.
- The train tracks of the Baltimore & Ohio Railroad, which nearly made that early highway obsolete.
- U.S. Route 40, built along the same route to accommodate the expanding automobile traffic of the early twentieth century.
- I-70 — the first Interstate Highway commissioned to transect the nation.

A bit further west of that bridge on U.S. 40 is the Zane Grey National Road Museum, where panoramic scenes with miniature people and animals tell the story of how this first federally funded highway in the Northwest Territory united the cities of the east with the wilderness territory beyond the Appalachian Mountains and helped to forge a nation.

Miniature scenes depict those early trailblazers felling the timbers and laying a corduroy road that would later be traveled by farmers and traders moving their stock to eastern markets and also by pioneers and adventurers moving westward toward a new life.

Another wing of the museum displays the wagons, bicycles, horseless carriages, and early automobiles that carried these travelers toward their dreams.

Today, one can make the journey from Wheeling, West Virginia, on the Ohio River to St. Louis, Missouri, on the Mississippi River with one full day's journey on I-70, or just a couple of hours by airplane. We seldom consider the long weeks and hazardous conditions faced by those early pioneers as they opened up the wilderness. With the threats of foul weather, wild animals, isolation, and occasional bandits and hostile natives, it was not a journey for the faint-hearted. Indeed, few would have dared the challenges were it not for the hopes and promises that waited on either end — the prosperity of the city markets for those traveling eastward on the trail, and the open skies, cheap land, and new opportunities for those going westward.

From the time God blessed humanity to "go forth, be fruitful, and multiply" men and women have sought out new territory in which to live out our human hopes and dreams. We have climbed mountains, crossed rivers, traversed deserts, sailed oceans, and trekked through the heavens. We have fought weather, wild animals, and hostile enemies, and we have buried comrades along the path. Many have turned back to safer havens and countless others preferred to never venture forth at all.

Not all our human journeys are measured in miles; not all "promised lands" can be plotted out with map or compass; and not all obstacles blocking our progress have physical dimensions. Yet, whatever the journey or the hardships, knowing one's ultimate destination becomes essential to completing the journey. For that pioneering farmer in the "wilderness" beyond the Ohio River the hazards of the National Road were well worth the risk, and the tolls to be paid along the way were worth the cost because of the higher financial rewards to be gained in the urban markets. For the European immigrants coming westward during that same time, the hardships of the ocean crossing and the indentured-servitude that paid the cost of passage were made bearable by the hope of a new life and economic freedom in the untamed lands of the west. Though it's tempting to stay in the comfort of the inn along the road (and many, in fact, did stay and build their futures beside the trail), it is the hope and promise of the final destination that keeps the pilgrim focused on the journey. That hope and promise maintains the momentum, helps overcome discouraging circumstances, and keeps the traveler from getting sidetracked.

The trouble with many pilgrims of our present day is that we've lost sight of our ultimate destination. For far too many, the goal of life's journey is to disembark in the land of "retirement" and there enjoy a new home with a fancy car, and to pluck the harvest of a healthy pension plan. For others, fame and fortune signal "arrival" in the promised land. Some can only envision their fulfillment in a walk down the aisle with their perfect mate or through the achievements of their children. Some become so beleaguered in the daily battle for food, shelter, and human justice that any hope for a better world fades in the mists of despair and cynicism.

Throughout life's journey it is the vision of our destination that determines our course and direction, and either prods us to keep moving onward or stops us in our tracks. If we can imagine nothing better than the temporary comforts of the inn, we will build our future there. If we fear the uncertainties and dangers lurking beyond the horizon, we will lodge amidst the safe and familiar. But, if we believe the tales of riches from witnesses who have visited those far-off places, we will not be content to live only halfway there. We will journey onward until we find that place, no matter what.

When John, the elder, penned his letter to the churches of Asia Minor, his fellow travelers were staring at rough and hostile terrain just ahead. Under siege by local persecutions and empirical decrees, many were caught between divine allegiance and civic loyalties. The pagan culture of Rome embraced many gods, the emperor included, and viewed the Christian profession, "Jesus is Lord," as unpatriotic, even treasonous. They eventually saw the church as a threat to "homeland security" and began official measures to discourage its growth and practice. John, himself, was exiled on account of his faith to Patmos, a rather inhospitable island in the Aegean Sea. Many believers to whom he writes had experienced the loss of their jobs and property, some had been forced to sacrifice family relationships

463

along with the economic security that went with them. Some had been beaten and others killed. Nearly three generations after Easter, Jesus had yet to return to put the world in proper order.

The trail ahead for Christian living did not look promising. Some had chosen to settle in the comfort and convenience of cultural accommodations and co-opted loyalties; others had simply turned tail and headed back to their old lives. Those who chose to travel onward were burying comrades along the trail. To keep his fellow pilgrims focused and moving toward holy terrain, John the Elder, needed to remind them of their ultimate destination. So he told them a traveler's tale of his own experience in the realm of heaven.

"I saw a new heaven, and a new earth," he says, "for the first heaven and earth had passed away, and the sea was no more. And I saw the holy city, the new Jerusalem, coming down out of heaven from God ..." (Revelation 21:1-2a).

Centuries after John's vision, explorers of the New World prompted a migration across the hostile Atlantic to the Americas with accounts of material riches and mysterious people in uncharted lands. Those who followed in search of their own wealth and political freedom often cut a wide swath of violence and destruction in their attempts to build the world of their dreams. But in the Revelation to John it is not material rewards but the glory of God's presence that awaits those "conquistadors" who persevere in faithful obedience. The abiding place of God's dominion is not built by human hands or ordained by human decree, nor won through human conflict; rather the holy city comes to us, a gift of divine grace, coming from heaven rather than arising from earth.

John does not give details about just how he got there to see that new heaven, for even that transport was divine gift, but he does bear witness to what was seen. It is a vision we need to grasp — a traveler's tale we need to hear and understand. *This world is not our ultimate destination.*

Like the believers of John's day, faithful travelers on today's Christian journey even yet find themselves to be "outsiders" in modern culture. The world around us is increasingly shoving God to the periphery. Fewer and fewer people know the Bible or are

464

interested in its teaching. It's okay to be religious we are told, but don't share your faith. It's nice to go to church, but don't let it interfere with the work schedule or the youth soccer league games. Speaking out on biblical values can be tolerated so long as we remain "politically correct" and don't "offend."

Historically, God's people have always journeyed with the tension of living *in* the world but not *of* it. At times we are able to live peaceably in our neighborhoods, to contribute to the welfare of the community, and to honor both God and country. Sometimes we cannot. Always we must keep in mind the true citizenship professed at our baptism — our citizenship in God's domain.

In the words of the old spiritual,

> *I'm just a poor, wayfaring stranger,*
> *traveling through this world of woe,*
> *But there's no sickness, toil, or danger*
> *In that bright land to which I go.*

If we believe that the material possessions and comforts and success and approval of this world are the best we can achieve, we will invest our life's energy here, and never know our ultimate home. It is a poor investment, says John, because this world, and all that is in it, is temporary. It is polluted by human sin and rebellion and it is rotting away. Were that the final chapter in the human story, it would be a tragic story indeed.

But in its place, John assures us, there is a new creation, waiting to be spoken into existence by the Creator who brought life and order to the present heaven and earth. Human sin cannot thwart the plan of the Creator to make all things new any more than human cruelty and power could keep Jesus in the tomb. God will once again "tent" or "tabernacle" with human beings, and human beings will once again commune with God face-to-face with nothing to keep us apart: no tears, no mourning, no crying, no death.

When we are confident in the hope of "that bright land to which I go" we will not be deterred by the distractions along the way — not by the temptations of safe and comfortable lodging on the side

465

of the road, nor by the fears of rough terrain or hostile forces that stand in the way.

But in the meantime, we have to keep moving. We have to guard against losing our way, and we must daily commune with God and fellow pilgrims in order to sustain our strength for the journey. Whether newly baptized or going on to perfection, it is our job to encourage, admonish, and sometimes even carry our fellow travelers toward our destination. Staying immersed in scripture and connected to each other we are challenged to remind one another, joyfully and frequently, of our ultimate destination. This world is not our home, but we've "got a mansion, just over the hilltop."

Were we left alone to find our way to that mansion, the perils might indeed overwhelm us. But just like that old National Road, another has traced out the path, and generations of others have gone on before us, clearing the way and laying a foundation. Like the trails blazed by those early conquistadors in the Americas, the path to the New World is marked with blood — but not the blood of helpless victims, or hostile enemies, it is the blood of Christ offered out of his love for us. Jesus, the "pioneer and perfector of our faith" laid the clear path when he came to dwell among us and to confront the wilderness of the human condition. With his life's blood he marked the trail to the dwelling place of God — the path of righteousness, of love, and of radical obedience to the call of the Spirit.

With each year's celebration of All Saints, we recognize with gratitude the pilgrims of faith who have preceded us, and who by their own struggles and victories have made the path a bit smoother, a bit straighter, and a bit easier to follow. We name their names, recall their faces, and tell the best parts of their stories. Let's pause for a moment to examine our own journey, to make the necessary course corrections so we can faithfully follow. Then let's strive to leave our own markers of sacrificial giving and righteous living to point the trail toward the generation that will follow us.

With each day's travel in faith we strive to draw closer to Christ and to catch a glimpse of "the holy city seen by John." If we will but pause to listen we can hear those saints singing praises to God and calling out encouragement to those of us still on the trail. To quote the hymn, "Beams Of Heaven As I Go," by Charles Albert Tindley:

Beams of Heaven as I go through this wilderness below, guide my feet in peaceful ways, turn my midnights into days.

When in the darkness I would grope, faith always sees a star of hope

and soon from all life's grief and danger, I shall be free someday.

I do not know how long 'twill be, not what the future holds for me.

But this I know — if Jesus leads me, I shall get home some day.

Grace To You, And Peace

The weeklong pastor's training event was about halfway through its course and the pastor coordinating the event was enjoying her break with a leisurely stroll across the grounds. But what began as a beautiful leisurely spring day soon turned somewhat anxious when she returned to her room and found a message taped to her door, "Call the bishop's assistant as soon as possible." She spent part of the afternoon playing phone tag between class sessions. "Whatever could it be?" she pondered.

The week was flowing smoothly and the participants seemed pleased with the whole event. All had been well with her congregation when she had left the previous Sunday. She could not think of a single reason the assistant to the bishop would be urgently trying to reach her. She reviewed the previous weeks in her memory. "What have I done now?" she thought and "Who is upset about it?"

When connections were finally made, her worst fears were banished and the day turned sunny again. The matter turned out to be important, but was, in fact, an opportunity rather than a punishment. The pastor learned a lesson about negative thinking.

Most of us have likely had those, "What have I done now?" moments — a mysterious summons into the presence of someone with authority over our lives or careers. Maybe it was the time in second grade when the loudspeaker summoned you to the principal's office and you were sure it was big trouble but you didn't know what you'd done wrong. Maybe it was seeing a police cruiser pull into your driveway — just to turn around. Perhaps it was an invitation to your boss's office amidst a weak economy or a corporate buyout.

When a personal summons comes from someone with authority over your future, it is a whole lot of scary! Take, for instance a fellow named Denny Robson of Bethesda, Ohio, who sent invitations to the family's annual reunion picnic in the form of a very official-looking court summons — with all the legal jargon included. Only by reading the fine print could the cousins get the joke. Most had a good laugh, but a few were ready to grab their passports and flee the country.

The book we call "The Revelation to John" is written in the form of an official letter customary to the author's place and time. But, in many ways, it is a kind of summons. Just who "John" is — whether the "beloved disciple" or someone else — the text does not say, but we can be sure that his audience knew. Just as the name of Paul or Peter would have been recognized, his name carried its own authority; no other credentials are given or needed. The "seven churches" to which the letter is addressed are named in chapter 2. But, of course, there were many more than those seven who were meant to hear and to heed. Certainly our congregation is one.

As best we know, The Revelation to John was written near the end of the first century. By that time, those who confessed "Jesus is Lord" were facing increasing conflict with Roman officials demanding public professions of faith in the emperor. John, himself, was one of the casualties, exiled to the barely hospitable island of Patmos in the Mediterranean Sea on account of his testimony. The churches are struggling with many of the same issues that plague congregations today: waning passion, compromised loyalties, internal conflicts, misplaced priorities. "Church growth" was no easier then than now.

We can imagine perhaps how those congregations might have felt by this personal summons. "What now?" they might have asked. "Why us?" and "How bad is it going to be?"

That is what makes John's salutation so striking. *"Grace to you, and peace,"* he says. We recognize the greeting from other places in the New Testament, but hardly any other literature.

470

- Grace: defined as unmerited favor. In our world favors are earned with a price. The rule is "You scratch my back and I'll scratch yours."
- Peace: the conflict is resolved and wholeness is restored. That's a scarce word these days on CNN.

"Grace to you, and peace." Such a pronouncement is as much a surprise to us as it must have been to them. These are hardly the words we expect to hear coming from the school principal, from the attorney's office, or on the lips of our employer. Are those the words we anticipate hearing from God as we approach the throne in prayer?

Over the last few weeks we have been pondering the Jewish experience of the Old Testament tabernacle and its priesthood, as interpreted through the book of Hebrews. The temple, the priests, and the cultic ceremonies embodied the scriptural pathway to God for a people "a long time ago and far, far away." What paths do we modern folk trek to connect with God, given all the stuff that stands between? And once we have arrived, just what pronouncement do we expect to hear from the Almighty?

Far too often, we approach in a manner like the Cowardly Lion in *The Wizard of Oz*, expecting a thunderous disembodied shout, "How dare you approach!" Perhaps one reason we spend so little time and energy on the hard path of intimate prayer is that we expect the same condemnation from God that we too often hear from the people around us — and even from those voices inside us. Too often we approach intimacy with God expecting a job-performance review instead of a candlelit dinner with our true love.

Do we hear the words? *Grace to you, and peace* from the one is and who was and who is to come ... and from Jesus Christ, the faithful witness.... Despite the trials and challenges confronting us, despite the reality of our own faults and failures, *God is not out to get us!* (or anybody else for that matter). This Jesus, "who loves us and freed us from our sins by his blood, made us to be a kingdom of priests serving his God and Father."

A new priesthood has been established by God, initiated by the sacrifice of Jesus Christ, our great high priest. No longer does

471

our sinfulness stand between us and our holy God. Through Jesus we now have direct access to enter God's presence with no fear of punishment and no words of condemnation.

But the story goes on — *we* are now called to priesthood. We are anointed to be intermediaries between divine love and an unholy loveless world. Through Christ and his commissioned royal priesthood a new regime has entered the human realm. Unlike Rome, we do not adore political and military power, nor give homage to its idols.

Hold up a second. Is that Roman power, as in "Hail Caesar"? Or is it "Hail Furer" that we dare not utter? Or maybe it's "Hail to the Chief" that we ought beware!

Different centuries, different countries, different titles — it doesn't matter — Jesus is Lord of all! Jesus, in his love for us and his complete submission to divine love is yet the King of kings on earth — even of those who pierced him, and those who continue to pierce him and his followers even yet.

That's why John was in exile on Patmos. That's why believers were suffering, and are suffering even today — because they recognized the superiority of love's power and refused allegiance to anything less, to any *one* less.

That is the foundation of our priesthood. That's the job — announcing forgiveness and healing to sin-sick souls, sharing divine love with human beings, and guiding those human beings into the glory of divine love. What a calling!

That is your job — every day, should you decide to accept it: pronouncing grace and peace rather than doling out criticism and condemnation. What would it look like? What if we replaced competition with co-operation in the workplace — or the marketplace? What if we spoke only words of forgiveness and encouragement to our families despite the negative comments or spiteful deeds? What if we came to our church board meetings offering words of praise for a job well done, and offering help when it isn't? If we intend to live together by the dominion of Christ's love for all eternity, we'd best get used to it now!

That's our job: to be a royal priest rather than a royal pain. You are the only access to divine love that some person might have. Let that message be one of grace and peace each and every day that you live, and deliver that message with confidence and joy as long as you live. Accept that commission, and the grace and peace and glory of God *will* abide in you. Amen.

Our Prayers Are Our Thanksgiving

I pledge allegiance to the flag of the United States of America, and to the republic for which it stands — one nation under God, indivisible, with liberty and justice for all.

How many of us memorized these words as part of our morning classroom ritual in elementary school? Probably most folks gathered here. Some of us still recite this pledge within a civic group, or the volunteer fire department, or some other public gathering. On occasion, a few even stop to reflect upon what we are actually promising when we speak these words. Mostly, however, they are just part of our public life — a civic tie that binds.

At least this was the case until the last couple years, anyway. Recently, the flag and its pledge have been a matter of public controversy — particularly the "one nation under God part." As you may remember, a while back a fellow by the name of Michael Newdow decided to challenge the pledge as a violation of the "separation of church and state." In 2002, the U.S. 9th District Court declared the pledge in its present "under God" form to be an unconstitutional endorsement of monotheism. The decision was not unanimous, and produced a groundswell of protest amongst politicians, radio talk show callers, and in many community "watering-holes" throughout the country. Pepsico even offered a short-lived "godless" version on its Pepsi cans, which was soundly resisted by thousands of protests. Despite the fact that the original pledge lacked that controversial phrase, the likelihood is that most Americans

475

memorized this pledge in its present form, and after fifty years it is not going to come out of their brains or their lips in any other version — regardless of any court's declaration.

Regardless of the final outcome of this case in the judicial process, we recognize that our "indivisible" nation is, in fact, divided over this issue. This should come as no surprise. The deeper dilemma to which this whole controversy points is not new to our nation's history, nor to the Christian community. Just what is the proper relationship between God and the state? And more personally, how do we faithfully live out our "dual citizenship" as Christian Americans?

During times of national crisis, governmental leaders exhibit little hesitation at invoking God's presence and power. The congressional "God Bless America" performance on the steps of the Capitol bears witness to this. Yet our courts have been equally willing to banish prayer and other religious expressions (like Nativity scenes and crosses) from our public arenas. American Christians themselves are not unanimous in their opinions on church-state relations; and biblical history is even more ambiguous.

The national holiday we celebrate as Thanksgiving is itself an example of the sometimes collaborative and sometimes conflicted relationship between people of faith and their political leadership. Officially declared a national holiday by President Franklin D. Roosevelt in 1939 (amidst the Great Depression), Thanksgiving as a nationwide celebration was earlier endorsed by Abraham Lincoln in 1863 (amidst the Civil War). Even earlier, after only months in office, President George Washington declared a day of national thanksgiving and prayer as his Presidential Proclamation Number One. "It is the duty of all nations to acknowledge the providence of Almighty God," he said. That would seem to be an endorsement of monotheism if ever there was one. In such times of national peril, the state is a bit more eager to acknowledge and even appeal to a higher power.

Yet, it would serve us well to remember that those "Pilgrims" whom we historically honor on this day (that's the name they gave *themselves*) were, in the old world, known as "Separatists" and "Puritans." Their attitude toward civil authorities was less than a

476

generous endorsement. The goal of their quest to the Virginia colony was to establish a community based on their religious values. (Yes, they missed the target and found Plymouth Rock instead.) Unwelcome and untolerated in the Church of England because of their extreme views, they saw the "New World" as a place where they could establish the kingdom of God on their own terms. Rather than a separation of church and state, they sought to build a community where their version of church *was* the state. Those Separatists who remained in England eventually overthrew the monarch to establish their own brand of church-state union under the leadership of Oliver Cromwell. (Some might say they missed their mark on that shore, too.)

However, successful or not, we know that their quest to build an earthly political domain governed by religious dictates puts these Separatist/Pilgrims in good historical company. We also must recognize that this tension of church and state did not begin with the European Reformation. It has been with God's people nearly from the beginning.

In the early chapters of Exodus, Moses stands before Pharaoh and utters God's command, "Let my people go!" Despite Pharaoh's pursuit, they depart across the Red Sea. Definitely a separation of church and state.

After Moses led the Hebrews from bondage in Egypt he led them to Sinai to receive the law. "I am the Lord your God, who brought you out of the land of Egypt," pronounced the First Commandment, "you shall have no other gods but me." As God's appointed leader, Moses guides the people as both prophet and judge. No separation of church and state there.

A few generations later, in the waning days of the judges, the people formed a loose military confederacy under a monarchy. A king was selected and crowned. But it was the prophet Samuel who anointed Saul, and later David, per the instructions of Yahweh. Church and state collaborated in strong alliance to take on the nation's enemies and "ensure domestic tranquility."

Then along came the destruction of the Jerusalem temple and the Babylonian exile. "How shall we sing the Lord's song in a foreign land?" The prophets urged the exiles to pray for the king

477

and respect the civil authorities as instruments of God's divine will. Definitely a separation of church and state and yet peacefully co-existent for the most part.

The history goes on — with God's people sometimes at odds with the government — as with the persecution under the Greek dominion of Antiochus Epiphanies, and sometime in charge of the government — as with the Maccabean period.

Then, of course, there was Rome and the early Christians.

The pastoral epistles to Timothy and Titus were not to be read as theological edicts on the nature of church structure. These letters were directed toward real faith communities wrestling with particular problems. Like that group of Separatists at Plymouth Rock, these congregations were seeking to forge a life of faith and obedience to Christ amidst unfamiliar and sometimes hostile territory. Since Christ had not returned to take his followers to heaven's realm, the church was forced to grapple with the very real challenges of establishing heaven's dominion in their earthly domain.

The role of human leaders in these earthly Christian colonies presented quite a challenge, especially since human leaders were emerging from the woodwork spouting fancy doctrines and mandating religious rituals to anyone who would listen. Like the Mayflower Compact of Plymouth history, the Letter to Timothy was written to clarify the principles on which this Christian colony was to base its common life.

While much of First Timothy deals with the nature and role of human leaders *within* the community, its writer is also mindful of the relationship that the church and its members have with the larger political dominion of the Roman Empire.

From its earliest days, the church experienced Roman authority as a mixed blessing. The common language and political stability of the first-century Empire had proven advantageous for a rapid spread of the gospel "to the ends of the earth" (or at least the edge of the empire). Sometimes, however, that movement was the result of persecutions. Roman stability and uniformity was predicated on rigid demands for civil duty and public order, and there was little room for divided loyalties or dissenting opinions. Those who professed, "Jesus is Lord" were not treated kindly in the realm that demanded "Hail Caesar." Gathering as we do to worship God, with the Christian flag on one side of the altar and the "Stars and Stripes" on the other, presents many of the same challenges in our world. Maintaining dual citizenship without divided loyalties is as much a challenge for today's congregation as it was for Timothy's. Can it be done, and if so, how?

> *First of all, then, I urge that supplications, prayers, intercessions and thanksgivings be made for everyone, for kings and all who are in high positions so that we may all lead a quiet and peaceable life in all godliness and dignity ... For there is one God, there is also one mediator between God and humankind, Christ Jesus, himself human, who gave himself as a ransom for all.*
> — 1 Timothy 2:1-2, 5-6a

In these brief verses from the epistle to Timothy two principles for practical Christian living are made abundantly clear: 1) We are to support our leaders in prayer. A stable nation benefits everyone. 2) Our "pledge of allegiance" is ultimately to Christ, who mediates God's divine grace and power to all nations and people. Any leader, nation, or institution that does not recognize or place itself under God's authority is not worthy of a Christian's ultimate allegiance.

In 1620, the Separatists of Plymouth signed the Mayflower Compact declaring in it their loyalty to King James and England, "by the grace of God." Another group of patriots would disavow their loyalty to another English king, 150 years later, because they believed the higher biblical principles of liberty and justice were at stake. From time to time through our history other Christians have done the same, and Christians themselves have not always agreed. Sometimes those dissidents are viewed as rebels and traitors, and sometimes as prophets.

A good example is our national declaration of "war on terrorism." Many of our congregations' sons and daughters, the children from our youth groups, have answered the call to military service and have put life and limb in peril on the front line. With each service of worship we pray for their physical safety and spiritual

479

protection. Yet with each day's news we see the death and destruction of other people's sons and daughters, and we lament the fundamental atrocity of war as contrary to God's intent for human welfare. Bishops, pastors, and church members write letters of comfort and compassion to soldiers, along with letters of protest to Washington, D.C. Both are grounded firmly in scripture and our own national history.

What is our civic obligation at times such as these, and what are the demands of God's call for justice and peace? What are we to do?

First of all, brothers and sisters, *I urge you to pray.*

In the secular realm of our culture it may be permissible, if not politically correct, to pray as a last resort when human efforts have failed. For those with dual citizenship, however, prayer is our first and best hope for homeland security and domestic tranquility. In the protocol of Christian worship, we are invited not only to ask, but to acknowledge. Our prayers are not just petitions but thanksgiving. We are called to pray for *all* our leaders, not just those whose politics suit our theological stance. We are urged to offer intercessions and supplications not just for *our* soldiers and their families, but for *everyone — even our enemies.*

As one Bible scholar comments, "That's casting a wide net!"

Imagine if we took these verses seriously in our civic life:

- Thanksgiving for political leaders. That surely beats the mudslinging and name-calling so prevalent amongst presidential and congressional elections of recent years. That could pave the way for some interesting political ads — the kind we might even listen to instead of flipping the channel or deleting from the answering machine messages.
- Prayers for everyone? Does that mean Saddam Hussein and Osama Bin Laden along with President Bush? Should we include intercessions for the Iraqi prisoners of war along with Americans? Does that include the mother of the suicide bomber as well as the victims and their families? How would *that* kind of prayer go over as the invocation for Congress?

480

Just what kind of prayer life is required for us all to "live a peaceable life in all godliness and dignity"? Certainly more fervent prayer than the perfunctory benediction offered at the civic luncheon or a chorus of "God Bless America" on the steps of the Capitol.

Such fervent prayers are dangerous. They are dangerous because they challenge our social boundaries. They are dangerous because they can change *us*. Such prayers of thanksgiving shift our focus from what's *wrong* (petition) to what is *right* (thanksgiving). Such prayers of intercession shift our focus from ourselves to *all* God's children.

The very devotion to Christ and his dominion that so often puts the church at odds with the world nevertheless demands from us a compassion that embraces that same world. Such devotion is dangerous, at least in the secular world-view that sees religious passion as divisive. In our worship we stand squarely upon our confession, "There is one mediator between God and humankind" (and no other), and in the eyes of the world that makes us separatists and even troublemakers. But in Christian mission and service we are empowered to see beyond all that divides us. "This is right and acceptable in the sight of God our Savior who desires *everyone* to be saved and to come to the knowledge of the truth."

Such devotion is powerful. It can change the world. Pharaoh of Egypt and Nebuchadnezzar of Babylon, Caesar of Rome, and Hitler of Nazi Germany are gone. Those who would rule with their same brand of tyranny will likewise follow them to destruction. But Jesus reigns supreme. Christ Jesus — who gave himself as a ransom for all — Christ Jesus reigns eternally. His is the power to restore a rebellious humanity to a holy God. His is the desire to reconcile embattled nations. He is the one who claims our deepest allegiance by the power of his love. His is the promise to ultimately establish "liberty and justice for all" for all eternity. Ours is the challenge to pray for it, to watch for it, to give thanks for it, and to live for it. Thanks be to God.

Lectionary Preaching After Pentecost

The following index will aid the user of this book in matching the correct Sunday with the appropriate text during Pentecost. All texts in this book are from the series for the Second Readings, Revised Common Lectionary. (Note that the ELCA division of Lutheranism is now following the Revised Common Lectionary.) The Lutheran designations indicate days comparable to Sundays on which Revised Common Lectionary Propers or Ordinary Time designations are used.

(Fixed dates do not pertain to Lutheran Lectionary)

Fixed Date Lectionaries *Revised Common (including ELCA)* *and Roman Catholic*	**Lutheran Lectionary** *Lutheran*
The Day Of Pentecost	The Day Of Pentecost
The Holy Trinity	The Holy Trinity
May 29-June 4 — Proper 4, Ordinary Time 9	Pentecost 2
June 5-11 — Proper 5, Ordinary Time 10	Pentecost 3
June 12-18 — Proper 6, Ordinary Time 11	Pentecost 4
June 19-25 — Proper 7, Ordinary Time 12	Pentecost 5
June 26-July 2 — Proper 8, Ordinary Time 13	Pentecost 6
July 3-9 — Proper 9, Ordinary Time 14	Pentecost 7
July 10-16 — Proper 10, Ordinary Time 15	Pentecost 8
July 17-23 — Proper 11, Ordinary Time 16	Pentecost 9
July 24-30 — Proper 12, Ordinary Time 17	Pentecost 10
July 31-Aug. 6 — Proper 13, Ordinary Time 18	Pentecost 11
Aug. 7-13 — Proper 14, Ordinary Time 19	Pentecost 12
Aug. 14-20 — Proper 15, Ordinary Time 20	Pentecost 13
Aug. 21-27 — Proper 16, Ordinary Time 21	Pentecost 14
Aug. 28-Sept. 3 — Proper 17, Ordinary Time 22	Pentecost 15
Sept. 4-10 — Proper 18, Ordinary Time 23	Pentecost 16
Sept. 11-17 — Proper 19, Ordinary Time 24	Pentecost 17
Sept. 18-24 — Proper 20, Ordinary Time 25	Pentecost 18

Sept. 25-Oct. 1 — Proper 21, Ordinary Time 26	Pentecost 19
Oct. 2-8 — Proper 22, Ordinary Time 27	Pentecost 20
Oct. 9-15 — Proper 23, Ordinary Time 28	Pentecost 21
Oct. 16-22 — Proper 24, Ordinary Time 29	Pentecost 22
Oct. 23-29 — Proper 25, Ordinary Time 30	Pentecost 23
Oct. 30-Nov. 5 — Proper 26, Ordinary Time 31	Pentecost 24
Nov. 6-12 — Proper 27, Ordinary Time 32	Pentecost 25
Nov. 13-19 — Proper 28, Ordinary Time 33	Pentecost 26
	Pentecost 27
Nov. 20-26 — Christ The King	Christ The King

Reformation Day (or last Sunday in October) is October 31 (Revised Common, Lutheran)

All Saints' Day (or first Sunday in November) is November 1 (Revised Common, Lutheran, Roman Catholic)

U.S. / Canadian Lectionary Comparison

The following index shows the correlation between the Sundays and special days of the church year as they are titled or labeled in the Revised Common Lectionary published by the Consultation On Common Texts and used in the United States (the reference used for this book) and the Sundays and special days of the church year as they are titled or labeled in the Revised Common Lectionary used in Canada.

Revised Common Lectionary	Canadian Revised Common Lectionary
Advent 1	Advent 1
Advent 2	Advent 2
Advent 3	Advent 3
Advent 4	Advent 4
Christmas Eve	Christmas Eve
The Nativity Of Our Lord / Christmas Day	The Nativity Of Our Lord
Christmas 1	Christmas 1
January 1 / Holy Name Of Jesus	January 1 / The Name Of Jesus
Christmas 2	Christmas 2
The Epiphany Of Our Lord	The Epiphany Of Our Lord
The Baptism Of Our Lord / Epiphany 1	The Baptism Of Our Lord / Proper 1
Epiphany 2 / Ordinary Time 2	Epiphany 2 / Proper 2
Epiphany 3 / Ordinary Time 3	Epiphany 3 / Proper 3
Epiphany 4 / Ordinary Time 4	Epiphany 4 / Proper 4
Epiphany 5 / Ordinary Time 5	Epiphany 5 / Proper 5
Epiphany 6 / Ordinary Time 6	Epiphany 6 / Proper 6
Epiphany 7 / Ordinary Time 7	Epiphany 7 / Proper 7
Epiphany 8 / Ordinary Time 8	Epiphany 8 / Proper 8
The Transfiguration Of Our Lord / Last Sunday After Epiphany	The Transfiguration Of Our Lord / Last Sunday After Epiphany
Ash Wednesday	Ash Wednesday
Lent 1	Lent 1
Lent 2	Lent 2
Lent 3	Lent 3
Lent 4	Lent 4
Lent 5	Lent 5
Sunday Of The Passion / Palm Sunday	Passion / Palm Sunday
Maundy Thursday	Holy / Maundy Thursday
Good Friday	Good Friday

The Resurrection Of Our Lord / Easter Day	The Resurrection Of Our Lord
Easter 2	Easter 2
Easter 3	Easter 3
Easter 4	Easter 4
Easter 5	Easter 5
Easter 6	Easter 6
The Ascension Of Our Lord	The Ascension Of Our Lord
Easter 7	Easter 7
The Day Of Pentecost	The Day Of Pentecost
The Holy Trinity	The Holy Trinity
Proper 4 / Pentecost 2 / O T 9*	Proper 9
Proper 5 / Pent 3 / O T 10	Proper 10
Proper 6 / Pent 4 / O T 11	Proper 11
Proper 7 / Pent 5 / O T 12	Proper 12
Proper 8 / Pent 6 / O T 13	Proper 13
Proper 9 / Pent 7 / O T 14	Proper 14
Proper 10 / Pent 8 / O T 15	Proper 15
Proper 11 / Pent 9 / O T 16	Proper 16
Proper 12 / Pent 10 / O T 17	Proper 17
Proper 13 / Pent 11 / O T 18	Proper 18
Proper 14 / Pent 12 / O T 19	Proper 19
Proper 15 / Pent 13 / O T 20	Proper 20
Proper 16 / Pent 14 / O T 21	Proper 21
Proper 17 / Pent 15 / O T 22	Proper 22
Proper 18 / Pent 16 / O T 23	Proper 23
Proper 19 / Pent 17 / O T 24	Proper 24
Proper 20 / Pent 18 / O T 25	Proper 25
Proper 21 / Pent 19 / O T 26	Proper 26
Proper 22 / Pent 20 / O T 27	Proper 27
Proper 23 / Pent 21 / O T 28	Proper 28
Proper 24 / Pent 22 / O T 29	Proper 29
Proper 25 / Pent 23 / O T 30	Proper 30
Proper 26 / Pent 24 / O T 31	Proper 31
Proper 27 / Pent 25 / O T 32	Proper 32
Proper 28 / Pent 26 / O T 33	Proper 33
Christ The King (Proper 29 / O T 34)	Proper 34 / Christ The King / Reign Of Christ
Reformation Day (October 31)	Reformation Day (October 31)
All Saints (November 1 or 1st Sunday in November)	All Saints' Day (November 1)
Thanksgiving Day (4th Thursday of November)	Thanksgiving Day (2nd Monday of October)

*O T = Ordinary Time

486

About The Authors

Donald Charles Lacy recently retired after more than four decades serving United Methodist churches in Indiana. He is the author of ten books, as well as hundreds of smaller pieces, several of which appear in his recently published *Collected Works* (Providence House). Lacy's sermons have appeared in many outlets, including *Great Preaching 2001, Keeping the Faith: Best Indiana Sermons* (2003), and *The Minister's Manual 2004*.

John T. Ball has served numerous United Methodist congregations throughout western Ohio. A graduate of Ohio State University and Boston University School of Theology, he has had articles published in *Circuit Rider, Christian Ministry*, and *Emphasis*. Ball is the author of *Barefoot In The Palace* (CSS).

Maurice A. Fetty is the interim senior minister of Park Congregational Church (UCC) in Grand Rapids, Michigan. He previously pastored congregations in Indiana, Michigan, Minnesota, and New York. Fetty is the author of numerous CSS titles, including *The Feasts Of The Kingdom, The Devilish Dialogues, Money And The Kingdom Of God*, and *Sex, Love, And Marriage*.

Richard Gribble, CSC is an associate professor in the department of religious studies at Stonehill College in North Easton, Massachusetts. The author of more than a dozen books and over 175 articles, Father Gribble is the former rector/superior of Moreau Seminary at the University of Notre Dame. He is a graduate of the United States Naval Academy and served for five years on nuclear submarines before entering the priesthood. Gribble earned his Ph.D. from The Catholic University of America, and has also earned degrees from the University of Southern California and the Jesuit School of Theology at Berkeley. Among Gribble's previous CSS publications is a three-volume series on *The Parables Of Jesus*.

Lee Ann Dunlap is the pastor of Pleasant Grove United Methodist Church in Zanesville, Ohio. She is a graduate of Mount Union College and the Methodist Theological School in Ohio.